WILLIAM DONALD SCHAEFER

William
Donald
Schaefer

A Political Biography

C. Fraser Smith

William Donald Schaefer
Mayor God Complex

To Greg Crawford
Best Wishes
C Fraser Smith

The Johns Hopkins University Press
BALTIMORE AND LONDON

For Mary Gillespie and Colin Smith
Nino and Armida Canzian
With Love

© 1999 The Johns Hopkins University Press
All rights reserved. Published 1999
Printed in the United States of America on acid-free paper
9 8 7 6 5 4 3 2 1

The Johns Hopkins University Press
2715 North Charles Street
Baltimore, Maryland 21218-4363
www. press.jhu.edu

Library of Congress Cataloging-in-Publication Data will be found
at the end of this book.
A catalog record for this book is available from the British
Library.

ISBN 0-8018-6252-3

FRONTISPIECE
Smiling on the Outside. Schaefer was devastated by his 60
percent to 40 percent victory in 1990, a sharp drop from his 80
percent majority four years earlier. One of these roadside thank-
you sessions led to one of the governor's biting letters—after, he
said, a motorist had made an offensive hand gesture. Richard
Tomlinson, Governor's Press Office.

CONTENTS

Preface and Acknowledgments   *vii*

I / Uncle Willie's Boy

1   "Dummy"   3
2   Apprenticeship   29
3   Schaefer's Turn   61
4   Charm City   94
5   Caretaker   115

II / Renaissance

6   The Cheerleader Cometh   143
7   Wild Man   169
8   Reinventing Main Street   194
9   "The Best Damned City"   219
10 Moving On   244

III / Exile

11 A Gift   271
12 Homeless   292
13 Tailspin   314
14 Hitting Bottom   330
15 Return of the Native   355

Notes on Sources   387
Schaefer's Rules   395
Index   397

Illustrations follow page 218

From the days of Tammany Hall in New York City, American mayors have been larger-than-life figures, loved for their style and foibles. Fiorello La Guardia practiced the politics of joy, and few ever embodied the character and color of a city more completely than he. James Michael Curley made the mayoralty of Boston synonymous with Irish progress in a new land, and if he stepped over the line into illegality, he did so in the name of justice and the people, didn't he? They called him "the Rascal King" and elected him from a jail cell. Pendergast of St. Louis, Daley of Chicago, Koch and Lindsay of New York, and Lee of New Haven must also be placed in the pantheon of civic fathers. Kevin White of Boston in a later generation, a man who was thought to have enough talent to warrant a place on the national stage, came to be called "America's Mayor." More recently, that title was bestowed on Ed Rendell of Philadelphia.

In the latter part of the twentieth century, as cities began to decline, a few of America's mayors tried to lead a counterattack against decay and despair. Some of them moved into positions of power and daily stewardship unknown to their lusty forebears. The best of them shed the merely ceremonial to assume the role of super development chiefs, marshaling public and private resources to reverse or at least resist the forces of decline: blight, poverty, drug dependency, and crime. Between White and Rendell came a group of leaders one urban scholar refers to as "the Messiah mayors." William Donald Schaefer was the foremost exemplar: the most idiosyncratic, driven, and deeply committed of these "saviors" and "miracle workers." The labels of that era were born of hype, thrown off by perfervid public relations types, a press secretary—or even a reporter— looking for a way to define what was happening in America's cities. In most cases, the language was far ahead of the progress. People spoke the word *renaissance* as if reclamation of a single set of downtown blocks was equal to a rebirth. Unless they were totally swept away by the excitement, they knew that their language included more hope than actual achievement, but they were obliged to pretend they had witnessed a mighty stirring. No one insisted more vehemently than Schaefer, who brought to his office a religious belief in the power of salesmanship and hyperintensive management. You had to sell your city. You had to run it like a corporation, rule it like a regiment, rail against the naysayers. You had to attack on every front. You had to rage against the night of decay and welfare dependency, high school dropout rates, and trash until you were seen as slightly mad. Then you made madness your tool.

By 1986, Schaefer had become not only the most accessible and unbeatable of local politicians, but a man of national stature. Without really wanting to, Schaefer left Baltimore after fifteen years as mayor to become governor of Maryland. Not many mayors (not White, after all) moved on to run their states, but Schaefer's bond with the citizens of Baltimore, even those who had fled his city, extended across the entire state. He easily defeated his highly regarded Democratic primary opponent and beat the Republican candidate by a record margin. He immediately assigned himself the most costly and controversial public works projects, passed them, and went on to defeat the National Rifle Association on a handgun control bill that few public figures would have backed. He won a second term in 1990, a year in which incumbent politicians at every level were losing or nearly losing. Schaefer won by 60 percent to 40 percent. He saw this as repudiation.

The canny madness of Schaefer engulfed him then, and he appeared near mental collapse. As always, though, he recovered. He was maniacal, unpredictable, and politically incorrect—aggressively so. He knew that his rough edges were assets. He was, like every modern politician, an actor, ever on stage, projecting his own image as he promoted his city.

After handing over the governor's office to Parris Glendening, Schaefer could not adjust to private life, so when the fabled Maryland Comptroller Louis L. Goldstein died in the summer of an election year, Schaefer decided at the age of seventy-six to be Louie's successor. The voters knew that Schaefer was not technically qualified to be their tax collector or day-to-day guardian of the state's credit rating, but they wanted his judgment and missed his energy.

Schaefer was a 24-hour man, a 100 percenter, an underachiever who was maddeningly unsatisfied with the grandest accomplishment. To keep pushing, to remain optimistic, to assault his friends with new demands required a lack of balance. His genius was to see this; his strength was to endure it. The feckless, distracted citizenry, he sometimes felt, did not deserve him. He used people mercilessly, appropriating their talent and their time and pretending not to notice the toll on them. He was self-indulgent and even a bit cruel to those who served him. He had too little regard for process, but his free-wheeling operation was never a self-dealing one, and he managed, by luck and obstinacy, to keep the scalawags who had helped put him in office away from the trough. On the contrary, few leaders commanded such an outpouring of work *for* the city and state. He was an honest man, committed to public service. To be sure, he wanted the ribbons, the statues, and the accolades—proof that he was worthy. He knew the costs and calculated that they were worth the pain he accepted and inflicted.

His life in politics had been vouchsafed by do-gooders, clubhouse operators, slick businessmen, and neighborhood leaders. He managed to find the best in each of these without being a servant to any. He was a classic 1950s-style can-do man, a veteran of World War II, a holdover from the time in American life when learning from experience and from respected elders was a way of life. He was a career politician who ran for office to serve—to work for people, to care about their welfare. He wanted to think of himself, and to have others think of him, as a distinguished city father, a public servant. He seemed to be the last Baltimorean to see how well he had succeeded.

AS A REPORTER for the *Baltimore Sun*, I found that my relationship with William Donald Schaefer was seldom a happy one. We were adversaries. My role was to report what he was doing and how he was doing it. His was to get a message of hope through the static of a sometimes cynical and distracted media. To that end, he suffered our company for periodic breakfast chats in his ceremonial room, speaking on the record, often making news. But sometimes, he got so upset he couldn't finish his Egg McMuffin. He wanted to recruit us into his sales force. We were offended. We had our objectivity and professional standards. Didn't he see that? When he failed to get any converts, he tried to invade our consciousness. He wanted to be there when we sat down to write, and, our best efforts notwithstanding, I think he probably succeeded. His press was good even when we thought we had caught him, once again, doing something silly. Silly was in the eye of the beholder, and the beholders of Baltimore (and later Maryland) loved what they saw. His PR apparatus was in a different zone, churning out campaigns and public events faster than any of us could process and absorb them. Bread and circuses, the critics said, efforts to make the bedraggled citizenry happy in spite of its many problems.

Ironically, though, public relations could pile glitter on top of substance. What did he have to hide? Unsolved problems? Surely. But possibly, himself, as well. His flair and energy were all there on the surface, and everyone saw them. But his wit, humor, and instinct for the right move were masked by the pageantry. At the same time, he deliberately concealed these traits. He realized what Governor Adlai Stevenson and Congressman Morris Udall did not: Humor is not always a political asset. To be witty was sometimes to be a bit obscure and therefore suspect. Since he was dead serious about his work, he would not allow himself time to laugh.

As colorful as he was, Schaefer could be a nightmare for a reporter to cover. He never uttered a cogent quote or a striking crystallization of an idea or project. Yet he was a sublime communicator. What he always seemed to be saying to reporters, the business community, and the city at large was "Could I get a little help here?" He was always trying to get everyone else as excited and energized as he was—a doomed endeavor, no doubt. Sometimes, I thought his devotion was a bit overweening, even suffocating. I had my own question: "How about letting us alone for a minute."

Not many Baltimoreans want to be left alone in that way now. Schaefer knew how to keep the streets clean. He knew, that is, that the streets would fill up with detritus if he didn't have a Trashball campaign or a neighborhood-by-neighborhood assault on garbage. He knew that graffiti would metastasize if he didn't appoint graffiti patrols to wipe it out within twenty-four hours. Schaefer's monuments were ballparks and waterside shopping malls, but his fundamental contribution was knowing how to run the government and how to motivate the bureaucratic governors— the cabinet secretaries, the department heads, the citizenry. If the garbage wasn't being handled properly, he would follow the trucks to find out why.

This is all folklore, old anecdotes that Baltimoreans have heard to the point of screaming. And, of course, he was colorful, a sublime, even gifted actor. He was a great protagonist for a book about government. I thought his story would be a tonic for those who still want to believe that government can be a positive force in our lives. I tried to get started on such a book before he left the governor's office. I wrote him a letter. He didn't respond. He was too busy, had too many problems. There was always too much to do. Who said he was getting out of public life anyway?

But a year after he was "deposed" (his word), one of his close aides, Marion Pines, said that he was ready to talk. Over lunch at the Johns Hopkins Club, she gestured toward me and told Schaefer, "This man wants to write a book about you. Are you going to cooperate?"

"Oh, sure," he said, as if hearing that idea for the first time.

I decided soon enough that my story was really about leadership, not salesmanship—though I suppose that is part of it. His critics called him a "bricks and mortar man," and was he ever. But what he really built were momentum, spirit, belief, hope—all intangibles, all the things a leader must build and the hardest building there is to build. He succeeded for reasons I hope will be clear in this book. He ran on the highest-octane human fuel: self-doubt, anger, and the clarity of those who believe in their own vision. He knew that conflict and controversy were a part of the alchemy of progress.

ALTHOUGH THIS SHOULD not be regarded as an authorized biography, Schaefer made himself available for lengthy interviews whenever I sought them (with an interruption or two when he heard that I was interviewing people he didn't like). I hope I have done him and his record justice.

I must also thank the members of his staff who spoke eagerly about their former boss. Of these talented people, I am indebted most to Lainy LeBow-Sachs. I am also grateful to Gene Raynor, Schaefer's friend and Maryland's dean of elections; Chuck Fawley, Schaefer's driver and fast-food gourmet; Paul Schurick, whom—fortunately for him and for Maryland—Schaefer failed to fire; Sandy Hillman, whose job was to give Baltimore a new industry from scratch (tourism); Mark Wasserman, Schaefer's eloquent development chief; Rick Berndt, the German General; Mark K. Joseph and Mark L. Joseph, whose jobs for the city were multiple; Janet Hoffman, whose political skills were dazzling; and Joan Bereska, whose ideas, stage management, and whipcracking devotion to Schaefer put her own stamp on Baltimore's renaissance. Regrettably, I could not speak with everyone who worked closely with Schaefer over the forty years he has served in public life, and to the rest of that legion, I apologize.

I am indebted to my friends in the *Sun*'s news library, particularly to Paul McCardell, whose eager, smiling assistance put him at risk of further requests, which were always cheerfully accepted, and to Dee, Carol, Jean, Bobby, and Andrea. I have leaned heavily on my colleagues at the *Baltimore Sun*, particularly Sandy Banisky and Doug Birch. My thanks also go to Bill Zorzi, Tom Waldron, Antero Pietila, Barry Rascovar, and Blair Lee IV, political seer and student of Maryland politics, who offered invaluable observations on the manuscript.

I thank also Emily Murphy, photographs chief at the Maryland State Archives in Annapolis, and Ed Papenfuse, her scholarly boss.

I am most grateful also for the encouragement and patience of Bob Brugger, history editor, writer, and historian at the Johns Hopkins University Press; to Barbara Willette, whose meticulous editorial judgment and skill freed the book of many problems; and to Anne Stewart Seitz of York Production Services.

I owe most to my family: my wife, Eileen, my children, Alexandra, Anna, Emily, Jacob, and Jennifer; and my grandchild, Hannah (aka Beanie).

May I exempt all but myself from any errors and oversights that may have intruded.

I

Uncle Willie's Boy

CHAPTER 1

"Dummy"

In the spring of 1971, City Solicitor George Russell scolded the voters of Baltimore for their thoughtless habit of honoring political bosses. Running for mayor in the primary against that year's representative of the Democratic machine, Russell sounded the time-honored appeal of reformers. Couldn't the voters be a little independent for once? he asked. Couldn't they see what was happening to them? "You can't send a dummy down to City Hall by divine right of ascension," he said.

But you could, and Russell knew it. His own career in politics had been promoted by some of the same forces that now served his opponent, City Council President William Donald Schaefer. The bosses had helped to secure Russell a judgeship and the post of city solicitor from which he was seeking the mayoralty—somewhat prematurely perhaps and without the organization's by-your-leave. In the past, he too had relied upon men the newspapers called "well-connected," "power broker," and "kingpin." And now they were getting behind Schaefer, a man of modest accomplishment save for the alliances alluded to by Russell.

Schaefer owed much to men with a certain dark aura, with reputations for self-serving, antidemocratic manipulations. Though sometimes called "bosses," these fixers were small businessmen, shopkeepers, and bar owners with their hands in a dozen enterprises. One of Russell's backers, William L. "Little Willie" Adams, had been a numbers man before sliding gracefully over into real estate development and politics. Schaefer's patron, Irvin Kovens, sold furniture and television sets, dabbled energetically in the bar business, and was available for other ventures. Politics had come into Kovens's life after a governor, William Preston Lane, instituted a sales tax in the late 1940s. Kovens's dislike of this levy brought him into the elections game and quickly afforded him a two-part epiphany: He saw that he could wheel and deal in the clubhouse world of Baltimore politics, and he found that it gave him a certain stature.

Kovens and his colleagues would take over from Jack Pollack and other Baltimore bosses who had decided by quadrennial reflex which dummies or geniuses would ascend to high office and when. An election was a certification of their choices. The fewer the candidate's qualifications, the greater the honor. Sometimes the bosses selected well, better than they knew—as they were about to do in 1971. Their motives were commercial and personal, almost never ideological or even partisan. If their Democrat lost in the primary, they might take a Republican. Their vision was to be with the winner. There was money to be made, of course, but few critics realized how much the game itself mattered. The worshipful attention of those they helped; the camaraderie of the teams they captained; the knowledge that they had "made" a mayor, a governor, a judge, or even a laborer in the public works yard; the thrill of a done deal, a favor granted, a wish whispered and obeyed—all of these things gave them an adrenaline rush.

Setback

George Russell's appeal for independence went unheeded, and many in Baltimore, the lowly and the elite, winced as the primary results rolled in. Civic stalwarts such as the developer Jim Rouse were more appalled than Russell. They knew Don Schaefer as a man of remarkable piques and public rages—and "nothing more than a title search lawyer," as Rouse sniffed. "Schaefer was thought of as being unstable," said Bob Embry, then the city's housing commissioner. "He'd last about two seconds before he started chewing the carpet." Rouse imagined City Hall in the hands of dolts and knaves, men of no scope or imagination who could rally no one to the city's aid. He saw Schaefer vaulting over talent and good sense—personified by Russell and Embry—to become the city's leader. The general election remained, of course, but Baltimore Republicans were hopelessly outnumbered. Schaefer would be the new mayor.

Jim Rouse had reason to feel aggrieved. He wanted to save the nation's cities, beginning with Baltimore, and he thought of himself as an ideal sort of activist—even a mayor in time. He thought cities and the nation itself were doomed if they could not preserve their role as a higher order of efficient human organization, capable of wondrous synergy, of ideas, of self-reliance, and of leadership. In time, Rouse's dream would seem ironic, a search for redemption, since he had been a progenitor of America's suburban shopping mall, which, along with superhighways, robbed American cities of citizens and even their reason for being. If a salvage operation was to succeed in Baltimore, though, Rouse needed what Kovens and Pollack and Adams needed for their objectives: an ally in public office. Strong-minded, creative, and charismatic, Rouse was an Establishment revolutionary who charmed venture capitalist lenders and politicians alike. A gifted speaker and a dreamer, he made his ideas compelling, seemingly doable, and urgent. At the end of Rouse's life, President Clinton awarded him the Medal of Freedom for his commitment to housing the poor and reviving their neighborhoods.

But Rouse was not as well informed as he might have been about Baltimore's next mayor. He did not really know the man whose election so disheartened him. A title searcher in name only by then, Schaefer had become a full-time public servant with a sleeve full of civic duty stripes conferred by a number of organizations, including the Citizens Planning and Housing Association, through whose councils passed many of the city's most effective elected officials. The CPHA credential was an undeniable bit of proof that one had done well in the pursuit of good government. As parochial as he was, Schaefer had moved far beyond his own neighborhood group, the Allendale and Grantley Improvement Association, to establish broad and deep grassroots credentials, deeper than the peripatetic Rouse's by far.

The developer would have been puzzled to know that the bosses of Baltimore found Schaefer a bit odd as well. The guy spent weekends in his City Hall office and consistently voted against his machine-made predecessors: Theodore Roosevelt McKeldin and the Tommies, Old and Young. Schaefer served in the council under both Thomas J. D'Alesandro, Jr. (Old), and his son, Thomas J. D'Alesandro III (Young). For different reasons, these men and their pals had as low an opinion of Schaefer as Rouse did. Like Rouse, though, they assumed Schaefer to be a wholly owned political subsidiary of Kovens—otherwise, Kovens would not have "made" him.

Virtually no one found the Democratic nominee gifted, bright, or prepared to be more than a caretaker. Schaefer was well aware of that thought and lashed himself with it for years, so determined was he to prove the world completely wrong. "The Sunpapers said the city could make do with me for four years and then elect somebody good," he said later with undiminished bitterness. In the beginning, the *Sun* had written about him in terms that were "dismissive," according to one of its editorial page editors. But the *Sun*'s reporters, having covered him closely in the City Council, were impressed by his skill at dealing with them and with members of the council, important indicators of his ability to handle both as mayor. Nor did the *Sun* put the Kovens of those years in the same category as did Rouse. Kovens appeared to be a virtual reformer in contrast to Pollack, a one-time rumrunner and grafter whose control of politics was breathtaking. Pollack's courthouse connections alone may have saved him from a murder indictment in the 1920s. But Rouse and others in the city made no distinction between Kovens and Pollack, who had been partners in both business and politics. In the public mind, the two were indistinguishable, so many saw the new mayor through a smudged lens.

Overnight Sensation

Schaefer had been around City Hall for sixteen years, four of them as council president, learning how city government worked. He seemed to be on all the committees, a bit of a nebbish who weathered the periodic power shifts generated by bosses or boss pretenders working toward council dominance. Described by a veteran city hall reporter as the best argument yet advanced for the divine right of kings, Baltimore's nineteen member council was a fine place to accumulate knowledge and experience without too much competition or scrutiny. Council seats were stepping stones or sinecures, not classrooms—until Schaefer arrived. Boss rule may have helped to send the council's overall image into decline, but in the heyday of Kovens, in the 1950s and 1960s, it had many talented members. Later it grew pathetically bombastic, dilatory, incoherent and sometimes corrupt. Several of its members, including its president in the mid-1980s, were indicted and convicted of political corruption, bribe taking, and the like. It was no wonder someone like Rouse was concerned when it produced a mayor.

But the idea man might have been reassured had he spoken with members of a third force then emerging in Baltimore civic life: a cadre of young idealists who organized a series of forums to give the Schaefer campaign and its candidate an intellectual zest. These young strivers had been drawn together first for issue breakfasts by Ted Venetoulis, a political science professor and organizer Schaefer had recruited to be his campaign manager, and later by Sally Michel, a civic leader and the wife of a Baltimore businessman. Michel had met Schaefer after winning lunch with him in a fund-raising raffle. She and Venetoulis joined Harvard-trained lawyer-developer Mark K. Joseph to lead a group of Ivy League backers who came from the city's middle and upper middle classes, people who were not part of the Baltimore worlds, east and west, that produced D'Alesandro, McKeldin, and Schaefer. The machine gave them a luxury: They would have time to prepare the winner to do the job he was running for and, thanks to the bosses, certain to win. Joseph brought in experts and drafted issue papers with Schaefer at his side—sometimes to the exclusion of campaigning. "He's got to win this damn thing first!" Venetoulis would shout. Schaefer resisted door knocking but sat patiently with Joseph, taking notes on a lawyer's yellow foolscap pad and saying little as the experts talked. He was never embarrassed to be a student, either in those days or later in his career. He would restate particularly penetrating lessons and declare, "I had to learn that" or "I remembered that." Schaefer's interest in housing issues and community development paralleled their own, and they sensed a unique determination and drive in him, though it was obscured by his sometimes awkward, quirky, and tempestuous eruptions on the council stage. They were doing what Kovens had done from the other end of the political spectrum: making a mayor, shaping him to their own specifications.

But none of them—not Rouse, not the *Sun,* not the young good government types, not the clubhouse boys (b'hoys in the odd lexicon of Baltimore politics)—had any real appreciation of the man they had elected: his passion, his capacity for work, his temper, or his odd charisma. After sixteen years in public office, he was almost unknown in the city that elected him mayor.

Uncle Willie

When William Donald Schaefer was born on November 2, 1921, his parents lived at 1004 West Lanvale Street in Old West Baltimore, a fine old central city neighborhood with small parks and stately three- and four-story brick and brownstone townhouses. His father, William Henry Schaefer, and his mother, Tululu Irene Skipper, were married on November 8, 1918. The minister was Confederate veteran Henry M. Wharton, pastor at William Schaefer's church, Brantly Baptist. Tululu's father, Fielding Copperton Skipper, was known as Fred. He and his wife Clara lived on the west side of the city. Schaefer's paternal grandparents, Louis and Emma, lived at 701 Dolphin Street, in the same building where Louis, who had started out as a produce clerk, ran one of the many small grocery stores he owned during his life. Schaefer's father worked there as a clerk for several years while studying to become a lawyer. Schaefer does not remember ever visiting the store, though it might have seemed a natural and pleasurable thing for a young boy to do, given the prospects for being spoiled with the odd candy or apple—not to speak of the grandparents' affection. Some said Tululu and her in-laws did not get on well, so perhaps that explains why her son was a stranger there.

Willie and Tululu had grown up together in that same old West Baltimore neighborhood, attending the same schools and a Baptist Church on Schroeder Street. In time, William Henry Schaefer noticed Tululu Irene Skipper and wrote letters to her brother, his friend, Clarence, expressing his feelings. The letters were lyrical, poetic expressions of a young man's intentions. He was certain he would marry Tululu, and eventually, he did. He was thirty-three; she was twenty-seven.

Schaefer's father seemed the ideal husband, cooking and doing dishes, chores not always accepted by the men of his era. His niece Anita Skipper remembered Willie mashing the potatoes. She saw him presiding over that chore often because, on Thanksgiving, the Schaefers entertained her family on Edgewood Street. At Christmas, the Schaefers went to Anita's house in Anneslie. Anita was in the Schaefer household almost every day after school as well because she attended St. Pius School, then just around the corner. Don was a handful, she said, willful and prone to tantrums. She teased him about it later: "You'd run your bicycle into the wall if you didn't get your way." Anita thought Willie was the disciplinarian but also the more affectionate parent. If father and son were together, she said, one or both had an arm around the other. Everyone called him Willie or Uncle Willie—and so did his son, a daring thing for a child, perhaps, but for the Schaefers, it seemed a natural thing to do and everyone was comfortable with it. Tu-loo, as she was known, was far less demonstrative, a failing that she would acknowledge and lament to Anita later.

A Sunshine House

When Schaefer was seven, his parents moved to what then was the far western edge of the city, the virtual suburbs. Their house stood in a row of relatively new houses perched on a slight ridge of land running north and south and perpendicular to Edmondson Avenue, a major east-west artery to and from downtown Baltimore. The neighborhood quickly became known as "The Hill," perched as it was on the crest of a rowhouse wave that swept up a broad and steep incline from a stream known as the Gwynns Falls west of the city.

The Schaefers' new place was a Keelty-built "sunshine" rowhouse, so named because every room had a window. James Keelty was the Jim Rouse of his time, blanketing the city's western hills with his bright new product. In time, a brier hedge ran across the front of the Schaefer address, defining the end of a sharply sloping front yard, modestly terraced with landscaping timbers into five- by ten-foot plots. Campaign workers joked later that they would be convening "on the upper terrace" for an important announcement, as if they were headed for the Kennedy estate in Hyannisport.

The modest house had a vague entrance hall opening immediately into the living room with a large, cherry red brick fireplace. Fake logs turned against a light in the ornamental hearth. A grandfather clock stood at the east wall. French doors led to the dining room, but the family usually took meals in the small kitchen, sitting around a porcelain-topped table of creamy white and raspberry hues. The ceilings of both rooms had the look of hand-troweled plaster, and there were handsome parquet floors, though in later years they were carpeted. The kitchen had no cabinets; supplies were kept in a small room leading to the back door.

The house had four small bedrooms on the second floor. Schaefer's parents took one of the smaller ones at the rear of the house, leaving the largest for Louis Schaefer, who moved in several years after Emma died. Schaefer's room was in the back of the house, adjacent to his parents'. The fourth bedroom, at the front of the house, was used as a sewing or sitting area. Except for mealtime, Grandfather Schaefer—very proper in every sense—seldom came downstairs. "He had shaky legs like I do," his grandson said. He noticed another infirmity as well. "My grandfather Schaefer's eyes were getting bad, so I would fold Reynold's Wrap around pennies and give them to him and say, 'Here's a dime. Give me two nickels.' He'd open up his little change purse, I'd drop the dime in and take two nickels. I did it a few times and then stopped." Did Schaefer think the older man was fooled? "Oh, yeah. He trusted me." He called off his scam apparently because the thrill was slight and the profit insufficient—or because it was a safe way to experiment with being bad and to realize on his own that this was not a kind thing to do. It would not be the last time he indulged or amused himself at someone else's expense. He was remarkably generous to his friends, but he could occasionally use people without remorse—with delight, in fact, when it suited him.

A Penance

Schaefer's father read Tennyson and mysteries and other books in great quantity. Tululu determined never to touch the volumes that were stacked around her husband's easy chair or on the dining room table. She, too, was a frequent visitor to the local library and may have thought it perfectly fine for her husband to have ready access to various books that were in the process of being read. Their son did not follow them in this recreational or academic pursuit, though he was a regular Bible reader and would become a compulsive reader of newspapers. Whatever Tululu's concessions to clutter, the Schaefer house was immaculate when company was coming. "The house had a precise touch to it, the lawn carefully taken care of, a tiny backyard," said the sportswriter John Steadman, whose mother was one of Tululu Schaefer's best friends. "The house was so inviting. His mother greeted you with a lot of hospitality. She was very refined."

Uncle Willie made an even deeper impression on the young Steadman. When Steadman's father, William, a Baltimore fire chief, died near the end of the Depression, Uncle Willie became the Steadman family's financial advisor. "My mother was grief stricken and not wise to the ways of the business world. He came in and told her what to do with the insurance money, what banks to use. As a fallout of the Depression you never dared put your money in just one bank." Notwithstanding the Schaefer family's kindness, visits to their house on Edgewood were "a penance" for Steadman. He and his mother made the grueling trek with some regularity, transferring twice on the trolley lines. His mother's friend was a welcoming and refined figure, to be sure, but her house seemed to Steadman a bit stuffy. "We would sit in the living room and have a glass of ginger ale and a piece of cake. Don and I talked but there wasn't any rapport. I was interested in Hank Greenberg and Mickey Cochran. I don't think he knew who they were. If the subject was the Orioles, he wasn't interested." Oddly enough, Schaefer fancied himself a ballplayer later—an indifferent hitter, but fast and good with the glove, he thought. He and his friends played their games on a field canted precipitously south and east—their neighborhood being the Hill, after all. No one complained, he would say later, using those games as a perspective against which to measure the demands of neighborhoods for level playing fields and top-drawer equipment.

Only Child

After Louis Schaefer's death in 1937, Schaefer, not his parents, moved into his grandfather's somewhat larger bedroom at the front of the house. His parents seem to have given no thought to occupying the larger room. "I was an only child. I was the center of the life of my mother and father." Indeed, he would live most of his life confident that he was and should be the focal point of everything that happened around him. Restrictions applied to him as well, suggesting an Only Child Law that required the offspring to honor his parents' every demand: He had to stay at home, to become a lawyer as his father had done, to remain unmarried, to work with puritanical zeal, to achieve high honors and to be honest. Schaefer became both native son and city father, a combination of images reflected back to him by family and neighborhood. He adopted Baltimore, treating it with the singular attentions his parents had lavished on him. Even before they were gone, he expected others to adopt and humor him, to make allowances for his quirks as if they were the price of his devotions — always to give him the front room. Perhaps, even then, it was clear that he needed the space. During his council years, his bedroom would be so jammed with stacks of file folders and papers that he could hardly move. When he was mayor the dining room, too, filled up with his things — Christmas presents stored there by the preoccupied recipient, who did not get around to opening them.

Except for the war years, Schaefer would live on Edgewood into his seventies. At one point he hung his shingle—"William D. Schaefer, Lawyer"—over the front porch railing. But he protected his mother's privacy even as he became a public man. Only after her death did he agree to announce the start of a campaign from the concrete steps with the pink hydrangea to the left, the black pipe stair railing on the right, and the tiny terraces below.

The Hill

The Hill had several small groceries and confectioneries, a major city bakery, a movie theater, and a dry cleaner. Elementary School 88 stood at the crest of the rise along Edmondson Avenue, farther to the west behind the Schaefer house, and was at the time he attended it, virtually the only building of consequence in the neighborhood. A cleaning and dying firm moved into the middle of the block on Edgewood, causing a stir apparently, because the man who would preside over such matters as an adult recalled it as a "non-conforming use," not usually permitted in a residential zone and existing only as an exception. Everything else on Edgewood Street conformed to unwritten, perfectly understood standards, and everyone, it seemed, worked hard, prospered, and went to church on Sundays. Schaefer and his mother walked two blocks south, crossing Edmondson, and on to Bishop Cummins Memorial Reformed Episcopal Church. Uncle Willie, though not a regular churchgoer, was a Baptist and attended Brantly Baptist. "He read the Bible every night and prayed, on his knees every night, as did my mother. My mother believed in the hereafter. This was just a temporary stop. Heaven was her home. She believed that until the day she died." Schaefer's own life would be firmly focused on the here and now, but he would occasionally have a bout of religious fervor. As a boy, he was a member of the Church's Junior Boy's Brigade. "You had a little sailor outfit, a sailor hat and suit," he remembered. He wore it dutifully and even later reported no feeling of humiliation at being so dressed. But perhaps the sometimes profane, prankish, and authoritarian man he turned out to be was statement enough.

If the neighborhood had published its collective goals, they would have been simple and straightforward: Keep your place nice; make money; send your kids to college. Directly across the street lived the Joynes family, who owned a little candy store. "He made money. Sent all his kids to college," Schaefer recalled. Individual shop owners thrived there in the days before supermarkets. Next to the Joyneses were the Bopps, a large family with three daughters. And next to them, the Weldons, who had a son and two daughters. Schaefer remembered Weldon as an expert in ceramics. Weldon's son Neal, Schaefer's friend, was killed in World War II. A grocery store owned by Abraham Green stood at the south end of the street. Green put his kids through college too. "They were good people," Schaefer says. Across Edmondson was Beck's Bakery, where the Schaefers and many in Baltimore bought their bread and cakes. Another grocery store stood on the other corner and was run by Henry Thomas, who had a wooden leg. His children, too, went to college.

At the southern end of the street, on the northwest corner of Edmondson Avenue, stood a vacant lot with an underground spring. A grocery store was there and then the Edgewood Theater, bringing a number of opportunities. On Saturdays, Schaefer and Doris Linthicum, his first girlfriend, who lived across the alley behind his house, would see the first of the talkies and then the matinee specials with titles that he remembered precisely: *Tarzan, King of the Jungle* and *Jack Armstrong, All American Boy*, among others. He could afford the quarter admission because he was one of the chosen neighborhood boys who delivered movie circulars. "That was a big deal. You were a hotshot kid." He was careful to say, however, that he had been only a fill-in, not really in the front rank of runners, the regulars. He did not wish to seem boastful, perhaps, or to make himself a target by claiming more status than he felt he had earned. Later in his life, Schaefer's movie partner and all-purpose companion was Hilda Mae Snoops, whose family lived on a block north of Schaefer's on Edgewood. He hardly knew her when he was a boy, but their grandparents were acquainted. Hilda Mae would be a lifelong link to the old neighborhood.

Four O'Clocks

Every house had a canvas awning, striped or solid colored, which was pulled up every night and rolled out every morning. People talked across adjoining porch rails or over back fences. If you had a problem with your sink or toilet, Hartge Levine, the plumber, would come over and fix it. He lived a couple of doors north on Schaefer's side of the street at 626 Edgewood. "He made money, too." Eventually, Hartge's wife would decide that the neighborhood was changing and they needed to move out. They went to Baltimore County, and within a year, Hartge was dead. When Schaefer and his mother thought about moving later—and she resisted—he remembered Hartge and agreed that it was a bad idea. Uncle Willie competed horticulturally with Edgar Amey, a steamfitter who lived one door south on Edgewood. "My father'd come home every night and go out and garden. He had zinnias, marigolds, morning glories, and four o'clocks." Willie put cedars in the back of the small yard, and rose bushes lined the southern side so that Amey would have a good look at their size and brilliance. "They had a tremendous amount of pride in it." The mayor who grew up watching these two men jockey for backyard bragging rights saw and honored the same spirit across an entire city. To make his appreciation tangible, he established an Order of the Rose, a distinction (accompanied by a certificate) that was conferred upon those who brightened their corners and alleys. As mayor, he would tour the neighborhoods looking for worthy new members. He was a bit chagrined to report, nevertheless, that a woman from the Hill came by to see him one morning with a complaint. Could he do something about his shutters? They needed painting. Hadn't he noticed? It was acceptable in those days to bring such a thing to the attention of a neighbor—who would, everyone was certain, be grateful.

Virtually 100 percent of Hill residents were white in those days, and Schaefer, for one, was quite conscious of black-white boundaries: the Gwynns Falls, Hilton Street, and other lines of demarcation which neither blacks nor whites would cross before World War II. Schaefer knew these barriers well and for virtually all his childhood and youth, until he entered the Army, gave little thought to the consequences for him or for his city. In 1932, for example, Schaefer's class at Public School 88 put on a minstrel show. The playbill announced, "The 5a Class presents the Lyndhurst Chocolate Drops (Something sweet for your Tooth)." The cast was as follows:

Class Interlocutor, William Woods

End men

Bones—Richard Nally

Sambo—Bob Dougherty

Amos—Thos. Urspurch

Tambo—Donald Schaefer

Also Sandy, Rat, Slim, Remus, George Washington, Nosslecomeoff and Mrs. Sambo.

The record of this somewhat common form of entertainment, preserved in a playbill that was printed for the occasion and kept in a family picture album, suggests no concern that anyone would find it remarkable, much less offensive. In those days, few would have. Feelings of superiority and a license to hold derisive attitudes unthinkingly permeated young lives in many ways. Jim Rouse, only a few years older than Schaefer, remembered his own reluctance to mingle with blacks when he was a young man growing up on Maryland's Eastern Shore. In Hawaii, years later, Rouse saw the reality of a diverse world, a culture of many ethnic groups coexisting effectively, he thought. Schaefer saw the same thing in the army. He recognized and sympathized with the pain and pride of a black sergeant whose soldiers were judged capable of only the most menial and simple tasks, setting up tents and the like. Schaefer was impressed with the pride of a man who refused to accept such a demeaning stereotype. That recognition might not have been possible on Edgewood Street.

His Old Man

In some ways, public office was one majestic adult education class for William Donald Schaefer. And sometimes what he learned, what he saw and embraced for the first time, were things many people learn before they leave home. Schaefer seems to have been watched over vigilantly by his mother and sternly by his doubting father. The degree to which he was shaped by this surveillance seems to have been a mystery to him. Years into his four-term mayoralty, he sat one day for a photograph, wearing a cowlicky toupee, glasses, and wide suspenders and holding a cigar—an early foray into the realm of public theater. Well on his way to becoming a mayor of many faces, he was on this day H. L. Mencken, social critic, *Evening Sun* columnist, and confidant of the nation's literary elite. The two Baltimore-born German Americans had never met. Mencken's career ended in 1948 when he had a stroke, and Schaefer, though an inveterate newspaper reader when he became a politician, seems to have been oblivious to the news in his early life. He had no sense of Mencken as a Baltimore presence. Would he have been consigned to Mencken's "Booboisee"? Perhaps—certainly on the day of the picture taking. Suited up and sitting for the photographer, the mayor of Baltimore achieved a fair approximation of the famous writer. Schaefer looked at the developed pictures later and saw something else entirely: "Oh, my God, that's my father!" The blunt and freckled fingers, the long and ruler-straight nose, the penetrating blue eyes sent flickers of recognition years after the older man's death. Schaefer was still living at home, surrounded by memories of his father, but he thought he had grown into a likeness of Willie without noticing. To others, the likeness was not as striking. Willie Schaefer affected a certain style in his straw boater with lacquer-stiff brim, worn according to Baltimore protocol from May 15—aka Straw Hat Day—until Labor Day, the official end of the season. Like Mencken, Schaefer père was a cigar man. If it was a particularly good cigar, the elder Schaefer would finish it off in his pipe, a habit of frugality as well a way to continue the smoke. "He lit up in the morning and kept smoking until his arm flopped over toward the ash tray just before he went to sleep at night," his son said. Always concerned about his health, the future mayor did not smoke or drink.

By the time the family moved to Edgewood Street, Uncle Willie had left the private practice of law and was working for Maryland Title Guaranty, a firm located across from the main downtown courthouse. His company's job was to provide unclouded ownership of houses to its clients—not something that was ever necessary for him because, according to his son, William Henry Schaefer preferred not to own. His son does not know what concerns led his father to adopt such a view. Some years after his Uncle Willie's death, Schaefer bought the house at 620 Edgewood.

"Wild Man"

As a schoolboy, Schaefer rode city trolleys to City College, Baltimore's preparatory high school, on East 33rd Street, a considerable distance from the Hill. His companion was often Charlie Eckman, later a sports and radio personality in Baltimore, who recalled that they would be accompanied often by uniformed girls on their way to Seton High, on Charles Street, near the Johns Hopkins University. "The girls would kid him, and old Schaefer would get all flustered." Eckman remembered him as sincere and serious, an occasionally assertive person but one whom no one knew well. "He was quiet, unassuming, but when he did have something to say everyone listened."

The City College yearbook for Schaefer's senior year says that he was known as "Don" and described him as "neat," apparently in the sense of tidy. He played soccer and lacrosse, sang in the glee club one year, served on the student advisory council one year, and was a member of a committee called "Journey's End." He wore his thinning hair in a sort of pompadour that rose an inch or so above his triangular face. By his last year of high school, the hair had already retreated a quarter of the way back on his large head. For most of his adult life, he visited a neighborhood barber every other week without fail. He prided himself on hewing to the military view of appearance. His crew cut grew more and more sparse, however, and in time, there were only wisps to cover the imposing freckled forehead.

He had enough of a temper to make an impression on his schoolmates, and the yearbook reports he had acquired an unlikely nickname: "Wild Man." He had earned it on the soccer and lacrosse fields. He brought

almost no athletic talent to these sports, but he had nerve and a willingness to disrupt. His teammates knew that when Schaefer ran onto the field,
a show could be expected—something useful for the City College side,
since it might take advantage of the other team's shock. "I was a tough
player. When they wanted someone to play dirty—if someone on our team
was getting beat up—they'd let me go in. I'd smash 'em up. They let me
play midfield. When I scored my first goal, I almost fainted." This penchant for the outrageous would color Schaefer's leadership style, giving
him great advantages over those who regarded certain behavior as unacceptable: pointing an assault rifle at a reporter, shouting at a U.S. cabinet
secretary in Washington, cursing governors of his own state, shunning his
own cabinet members if they offended—being unrestrained whenever it
might suit him.

Wild as he may have been on the athletic field, he achieved some academic distinction. "I didn't care if I made the honor roll. But I really wanted
to do it for my parents. I was a goody goody. I worked hard. I studied hard.
I had to. I had to prove to my parents I had some brains. I had to fight to
get on the honor society." Schaefer constantly poor-mouthed his mind and
the quality of his education. Many of his political and business associates
concluded that he had a monumental inferiority complex. Yet he was on
the honor roll at City College, the city's best public high school, and he
later missed by only 0.1 percent a place on the honor roll at the University of Baltimore Law School. When he spoke of schooling, Schaefer often
skipped the honor roll stories to tell how he was almost suspended from
City College. His German teacher wanted to expel him for an infraction
he insisted later he could not recall. He would say only that his father had
to intervene to keep him enrolled. Whatever he had done, he had done it
while studying German, not the language of the weak minded. However,
he showed little interest in history, art, ideas, or even the dominant events
of the day.

A happier yet revealing moment came with an award from the United
Christian Citizens' Organization, again for something he cannot remember. "It was just a little certificate, a little tiny certificate, nothing big. But
you would have thought I got a Medal of Honor or something. My father
couldn't imagine that his son would get this award." He told the story as
if he had been a bit wounded by Willie's surprise at such a modest tribute—as if the old man's expectations were low, certainly not as high as
his own. Irene Vincent, who dated Schaefer in the 1950s and remained
close to his mother until Tululu's death, says that Schaefer's father, how-

ever devoted, was not about to spoil his son. "I do think his father was harsh. Germans have this tradition of being hard on their children. Willie would tell him, 'That's stupid. That's a dumb thing to do.'" Someone at the title company remembered a call from Mr. Schaefer one day. He was looking for his son and was told he must be in the law library. "Don't try to kid me," he said, "I'm his father."

First Lady

Schaefer had been struck by the physical similarities between his impersonation of Mencken and his father, but others found even more resemblance between mother and son—the high forehead, the shape of the mouth when they smiled. "I always called her an older, female version of him," said Joan Bereska, the first and most important of his City Hall aides; no one knew the Schaefer of those early years better. If the work ethic came from Uncle Willie, Tululu supplied doggedness and determination. "Many of the characteristics he has are her characteristics," Bereska said. "Get on course and follow it; don't give up until your job is finished." Schaefer was as stubborn, demanding, and caring, as she was. He took her counsel further: Never relent. Never settle. Nothing is enough. You will never, ever accumulate enough laurels to rest on. Photographs in the family albums suggest that Tululu was a vivacious, outgoing woman. Certainly, she and her only son were close. On May 14, 1933, Mother's Day, he sent a card with this message: "Mother Dear, Just a tiny greeting with a lot o' joy To one who's always, Mother, Your loving little boy." In the lower right corner he signed, "Donald." Tululu wrote on the back, "From my little boy."

But, Anita Skipper noticed, something was missing for both mother and son; there was a reserve between them, an arms-length relationship that neither seemed to want. In a 1936 letter to his mother, who was away in Atlantic City, Schaefer reported going to a baseball game with his father. He seemed almost at pains to speak of the outing without romance or hint of real excitement, about the game or his father.

Dear Tululu,
 Are you having a nice time? I know you are but that is a good way to start a letter. Willie and I went to baseball Tuesday. Great game. Oriole lost.

I have a chance to swim in the South Atlantic Association meet. The "Y" coach gave me an application for registration. I swam some races so I got it. When you get letters down there it looks important? Have a good time.

Yours Truly,
Donald Schaefer.

His formality may well have been a teasing one, a reflection of the formality with which his mother addressed him, or an attempt at the age of thirteen to seem more businesslike or older than he was. His father operated with similar reserve. He sent this birthday card to his wife in 1933: "To Greet you and hope this birthday and all those yet to come will bring an abundance of joy, good cheer and contentment." His son's approach to correspondence would continue to evolve, finding its most colorful and provocative form in high government office.

Known to some on Edgewood Street as "the first lady of the neighborhood," Tululu occasionally helped people with small gifts of money. "Not everyone was so well off, but I guess she thought she could afford to do a little extra. She gave a lot, but she looked for nothing in return. She was definitely a person of good will," a neighbor told *The Sun*. She had cats, as many as four at a time. Strays seemed to find their way to her door. Her son became a cat lover, too, but was always learning that he didn't have time to care for them. Like her husband, Tululu loved flowers and worked in her garden often. In city hall, her son's office was filled with African violets.

Schaefer devoted himself to her as his father had. Even as mayor, he called home every night at 9:00 to tell her where he was, what he was doing, when he might get there. She waited up for him. One night, after he had been mayor a few years, the city's symphony orchestra went on strike. Leon Sachs, a Baltimore lawyer whose son Steve would later run against Schaefer for governor, was deputized by the mayor to negotiate with the union. Leon Sachs would telephone Edgewood Street every night to give Schaefer a status report. One night, Mrs. Schaefer answered. "He's not here, but I'm expecting him," she said. "I've got his covers turned down." Schaefer was well into his fifties by then.

Tululu Schaefer was a woman of absolute likes and dislikes, according to her niece Anita—"busy, busy, busy with her feelings exposed on everything," very much like her son. She was not visibly involved in his political life, though on occasion she helped with a campaign, and according to Anita, she knew all the issues and all the political players—and loved to visit with them over lunch at Horn and Horn, one of the favorite lunchtime political listening posts. She sometimes pretended to know nothing of politics and even to dislike her son's career choice. But she actually held strong opinions on current affairs in Baltimore and, on occasion, made them known to members of the council she met on her frequent sojourns downtown. She told a reporter once that Donald had always wanted to be a lawyer, but she knew very clearly what a disaster that enterprise had been. He often did not send bills and refused to go after clients who owed him money. Tululu had no such compunction. She went to his office almost every day after he had been elected to the council, and her main assignment—a self-assignment—was to make collections. After one election, she told reporters that politics really meant little to her son. She seemed to think the law a more worthy vocation, long after he'd made his own preference clear. Given a second choice, Schaefer said later, he'd have chosen business and would have been a corporate executive, a CEO. He had great respect for the D'Alesandros, but he revered men like H. Vernon Eney, a distinguished lawyer and civic activist. Aside from his father, men like Eney and Bill Marbury, the famous Baltimore lawyer, were his role models.

"A Shore"

His family was not wealthy, but Schaefer insists that he was untouched by the Depression and could not remember observing any of its grim manifestations on the streets of the city. "We had a nice house, nice furniture. I had nice clothes and enough money to get to school. We weren't overflowing with money, but the Depression didn't touch me." Almost no one went through that period without some searing image of privation and pain, but Schaefer insists he was an exception. He was not conscious of FDR, the New Deal, unemployment, bread lines, or any of the painful episodes endured by others. He had no Depression stories, no tales of impoverished uncles or cousins, no awareness even of the tumult around him. He did think his father was a resolute company man partly because Maryland Title Guaranty Company carried him through those frightening years without pause. And, of course, if his parents were able to shelter him so totally from such a major event, they must have been at least as devoted to him as he always said.

His mother's parents had what Schaefer and other Baltimoreans of that day called a "Shore," a summer retreat on the water, in this case a cottage on Marley Creek in Anne Arundel County. All the land there was owned by the B & O Railroad, which rented small plots to vacationers. To get there, the Schaefers would ride the streetcar to Curtis Bay, where they boarded a small boat for the hour-long cruise. His grandmother's brother Harry Skipper was in the signboard business, so the "Shore" featured out-sized shutterlike arrangements fashioned from discarded goods from Great Uncle Harry's business. Above the front porch were the words "Oh Yes." "There were about ten summer homes. No electric. No indoor plumbing. No nothing. It was just a summer house. My father and I used to row around in what was known as the Furnace Branch. We'd anchor on the sand bar and catch striped bass, white perch and yellow perch." Breakfasting on Willie's catch was one of many Marley Creek treats. Shore life was filled with the joys a young boy covets. His Uncle Harry raced speedboats on the creek. When boats weren't tearing about, Schaefer watched the Nuffer girls, Dorothy and Elsie, who could swim across the river and back. Schaefer couldn't keep up. "I tried to swim across with them and made it about halfway." Family albums include several shots of a teenaged Schaefer, wan and skinny, wearing an all-black bathing suit complete with sleeveless shirt.

Bubba and Fred

Schaefer's maternal grandmother—he called her Bubba—would position herself, somewhat regally, in the front room of the cottage. She had asthma, but it did not keep her away from what seemed an idyllic, if rustic, retreat. "The outhouse was over the water. No one bothered with environmental (or health) things then. The sea grass was so thick you couldn't swim through it. You'd walk along the beach and pick up the soft crabs in the shallow water. We tore out the grasses because we couldn't swim. You had to build a channel through the grass so you could get into deep water." When environmentalists told him later that chemicals dumped into the Chesapeake Bay were killing the crabs and rockfish by decimating these underwater thickets, Schaefer had a personal and historical reference that many people lacked. He knew how lush the aquatic vegetation had been, how the grasses had flourished before phosphorus fertilizers and detergents washed into the bay in later years, helping to eradicate the fish he had caught as a boy. Though he was a big city mayor, an urban politician, he had a feel for the water and its ecology that made him a natural ally of the antipollution forces. He was better on efforts to control development, pollution and other negative impacts on the Bay than virtually any other governor, thought Will Baker, head of the Chesapeake Bay Foundation. Nothing seemed to please Schaefer more as mayor and later as governor than moving around in his small boat, catching the odd flounder. He kept fishing all his life, heading off toward Ocean City and Assawoman Bay, which he shortened to "Ass-a-wan."

His grandmother died at her camp one day, and Uncle Harry came to the house on Edgewood Street to tell his niece. "I can remember how shaken he was. They buried her from her house in Baltimore. She was laid out in the front room. That was when they put crepe on the front door handle. That's how you knew there was death. There'd be crepe hanging about two thirds of the way down." After Bubba's death, another grandfather, Tululu's father, moved into the Schaefer household for a short time. Though a smallish man, Fred Skipper was a boilermaker whose job required him to climb inside the behemoths he tended. "He came home every night absolutely black," Schaefer remembered. It was yet another image of a man committed to his work.

Last Meal

When the United States entered World War II, Schaefer was in law school. He chose to stay and finish, though at least one of his close friends, Eddie Davis, left immediately to enlist in the marines. Schaefer later said, "He thought it was his duty. I had an opportunity to finish and I did." Was he pragmatic, self-centered, oblivious, sheltered? Not then as fully invested in patriotic things as he would be after the war, Schaefer allowed himself to wait a few months before attempting to enlist in the navy but he was unable to get the specialty he wanted, cryptography. In time, he was drafted into the army. He prepared to leave for war and for his only extended period of living away from 620 Edgewood Street, Baltimore, Maryland. Just hours before he left, he and his parents sat down for dinner in their kitchen. "Well, this is the last meal before I go," Schaefer said, and the stern Willie began to sob. "He couldn't control his crying and left the room."

Several of Schaefer's young friends were killed in the war. The toll was high. Years later, after Schaefer became mayor, Tululu received a letter that evoked the dread she and her husband had felt that night in 1942. Betty Wise Lonergan, who had grown up across the street, sent a snapshot she had taken on the sidewalk in 1930. "I remember well how Donald refused to be photographed. He probably never knew he was in the picture." Schaefer is wearing high-topped shoes, a V-necked sweater, and a tie. He does not appear to be ducking the camera, but he is on the very edge of the picture. "I know you must be very proud of your son," Lonergan wrote. "I'm sorry my brother never lived to follow his career. I often think of the good times we had on Edgewood Street. You may not remember seeing me in the Valencia Theater after the war, but I told you then that Harry, Jr. was killed in Germany in April 1945. He was a captain and company commander. We miss him."

Jeri Fowler, Anita's sister and one of Schaefer's playmates at the "Shore," came along to Camden Yards the day after that last meal to say goodbye. Thousands of Baltimoreans debarked from that same spot, and like the Schaefer entourage, many of them were crying uncontrollably. From Camp Meade, Schaefer traveled to Camp Grant in Illinois, where he found himself in a career selection line. One trainee went to the Air Force, the next to the hospital corps. Schaefer went to hospitals. As a trainee, he had a tough time. "I was not used to living with a bunch of guys in cramped quarters." One day while he was serving as company commander, he marched his men into the battalion in front of his on the parade grounds. But he had an IQ that qualified him for Officer Candidate School, and he became a "ninety-day wonder" (that is, he was turned into an officer without the usual training). He was shipped first to New Orleans and then to Palm Springs, California. There, he was made adjutant—a job that demanded an authority figure—which Schaefer found he enjoyed thoroughly. It set him apart a bit, but he tended to be a loner anyway in those days. Other officers had families or girlfriends and, when allowed, went to town. Schaefer was single but stayed on base, a kind of permanent officer of the day.

In short order, he adjusted fully to the military life. "I was full of GI. We made the nurses get up and do the formations and raised hell if they didn't." Soon, his unit was headed back across the United States and on toward England. "We sailed on the *America*, a fast boat, faster than the subs, so it went by itself. When we got to Liverpool, we saw the first damage by the Germans." By truck, Schaefer's group went to Blanford in the south of England. "We set up a 700-bed hospital to be ready, it turned out, for D-Day." Not entirely certain what lay in store, Schaefer and the others saw the parade of troops and planes. In short order, they were tending to 1,500 wounded men. "We had guys with their arms shot off, a kid with the skin cleaned off so you could look in his belly. But the mortality rate was very low."

Occasionally, Schaefer could do something for someone he knew. A friend from the Hill, Alonzo Darden, was one of the patients. Darden's neck wound was a ticket to the States, something Schaefer tried to expedite. "If you could help a guy, you did." Another Baltimorean he met there was patched up and returned to the front, where he was promptly killed. Once again, as with the Depression, Schaefer gave little thought to his status—a noncombatant, exempted from the killing fields. He accepted an opportunity to fly on a bombing mission but then did not go. The plane did not return.

Military rules governing hospitals changed during the war so that nonmedical personnel could be executive officers. A commander had to be a doctor, but the second in command didn't. Schaefer was promoted and, for the first time, began to think about a life in which the lives of others could be positively affected by his own hard work. "In a hospital unit you really did something. You saved lives, made decisions about sending people home or back to the front." He enjoyed having his judgment tested and relied upon. He learned about people as well. Some had an aura of unapproachable authority or skill, but you saw their frailties: the officer who drank pure alcohol and grapefruit juice, for example, and the officer who got a nurse pregnant with twins. Orders often seemed brutal. During the Battle of the Bulge, the hospital service received a recruiting call, a demand for men to proceed to the front—as cannon fodder, Schaefer thought. "Most of these men had basic training but no real military training. They were not sent ultimately. They hadn't shot guns in years. They would have been killed instantly." He was not wired constitutionally to question authority, but he was also unwilling to stifle his own views. The Only Child had the right to speak the truth as he saw it, whether or not offense was taken. In the army and for years after, the willful and imperious General George Patton held a principal spot in Schaefer's pantheon of heroes.

Cookie

While Schaefer was gone, Willie kept his son's Plymouth in tune. "Every week he would take it out for a ride. He'd go up Edmondson Avenue and then bring it back down. He wasn't a very good driver, so he couldn't get it in the garage. He'd get Murphy across the street to help him." And every day, Willie Schaefer wrote his son a letter. "Every day," Schaefer would say, savoring that recollection. Sometimes the letter contained only the briefest message: "Hope you are well" or simply "Hello." Once, his father forgot the letter until he was already on the Number 14 streetcar and headed up Charles Street toward Lexington, where it turned west toward Edmondson. He got off, went back to the office, and composed his note.

The dutiful son wrote back, often sending pictures of himself, pictures of tourist sites and a number of shots of "Miss Cook," also known as "Cookie," as Schaefer noted on the back of one snapshot. Lolita B. Cook of Columbus, Ohio, was introduced to the Schaefers of Edgewood Street in Baltimore by these pictures. If there were letters, they have not survived. But the photo albums are an eloquent chronicle of what surely was a singular period in this young man's life. As second in command, Schaefer knew he needed to maintain a certain distance from those he supervised. Officers are taught that familiarity breeds contempt, so they were ordered not to fraternize with the troops. "You didn't get close to anyone. You just didn't. You didn't get close to nurses. You had be a little tougher." Schaefer thought he should be careful even when dealing with other officers, lest he lose some of his authority. "I was pleasant with them but I didn't go to parties. I just didn't."

With Ms. Cook, he made an exception. "She was in the same unit but they were way off to the side"—but, happily for him, not always. He sent pictures of himself with his new friend at the beach, in front of hotels, by Westminster Abbey, at Big Ben, in Ireland. On the back of one snapshot, Schaefer reminded his parents that he was in a war zone, though most of what they got was well-removed from the violence and the carnage. He sent a picture of bombardment rubble, a house splintered and spilling into the street, offering understated praise of the English resolve: "Buzz bomb dropped in and people just carry on."

Schaefer's notations on the backs of these pictures are full of self-deprecation and irony. "Ain't that a great picture of the big building?" he wrote on the back of one photo. He was standing with Cookie, Big Ben in the background. In another shot, a London policeman was bending over to pick up something in an almost acrobatic pose, one leg pointing out behind him. "Nice posing by the Bobbie," Schaefer observed. Referring to his own expression in a picture with Cookie, he said, "I look like I'm slightly off my nut." Was he? We really can't tell, though he seemed to be with Cookie often and sent his parents pictures showing them in many different places. "I liked her," he said without elaboration many years later. "You needed someone to talk to."

Schaefer identified his friend on the back of one picture as "Miss Cook." The absence of a first name suggests that his parents already knew it, most likely from a letter. As much fun as he was having, as far from home as he was, Schaefer was letting his mother and father into the secret—part of the way, at least. He was teasing again, no doubt. Away at war, occupied with the urgent business of treating the wounded, Schaefer presented himself in these pictures as a companionable, fun-loving young suitor possessed of a certain worldly detachment even as he seemed immersed in a relationship, however undefined. He seemed every bit the dashing young captain, handsome, charming, and mature. At the same time, his bearing included a certain reserve, a control and objectivity that must have been reassuring to his parents. On the back of a shot of the lovely Cookie pulling on his arm, he wrote, "Dragging me out of the hotel (or in)." Some young men might keep such sectors of their lives off limits, but Schaefer drew his parents in. He sent a snapshot taken on a London street of an unidentified young woman, whom he seemed not to know but saw walking along and could not resist photographing. His notation read, "Some babe . . . Didn't do so good. Oh, well."

In another shot, he posed in front of what look like the White Cliffs of Dover. "Got my pants pressed," he said, referring to how sharp he looked. All of this showed his well-observed fetish for order and tidiness, a neat freak in his military element. As mayor, he never left City Hall without having on a freshly pressed pair of slacks. Later in life, he would seem almost pathetic as he referred to others—notably Maryland Governor Harry R. Hughes and New York mayor John Lindsay, who were both tall and slender—with pitiable envy. He dismissed them both as empty vessels who merely "looked good in a suit." Schaefer might have been lamenting the loss of an equally svelte figure. As a younger man, the albums reveal, he had dressed smartly and elegantly. In one photo, he stands with his mother at Atlantic City in a checked suit, pants creased to a knife's edge and cuffed, jacket sharply tailored. His shoes are two-toned, his collar and tie precise. He was equally striking in his uniform.

As a politician, he had no tolerance for criticism directed at him by others, but in private, he poked fun at himself. He sent along a shot of himself leaning against some sort of railing, "Me, asleep." Sometimes, he was content to let the picture speak for itself. On the back of one, featuring the lovely nurse yet again, he wrote only, "W. D. Schaefer." On an accidental picture focusing on a pike-tipped iron fence, he wrote, "Cookie took it. Great picture of a fence. It is supposed to be the Tower of London—You know where Anne carries her 'head tucked underneath her arm'. WDS." The album also includes a picture of a lovely child, perhaps four years old, whom he called "Our war orphan," as if caring for such a victim of war was sappy or to step back from claiming too much credit. Operations in progress, soldiers recuperating, and coffins draped with American flags, lined up and ready for loading on ships, are also among these photos. One of his albums, apparently maintained in England, includes a shot of his parents labeled "Decoration Day, Tululu and Willie." His father looks quite girthy in this picture, as heavy as his mother is slim. This album includes a picture of his mother with the family dog sitting on the back steps. But Lolita B. Cook is the real star. Near the end is Cookie in civvies outside "Ye Olde Tea House, A.D. 1616." And finally, there is Cookie holding a package on a bridge at the shore with Schaefer's notation, "Ah, my lady, Holding the Fudge."

A Traveler

When the war in Europe was over, Schaefer could not immediately return to the United States. Soldiers and officers came back when they had accumulated sufficient points, which were earned with length of service, combat, and other qualifying criteria. Instead, he was selected to go to the Far East, assigned to a psychiatric hospital. But the United States dropped atom bombs on Hiroshima and Nagasaki, and Schaefer's unit stayed in Europe. His remaining months in service seemed something like a Grand Tour, complete with a visit to the war crimes trials in Nuremberg. He saw Nazis in the dock, including Herman Göring, the master propagandist, before he committed suicide. He says that he had no sense then of looking upon evil incarnate. They were merely prisoners accused of unspeakable crimes. Schaefer visited a German castle and remembers being warned not to steal anything—an embarrassing indication that Americans had apparently shown themselves to need such instruction.

While Schaefer was still in Europe after the war ended, Miss Cook came to Baltimore to visit his parents. When he returned, she visited again, and Schaefer went home with her to Columbus. But the relationship did not continue. Schaefer says that he and Ms. Cook did not have any agreement, certainly no engagement, and no commitment was ever exchanged. Perhaps she was just "someone to talk to." He moved back in with his parents and, in time, learned that Cookie had married.

After that, Schaefer had many girlfriends—"the prettiest ones," according to his cousin Jeri, who often threw parties at an apartment in a mansion at Charles and Madison streets on Mount Vernon Place, where she and her friends were housesitting. While he was in Europe, Jeri had written to Schaefer almost as often as Willie had, and he had written back, never mentioning the pain he saw everyday—or Ms. Cook.

"Don had many girlfriends. He played the field. But he left them all waiting longer than they could wait. They wanted a family, kids," Jeri said. Why Schaefer held off the advances of Cookie and others they knew was a mystery to Jeri and Anita, but they were certain that he was as attracted to women as any man they knew.

Like a Sailor

When Schaefer returned to Baltimore in late 1945, having reached the rank of major, the young veteran and his parents sat down at the kitchen table at which his impending departure had caused so much pain three and a half years earlier. The returning soldier had by then adopted something of the military's occasionally colorful approach to language. "Pass the Goddamned salt," the young man said without thinking. If that outburst might have provoked another outburst of tears, Schaefer did not notice. His parents barely looked up and said nothing. "Right away I realized what I had done. I didn't do it again." Such a lapse might well be attributed to the absence of Miss Cook. She had been such a constant in his life, traveling with him to so many places, sharing so many adventures and sojourns away from their grim task at the hospital, that one could understand why he was a bit cranky. He could have been having dinner with her at the Norfolk, after all.

Three years of military service, even as an officer and gentleman, apparently had elevated Schaefer's penchant for profanity to the level of reflex. He would later, as governor, be accused of spending like a drunken sailor. He certainly swore like one. Called a momma's boy on into adulthood, Schaefer had a rough side to offset what he called his goody-goody side. He relished it and embellished it, thinking it made him a part of groups that might otherwise have rejected his serious approach to most things. His profanity was inventive and seldom censored by him. When the author of an important stadium study went to Hawaii without leaving a copy for then Governor Harry Hughes, Baltimore's mayor told reporters, "I had to get the first asshole off the beach so I could get a copy of the study to the asshole in the governor's office."

Apprenticeship

From war crimes trials and the bedsides of grievously wounded soldiers and from his days with Cookie, Schaefer returned to what he called "an average life in an average city." He remained a churchgoer and a member of the Mystic Circle Lodge #104 A.F. & A.M. He also joined the Montfaucon Post of the American Legion and the Veterans of Foreign Wars and belonged to the city bar association, without ever thinking of these memberships as political building blocks. He saw no neighborhood or interest group network forming, no venues for promoting name recognition or money raising, though he was working with the Improvement Association and, in time, joined the Citizens Planning and Housing Association. Serious civic strivers and ambitious pols in Baltimore needed to earn their CPHA merit badge, but Schaefer, oblivious to so many things, might not have known that. All his joining seemed inherently political, but it was also inherently American and inherently Schaefer. He wanted to feel productive in his "average life"—to find recognition and honor that would be worthy of his father's praise.

At Maryland Title and in the courthouse record office, a repository of real estate transactions representing the land ownership history of Baltimore, Schaefer worked again with his father, this time as a lawyer. He met two recent graduates of the University of Maryland Law School: Norman Waltjen, a somewhat aristocratic World War II fighter pilot, and Mary Arabian, a smallish, dark-haired woman with an ironic view of life. They formed a three-person firm and found an office on the seventh floor of the nearby Munsey Building. Schaefer decided that his name would be first, followed by Waltjen's and then Arabian's. She did not object, guessing that the last name in the list would be the one most callers would remember. These three lions of the law had but two desks; Arabian occupied the one near the door. The firm could not afford a secretary, so she allowed herself to be the official greeter and phone answerer.

As a law firm, Arabian realized quickly, the three friends were hopeless. "Just kids," she said. "We had a lot of fun. That's what we mostly did, have fun. We didn't work. We didn't have many clients in the beginning—or at the end." Schaefer's father often asked his son if "that girl of yours" needed a title—title search work, in other words. She always did. Willie would then call her and say, "Come on over here, I've got one for you." So without much threat of paying customers, they met for a leisurely breakfast almost every day with Milton Wisniewski, another title searcher and settlement expert, who joined in the casual prospecting for business at Bickford's, known as Number 10 Downing Street in mocking honor of Boss Pollack, who held court there. The place hummed with deals of every kind, including much real estate business, some of it of marginal legality. Brokers bought and sold property before getting into the official chain of title, thereby escaping the need to pay filing and recordation fees. A young lawyer had to be agile to avoid getting used, Wisniewski saw. "They'd send work my way, a title, and then two days later they'd say, 'I sold the property. Forget it.' It was not illegal, but it was unfair. I'd do the work, but then my guy was out of the deal. It could get pretty convoluted. There was a brokerage house across the street in the Equitable Building where some of these same men would spend the rest of the day watching their investments."

Catching Up

On some days, Milton, Don, and five or six others would repair, as early as 11:00 A.M., to the HiHo or the Two O'Clock Club on the Block. More an artist than a lawyer by temperament, Wisniewski would often take a book.

One morning, Schaefer went to court to watch a proceeding against a Block acquaintance, Blaze Starr, the stripper. As a youth—even as his father was searching for him, perhaps—Schaefer had made an occasional jaunt to the Block. Now he read in the morning paper that Starr had been arrested on a charge of distributing pornographic materials. When he arrived at the appointed courtroom, he could not find the accused. The lacquered benches were empty except for two young women in gingham dresses sitting demurely with an older man at the front of the room. Schaefer walked closer and realized that the dancer had been reconstituted as "a milk-fed country girl, fresh as the dew." Such a sweet young thing could hardly be in the porn trade! Smart lawyer, Schaefer thought. Starr walked. Schaefer, who never tired of watching Starr perform, kept up with her over the years.

With little lawyering of any kind on his agenda, Schaefer could afford to watch other cases or join Milton at the HiHo. Schaefer tended to be the group's clown, a role that his cousins Anita and Jeri saw as well. Good at one-liners and near pratfalls, he might have been regarded as a wit, but he never spoke enough to prove the description apt, Wisniewski thought. At the same time, he thought Schaefer had a kind of charisma—an assurance, an aura of purpose, though hidden behind some unusual behavior. On weekends, the HiHo and Guaranty gang would often drive to Ocean City, where they would meet a number of young women, many of them part of the Title Guaranty family. They would stay at the George Washington Hotel or the Cavalier. Occasionally, Schaefer's mother would come along. Everyone welcomed her, Wisniewski said. She was a warm, reassuring presence, not at all resented, he thought, but "someone you wanted to hug." Wisniewski loved sharp cars and liked to have one at the beach. He noticed that Waltjen had a 1947 Chrysler convertible. So Milt bought a 1948 model, a Windsor, with Scotch plaid upholstery. When he drove down to Ocean City the next weekend, he pulled into the George Washington's parking lot and "Guess what was parked next to me? One of the first postwar Cadillacs, Waltjen's latest acquisition." He hadn't done it to keep up with the Wisniewski's. "He didn't care. I didn't matter in his eyes."

This band of young men, veterans usually, like Waltjen, Schaefer, and Wisniewski, seemed to be reaching back to capture lost days and hours. Fights with water pistols broke out occasionally with Schaefer as the almost willing target. "Donald would pull a sheet up over his head, and we would soak him with the toy cannons—to the consternation of the Cavalier's owner, Mrs. Quillen. 'I can't believe this,' she shouted. 'You call yourself lawyers. Look! The wallpaper's coming off!'

"Schaefer never complained about being the target," Wisniewski said. "He would never say 'You bastards!' or anything." Schaefer and Wisniewski double-dated occasionally, and Schaefer showed up once in Ocean City with an attractive woman who Wisniewski thought was a divorcee, vaguely scandalous in those days. When the couples parted around 10:00 P.M. that evening, Schaefer said he would meet his lawyer friend at the end of the pier around midnight. Wisniewski was there on time, but Schaefer did not show. At 1:00 A.M., Wisniewski had a beer and a sandwich, but still no Don. Wisniewski fell asleep and did not awaken for several hours when, with the sun rising, he saw Schaefer waddling toward him—"That's the way he walked even then."

"Where did you go?" asked the groggy Milt.

"Oh, we parked the car by the inlet."

"What did you do?"

"We just talked. She's a widow. She has two kids."

Widow or divorcee, Wisniewski thought, she was gorgeous. "I envied the rascal. But as usual he wouldn't talk. You'd think he'd tell you a little. I couldn't get a thing out of him. So he had his secret life. It was his business."

Wisniewski found his friend "a serious guy," who thought some things were too trivial or too personal to talk about. Schaefer occasionally went to Ocean City with others, including his Democratic friends, among them future congressman Danny Brewster. On one such trip, Schaefer endeared himself to Wisniewski when he rescued Milton's future wife, Anne, from unwanted pursuit by Brewster. "Don just stepped in, and Anne never forgot it," he said. Wisniewski was then running away from marriage, but Schaefer knew that he cared about Anne.

An Absolute Animal

As law partners, Schaefer and Arabian often walked down past the Block to the harbor, peering at the water framed by the collapsing warehouses. After a trip to San Francisco, Arabian wondered aloud why Baltimore couldn't aspire to the romance of that Pacific port city with its mystery-laden fog, its glorious bay, and its slanting streets. Years later, during an interview, she told a newspaper reporter that Schaefer's Inner Harbor vision dated from those days. "'This could be just like San Francisco, he said." Actually, of course, it was Arabian's observation. "I said *he* said it, but *I* really said it. He brought up the subject because he knew I had been there and had been raving about it." Like many of the women in his life, Arabian subordinated herself to her friend and partner—taking the last place in the firm's title, pretending to be a secretary, and giving good quotes to reporters.

When it came to dealing with the distressed souls who actually found their way to the offices of Schaefer, Waltjen, and Arabian, Schaefer quickly judged himself ill suited. He internalized their pain, refused to send bills to divorcing women—and knew he could not be as effective as a result. He needed a more dispassionate stance to judge the facts properly. He began to see that his emotional involvement led to embarrassment. One wealthy, prestigious client insisted that he had been wrongly accused of drunken driving, an offense that was about to cost the man his law license. "I fought for him like an absolute animal; it became a matter of principle. Then I found out he was really lying to me. He had been drinking, had hit another car. And he had a long series of license violations. When that realization came, it was like hitting me over the head. If I hadn't associated myself with him, the surprise wouldn't have made news to me. So, he lied to me, so what? . . . But it affected me." Schaefer wanted to trust people, to rely on them, and he always was affected by disloyalty. He began to look at people more carefully, with caution if not suspicion, a useful habit for the new life just ahead.

He remained a faithful communicant of Bishop Cummins Memorial Reformed Episcopal Church, a member of its vestry as a young man and moving into even more responsibility as he grew older. The congregation was jolted in those years when the treasurer absconded with $10,000, an enormous sum of money for a small church. Schaefer spoke to the pastor, Milton Erickson.

"Are you going to prosecute him?"

"No," the minister said.

"Why not?"

"I feel sorry for him. And he's going to give us back the money."

Schaefer thought Erickson most naive. The money was not, in fact, returned, but Bishop Cummins did get a new treasurer: William Donald Schaefer. He insisted that the church buy an insurance bond to protect itself lest he, too, take the money and run. He would not always demand such legalisms, growing supremely confident of his own probity and judgment. As a public official, he eagerly assumed the burden of spending other people's money, deciding for them what was in their best interest.

Meanwhile, the church congregation was growing, and an addition was to be built. The church wanted to buy a bit of adjoining land but ran into the power of City Hall. Others coveted the property and competed for it with the church. Bishop Cummins offered the most money, but the city sold the lot to the second highest bidder. This was a dirty trick, Schaefer thought then, a move to favor someone's political friend. Suddenly, the young lawyer and World War II vet was an aggrieved citizen, stirred by injustice.

At about the same time, he was angered by reports that a councilman had eased a relative into a nonconforming commercial use along Edmondson Avenue on The Hill. Suddenly, he was doubly outraged. Whatever he knew about civic life did not comport with events unfolding in his neighborhood. In the scheme of things, these were the mildest of pinpricks against the fabric of municipal law and life. But Schaefer decided he could do better and, shortly afterward, called a meeting of his partners to announce his intentions. He may well have been offended, but he and his mates were in danger of going hungry. They needed to get started, and law firms often gained clients when one of the partners was in the news. Someone was going to have to run for office, he said, and it was going to be him. Arabian and Waltjen became his campaign staff, and they hit the streets along with Alvie Unglesbee, Schaefer's colleague in the Grantley Improvement Association. The whole political enterprise was laughable, Arabian thought. "We were just kids. We didn't know what we were doing." Schaefer went after his new career with almost no training, no experience, not even the most casual interest in the affairs of government. What you didn't know could hurt you in Baltimore where politics was a nuanced and sometimes brutal world populated by the cunning and resolute, men who had done the work from near infancy. But this man, for whom the Great Depression had passed without notice, offered himself to the voters of Baltimore's Fifth District as a blank slate.

Running

For the serious student of the game, the D'Alesandros were Lesson 1, the First Family of Baltimore politics in the 1950s and 1960s. They worked their fields as carefully and devotedly as Uncle Willie tended his bed of zinnias. Young Tommy had been a precinct executive at the age of nine, working the polls with his mother, Nancy. They knew they could not survive without attention to the smallest detail of the family business, so, without finding it remarkable, they knew everyone's name and polling place—church, school, or firehouse. They knew where everyone worked, where they went to church, what bar they favored, and, almost always, whom they had voted for since the first year they could vote—and they kept the rolls up to date. As Old Tommy, the illustrious mayor of Baltimore, headed home one evening in the late 1950s, his driver stopped for a traffic light on Pratt Street near Little Italy, his neighborhood, the First Ward—all-Italian, all-Democratic, all-D'Alesandro. Their friend Tony, proprietor of the neighborhood dry cleaning establishment crossed the street in front of them. The mayor turned to his son: "How old do you think Gloria is . . . Tony's Gloria?" Young Tommy said he didn't know.

"Why don't you go over tomorrow and find out," his father said. The next morning, Young Tommy walked over to Tony's. After the usual pleasantries, D'Alesandro said, "Tony, how's Gloria?"

"Fine, fine. She'll be twenty-one on Thursday," her father said. "She'll be going to the elections board right away." Gloria could now join the neighborhood. She could vote. D'Alesandros knew birthdays.

Schaefer grew up on the other side of the city—and on the far side of the political world. He had no political nurturing whatever. D'Alesandro's father had named one of his sons Franklin Delano and called him "Roosie." FDR got little attention in the Schaefer household and William Donald says he knew virtually nothing about the man who gave the United States the hope and sustenance it needed to survive the Depression. Hungry men lined up outside D'Alesandro's house in Little Italy, hoping to find work. Schaefer claims he never saw a hungry Baltimorean in his neighborhood or even as he rode through the city on his way to school in those days of privation and fear. He was in his late twenties before he knew a precinct executive or what a precinct executive did. He had no idea whether his next-door neighbor was registered to vote, let alone the birth date of a shopkeeper's daughter. He and Uncle Willie exchanged only the briefest observations on public life, though his father might have known some-thing of Boss Pollack and his crowd of seat warmers in the courthouse. Schaefer remembered only one political observation: Mayor Howard Jack-son had run afoul of booze, his father had observed, passing out in pub-lic and embarrassing himself and his office. Schaefer's only other brush with politics came via church when one day Baltimore Mayor Theodore Roosevelt McKeldin spoke at Bishop Cummins Church. Schaefer had been curious at least, but he remembered only that it was Good Friday and that he sat in the balcony, which was opened specially to accommodate the crowd.

Now, motivated by the injustice visited upon his church—and perhaps by the need for law clients—Schaefer filed to run for the House of Dele-gates in the Fifth District, which in 1950 swung from North Charles Street through Roland Park, continuing into far West Baltimore, and then dipping down past Edmondson Avenue to Frederick Road. It was the second largest of the city's six districts. The contention that Schaefer's law firm needed some rainmaking—with lawyer advertising prohibited by the bar association—is supported by the office he sought. A member of the state legislature had little opportunity to right a local wrong, but seats in Annapolis were easier to come by than city office because city councilmen were far more influential, their seats more highly prized, the competition stiffer.

Schaefer, with the help of his friend Alvie Unglesbee, an officer in the neighborhood association, ran against twenty-seven other contenders for six available seats. Arabian and Waltjen knocked on doors, dropped his campaign card. Schaefer was obliged to file and appear on the ballot as William D. Schaefer, a damaging requirement, since he was known (if at all) as Donald Schaefer. Baltimoreans with any political aspiration knew enough to register under the name people recognized. With no party backing, no money, and no thousand-member D'Alesandro-like team, he needed a name people knew at least. Nevertheless, Schaefer finished ahead of thirteen candidates, a total of 5,053 voters pulling his lever. Of course, fourteen other candidates finished ahead of him. When he lost, he said, he simply went back to his law office in the Munsey Building.

He continued to work for the community association but made no effort to thrust himself toward the front of the pack even as his enthusiasm for the practice of law waned. Yet when he tried again in 1954, he had some confidence of victory. He told his steady date, Irene Vincent, that he would take her to a celebration after the polls closed. This time, his share of the vote increased to 5,858, up almost 15 percent, and he finished seventh, beating one incumbent but just out of the winning six. On his own, without clubhouse credentials, he had attracted more than 5,000 votes twice—enough to make him seem worthy of attention from the bosses, men who always had talent scouts watching, the better to head off threats to their chosen candidates. All of this might have been consoling, but Schaefer apparently went into a deep funk. He failed to call Vincent, who had no idea what had happened until she saw in the morning newspaper that her friend had not won.

But Schaefer had made an impression. Edgar Silver, a young lawyer who won a delegate seat in 1954, started talking about him. Silver knew that talk mattered; he saw that it could generate action on large and small scales. Silver achieved in politics the way D'Alesandro did, working his way in from the precincts around his family's house on Auchenteroly Terrace near Druid Hill Park in the city's Fourth District. He was with and then against the mighty Pollack. He saw the value of putting people together with important other people and claiming credit for the results: an endorsement, a job, a judgeship, a meeting, a hospitable climate in which something could be accomplished.

"You ought to take a look at this guy I know," he told Irvin Kovens. "He ran for House of Delegates. Clean-cut, hard-working guy." Silver knew that Schaefer had other qualifications the Kovens organization wanted: Schaefer was not Jewish, and he lived in the southern end of the sprawling Fifth, where the organization was weakest. A Gentile was needed to provide ethnic balance for the virtually all-Jewish team led by Kovens: Phillip Goodman, Leon Edelman, Leon Abramson, and Sol Liss. The Fifth was a mighty clubhouse, an extraordinary seedbed of Baltimore and Maryland leadership, eventually producing two governors, an appellate court judge, and any number of city and state lawmakers—not to speak of a king-making, bank-rolling boss.

Schaefer and Kovens had met. In what might have been his only overtly political act aside from actually running for office, the two-time loser joined the citywide Democratic Club, and every Sunday after church, he drove to a meeting of Democratic leaders at the Emerson Hotel. Pollack and Kovens were always there. Kovens had the bearing of command. "All of a sudden in he came. He was six foot two. He had a foot-long cigar in his face. Everybody, everything stopped and he was like a honey pot. Everyone ran to Mr. Kovens. They all wanted something: Will you take care of this for me? Will you do this, Mr. Kovens?" There was a parking ticket basket into which all the precinct workers tossed citations that needed attention. Status accrued to those who could "fix" such things. Offenders were instructed to show up; then, usually without prompting, the matter would be dropped or the penalty reduced as a matter of course without any involvement by Kovens or his men. They invariably got the credit, though. On such illusions was power built.

Terms

After one of the Sunday meetings, the great man approached the nobody. "I want to see you," he said.

"All right. Yes sir," Schaefer replied.

He called at the Kovens home that evening. "We need someone in your part of the ward to run for council," Kovens said. Schaefer said he'd like nothing more. Kovens talked about the Fifth and the team he'd assembled—smart, able people who were certain to move ahead, to be successful. When a pause came, Schaefer said, "I want to tell you my terms."

"Your terms?"

"Yes, sir."

Schaefer says Kovens stared at him for a moment. "He must have been laughing himself to death," Schaefer thought, but he went on: "Everything political is yours. Everything in the area of voting is mine."

He told this story repeatedly over the years, knowing that few believed he could have retained any independence once such a deal was struck by a man like Kovens. With help came control, ownership. At least, that was Kovens's image, passed on to him by men like Pollack who put people into judgeships and other positions after having them write and sign undated letters of resignation so that they could be dismissed if they opposed the Pollack line. But here was a young, untutored supplicant negotiating away at least a part of his yet-to-be won authority, the political part. Schaefer's terms suggested utter ignorance of, or utter disregard for, the rules of the clubhouse. Newcomers didn't have terms. Even if they did, they could hardly make a distinction between the political and business needs of a man like Kovens. The two were inseparable. Politics *was* business. But Schaefer gained something simply by daring to assert himself. It worked for him the way many things worked for him because it was unexpected— and because Kovens was, relative to the knaves and grafters then operating in Maryland, a reformer.

"I'll listen to you, but if I think something is right, I'll vote my way no matter what," Schaefer says he said. Thus did a thirty-two-year-old Court Square lawyer become Kovens' designated Gentile, a made political man. He called at the boss's house as a hopeful without portfolio, experience or network. Yet he had won 5,585 votes in the immediately previous election, an impressive number, and not that many fewer on his first try. Schaefer had a constituency, and he had nerve. "I don't think anyone ever went in to him and said I'm going to vote the way I want. I expect you put up a lot of money for me. I expect you to bust your back for me. I want you to support everything I do. And I'm going to do what *I* want to do. I think he might have been stunned." The tale gains credence from a retelling by Kovens himself. Edgar Silver got a phone call from the bemused boss the very next day. "That's a strange guy you've got there," Kovens said. "He told me he wouldn't do anything he wouldn't be proud of in church."

"That was his interpretation," Schaefer said. "That's how he put it. He gave it the right spin for him. But that's not what I said." As impudent as Schaefer's demand might have seemed, it was not beyond a Kovens to modulate his own ego, not beyond his imagination to see that a man so guileless would look independent and be of even more value to him — not at all beyond his calculation that he would own Schaefer soon enough. Here were the mirror and the smoke, the little deal between boss and tyro, terms agreed to mutually but defined and interpreted variously.

"William Donald, William Donald"

Kovens was becoming a dominant political force, strong enough to challenge the notorious Pollack, a liquor running, patronage-wielding bully who truly was a boss, a man who made hostages of governors as well as mayors. He ran a ruthlessly tight organization that counted the D'Alesandros as loyalists. "I knew what Pollack was," Schaefer said. Any adult Baltimorean, even one as oblivious as Schaefer, knew something of the most notorious of Baltimore bosses. Pollack was referred to occasionally in newspapers by nicknames, a certain sign that he was thought of as a ruffian: "Yankel" or "Big John" or "J. P." but usually just "Jack." Schaefer met the fourth Ward leader at those Sunday morning Democratic conclaves. He would sit, Schaefer said later, "like a bird of prey and start quoting Shakespeare." Pretty ridiculous, Schaefer thought, for someone as notorious as Yankel. James H. "Jack" Pollack had been arrested repeatedly for violations of the motor vehicle laws. He seemed uncommonly inept behind the wheel, forever finding himself in collisions of some sort — often, unluckily, with police vehicles. The arresting officers frequently found quantities of "strained mash" sloshing in twenty-gallon containers on the back seat of Pollack's car. Thus his record included numerous Volstead Act (Prohibition) violations.

A prize fighter of local reknown in his youth, Pollack was occasionally charged with assault on police officers during these rum-running incidents. Once, during a robbery, police said Jack Pollack had shot a man to death, one Hugo Caplan. Police records of this event suddenly disappeared. It was no unanticipated by-product of his move into politics, then, that he quickly gained a presence in the courthouse. He controlled judgeships, clerkships and all manner of patronage appointments, and the winner of each job was expected to give to Pollack, along with the unsigned letter, a tribute of cash, perhaps a weekly one — a kickback. In times of trouble, when one of many charges against him was scheduled for hearing, a Pollack man would likely be nearby to help. Jack became the man to see for jobs in the halls of justice, in the legislature, and elsewhere. He was seldom convicted of any offense—and once, after the Caplan shooting, the Baltimore City State's attorney apologized to him publicly.

In the patronage play Pollack directed, jobs and votes were the thing. As his precinct level mastery deepened and expanded, he discovered that money could be made with less threat to himself and others via politics. At first, he served the Northeast Baltimore boss, Willie Curran, with distinction. But then Pollack transformed himself into a businessman who wore bow ties, met downtown for lunch with his lieutenants, and held a lavish Christmas party, which became an institution for pols and reporters. The newspapers would recount his police record periodically, and Curran would defend him. When Pollack was named in 1934 to the State Boxing Commission, the *Sun* called it "a sad commentary on Maryland politics." Willie Curran disagreed: "He is a high class fellow, all the better for any little roughness in early life." Fittingly, Curran's portrait was hung in a Supreme Bench courtroom, but Pollack became a more prepossessing figure on the Baltimore political field, fighting the patronage wars as fiercely as he fought to allow that strained mash its fullest evolution.

Pollack was a skilled practitioner of every electoral trick. His representatives scoured every alley house and bar for those votes that, one upon one, delivered prodigious margins for his favored candidates. For two decades, he owned the fourth councilmanic district of Baltimore, which gave him ownership of much more in the days before the U.S. Supreme Court decreed in 1964 that democracy worked only when wards or precincts had roughly the same number of voters—one person, one vote. Before that decision, control of a single Baltimore district, if it was the right district, gave a boss important control not just in city, but also in statewide elections. Pollack's mastery peaked in the gubernatorial race of 1950, when he "took" Democratic incumbent William Preston Lane. Lane's levy of a sales tax was a grave threat to his reelection prospects, but no issue and no grievance rivaled the organization's orders. Lane won Pollack's district in the primary that year by better than 2 to 1, even as the rest of Baltimore went for Lane's opponent. Then Lane made a big mistake. He fired a Pollack loyalist named Reuben Caplan in a dispute about patronage at the Orphan's Court in Baltimore. Pollack retaliated, in effect firing Lane—dropping him from the Yankel ticket. A profound change of mind swept over the Fourth District. Having found Lane the best candidate a few weeks earlier (and having backed him handsomely in 1946), voters discovered the virtues of Theodore McKeldin—a Republican, of all things. Lane had beaten McKeldin in 1946, but when Lane fired Caplan, Pollack took another look. In Pollack's home precinct, the thirty-third of Ward 15, voters went for McKeldin big—17,346 to 9,282, a two-to-one margin. Only weeks earlier, the results had been essentially the opposite, Lane winning over his Democratic primary opponent by about the same margin. Pollack's control was surgical: Voters replaced Democrat Lane with a Republican, but the palm card, a hand-held guide for voters, directed them to all of Pollack's still-favored Democrats farther down the ballot. All of these worthies were elected. Lane was out. Pollack's man, Reuben Caplan, remained in public life, serving later with Schaefer on the City Council.

A Kovens Man

Another prominent beneficiary of Boss Pollack's labors was Old Tommy, who had served in the Maryland House of Delegates, as mayor of Baltimore, and as a U.S. congressman. Old Tommy, it was said, never left his Fawn/President Street–Little Italy base, and it never left him. Similarly, Pollack clung to his Anoka Avenue manse. Richard J. Daley lived on in his pin-neat house in the blue-collar Bridgeport neighborhood of Chicago. Base was everything.

This was not necessarily an advantage for Schaefer as it turned out. Over the decade of the 1950s, a West Baltimore politician's carefully cultivated home turf could vanish. The fourth and fifth councilmanic districts became far less white and less Jewish almost overnight. To compensate, Pollack tried to push over into Kovens's territory but failed. And in 1959, his drive to give himself and Old Tommy one more romp in City Hall was thwarted by J. Harold Grady, who was backed by Kovens. Pollack and Kovens had been in business together, co-owners of a laundry that tried to corner the restaurant tablecloth business. Kovens would later covet and win a seat on the city's liquor board—by the grace of Mayor Ted McKeldin—the better to enforce his linen franchise, perhaps. It fell to young Councilman Schaefer to chose between these two men, the imperious Kovens and the "bird of prey." Though others saw little difference between them, Schaefer found Pollack's hand far too heavy. "Pollack asked me to be with him once and I said, 'No, I'm a Kovens man.' He never spoke to me again. When you got on Pollack's ticket you did what he said. Kovens never did that. Kovens never did anything like that," Schaefer insisted. The political sun was setting for Yankel and rising for Kovens, a man with more than the usual assets of boss leaders. At his store on Baltimore Street, he sold kitchen sets, couches, televisions, and chests of drawers to welfare families. Merely in the course of his daily business, then, his personal network—his constituency—grew. In the rear of the showroom, a clerk sat behind a window beneath a neon sign that said "Cashier." Kovens had thirty-five collectors who went out into his domain to gather up the dollars paid for these household goods on time. A fine way to know and to control the thinking of a precinct or a district, thought Edgar Silver: You tended to your constituents every day of the year, and they would become beholden to you. Kovens had multiple networks—his employees, his political runners, and a loose collection of partners, which included Pollack and "Little Willie" Adams, for whom the numbers game had evolved into real estate development. Little Willie and the Furniture Man became a potent twosome, a combination of money, votes, and brains—often, over the years, devoted to the promotion of William Donald Schaefer.

Pollack fought on to keep his empire any time it was threatened. He put one "Schaffer, Max" on the ballot for City Council in 1955 to dilute the vote for "Schaefer, William D." Here was a staple from the boffo archive of ballot tailoring, a ploy known in Baltimore as "name's the same," an effort to confuse the voter into pulling the lever for a candidate whose name was similar to that of the candidate he or she really preferred. Schaffer? Schaefer? Shaffer? Who knew? One year, Kovens and Raynor, then a clerk in the elections office, drove to the home of one of these Schaefers to encourage his retirement from the field. At Kovens's insistence, Raynor says he went to the door with the form, and the mischievous candidate appeared, drunk. Raynor got the needed signature, returned to the car, and drove back downtown with Kovens.

In 1955, the candidate countered as well, attempting to have his name changed officially to William Donald Schaefer. The court ruled against him. Was the judge controlled then, as were many on the Baltimore bench, by Pollack? It would take four years for Schaefer to make the change, an effort that, somewhat ironically, began to cement his three-part banner into the mind of Baltimore voters. In the meantime, he and the Kovens team went ahead with the change on the street, in the public mind, and on their election day palm cards. Kovens's men accomplished what the court had declined to do at some potential sacrifice to their own well-being, actions taken only at the insistence of a Kovens. It was not unheard of for candidates to work solely for themselves, encouraging their supporters to "single shoot." This was a tactic employed by ostensible allies who might quietly urge their backers to vote only for them even though, if a district was electing three council members, a voter had three choices. If only a single vote was cast, however, only one candidate was helped. But the Kovens team actually was a team, strong enough to bring along the newest of its members. "They were so afraid I would lose. We used to go around and say, 'Be sure it's William Donald, William Donald, William Donald.' By the end of it all, I had four names. I was known as William Donald, William Donald." Part of his political vulnerability had become a strength: Now he had a distinctive, three-part name with a certain aristocratic flavor, complete with everything but a Roman numeral.

Getting 10,928 votes in his third outing for public office, Schaefer ran third in a field of twenty-three. The importance of being on the Kovens team could not have been clearer. Behind the fourth-place finisher, who took 10,514 votes, the next best contender, Frank Flynn, had 8,767 votes, nearly 2,000 fewer—and Flynn was an incumbent. These numbers, seen in the context of his 1950 and 1954 defeats, left Schaefer certain of his debt to Kovens.

Schaefer had thought of himself as a loser and knew he would never win, even with Kovens's help. He fretted, fumed, and paced to the point of nervous exhaustion. Years later, Schaefer recalled, he refused to appear at his headquarters until he was certain of victory. "Look at Shaky," Kovens said to one of his other, more confident charges. "He thinks he can lose." Pre-Kovens, the big man was saying, Schaefer could have lost and did. In the general election several weeks later, Schaefer finished first.

The Boss quickly got his new councilman his first aide, a driver and advance man named Remy Marks. Kovens, Schaefer said, put Marks on the liquor board staff and then had him assigned to Schaefer. He was from the lower end of the district, too, knew a lot of people, and could introduce the new man around in neighborhoods where he wasn't well known. "This is Don Schaefer," Remy would say. "He's a Kovens man." And people would say, "Oh, okay, all right." Schaefer had arrived. He had a political Man Friday. Such men were called "Up-Ups" by one student of clubhouse lore and language: An Up-Up (also known as a coat holder or body slave) drove the candidate, entered the meeting before the candidate, sat in the front row, and waited for the candidate to arrive. When that moment came, he would turn just a second or two earlier, smile to the audience, and, while raising his outstretched palms toward the roof, murmur ever so gently, "Up, up." The people would stand as if a bishop had blessed them with his presence.

A Talent Pool

Schaefer joined an immensely talented group of men on the City Council of 1955, men of promise and drive, many of whom would move on to exalted careers. In some ways, this council would represent a high point in Baltimore City government. After its members left—for judgeships, for business opportunities, to run for higher office—the next wave of city representatives would be a cut below. Schaefer's colleagues eventually would include Peter Angelos, a fierce advocate who made millions as a Steelworkers Union lawyer, winning cases against big steel for allowing conditions that infected workers with asbestosis. He had run unsuccessfully for mayor and council president before settling down to practice law and await his moment. He would later become principal owner of the Baltimore Orioles, saving the team from out-of-city ownership, and a force in state politics. Another colleague was Sol Liss, who went on to serve as an appeals court judge in Maryland and to chair an important study of the Chesapeake Bay. Robert Embry, the imaginative and feverish advocate of the city, might have been Jimmy Carter's Secretary of Housing and Urban Development but for political considerations. Leon Edelman, a pioneer in civil rights, proposed open housing laws and stood as the only favorable vote for his own measures, which were too liberal for the 1940s. Henry G. Parks was a tough black businessman whose Baltimore-based sausage company had name recognition far beyond the city, a man who said that racial discrimination had kept him from running General Motors or some other major corporation. A later colleague, Barbara A. Mikulski, a social worker and neighborhood organizer who later won a seat in Congress, became a star in the firmament of national liberalism—and then the first woman elected to the U.S. Senate in her own right. Kweisi Mfume, one of the most skilled politicians in Baltimore history, came up from poverty to win a seat in Congress, to head the Congressional Black Caucus, and to become president of the National Association for the Advancement of Colored People. As this wave of talented members retired or moved up, the power of the mayor peaked under Schaefer, who was another product of the council's glory days.

Noise

The new councilman began making noise and news on August 11, 1955, when he demanded "immediate correction" of a serious neighborhood complaint: high weeds sheltering rats on city-owned land adjacent to a playground in the 900 block of Allendale Street in his home district. This was the very heart of the area that elected him, his base as surely as Little Italy was D'Alesandro's. Councilmen did address overarching policy issues with some frequency, but their focus always returned to neighborhoods: the homeowners, their children, their rear alleys, their pets, their automobiles, streetlights, wrecked and abandoned cars, potholes, and troublesome bars. Schaefer approached it all with relish. He pushed for more lighting along Edmondson Avenue. He wanted stiffer penalties for dog poisoning, a crackdown on firing weapons in the city, and an end to excessive car noise. And he was immediately more assertive than the usual new member. When his bill calling for more trash collection failed, he loudly accused the city's sanitary engineers of "knifing Baltimoreans in the back." He engaged Fourth Ward colleague Liss in what the *Sun* called "a thunderous" exchange on the advisability of incarcerating young offenders for liquor law violations. A sound approach, declared Liss. Schaefer thought better recreational opportunities were a more sensible way to address the problem.

Epiphanies

Jim Rouse thought of Schaefer as a creature of "the city's worst scalawags," but others were intrigued that he regularly opposed measures that Pollack advanced via Old Tommy. Indeed, Schaefer's was often the only "no" vote on Old Tommy's bills. By the time Schaefer was up for reelection, the *Sun* endorsed him without reservation: "Not only is he a member of the anti-Pollack faction, he has consistently stood up in councilmanic debate as the lone opponent to most of the ill-advised bills hustled through on heavy D'Alesandro majorities. Mr. Schaefer surely deserves re-election."

The Pollack-Kovens rivalry and perhaps Schaefer's rising prominence provided a challenge to the first-term councilmen's judgment in early 1959. Kovens's men decided they might knock off one of Pollack's most important legislators, state Senator Paul Dorf, a man whose importance to Pollack was extended by actual family ties. Dorf was married to Pollack's daughter Rona. So, of course, beating him would have been even sweeter. Maybe, it was thought, Schaefer was the man for the job. The forces of Kovens, Goodman, and Abramson—so anxious for Schaefer to win, so determined to elect a man who could give them balance—now determined that he was valuable for another purpose: hurting Yankel. It is a boss's prerogative to take risks with the future of others, to be sure, and this was one of those moments when a misstep could end a career. Flattered, no doubt, Schaefer at first acquiesced. He announced his candidacy and seemed headed into a brutal, unwinnable fight when he suddenly withdrew, filing for reelection to the council. He sensed the peril and drew a line: He would be devoted and loyal, but he would not commit suicide— another one of his terms, it turned out. His view of it in retrospect kept love and loyalty for the Kovens crowd alive. "They would have worked hard for me," he said, "but it wouldn't have been enough." Better, much better, for Schaefer to continue along the path that had become so pleasing to him.

In both the primary and general elections of 1959, Schaefer led all the other council contenders in the Fifth District, finishing well ahead of the other three incumbents. And, of course, Paul Dorf crushed whoever it was the Kovens men finally sent out against him.

Life was changing in many ways. Sophistication and self-knowledge were growing. "Mr. Kovens used to take me to all the rich clubs, the Suburban Club, all the clubs. I enjoyed going. I used to be walking behind him and I loved it. Everybody came over to him and he'd say, 'Say hello to Shaky. Shake hands with Shaky. Shake hands with Shaky.' They'd all shake hands. He'd always be at the top table. I'd be sitting somewhere near him. I didn't have to sit beside him. Somewhere near him." Schaefer's submission to the aura of Kovens power seemed complete, but it was not. Even as he had bargained with the boss for some measure of independence, Schaefer made a bargain with himself. "There was a time when I had to figure out that this was not my life. I didn't have any money. But I told myself, 'Don't try to get up where Mr. Kovens is. Stay in your own area. Keep your mind where you belong.'"

In this crucial matter, Schaefer had far more insight, far better instinct for survival than the man who was supposed to be manipulating him. Schaefer seldom let anyone buy his lunch or dinner, an effort of some will, since public officials can always expect someone to pick up the tab. He never agreed with the old line uttered piously by his colleagues: "You can't buy me that cheaply." Schaefer sensed that "cheaply" does it most of the time, as each beer and burger adds up to an accretion of bias, an atmosphere in which favors may be requested and granted without thought. One is bought without ever knowing it. A quirk of his personality, invaluable for politicians perhaps, was a thoroughgoing lack of trust. Always most comfortable with large groups, Schaefer would sit with allies or enemies always wondering what they were plotting. He might well have succumbed to the subtle cooptation that was practiced with such skill and ease by men like Irv Kovens. But he sensed danger in privilege unearned, in the entrée he had now, and in the wealth of those he was meeting. He could think of himself as a visitor or an interloper but not as a member of these clubs. "That's when people own you," he told himself. Schaefer insisted that the bargain held, though he knew it was tested repeatedly—and, in truth, he was, by design, not a good witness. He did not wish to know what Kovens was up to. "He knew when to leave the room," is the way it was usually put. Don't hear the deal done—for surely even Schaefer knew that deals were the oxygen of men like Kovens. "He never involved me in anything. I don't think he ever expected me to do anything that just wasn't right and proper."

"Be Honest, Work Hard"

Remy Marks was not Schaefer's only aide, of course. And not the most important by a long shot. In this period of his development, beginning in March 1957, he made another career-building associate, Joan Bereska, who was as committed a worker as he was and just as smart. An employee of the Citizens Planning and Housing Association, she took Schaefer the bills and the positions of the CPHA, and he pushed them. She attended the council meetings and learned how that body worked. She began to get involved in the daily operation of his office. Like Kovens, she was a stabilizing force, a talent and a resource that expanded his reach — the rooster that soothed the skittish racehorse, one of her friends said. A young woman of some privilege, Joan Bereska, née Burrier, grew up near the old mill village of Hampden with its stone company houses and its chockablock neighborhoods of refugees from the privations of West Virginia, where the company housed its mill hands. Her family kept a horse, which she rode in Druid Hill Park. She had a bit of a prep school look, and she was smart. At first, she was an employee of the CPHA, then of the Girl Scouts, but Schaefer had the ability to expropriate people, to annex and own them. Bereska gave up a $14,000-a-year job with the Scouts to become Schaefer's super-charged assistant at a $3,000 pay cut. Her life merged with his public life almost completely. Over time, she handled almost everything, from dressing down unruly public works employees who balked at the latest PR stunt to making sure Schaefer had ginger ale and nothing stronger in his glass at cocktail parties. Schaefer had a far better instinctive sense of how to protect himself personally and politically than she, but in virtually everything else, she was his equal.

The young councilman began to progress steadily on the council, offering workaday bills, seeing a fair number of them passed, and winning minor promotions. In a tribute to his independent voting, city comptroller Hyman Pressman had a rubber stamp made with every councilman's name on it except Schaefer's. Some thought the Fifth Ward representative was a bit of a nerd, but he was getting a profile, intentionally or not, and solidifying his ties with Kovens, who was striving to succeed Pollack as the city's big political force. His life outside the office remained an "average" one, and he continued to live with his parents on Edgewood Street. He and Irene Vincent continued their relationship, though it had its ups and downs. They traveled frequently to the beach in his modest little gray Dodge, and she occasionally visited with his parents.

Just before Easter in 1958, Schaefer and his father were trimming the hedge in front of the house. "Why don't you get us a bag for the clippings," his father said. When Schaefer came back a few minutes later, his partner was not there. Schaefer looked up and down the block and then started down the steps. He found Uncle Willie lying on the sidewalk.

"Dad's down. He's down on the sidewalk," he shouted to his mother, who called the rescue service.

Hartge Levine came down from his porch and put a pillow under the stricken man's head. Seventy years old by then, Willie Schaefer had had a heart attack, and the doctors at Lutheran Hospital were unable to help. "Just like that he was gone," Schaefer said. Schaefer wasn't aware of any heart problem, but Willie, who was a smoker and overweight, had been treated for heart disease for six years.

Hundreds of people turned out to pay their respects at Ticknor's Funeral Home on the corner of Pennsylvania and North avenues. They needed an extra room to hold the flowers. Schaefer was impressed all over again with the respect and admiration his father attracted, and, he says, he learned another of life's lessons. He'd always thought visits to funeral homes and dutiful expressions of condolence were intrusive and as difficult for the deceased person's family as for the sympathizer. Now he found these attentions comforting. Despite that final lesson from his father, Schaefer never got over the difficulty of dealing with the death or even the impending death of his friends. He visited them with fear and loathing or skipped the visit altogether. Often, he tried to hang onto some fragment of the departed, visiting the graves of his closest departed friends, usually on New Year's Day. He brought wreaths and news of the previous year's events, and he felt he could hear his good wishes reciprocated.

Schaefer was thirty-seven when his father died, three years into his first council term. Over the years, Schaefer told of his father's advice: "Be honest, work hard. He felt if he didn't work six days a week he was stealing from his employer." His son would do better. He would work seven. When Schaefer met criticism in his public life, some of it severe enough to be considered ridicule, he seemed puzzled as well as angry. Certain that he had followed his father's counsel without exception as mayor and as governor, Schaefer felt he should have been immune to criticism, as if those who questioned his methods or his motives were breaking a contract.

Accommodations

With Kovens and his Fifth District team to support him, Schaefer moved rapidly into the council's leadership rank, a remarkable bit of early success for a man who had arrived with virtually no knowledge of politics or government. And he began to see what life in segregated Baltimore was like if you were black. He and his colleagues ate lunch regularly at the House of Welch, a restaurant and bar at the corner of Holliday Street and Guilford Avenue, no more than a block from City Hall. After being elected to the council in 1963, Henry Parks would accompany them occasionally. His presence, though, was problematic. The African American Parks could not enter the restaurant's bar. Even earlier, Councilman Peter Angelos remembers going out for lunch and bringing a sandwich back for one of the council's black staff members. The man would thank him and say, "Wouldn't it be nice if I could just come with you?" Angelos then introduced one of the early civil rights ordinances, but he was not successful.

The city's most prominent restaurateurs opposed a 1962 bill that was designed to open restaurants and bars but actually kept them closed to blacks with an outrageous loophole: The law exempted barber shops, cemeteries, and also restaurants that did more business in liquor than in food—a convenient way to tolerate and extend Jim Crow's reign in Baltimore. Even that gap in the law was not big enough for many. Otto Shell-hase, owner of the very well-known Shellhase's Restaurant on North Howard Street, voiced a common theme of the opposition: "This is going to affect our livelihood." One could legitimately oppose civil rights progress in those days by invoking the needs of commerce. Schaefer was sympathetic to the financial concerns of such men and to the feelings of those in the broader community who thought mixing of the races was simply wrong. They weren't racists, he thought, they just didn't want to have to eat in the same restaurants or stay in the same motels with blacks. If one clung to such feelings honestly, he reasoned, it was understandable. It was a time when the prerogatives of business and the feelings of whites still counted more than decency and justice.

Thus came the spectacle of black and white Baltimore City Council members lunching together in a downtown restaurant, the House of Welch, but separating if they chose to visit the restaurant's bar. Schaefer said he was embarrassed and "very emotional about" the degrading treatment of Parks, a man he regarded as a gentleman—courageous, dignified, and tough. The humiliation of an individual, a person of rank and standing in the community, a personal friend, was hurtful and somewhat confusing to Schaefer. Yet, there is no record of on-the-spot protest by him or his white council colleagues, no determination to wipe out a circumstance they in fact had created with their ordinance. They left that to Parks, largely because, in those days, the thought of lodging a formal protest would not have occurred to anyone—any more than whites would have questioned a minstrel show. Parks himself and the council's civil rights pioneers, Rubenstein and Edelman primarily, had not been revolutionaries, though Schaefer said Edelman had been "a flaming liberal." Rubenstein, Edelman, Sol Liss, and Abramson were the council's natural civil rights leaders because, as Jews, Schaefer said "their people have been put upon all over the world." In those days, Jews were not allowed to join many of Baltimore's business organizations, including the Merchants Club on Redwood Street.

Parks had hoped to open completely "any and every" place of business catering to the public. Yet Parks was obliged in the interests of passing any bill at all to revise, trim, and reduce the scope of his proposal. He wanted to end what he called "the most obnoxious" restriction on blacks. It was time, he said, for the council to create a truly open city. The bill brought him into conflict with east side Councilman Joe Staszak, himself a bar owner. One afternoon, Parks and Staszak almost fought in Schaefer's office. Bereska and Schaefer separated them. Councilman Joe Mach, speaking for himself and the very powerful Young Men's Bohemian Clubs, was also there, adding to the tension with Parks. The dispute boiled through the afternoon and flared again later on the council floor. Staszak abusively challenged Parks's proposal, and Parks responded with a proposition: "I'll fight you here like a gentleman," he told Staszak, or "I'll fight you outside in the street, whichever you like." Schaefer admired Parks's courage but did not stand to speak for him.

The dehumanizing ploys that were then used to cope with white people's mindless fear had come through during council hearings on earlier desegregation legislation: Anton Wilke, an East Baltimore restaurant owner, said that he always took care to ease the concerns of white patrons when a group of Hopkins physicians came in, since often one or more of them was dark-skinned. "I always had to make it very clear that I had visitors from Calcutta, India, not from Pennsylvania Avenue," Wilke said. Councilman Liss stood. "I think the citizens of this city are entitled to as much consideration as people from India," he said. So did an array of religious and civil rights organizations, whose demands were taking the issue to a new level of explosiveness. Some began to worry that bars could become the sites of major demonstrations unless the ban were lifted. Pragmatism, if nothing else, would come to the aid of equality. On the night of the first climactic vote on Parks's bill, Schaefer introduced legislation regulating heaters that used solid fuel. Life went on even in the midst of traumatic social change. Parks's ordinance did not pass that year or in any other. Schaefer voted in favor each time it was introduced, but open accommodations were achieved in Baltimore only by an act of the state legislature that annulled the so-called tavern exemption in 1969. Baltimore clung to its "most obnoxious" discriminatory law until after Dr. Martin Luther King Jr.'s "I Have a Dream" speech, the Birmingham bus boycott, and King's assassination.

A Knife and a Dent

In 1951, when Schaefer's friend Walter Sondheim became chairman of the Baltimore School Board, it met for lunch at the Merchants Club on Redwood Street. Sondheim, as a Jew, could not have been a member. "A knife went through me every time I was there," said Sondheim. He finally said that he would resign rather than subject himself to that feeling again. The meeting place was changed.

Baltimore was a city that began to mark the falling of these loathsome barriers in the 1960s: the first ranking Jewish banker at the Mercantile, the first black partner at the preeminent law firm Piper and Marbury, the first department store to allow black shoppers to try on clothing, the first Jewish member of the Merchant's Club. The latter was a military man named Levy, Sondheim recalled, a high-ranking officer in the Coast Guard. By tradition, the powerful B&O named the captain of the port, and that person automatically became a Merchant's member. The B&O wrote a letter to the club saying that the new port chief was a Captain Levy. The railroad got a letter by return mail asking whether the man named Levy was Jewish. The B&O leadership refused to answer the question, and the Merchant's Club was integrated—slightly. A Jew was in, sort of; blacks were still barred; and women were provided a separate room.

Some people were apologetic about these rules. They said they opposed them but were simply unable to act for business reasons: their fear that customers would stay away or that Baltimore handicapped itself if it opened its restaurants and bars to blacks and surrounding jurisdictions did not. Sondheim worked to break down barriers in other areas: "We were trying to make a dent in the 100 percent segregation in housing, trying to get black tenants into traditionally white housing projects. The projects were segregated because the city was segregated, geographically segregated. The things we were trying to do seemed artificial, I guess, in the sense that busing was artificial, not in response to some great demand. We did it because we thought it ought to be done. I don't remember tenant pressure to do it."

At the start of what Schaefer called "civil rights days"—as if it was a national or local passage to be tolerated—he was tutored by Phil Goodman, one of his Fifth Ward mentors. Goodman took Schaefer aside one day and said, "'You know the civil rights thing is right and you ought to vote for it.' He said it in an offhanded way. He didn't tell me how to vote, he just said I should be for open accommodations." The Fifth was getting more and more black, of course, as was the city itself, so there was plenty of political motivation to vote "right" on these issues. Then and later, Schaefer's evolving public and political consciousness was shaped by his Jewish colleagues. Schaefer thought that anyone would have to accept the moral force and honesty of their civil rights advocacy. At the same time, he was tolerant of his three colleagues in the First District, in particular, who "were violently opposed to civil rights because they never had any black people down there. They had an old time prejudice." Schaefer might well have had it too. He had not known any black people until his army days.

No Dancing

In Baltimore later, Schaefer learned more in 1963 from Emma Gaskins Bright, who ran a neighborhood association and whose husband was a school principal. She invited him to a meeting to hear a young black minister, Dr. Martin Luther King, Jr. Bright was dealing with a blank slate. "I never knew who he was," Schaefer recalled: "Emma had an event, and he was to speak at the church. He wasn't that prominent then. He wasn't a great leader then, though I guess he was in the black community. He was some speaker. You'd think he was speaking directly from God." Emma Bright was Schaefer's friend as well as an ally, first in the neighborhood improvement world and then in politics. She adopted the young man from Edgewood Street, choosing a bit of responsive clay and attempting to mold into it some compassion and understanding. Schaefer knew exactly what she was doing and, in a sense, knew that he needed what she was offering: a friendly introduction to diversity.

At a dance one night, she stopped by Schaefer's seat with a proposition.

"Come on, Don, let's dance."

"Oh, Emma, thanks, but no, I don't think so."

"On come on, Don," she persisted.

"No, no, Emma, I don't dance."

Then she looked at him, smiled, and said, "Don, it doesn't rub off."

"I remembered that," Schaefer said, as if he understood her mild rebuke and found it legitimate. He saw the truth in Bright's invitation to let go of fear—fear that whites might turn to stone if they touched blacks or drank from the same water fountains or sat in the same movie theaters together.

The Road

Civil rights, poverty, and the power of neighborhoods were vectors of public life then directing themselves at city governments across the nation. In the mid-1960s, President Lyndon Johnson's War on Poverty was putting money and power in the hands of people who had had none, hoping to bring them into the political world then owned by D'Alesandro, Pollack, Kovens, and others. Schaefer and his colleagues on the council were left to rationalize it all, to catch the flak, and to find a way to preserve their own positions while honoring the aspirations of left-out neighborhoods. This required balancing that was illustrated in many ways, including efforts to make the city a more viable commercial entity by providing a more modern transportation system. Schaefer and others advocated construction of a new road from the center city to a circumferential highway (what would become the Baltimore Beltway). After all, with the suburbs growing around it, how could the city function without easy ins and outs? Baltimore might well have needed just such a road, but the cost was to be high. Schaefer wanted to feed it down the east-west corridor formed by two neighborhood streets, Franklin and Mulberry, lanes of city life crammed with rowhouses. The road would topple a wide swath of them, uproot and displace hundreds of poor families as if they did not matter. This was not Schaefer's intent, but the effect was clear.

Schaefer's chief opponent in this matter was a young social worker from East Baltimore named Barbara Ann Mikulski. A disciple of Monsignor Geno Baroni and other promoters of community empowerment, Mikulski began to practice her innate and professional skills at community organizing. She discovered in this endeavor another talent: an ability to make people listen, to communicate on television and radio—"electronic aggrandizing" she called it. Mikulski was a sound bite machine, a political speaker who gave TV and radio what it needed: the pithy or cutting or funny (usually all three) one-liner that told the story in seconds. Official concessions to neighborhood concerns, she said later, were a joke: "They were going to give us a snazzy turn-off into the Inner Harbor so that when you rode through, you could kind of look at the dead fish." All of this she put to work in a campaign to defeat "the Road," a plan conceived by Schaefer and others to put a highway across the heart of the city, from the western outskirts along Edmondson Avenue past Schaefer's neighborhood and down the Franklin-Mulberry corridor, thence through the center city neighborhoods of Federal Hill and Mikulski's own East Baltimore and Fells Point, which was not the trendy place it would become but a port district, sometimes called the Foot of Broadway. Mikulski and her group, known by the acronym SCAR, for Southeast Council Against the Road, took on City Hall and prevailed.

It seemed that this highway was going to take the homes of a lot of people in a couple of neighborhoods—the Poles, the Italians, the Greeks, the blacks—and give them almost nothing in return. . . .

They had all sorts of multicolored charts and graphs and slide shows about how great it was going to be. But a lot of us didn't think it was such a great idea. We didn't think it was fair to take houses from old people who had come to this country in search of the American dream and who had lived through the sweatshops and the Great Depression. We didn't think it was fair to take the homes from the black community that had fought at Hiroshima and Pork Chop Hill. The only way they were going to get loans in the segregated city of Baltimore in the 1950s was through the VA mortgage system. We didn't think it was right to destroy healthy neighborhoods so that suburban commuters could get in and out of the city faster. We didn't believe it when we were told this was going to be good for us. We were told, "Don't worry honey, we'll take care of you because it's going to be for everybody's progress."

One of the foremost preachers of that message of progress was Schaefer, who believed he could explain the necessity of doing all the things Mikulski feared. So it was the city and Schaefer versus an East Baltimore baker's niece who was beginning to understand and communicate to others the quality of her political gifts. In this campaign, the Road made Mikulski a household name. Mark Joseph, the developer, who was then a Schaefer aide, says that Schaefer knew he had lost long before he acknowledged defeat. But he also knew important federal aid depended on maintaining the illusion that a road was under way and conceded to the Mikulski forces only when Washington had sent all the money it had promised. He emerged from defeat with federal dollars—and a valuable lesson. Baltimore neighborhoods and Baltimore people did have spirit, dormant and underappreciated though it may have been. People would stand up and speak truth to power and authority—or respond to it if well directed. Schaefer would later insist that he had always been a proponent of Baltimore's neighborhoods—even though he was willing to knock a few of them down to accommodate a road. He had no compunction about pushing ahead with a controversial, unpopular project, whatever the pain to individuals, if he thought the greater good would be served. He might well have been right in this case, moreover, since Baltimore remained, with all its incapacitating remoteness, a difficult place to visit by car.

Ancient Ass

In 1962, Kovens told Schaefer that he could not be council president when Harold Grady resigned the mayoralty to become a judge. Another of Schaefer's Fifth Ward cohorts, Phil Goodman, was council president, and he would become mayor. Kovens wanted Young Tommy, who was then on the city elections board, to replace Goodman as council president. No member of the council was a threat because, under the charter, a councilman could not be appointed unless he resigned first. No one was willing to take that risk. Kovens wanted Young Tommy as a way of banking whatever candidacy fire still burned in his father's breast. Kovens hoped that a favor to the Younger Tommy would keep the Older Tommy out. In service to pragmatism, to Kovens, and to the protocols of machine politics, Schaefer waited his turn. But five years later, in 1967, D'Alesandro was running for mayor, and Schaefer was on his team in the council president's slot. They won the general election easily, carrying all 555 precincts. For Schaefer's swearing-in, Joan Bereska wrote a speech invoking the glory of history's greatest cities. "In ancient Athens, which was the best a city could be," it began. But Schaefer could not get beyond the first three words. "In ancien'a . . . ss," he would say, slurring the two words together and obliterating the "th" sound.

"No, no, no," Bereska would say. "Ancient ATH-ens. Ancient ATH-ens." Perhaps, they thought, a larger typeface for the script would help. "In ancien'aaayyss," began the new council president yet again. A Baltimore version of Pygmalion then ensued with Bereska playing Professor Henry Higgins to the fair councilman—except that he seemed unable to get it.

"I think we should just do away with that part," he suggested.

Unaccustomed as she was to opposing him, Bereska refused to accede. She liked the sound of what she had written and wanted the new council president to sound learned. People were always trying to give Schaefer a boost in class, a depth they feared he lacked. Finally, though, she went home knowing that her charge was falling short of the clarity they both wanted. When she arrived the next day at the War Memorial Auditorium for the ceremony, she thought, "What have I done to myself? He's going to screw this up and it will be my fault." She tried to submerge her fears by doing everything she could think of: putting up the decorations, making a seating chart, and attending to the refreshments—and returning to the elocution lessons. As the impending horror weighed in on her, she walked off the stage to the women's restroom, where she discovered something about the old auditorium: It had a fine sound system. Suddenly, she heard the speakers rumble to life and a familiar voice saying, "In ancient ATH-ens. . . ."

Loyalty

Willingly, eagerly, Schaefer accepted the scut work of public life, the problem-solving dilemmas that D'Alesandro dreaded. They were, by many accounts, a good team as Schaefer abandoned his earlier practice of setting himself apart from the mayor. D'Alesandro would not have indulged the famous Schaefer tantrums, and Schaefer seems to have known it. D'Alesandro actually did appreciate what the council president was doing for him while wondering at the totality of it. D'Alesandro said, "If I told him 'Tomorrow morning at 9 A.M., we're going to jump off the Maryland Bank building,' he'd say 'I'll be there at five of 9.'" Schaefer remembered D'Alesandro telling him, "I don't drink," and his own immediate reply, "Okay, I don't drink either." They did not agree about everything by a long shot, parting ways particularly on D'Alesandro's infinitely accommodating approach to African American strivings.

D'Alesandro thought Schaefer would have had difficulty if he had been mayor in those turbulent times. "He was there with me, but he didn't like the sort of out-front leadership I was taking. He thought we needed a slower pace. It wasn't anything he disagreed with as to the things we were doing, except the pace. But we didn't have the luxury of waiting anymore. We had to move with quick dispatch. Schaefer was a carryover from the old Baltimore. Baltimore was a very segregated city, very segregated. It was very ethnically diverse. Every section of the city still in the 1960s could be defined by language, by European roots, and by beliefs about the place of blacks and whites in American society. Blacks didn't have much leeway."

Young Tommy was pleased to provide that leeway—to bend and accede to the wishes of those who brought their grievances to City Hall in marches and demonstrations. Schaefer questioned whether giving in was the right response. "Tommy was too good-hearted," he said, giving in too easily and too often. Community action and civil disobedience were paralyzing the city, Schaefer thought. The upheaval after the assassination of Martin Luther King Jr., was the best and most dramatic proof that being a nice guy didn't always pay off.

King was killed in Memphis, Tennessee, on a Thursday, April 4, 1968. Washington, D.C., and Chicago were engulfed immediately by anguished retaliation and then by violence and looting for its own sake. In Baltimore, Mayor D'Alesandro ordered city flags flown at half-staff in King's honor, welcomed a plan for black city workers to stay at home "to show their unity of purpose and respect for their fallen leader," and said that his administration's major thrust was elimination of discrimination wherever it existed in the city. He expressed optimism that Baltimore could escape the turmoil that was sweeping the nation, asserting that there was "great rapport" among various groups. He was attempting to immunize his city by appealing to its people's best instincts.

By Saturday, though, the inevitable outbreak of stone throwing, arson, and looting hit Baltimore. Fires were started along Gay Street just east of downtown, within blocks of City Hall. Three Baltimoreans were killed as police and fire departments attempted to deal with the fires and window breaking that spread quickly north to Pennsylvania Avenue and then to west side neighborhoods. Schaefer was having dinner at the Greenspring Inn when a call came from D'Alesandro. He wanted his council president to meet him at the Fifth Regiment Armory, where a command post was established under the command of D'Alesandro and the Maryland National Guard. Schaefer could see the flames as he drove into the city. A young assistant U.S. attorney, Stephen H. Sachs, joined them, representing the federal government. By the second night, Governor Agnew and D'Alesandro were pleading with President Johnson for federal troops. Sachs listened as the mayor talked with a Johnson aide in the White House. "My fucking city is burning!" D'Alesandro shouted. "We need those troops!" The national guard and the city police were unable to keep up with the looters and arsonists, and D'Alesandro's call was honored with a total of 4,900 federal troops.

What Agnew called an "insurrection" ended on the evening of April 10, four days after it started. Property damage was estimated at $10 million. At least 900 fires had been started, and 1,660 looting incidents were reported. Shopkeepers stood in their doorways with rifles. Every available jail cell was filled. A near confrontation of angry black and white mobs was narrowly averted. Police reported instances of human kindness as well, including a white jewelry store owner and his elderly sister trapped in a burning store until black neighbors alerted police rescuers. Baltimore sought to console itself with the view that its troubles could have been worse.

"We had looting but not with the vengeance they had elsewhere. Tommy had done things in civil rights," Schaefer said later. "And some of the stores they let alone were stores that had been very good to black people. It was a selective sort of thing. And some of the cooler heads knew they were destroying themselves, burning down their own areas."

These riots should not have been a surprise. D'Alesandro's accommodations, rare and controversial as they had been, were almost irrelevant against the provocation of history, which demanded a response from people who felt that they had little recourse outside the streets. Baltimore's mayor realized this, but he was shattered by what he saw. The end of his public life had begun. At the same time, ironically, Spiro Agnew's tough public recriminations against Baltimore black leaders—who were insufficiently critical of the rioters, he charged—earned him status in the Republican Party and ultimately the vice presidency.

Schaefer knew what to do when the conflict ended: You had to go in and rebuild everything as quickly as possible. He had seen that dynamic in the military, in which returning a populace to some sense of normalcy and security in their daily affairs was a critical necessity if progress was to be made on other fronts. The areas that burned became targets for renewal. When D'Alesandro left office, mayors from the around the United States came to Baltimore for a dinner in his honor at the Lord Baltimore Hotel, an extraordinary tribute to a man who had sacrificed himself to find a peaceful way through the trauma of the 1960s. He gave that gift to Baltimore and to Schaefer. By the time Schaefer became mayor, the years of confrontation were largely over, and the fight for civil rights had moved indoors. Schaefer had his record of "right" voting to run on in a city with a growing black electorate.

Given his holdover views, he attracted some extraordinary supporters, including Juanita Jackson Mitchell, a Baltimore lawyer and wife of the nearly sainted Clarence M. Mitchell Jr., lobbyist for the NAACP in Washington. Both Mitchells became Schaefer advocates, encouraging others in their community to acknowledge his record. Schaefer himself seemed oddly unaware of his cachet. "Why are you for me?" he asked Clarence once when they were alone for a minute, as if he might have been regarded fairly enough as one of the enemy. Schaefer had not been a leader or a prmary peacemaker, and he had showed some sympathy for those who resisted equal rights, so he might have thought he didn't really deserve Mitchell's approval.

"You voted right," Mitchell told him. A man's reservations, a clinging to attitudes that sustained unequal treatment were of less concern to Mitchell then, as long as the man voted right. Many did not. "Don Schaefer had just the right combination of bull and mule and tenderness. And he had the ability to change his mind about things," said the Reverend Marion Bascom, pastor of Douglass Memorial Community Church — one of the city's most eloquent and courageous black clergyman and one of the city leaders upbraided by Agnew after the riots.

From Schaefer's viewpoint, one could hardly overstate the political value of an endorsement from Mitchell, revered in Baltimore's black community and referred to by President Lyndon Johnson as the 101st senator. Schaefer might well have simply accepted Mitchell's praise. But he tried to understand it, may have sensed some undeserved forgiveness in it, and may have grown in some way as a result.

Schaefer also owed much to the D'Alesandros, Kovens, and Goodman — to "the Machine," which had tutored him on how to vote in these matters. The man who had thought little about public life — who had missed FDR, Mencken, and the Great Depression — had been without a considered thought about race. He accepted the goals of civil rights dutifully and pragmatically, recognizing the injustices that propelled the movement without ever being an activist himself. Kovens and Emma Bright had given him almost everything a political figure needs: a distinctive well-known name, a position on the central issue of his time — race — and boss-enforced protections that would allow him to develop a daring leadership style.

CHAPTER 3

Schaefer's Turn

Proud residents of the Waverly neighborhood waited for Mayor D'Alesandro to officiate as their branch of the public library opened on 33rd Street in north central Baltimore. The mayor was late, not having returned from a day trip to New York. In his place on April 13, 1971, stood Council President Schaefer, who had occasionally served as acting mayor. When the appointed hour arrived but D'Alesandro hadn't, Schaefer walked to the front of the room. Smiling community leaders and the new librarians anticipated his inspirational words. Here was the sort of ceremony Schaefer loved, the sort he would perfect later, rejecting mere ribbons or spadefuls of groundbreaking dirt and demanding extravaganzas instead. At the penultimate moment on this evening, though, the dashing Young Tommy appeared in the doorway with a mischievous grin. "Getting a little ahead of yourself, aren't you, Donald?" he said.

When D'Alesandro left town, he sometimes neglected to tell his council president, wishing to avoid conferring on Schaefer the title of acting mayor. "The place could be in ashes by the time I got back," he would say, not entirely in jest. Already, the council president's emotional equilibrium was in question, because of his periodic bouts of temper on the council floor. "Schaefer was thought of as being unstable," said Bob Embry, by then the city's housing commissioner and a man many thought would be Baltimore's next mayor.

D'Alesandro's cutting remark—outrageous to Schaefer who was working so hard for the man—helped to create the feeling, accepted by Rouse and others, that Schaefer had risen about as far as he ought to in public life. He was a grit with a temper, a plodder without much sense of humor or talent. Schaefer made no effort to recast his public personality, to make people feel that he was not on the emotional brink. That perception, he sensed, had its value. But the criticism from D'Alesandro stung and spurred him on. "I saved his ass so many times. He never lost a vote on the council. His problem was that we fought like hell in private. Everything was smooth when the board met, but in the private meetings we fought."

D'Alesandro was always a bit bemused by Schaefer's devotion and work ethic. "I came back from the beach one Sunday and drove by city hall on the way to a dinner," D'Alesandro recalled later. "The light was on in his office, and I saw his little car parked outside. It had all kinds of stickers on it: Go Army, Beat Navy, stuff like that. I parked and went upstairs. It was seven o'clock on a Sunday and there he was, a single guy, working all by himself." Schaefer did Tommy's bidding loyally, if not always agreeing with his leader.

D'Alesandro had elected to absorb the blows from Baltimore blacks, believing that they were delivered with ample cause. Unlike Schaefer, D'Alesandro had been a target of ethnic snobbery. He was congratulated by an *Evening Sun* editorial writer for eschewing his father's moustache and for moving out of the Italian enclave of Little Italy. He knew discrimination and prejudice, overt and subtle, and while his father parried its blows with humor, Young Tommy chose to tackle it head on—honestly, as he thought justice demanded.

McKeldin had begun to address the inequities of life for blacks and Jews in Baltimore, but his responses were judged both revolutionary and insufficient. D'Alesandro faced the same contradictory reality but decided to err on the side of black demands. He named blacks to important public bodies on which they had not served before: Larry S. Gibson, a lawyer and political organizer, was given a seat on the school board, and Marion Bascom became the first black member of the city's fire board. These appointments and D'Alesandro's decision to fly flags at half-staff after King's murder were not widely popular moves, and they had immediate implications for the management of city affairs. "Tommy pulled the thorn of racial anger from the city's paw," said Wally Orlinsky, the former council president. The city's lobbyist at the general assembly in Annapolis advised him to stay away from Annapolis lest his stand on race interfere with the city's effort to win approval for state grants among the still unreconstructed legislative community of Maryland. "Schaefer owed Tommy a lot," said Peter Marudas, who served Baltimore mayors from McKeldin to Schmoke. Had Schaefer faced the same challenge, Marudas and D'Alesandro thought, he would have been defeated by it, and, worse still, the city might have had a real riot—one between groups of people, not simply people striking out at property.

But Schaefer had advantages over his predecessor. He loved the work, and he had no other life. D'Alesandro might have been burned out from the day he was elected. Even before he was a teenager, he had been holding his father's coat in city hall and a hundred other venues of local politics. He had done the political work of a lifetime before ascending, almost by primogeniture, to the office his father had held. Then he discovered, like a rank ward heeler in a patronage job, that you really had to work, that people hammered you even when you were doing your best. Every day brought another helping of irreconcilable unhappiness. "Every morning," D'Alesandro said, "Marudas brings me a heaping plateful of steaming shit. And the next day he brings me another plateful." These were the fare of a mayor's life in the 1960s, as black Americans fought to break the bonds of legal discrimination and to assert their claims to power where voting strength demanded it. Ted McKeldin had faced the same demands similarly and not without frustration. McKeldin's secretary, Mildred Momberger, remembered,

> He'd stand by the windows of the mayor's office and look out and he'd say, "There's so many things to be done out there, and yet all I've done all day is spend my time meeting such and such a group and trying to satisfy them. Maybe tomorrow I can get busy on so and so." The next day it would be another problem. And this is what we ran into the whole [second term 1963–1967]. . . . Everything had erupted. Of course he blamed . . . white people that these problems were not faced sooner. Why did we wait until they erupted into a volcano? These wrongs should have been righted over the years, and so he said that we were really to blame for this, that this happened as it did. But you can't right them all in one or two years. It takes time, but they should have been worked on long before. And we should have been listening to the black community probably to a much greater extent than we did."

The price of this neglect and insensitivity was paid with the 1968 riots. D'Alesandro took the upheaval personally. After he had been so open and flexible this was the thanks he got. He fell into despair. The legitimate antagonisms of black Baltimoreans, recognized with equal unhappiness by McKeldin, seemed to be aimed at D'Alesandro personally. A religious man who attended Mass at St. Vincent de Paul Church three blocks from city hall every day, D'Alesandro would be cherished by some of the city's black clergy as being a key to the peaceful transition from the smug insensitivity of the 1950s. In a city with its share of bigots, D'Alesandro might have followed in the path of Louise Day Hicks, the dough-faced South Boston housewife whose opposition to busing took her city to the brink of chaos; of Frank Rizzo, the militaristic boss of Philadelphia; or of Richard Daley of Chicago, whose scowling, jowly resistance made him seem an enemy of racial understanding. Schaefer's inclinations were closer to those of Hicks and Rizzo than to Tommy's. D'Alesandro had embraced the anger of African Americans, clasped it tightly to his mayoral breast as if hoping to extinguish it. Instead, his own zest for public service was smothered.

In the fall of 1970, the mayor asked Schaefer to visit him at Mercy Hospital, where he was being treated for a minor ailment. "Don I want to tell you something," D'Alesandro said, "I haven't announced it yet, but I want to tell you in advance what I'm going to do. I'm not going to run again." Though he must have noticed the mayor's sagging spirit, Schaefer protested, disbelieving, "No, you love this stuff. Your whole life is politics. You can't be leaving." A day later, he went back to listen again. D'Alesandro was determined. "Do what you've got to do," D'Alesandro said. Politicians were always making promises not to make political widows of their wives. D'Alesandro decided to keep his promise.

Role Model

Schaefer's zeal to run the city—and D'Alesandro's burnout—had been unmistakable to many. When they flew to Chicago in 1970 to inspect the mass transit system there, D'Alesandro seemed to the Greater Baltimore Committee's Bill Boucher uninterested, already disengaged. Schaefer found everything new and exciting. The council president was struck immediately by the enveloping sense in Chicago of government at work and by the constant reminders to citizens that one man was government in their city. Signs welcomed residents and out-of-towners alike with a tag line that went something like "This splendid amenity brought to you by Mayor Richard J. Daley and the people of Chicago." No public works project, no bus shelter or road repair project escaped the legend. If government was abstract, Daley was not. Daley was understandable, touchable, defiant—concrete. "That's the way to do it," Schaefer told Boucher. When he became mayor, Schaefer put *his* name on everything from benches at bus stops to potholes.

He admired Daley's style even after Daley had given his police department a shoot-to-kill order when riots broke out during the 1968 Democratic National Convention. A study commission held that the convention riots were provoked by Daley's police themselves, but Schaefer saw it from the viewpoint of a civic leader worried that he would be unable to prevent chaos in his own city. His preference for Daley's approach over D'Alesandro's contributed to D'Alesandro's belief that Schaefer would have been a disaster as manager of the civil rights confrontations in Baltimore. But Schaefer admired Daley's trains-on-time efficiency, the wide highways, and the Lake Michigan waterfront housing. "I saw a man whose whole life was wrapped around one thing, Chicago. I saw a mayor who lived in the same house for years, in a modest house, I saw a man who worked with the business community." In short, he saw a mayor much like the one he planned to be himself.

Unashamed to copy the projects and style points of mayors like Kevin White in Boston or Daley, Schaefer was equally quick to scoff at those whose approach offended him. He called New York Mayor John V. Lindsay a "glamour mayor"—nothing more, in other words, than a fashion statement. Lindsay had represented the Silk Stocking District in Congress and had walked the riot torn streets of Harlem in shirtsleeves—a "TV star," Schaefer called him.

Some of what Schaefer learned about the Daley operation puzzled him, though, because it did not fit what he knew of rules and regulations on the use of federal money. "Just do it, then convince Washington it's legal," Daley advised him. To his occasional detriment, as he grew more like Daley, Schaefer took that advice, risking censure from Washington but most of the time prevailing. He was on the urban action front, after all, and his word carried considerable weight in the halls of Congress. He took Daley's advice on intergovernmental relations much as he would borrow the idea of building an aquarium from Boston's White. Schaefer did not copy everything he saw in Chicago, though. He noticed that Daley's desk was elevated, giving the great man a bit of an advantage over those who called on him. Schaefer drew the line at putting lifts under his desk and chair.

Best Man

Given what he had seen of Schaefer over the years—including the Chicago trip—Boucher was not surprised to see the council president at his door in early 1971. Boucher was a man with all the business connections Schaefer then lacked, and, of course, Schaefer knew that only too well. Boucher was confident, jovial, and ironic, a liberal who got on well with businessmen despite his politics. Schaefer knew that Boucher was close to every CEO in Baltimore and hoped that what he said on this day would be heard by an audience of more than one. Schaefer frowned, lowered his balding head, and stammered out what amounted to a withdrawal statement. He was not yet a candidate, and he was not going to be one in 1971, he declared.

"I'm not running," he said. "No money."

After fifteen years on the council, Schaefer was still an unknown to the wider world of Baltimore. He needed introductions. He needed Boucher, who saw the political and the governmental worlds as parts of an ill-fitting whole that was cobbled together by the reinforcing needs of both. As executive director of the city's private business and civic development group, a chamber of commerce with money and the willingness to serve as an adjunct of City Hall, Boucher had access to the men with money to finance campaigns. Schaefer wanted this group to know what he was thinking, and he knew that Boucher would tell them.

Schaefer, Boucher thought, had a monumental inferiority complex, yet he was constantly working through his insecurities toward success as a political candidate, as a councilman and as council president. Here was a surly nebbish who seemed to fear everyone but never backed down and never let his insecurities defeat him. Schaefer spent much of his life acting out comedian Woody Allen's dictum that 90 percent of life is showing up—even if you were insisting that you couldn't. Boucher thought the business guys would be more comfortable with Schaefer than with the more intellectual Embry or with George Russell. It was another way in which the power brokers misjudged his abilities and the force of his personality.

"I don't know these people you work with," Schaefer told Boucher. What about Kovens? Boucher wanted to know.

"Irv's out of politics," Schaefer said. "Retired. He's in Florida, and he's not going to do it again. I can't run."

But Schaefer's withdrawal was feigned and came with an assumption: The businessmen of Baltimore, the people of means, those who would or *should* want him to run—with or without Kovens's backing—would hear of his concerns from Boucher. Schaefer was not a worldly man, but he was not naive. He wanted the money guys with him in advance. He wanted them to begin declaring for him, and he wanted them to do it on their own—or seem to. So he said he wouldn't run, absolutely couldn't, knowing that Boucher would go to the people who cared about all of this and get them into the game behind him. If they drafted him, even they would know that they had to bankroll his campaign.

Boucher actually had a better idea. He got on the phone to Dr. Edgar Berman, a Maryland physician who had been Vice President Hubert Humphrey's doctor. In 1968, when Humphrey was the presidential nominee, Maryland Democrats were embarrassingly cool to him. So Berman, Kovens, and then Maryland House Speaker Marvin Mandel organized the face-saving semblance of a campaign. They opened a Humphrey for President headquarters downtown on Charles Street and staged a few token events.

With Schaefer, there was a more immediate and direct political chore to be managed: not a pallid effort this time, but a real campaign designed to win in a difficult social context. Never impressed with the political acumen of the average business type and seeing no reliable stand-in for Kovens, Boucher asked Berman to call Florida. "Tell Irv he's got to get up here and put this thing together," Boucher said. A few days later, Irv was back. He, Boucher, and Berman had lunch at the Center Club. Lunch ended with Kovens's agreement.

"One more thing." Boucher said. "Will you call Donald and tell him?" One had to keep settling Schaefer down, Boucher knew even then.

Kovens made the call, and the two men met. "You're pretty late, Shaky," Kovens said. Schaefer agreed but, emboldened by his mentor's return, said that he was running anyway. "I'm the best man."

"You are?"

"I know the city," he said. "George is a good lawyer, a brilliant lawyer, much better than I am. But he doesn't know the city." All the earlier pretense of withdrawing was gone, and Schaefer was instantly confident that no one could possibly be a better candidate than he was. Within days, Boucher and Joan Bereska, by then Schaefer's all-around aide, made a visit to the store on West Baltimore Street. They walked up the worn, unfinished wood flooring into the main showroom, past a wrought iron railing, and toward the time payment collection booth in the back of the store marked "Cashier" in neon. They went up to the second-floor offices, where Kovens gave them names and phone numbers by the hundreds. As they rode back downtown, William Donald Schaefer's lieutenants looked at each other as though the campaign had been handed to them.

"A gold mine," Boucher said.

Bereska doesn't remember the moment, but she does not dispute the importance of Irv's return. What it meant was clear enough: Schaefer could run, stronger and more politically wealthy than ever. He had the Furniture Man and Bereska. Boucher had the business guys.

A Cashmere Coat

Kovens knew the game. He had played it from every angle. When McKeldin was governor, Kovens wanted access to him, and for that he needed the help of someone like Sam Culotta, a twenty-seven-year-old lawyer who was working as the governor's appointments secretary. Culotta saw Kovens with some regularity, chatting with him outside the governor's offices on Preston Street, where a petitioner without special entrée could sit for a considerable length of time. One day in 1952, they were talking about the upcoming presidential inauguration of General Dwight David Eisenhower, the World War II hero known as "Ike."

"You'll be there?" Kovens said.

"I can't go," Culotta replied. "I don't have a cashmere coat." Culotta's understanding was that one wore a tuxedo, a cashmere overcoat, and a top hat to inaugurations, which were held outside the U.S. Capitol building in the dead of winter. Actually, Culotta said, recalling the story later, he didn't have a winter coat of any kind.

"You're gonna wear mine," Kovens told McKeldin's man.

"Damned if he didn't have it delivered a couple of days later. I wore it, had it cleaned, and returned it," Culotta says. For a time at least, Kovens figured that he would have as good a chance of getting in to see McKeldin as anyone.

One of Kovens's many businesses was a men's clothing shop on Howard Street, and he would routinely give presents, drawn from his stock, to politicians he knew. When Schaefer admired a Burberry raincoat he was wearing years later, Kovens told Edgar Silver, "That son of a bitch wants my coat." He could hardly be angry, of course, since he had made clear that such gifts were available.

Kovens had perfected the art of the small favor, the memorable, ingratiating gift—nothing big, nothing to make the recipient feel uncomfortable for a moment. He saw that politics was rooted in the personal and tangible—primarily in jobs for families that were not far removed from the agony of the Great Depression. Politics drew men like Silver, whose most formative and enduring experience in life was standing in a line with his mother at a Metropolitan Savings and Loan on Pennsylvania Avenue to collect ten cents on the dollar for the $700 she had saved. The power of men like Pollack, Curran, and Kovens was rooted in such memories and in the knowledge that jobs were essential building blocks of organizational strength. Kovens was indefatigable, organized, and relentless in his creation of an entire environment in which his will could be worked. He wanted what the game could deliver: a phone line to the mayor's inner office, parking spots near the door at Memorial Stadium, where the Orioles and the Colts played. He wanted to have a word on critical decisions, insider status that he could brag about if not actually translate into action and profit—the appearance of power, which often turned into real power.

From his cramped second-floor office, Kovens selected city and state leaders for at least five decades. He was a charmer or a bully as the occasion required, a man who understood what moved people—including intimidation and threat. Schaefer found him a benevolent figure, a man who would rather find a street-level laborer a job than arrange some big-deal judicial appointment—but sometimes, the job that Kovens gave was one he took away from someone else. Schaefer's friend Walter Sondheim, an advisor to five Baltimore mayors over forty years, whose involvement with downtown renewal surpassed that of every political figure, talked with Kovens one day about a lawyer whose post Kovens wanted for one of his designees even if it meant evicting the incumbent—as it would have. "They apparently heard the guy was making a lot of money," Sondheim said. "Actually it was $7,500 a year, not bad then, but not what they apparently thought." Sondheim says he didn't blink. "I will call the mayor about this, and if he is so inclined he can have my job too," he told Kovens. Sondheim was then head of the Baltimore Urban Renewal and Housing Agency, a precursor to the Charles Center urban renewal agency. Sondheim and the lawyer, Eugene Feinblatt, kept their jobs. Feinblatt became one of the most important legal advisers in the city, working on a range of critical city projects, including negotiations to keep the Orioles in Baltimore.

Patronage and payoff, a singular dynamic, flourished in those days. Though politicians never dared to intrude openly on education, Sondheim was told that a principal's post could be purchased from the bosses for $150, a vice principalship for $100. Edgar Silver's judgeship was conferred by Governor J. Millard Tawes and George Hocker, Tawes's patronage chief—bagman, in political parlance. Hocker told Silver he would have to pay for the post. Silver demurred.

Even Ted McKeldin, thought of as a paragon of good government, had a fixer, Bill Adelson, a brilliant graduate of Duke University Law School and classmate of President Richard Nixon. Adelson was known as Sweetie Pie, Sweetie, or simply Sweets. McKeldin lamented to trusted aides that in politics, one did things one was not always proud of or tolerated them in men like Sweetie. Adelson, it was said, got a half-year's salary from the men whom McKeldin "made." If the job paid $10,000 a year, you paid $5,000 to get it. Then Adelson would let you know that you had it for four years only. In Annapolis, Sweetie was known as a dispenser of "the magic elixir," money that could make a bill live or die. In an era that was less concerned about such matters, Adelson did a bit of lobbying even as he was McKeldin's chief political advisor.

Tawes's man, Hocker, pushed the dodge a bit further. The governor, he said, had a "continuing campaign fund" that needed replenishing by those the governor appointed. Unhappy with Silver's resistance to his demand for money, Hocker called him repeatedly to restate the terms, once from O'Hare Airport in Chicago. "You know they're going to announce tomorrow you're being appointed to the municipal court," he said.

"Yes. Governor Tawes told me, and I'm appreciative."

"Well, you know—," Hocker began.

Silver says he jumped in. "Hold on George. The governor's giving this to me. We're close. I've been good to him in the legislature. And I've made up my mind I'm going to stop practicing law, so don't get me involved."

But Silver decided that he wanted the judgeship enough to pretend to acquiesce. Hocker was talking and Silver was thinking, "This bastard has the power to call Tawes up and pull it back."

"How much do you want?" Silver asked.

"I'm going to let you off easy, Edgar," Hocker said, "because you've been a good friend. Everybody likes you—so $5,000."

Hocker called again a few days later. "When are you coming up?" Hocker had an office at Saratoga and Light streets.

Silver said, "I really don't have it now. I'm getting it together from relatives." Whether he had the money or not, Silver suggested to Hocker that it was just a bit uncomfortable for him, a newly made judge, to be delivering a payoff.

"Ohhhhhhh, Edgar don't feel that way! This is for the campaign fund."

Then a ploy occurred to the judge-designate. "You know Phil Goodman don't you?" Silver said, referring to the city councilman. Goodman would deliver the money, said the new judge. He called Goodman and told him Hocker was trying to hold him up. "Okay, Edgar, I'll take care of it."

The dance went on for days—and Tawes did not make the appointment. Finally, Silver told Hocker, "Look, I delivered it to Phil." And then the judgeship came through.

A year later, Hocker saw Silver and said, "That Goodman was a thief, Edgar. He took your money. I never saw it."

"I'm shocked," said Silver.

Showing Up

In such an environment did William Donald Schaefer offer himself in 1971 to guide a city whose collective psyche had been scarred in the riots of 1968. As shy and self-deprecating as he could be in many areas, Schaefer was self-assured when it came to his work. He had handled some of Young Tommy's most difficult chores, eagerly and energetically, working at the job of councilman and later as council president. He spent twelve hours a day at it, essentially reinventing the job. Every week, he interviewed a city department head for a radio program he hosted. Each interview, aired at five o'clock on Sunday morning, was a lesson for the city—and for its mayor-in-waiting. In periodic council "reorganizations"— designed politically to subvert some opponent—Schaefer was usually untouched, keeping his committee assignments because people began to rely on his work habits and his knowledge. He was seen as a man of no achievable agenda, no threat, but he knew he was moving ahead of his colleagues. He was learning how to prepare budgets, how the scrambled zoning laws were failing, the importance of housing code enforcement, the need for a housing court, who the leaders were in the police and fire departments—and who could get something done for you in public works. If anyone thought he was a chump, so much the better. "It was fine with me. I was in power even though I was out of power."

Schaefer knew that the heads-up from Tommy at Mercy Hospital had not been an endorsement. D'Alesandro favored Bob Embry. In addition to connections with the world of campaign fund raising—those business contacts Schaefer wanted from Boucher—the thirty-three-year-old Embry had the intellectual preparation Schaefer felt he lacked and some of the requisite temperament, too. Or so it seemed. Embry would not have been a closed door to the surging black consciousness movement, for example. Embry might well have been the darling of the city's good government types, including the Citizens Planning and Housing Association activists. A graduate of Harvard Law School, and a man with big ideas about how to save cities, Embry thought he could stabilize a Baltimore that was wobbling toward financial and social chaos. Smart, young, and moving up, unlike Schaefer, he had been able to arrange early financial help for a campaign from an important Democratic Party banker and a city official who had great fund-raising credentials, men whose names suggested to insiders that he was serious and positioning himself well. Schaefer decided to meet his adversary. They had lunch at Bickford's, where Schaefer had a double salad and fried fish almost every day.

"I'm going to run," he told Embry.

"So am I," said Embry.

He did not have a high regard for Schaefer's consensus-building style. "On the council we were at loggerheads. He'd summon me into his office and tell me how to vote on things. I told him, 'You didn't elect me.' He had trouble with people who felt answerable to nobody and weren't because they didn't get elected by the organization." Schaefer claimed absolute sovereignty over his own vote but occasionally wanted to demand the votes of others. At the same time, though, he had been something of an idol for Embry, who admired the council president's hard work and commitment on housing and in the neighborhoods. "He wanted to do everything I wanted to do. Russell didn't have a thought in his head about what to do." If he stayed in, Embry thought, he might split the white vote while Russell came up the middle. "Schaefer'd been around for fifteen years. So who was I to run? He was dedicated to the city. I sort of decided it was selfish of me to be out there running. Why not let him? I learned later that Schaefer was thinking of not running. He thought I had the money. He was just going to go back and run for the council."

It was one of those confrontations of will that comes off with neither side aware of the other's insecurities. Schaefer always hid his fears masterfully, even when he had more of them than his adversary. Embry, who would get close to running again in the 1980s, claimed to have no misgivings about deferring.

But he was right about Schaefer's prior claim. In 1965, as a second term councilman, the machine's designated contender received the first Citizen Statesman Award from the Citizens Planning and Housing Association. He had been the council floor leader for a bill merging and streamlining urban renewal agencies; his raze-or-rehabilitate ordinance passed; he sponsored legislation leading to formation of the Historic Preservation Commission; with Councilman Francis X. Gallagher, he rationalized the city's housing code and code enforcement efforts, which had previously been managed by as many as five city agencies.

A month later, D'Alesandro made his retirement official. His father said that the whole thing had "gone sour" for his 49-year-old son. Schaefer got in publicly and officially two short weeks after that. "I know what the city's problems are," he said, "but I also know what the real possibilities are." He read his declaration of candidacy in a barely audible monotone, his head down, hardly looking up, as if he were a terrified high school sophomore running for student council.

The Ballot Tailor

The strongest candidate up to that point was George Russell, who had declared his mayoral intentions and demonstrated his potential by throwing a testimonial fund-raiser at a big downtown hotel. For Baltimore's first black city solicitor, this glittering event was a statement: This is the year for a black mayor in an increasingly black city. The well-dressed, well-spoken Russell, a talented lawyer, looked out to see some of the city's leading political operators and businessmen in his audience that night, including William L. Adams, a black businessman and close ally of Kovens, and Jack Pollack, Kovens's rival as political boss of West Baltimore. The smart money guys were getting ahead of the curve—or some of them were. The Russell group included Louis J. Grasmick, a lumber dealer and developer whose earlier political efforts had included a lead role in the campaign of segregationist George P. Mahoney in 1966. This had been the famous "Your Home Is Your Castle" race, which split the Democrats and handed the governorship to a Republican named Spiro T. Agnew. Agnew had gone on to become vice president of the United States, leaving Grasmick to find another political horse. He figured Russell was made for the times, Grasmick's latest main chance, and despite his earlier association with the all-but-racist campaign of Mahoney, he wasn't about to miss it. The event raised $125,000, an impressive sum for a mayoral race, more than sufficient to establish the bona fides of a black candidate anxious to prove he had deep support.

Schaefer needed a quick response. In a city still dominated by its white voters, he feared Embry more, but he saw Russell's potential. With the businessman-contributors supplied by Irv, with the help of Boucher and the resourceful Bereska, he threw his own party on January 25, 1971. His team announced a $67,000 take, less than Russell's but an adequate demonstration of fund-raising ability. Hedging their bets, Willie Adams and Pollack came to Schaefer's event, too. The money and the organization were coming together, a fact that was not lost on Embry, whose campaign had not managed to keep pace. While he seemed to enjoy D'Alesandro's support, Embry was not lining up the financial network that Schaefer had assumed was there for him. The smart money was biding its time.

Kovens took over. He raised money, of course, but that was the least of what he did. He shaped the field, winnowing in and winnowing out as the dynamics dictated, keeping out those who could hurt Schaefer (whites) and keeping in those who could hurt Russell (blacks). Much is said about turning out the vote, the impact of television, and the role of backers with money. But with bosses, the process began much earlier. If the strongest opponents could be convinced to stand aside or if relatively strong ones could be turned against an opponent in his base, neutralizing or splitting his support, the team could concentrate all its energy on the chosen dummy or genius.

Even more than Embry, who was merely talented, the Schaefer team worried about Hyman Pressman, the city comptroller, who had held the job as a Democrat and a Republican. He could win or take enough votes from Schaefer to elect Russell. A penchant for writing and reciting tedious doggerel had brought Pressman the title "Rhymin' Hyman." He was a fabulous campaigner who marched in every parade, danced with senior citizens, and picked any public fight that would enhance his image as a watchdog. In truth, he was a bit of a demagogue who was willing to throw rhetorical hand grenades, a gut-level fighter, and a thoroughly unpredictable figure who had drawn huge numbers of votes. After losing a Democratic primary for comptroller in 1963, Pressman was drafted to run on a "fusion ticket" in the general election. McKeldin needed Pressman's vote-drawing power to ensure his own election to a second term. The law that permitted this sort of opportunistic party switching was subsequently changed. But in 1963, Pressman used it to win and to become an institution in city hall. He subsequently returned to the Democratic fold, though he was a political entity unto himself, owing almost nothing to party. If Pressman had entered the Democratic mayoral primary of 1971, he and Schaefer would have split the white vote, and Russell would almost certainly have been elected.

This one, too, by all accounts, Kovens took care of. He spoke to Pressman or to one of Pressman's advisers, and on May 14, the comptroller announced that he was running again: for comptroller, and on a ticket with Schaefer. It was coming together, as Embry had seen. "Hyman didn't really wanted to be mayor," Schaefer thought. He wanted a high-profile job with room to cavort and recite, but he did not want the responsibility of running Baltimore. So his posturing was designed to attract Kovens's attention and to gain for him the money he would need to run and win— about $5,000, Schaefer thought. On that same day, May 14, Harry J. McGuirk, then head of the Stonewall Democratic Club—one of the machine's main pistons—declared his support of Schaefer as did Joe Staszak, the tavern owner who had tangled with Henry Parks and by then a state senator from East Baltimore. McGuirk's hoarsely velvet voice and deft bill drafting had earned him great respect among his peers and the nickname "Soft Shoes." Harry could come and go without notice. He always seemed to be there, but no one knew. Staszak acquired similar power with blunter instruments. In the general assembly, after voting for a bill that advantaged bar owners such as himself, he was asked, "Wasn't that a conflict of interest?"

"What conflict of interest?" he replied. "How does this conflict with my interest?" No legislator ever uttered a more memorable line.

Men of their people, McGuirk and Staszak were described in the newspapers as "conservative on racial matters," a characterization that apparently meant they would go slow on open accommodations in housing, restaurants, and bars and other matters of de facto or de jure segregation. Sometimes such people were called "safe." Anyone looking for signals about what sort of place city hall would be in Schaefer's charge saw that "safe" men like McGuirk and Staszak were with him, and they could listen to Hyman Pressman—all of whom gave Schaefer the appearance of being "safe" himself.

Pressman said, as he announced his alliance with the council president, "I will tell the militants that they can exercise the freedom of speech in a lawful manner, but if they break the law or destroy property they will go to jail." With Pressman out, Schaefer was safer. A state legislator from Baltimore's Bolton Hill neighborhood, Walter S. Orlinsky, was still talking about seeking the office, referring to Schaefer and Pressman as puppets of Kovens. So Pressman went after him, too, purporting to quote Shakespeare: "Things are not always what they seem. Skim milk masquerades as cream." Orlinsky's charge had merit, but in time, he bowed to the power of Kovens, who was also getting Pressman out. Kovens got the organization guys behind Schaefer. He raised money. And then, it was widely believed, he recruited Clarence Mitchell III to cut into Russell's vote. Clarence Mitchell III was the eldest son of the NAACP's revered Washington lobbyist, Clarence M. Mitchell, Jr.

Clarence M. Mitchell III, elected a state senator at the age of twenty-three, might well have entered the 1971 race for mayor even without Kovens's urging. He did not think Russell deserved to be mayor ahead of someone in the Mitchell family, who were sometimes referred to as the black Kennedys of Baltimore. The newspapers said that Clarence combined "boyish qualities with militant words," but he did not have the esteem accorded his father. Russell tried to flick his candidacy off as mere annoyance. Clarence was running, he said, "because Mommy and Daddy wouldn't buy him a convertible for his sixteenth birthday." From Kovens's point of view, though, Mitchell altered the psychic chemistry of the election. He was a candidate who *might* have represented a threat to Russell. His very entry changed the public discussion. Suddenly, the historical imperative, the hoped-for sense of inevitability, and the glory of firstness—of destiny—became a matter of self-neutralizing intramural rivalry. "Whether he knows it or not, he's acting as a tool of Kovens," a critic said.

Russell had a stronger claim than the younger Mitchell, judging by personal and professional attainment. A former judge who had become Baltimore City solicitor, he was the son of a postal worker who had seen Baltimore through many lenses. On weekends, Russell's father was a gardener for Dr. George Finney, whose son Reddy would become headmaster of the Gilman School, Baltimore's most prestigious preparatory academy. Reddy's brother Jervis became U.S. Attorney for Maryland. One of Baltimore's most astute political managers, Nick Schloeder, who was also the football coach at Gilman, learned of the Russell-Finney connection after he noticed that Reddy Finney and his father were contributors— $1,000 and $750, respectively—to Russell's campaign. Even the prospect of a collision of black candidates meant that everything was falling into place for Schaefer: harmony in the white Democratic machine, division among blacks, plenty of money, and a clear sense that Baltimore would be more comfortable with a bossed candidate than a black one.

For his part, Schaefer urged harmony. "It's not, as some are whispering, whether the mayor is black or white. The only question is who is best qualified to lead the city," he said—and, of course, who had the best political team. Schaefer's team had a certain stealth quality. Reporters did not recognize the names of his financial supporters, so new were those neighborhood workers to citywide politics. And while the newspapers certainly knew his staff members, their labors on behalf of the Schaefer campaign were carefully concealed. Many of them were government employees, disqualified from political activity not only by the demands of their jobs but by the Hatch Act, a federal reform law that was meant to keep the bosses from forcing employees into political servitude upon threat of losing their jobs. Led by Bereska, the ragtag army of volunteers went "skulking up back alleys" to the old Stafford Hotel on St. Paul Street. Its owner had offered a room to Schaefer for free, and there Bereska organized a boiler room political operation, a den of overworked loyalists who did the grinding organizational tasks upon which every campaign rests ultimately. The district and ward maps, the phone banks, the mailing operations, the schedules of rallies and meetings—everything was planned and executed from this subterranean command post. They brought their own chips and sodas—and their own light bulbs.

Adding Zest

In late June, Schaefer put the last organizational piece in place: He called Ted Venetoulis. Bereska called Teddy "the pizzazz." He was a handsome young hustler and frontman with a touch of the 1960s in him. "It took him a while to learn to take a bath," she recalled. As usual, though, Schaefer was working to field a many-faceted organization. He wanted to address the neighborhoods, the businessmen, even the intellectuals, though he seemed to distrust them. Venetoulis he trusted. Already an aging wunderkind in Maryland politics at thirty-four, Venetoulis was an organizer who had very nearly put at-large congressman Carlton Sickles in the governor's office in 1966. Then a teacher at Essex Community College, Venetoulis had already been an advance man in the 1960 campaign of John F. Kennedy, written several books on politics, and worked on Capitol Hill. But only one Baltimore pol of any significance, William Donald Schaefer, had endorsed Venetoulis's candidate. Sickles lost by a relative handful of votes, and when it was over, the campaign manager was grateful.

"Don, I owe you," he said. "I appreciate what you did. Call me."

In 1971, Schaefer called.

"You said you owed me."

"I know, I know, but . . ."

The two men agreed to have lunch at a restaurant in Little Italy. Schaefer arrived and suddenly began to empty his suit coat and pants pockets. Bits of paper, cards, envelopes, sheets of yellow legal paper, and telephone message slips fluttered onto the white tablecloth.

"What's this?" Venetoulis said.

"These people say they want to help me," Schaefer said.

He began to lay out who they were and what each one of them had promised to do for him if he ran. They lived in every neighborhood of the city. Venetoulis was not the only one who owed the candidate. The two men were dining in the heart of Maryland political deal making, the prime restaurant district east of downtown, a place of small, immaculate rowhouses and restaurants without which Maryland politics might have been far less dramatic over the last fifty years or so. Many deals were cut, ballot lineups cemented, and payoffs arranged over pasta at Sabatino's and its neighboring competitors. These were unofficial backrooms for reporters, elected public officials, vendors, contractors, and hangers-on of all variety. Baltimore County executive, governor, and vice president Agnew was a regular. The maitre d'hotel at one popular spot sold food stamps from the trunk of his car. Walter Orlinsky would utter a line for an FBI tape running inside the shirt of his luncheon companion: "See what you can do for a couple thousand," said Orlinsky, by then the city council president. The would-be city sludge hauler's agent then turned his recording over to federal authorities, who indicted and convicted the brilliant but hapless Wally for soliciting a bribe.

For Venetoulis, a reformer and theorist, the political confetti floating down from the Schaeferian pockets was compelling evidence: Just as when he had presented himself to Kovens fifteen years earlier, the man was running on more than ambition, more than the power of a machine. When Schaefer had announced his fund-raiser that winter, newspapers said the list of contributors included two hundred or so names its reporters had never heard of—as though that diminished the support or made it suspect. Venetoulis thought just the opposite. Schaefer was "well placed." He had Irv. He had the clubs. He had his pocketful of promises from neighborhood nobodies. He was beginning to raise money. Still, Venetoulis knew the dynamics of 1971 and applauded them, hoping that they were true—on one level. "Russell had stature. He was a good candidate and he had good support, too," Venetoulis thought. But there he was, having lunch with a man who was making the sort of insistent, "my turn" argument that usually wins out against abstract imperatives that are not similarly backed by money, experience, and organization. "Some people thought it was time for Baltimore to have a black mayor. Schaefer thought it was time for Schaefer to be mayor," says Gene Raynor, head of the Baltimore Board of Elections and a close Schaefer friend.

The Outer City

"The preservation of neighborhoods," Schaefer would say later during the campaign, "has absorbed much of my official energy." At least 80 percent of the city's housing stock was then in sound shape, though 20 percent was in steep and distressing decline. Intimately familiar with federal and local renewal efforts, Schaefer proposed to continue and streamline them—but to add what he called an "Outer City Conservation Program," a term that was designed to capture the attention of voters who felt left out of the huge antipoverty and employment training programs of the 1960s. His plan grew from both experience and belief: He knew that government could cure nothing unless citizens invested time and energy. "Furthermore," he declared, "we all benefit from the good sense citizens bring to participation, while the very involvement strengthens citizen confidence in government." Without intrinsic strength, he had concluded, government money would be wasted. Even as he was asking for people's votes, he put demands on them: Neighborhood groups—Waverly, Northwood, Govans, Roland Park, Mount Holly, Ednor Gardens, St. Agnes, and the various umbrella organizations—must be an integral part of the city's preservation effort.

"We will need a program of loans and grants for the outer city," he observed, rather pointedly. "This now exists in federal assisted areas, but it is not available in the outer city. I am committed to making such a program city-wide and will approach the federal government to attempt a change in their funding restrictions." At a time when the nation and its cities were still fearful of unrest—"long, hot summers"—Schaefer's platform was filled with simple assertions about what government and citizen could do, individually and together. If people felt hopeless and help-less—and he knew they did—someone had to find language that would communicate a professional, orderly, and doable program. "Propose the Possible," he wrote. "There are no magic answers. In these times and with limited resources, it is unwise to suggest otherwise. Unrealistic proposals and promises falsely raise hopes."

"Flea Money"

When Schaefer claimed during a campaign event that he had stayed in Baltimore to live among black neighbors, some jeered at him, as if he had said, "Some of my best friends are black." Why did he think he should get credit for choosing to live with black people? Yet it was a time when whites were fleeing the city. Schaefer was not. Reporters found "Russell for Mayor" bumper stickers on the cars parked on Edgewood Street, and someone there said that Mr. Schaefer need not expect many votes in his own neighborhood, which was then changing so thoroughly that he would need a new base if he were to survive in office. Over time, he made the entire city his base. But in this initial election, he fared much better than anyone expected on Edgewood and in other black neighborhoods, collecting about 20 percent of the vote when some predicted that he would do no better than 2 percent. Both Schaefer and Baltimore's black voters were wronged by this assessment. He was more popular, and black voters more discerning, than some allowed.

In later elections, black politicians learned that they criticized him at their peril. The Reverend Wendell Phillips, a motorcycle-driving veteran of the civil rights movement who was also a minister and a member of the Maryland House of Delegates, once started in on Schaefer during a 1978 campaign stop in a West Baltimore Church. "I took a few shots," he said, "and I heard this murmur. Pretty soon one of these ladies was shaking her head and telling me I ought not criticize the mayor." Phillips knew that the approbation of this audience was absolutely crucial for his own success. The rough demographic profile of a voter in increasingly black Baltimore during these years was sitting in front of him: a church-going black woman over age forty. Since no one else came close to Schaefer's level of commitment to the city and all its neighborhoods—and since that zeal was already creeping into the political subconscious of the city resident—he had an immediate advantage over almost everyone else in the race. He knew intuitively by then what a street or a neighborhood needed. In time, he would have a remarkable street-by-street knowledge of the city: which houses targeted for repair or demolition were where on a given block, for example.

Baltimore's population then was half black, half white. But whites who were registered to vote outnumbered registered blacks by 60 percent to 40 percent and the black turnout was notoriously anemic year after year. A surge in black voter registration in 1971 suggested that this disadvantage was changing. But was it changing fast enough? Orlinsky, who had made his own civil rights stands, suggested that everyone was involved in racial politics, like it or not.

Russell's ticket mate for council president, Jim Lacy, was a member of the Maryland Club, which did not serve blacks. "If you're elected," Orlinsky told Russell, "you won't be able to have lunch with your running mate at his club." A sophisticated man, Russell knew well enough what he was up against. The insider money and the political wise guys might offer him support, but they were men of the 1950s who were willing to indulge in snide racial humor, willing to offend, and certain they would not hurt themselves or their interests. By the same token, Russell carefully made clear that he was no revolutionary: "We can't destroy the system. There's a place for change within it," he said.

The candidates conducted themselves with dignity, with respect for each other and for their city, without pulling punches. Yet race was part of the drama, muted and rendered in code. Was Pressman calling Russell uppity when he said that the candidate had become "a pompous peacock whose head has grown to twice its former size since he became city solicitor"? Only a year earlier, Maryland had elected its first black person to the U.S. Congress. Antipoverty bureaucrat and civil rights firebrand Parren J. Mitchell—brother of Clarence, Jr. and uncle of State Senator Mitchell— was easily elected after the primary, but he found himself accused of racism by his Republican opponent. That tone, that level of invective hung in the air as Russell and Schaefer squared off a year later. Some people were upset, Russell observed, that a black man (himself) was riding around in a city car but not headed for the police station. That was about as cutting as he could afford to be.

There was ambient fear, a vestige of 1968's turmoil. A man named Olugbala demanded the right to speak during a candidate debate at the Village of Cross Keys, a sparkling Rouse Company development. Olugbala and others wanted to talk about inner-city issues. They wanted to speak in support of a Black Panther Party fund-raising drive that was regarded as extortion by the merchants toward whom it was directed. The candidates themselves hardly needed to speak of fear generated by blacks who were demanding respect. "Serious crime and brutal violence have become endemic in the city," wrote Bill Blatop, private citizen, in a July 9 letter to the *Sun*. "Narcotics are more or less openly peddled in the high schools and are now reported in the elementary schools; the schools themselves, in many cases, have become jungles in which neither pupils nor teachers are safe from physical assault and robbery; a trip on a transit bus may become an experience of mayhem; the school board has become an arena for racial and cultural conflict; the tax burden has become staggering."

This dreary assessment may have been a fair representation of the general public's view of Baltimore in that election year. People were afraid of downtown and stayed away from it. Schaefer's prospects might have been improved as a result of this fear, but he attacked the pessimists, taking them to task for negative thinking, supporters or not. He urged citizens to get involved, not to be overwhelmed by crime. He saw the problems, he said, but preferred to talk about the city's strengths. As a major defender of Young Tommy D'Alesandro's policies, he could hardly do otherwise. He was running on their record—and seeking to preserve some proprietary sense among the populace whose support he would need not only to win, but also to govern. Russell called Schaefer a Pollyanna, stopping just short of ridicule. The survival of Baltimore was at stake, he said, and his opponent's conjuring of a "happy city" was ludicrous. Here was a turning point election, Russell said, and his opponent offered bromides. Schaefer did make positive thinking a precept of his campaign, spelling it out in "Where I Stand," his basic campaign document: "Although the city faces many problems," he wrote, "we must adopt a positive, non-crisis attitude if we are to move thoughtfully and reasonably toward solutions."

Transition

Venetoulis saw all the elements on this troubled landscape but assumed that Schaefer would win easily because Russell simply could not overcome a still-functioning machine, which had been, in effect, expanded by Schaefer's neighborhood contacts. Nor did anyone, in truth, really feel that Baltimoreans who voted would elect a black man, no matter how talented or deserving. Better to elect a "dummy." With the election assured, at least in his mind, the young political scientist could look ahead and think about how his candidate might govern, knowing better than men like Rouse that

Schaefer was not controlled by the bosses—and was surprisingly talented. In a year like 1971, Venetoulis thought, a mayor needed qualifications that went beyond an ability to fill potholes, handle zoning changes, and get jobs. He knew that Schaefer had intimate knowledge of how city government actually worked. He had a remarkable base. Proof of it had been lying on the luncheon table. What the candidate needed was what Venetoulis called "intellectual zest"—and perhaps a better understanding of why Tommy had been so receptive to the black petitioners who had become virtually institutionalized in some cities.

Schaefer was about to become the first professional, modern, and full-time mayor of Baltimore—and one of the first in the nation. Uniquely for Baltimore, at least, he cared more about doing the job than simply having it. His immediate predecessors, Grady and D'Alesandro, had been handed City Hall by the bosses, and both handed it back. Venetoulis and Schaefer realized that the machine had given them a gift, and they wanted to do more than tend to the machinery of precincts, printing costs, and patronage.

Quantum Politics

In the campaign, Russell called Schaefer "the King of Concrete" and pointed to a pathetic symbol to make his case: the unfinished Road, looking like a huge section of the Great Wall of China plunked down in Baltimore. It would become a monument to the power of neighborhood organization and a curiously unfinished piece of government work, rising on the west edge of downtown with four- to six-lane promise and then disappearing, its squared-off western end dumping cars back onto city streets. All the more reason for Venetoulis to hope he might inject the largely unformed urban consciousness of William Donald Schaefer with a quantum of ideas. The organizer recruited some of the city's most energetic and thoughtful young lawyers to help. They put together a series of issue forums. Thus began "Breakfast with the Experts," a weekly session of policy discussions. What they got was more than the usual parade of position papers. They got the support of the cadre of civic promoters organized by Mark Joseph, a local lawyer, and Embry, part of a generation of bright Baltimoreans, JFK-era idealists who were anxious to have some part in the governing of their city. Mark Joseph was occasionally mistaken for his cousin, Yellow Cab's Mark Joseph. In addition to their names, they shared Schaefer's confidence. Many of them were women.

One of the earliest was Sandy Hillman, who came to Baltimore with her husband, Bob, who had been Embry's roommate at Harvard. She was miserable. She had been in Washington with an exciting job, pushing for passage of a bill that would offer special education help to poor children. She was sent to Capitol Hill to meet with Senator Richard Russell of Georgia. As chairman of the Appropriations Committee, Russell was, it was said, the second most powerful man in America. She and the senator had lunch in the Senate dining room. "Little girl, what you've got to do is get an editorial in the Atlanta *Constitution* that says to me, 'Senator Russell you must get beyond your bigotry, beyond your this, beyond your that, and make sure the poor children of Georgia can have the advantage of this legislation'." Hillman went back to her office, on fire with the opportunity to effect change. A newspaper friend called Reg Murphy, who was then editorial page editor of *Constitution,* and Murphy immediately ran the editorial Russell needed for political cover. Years later, Hillman met Murphy in Baltimore, where he had come to be publisher of the *Sun.* "He said, 'Hi, I'm Reg Murphy.' I started to cry."

But Hillman had been in tears about being in Baltimore as well. Embry pleaded with her not to abandon hope and introduced her to Schaefer. She wondered how he could succeed. Could he "spark the soul of a wary city"? Her first project with him was an effort to get emergency heating help for poor families. "No one's going to freeze to death in my city," he said as if to himself. Hillman's soul was "sparked," in part, because she was convinced that Schaefer's own heart was in the task. But she wondered whether he could do the same thing with an entire city—"a very complicated city," she thought.

Schaefer began, of course, by writing the names of all these passionate newcomers (and old comers as well) on folded yellow legal paper, business cards, and the backs of envelopes. He called these people later, as he had called Venetoulis, recruiting them for other tasks. This was his cadre of talented, energetic young men and women, imbued with the service ethic, who bonded to their unlikely leader. Schaefer was from Edgewood Street and the University of Baltimore. He showed up at work in mismatched socks, and his tie always seemed several inches too short, pointing out his incipient paunch. Occasionally, he had sweat marks on his shirts. His more buttoned down and color-coordinated election teammates became his labor commissioners, his school board chairs, his legislative assistants, his fund raisers and advisers. They were an extraordinary resource, a rich vein of youthful strivers who were completely devoted to making Baltimore best. Vene-toulis and others would see that Schaefer had a passion for problem solv-ing that his partisans could only marvel at. "Zest" was inadequate as a word to describe the energy level, the constant creative turmoil of his lead-ership. He was not an intellectual, nor did he claim to be, but he had in-stincts that made him see the utility and the value of art and ideas in his community. Venetoulis knew that issue papers were low-calorie political fare, a security blanket for reporters to skim and ignore, something for the League of Women Voters to praise. This was different. "We were building something, a base to go forward with," Venetoulis said.

Walking Around

One of Schaefer's earliest mayoral fund-raisers was called "a renais-sance of art," a title that was typical of the political money events he usu-ally put into some other context to put him personally at a remove from the givers. People were contributing to an idea, a concept of the city, a generally accepted goal, or accomplishments. Later, these necessary events would be called "Reflections" and billed as opportunities for the governed to look around and think happily about the progress their money and votes had made possible—while giving generously again. The process of raising money became, like the process of addressing issues, an organic thing. People were asked to write checks, not only for the campaign ahead, but also in recognition of what had come before. Fund-raisers became cel-ebrations, disguising the crass collecting of dollars. At the same time, Irv rounded up the usual wealthy suspects, men who owed him for some favor—the loan of a coat, a necessary phone call, a job—men whose names graced what would become the most potent and famous of all Rolodexes. "He was always on the phone to people. He sent out an urgent message: Raise the money. Raise the money. Raise the money," Venetoulis recalled. The money was needed for ads, for printing, for salaries, for elec-tion day expenses, for walking-around money.

Schaefer's own friends gathered in venues such as firehouses to ante up what they could afford. Schaefer, a fifteen year veteran of such events, still seemed to be embarrassed by the whole process and stood in the corner. His friends and reporters always characterized him as "painfully" shy. This was a curious start for the man who would later be called a cheer-leader, though it probably served him well. He did not seem driven by the high octane fuel of ego or ambition. He refused, one of his secretaries said, to "toot his own horn." His shyness continued, though in time he would become a one-man John Phillip Sousa band.

A Test

Near the end of the campaign, the Furniture Man came to the campaign manager with a deal. A wealthy contributor wanted to put up a substantial sum of money, but he wanted the new mayor to put him on the zoning board. The money was being offered, rather directly, to buy an appointment of great importance to men like Kovens, who wanted to be able to handle problems for the small businesses they owned or the small business owners who contributed to the candidates they backed.

"He was testing me," Venetoulis thought. Tests—or propositions, pick a word—came to almost everyone, except, apparently, to Schaefer. Sondheim, Venetoulis, Joseph, and others said that Irv did petition them for favors. Schaefer says he never knew of any such offer. Irv, he insisted repeatedly, never ever asked him for anything. But Irv asked others, including, in this case, Venetoulis, who said no—while knowing excruciatingly well the cost of saying no. In the 1966 Sickles-for-governor campaign that Venetoulis had managed, Kovens wanted a guarantee that Marvin Mandel, then a member of the House of Delegates from Baltimore, would be the next House Speaker. Sickles liked Mandel. He thought Marvin would be an acceptable speaker. What wasn't acceptable, Sickles explained, was a deal in advance. He said no to Irv, who immediately backed Western Maryland's Tom Finan, the third major gubernatorial candidate. Sickles then ran second to George P. Mahoney by 1,945 votes, a number that Kovens might easily have delivered to Sickles instead of to Finan, who everyone thought was destined to run third. If a principled stand ever cost a politician an election, this one did. Venetoulis thought about the Kovens offer over the years, wondering what he would have done if something similar arose in the future. He thought he would say yes. Not taking the deal created a big split in the Democratic Party, helping to make Spiro Agnew governor—and then vice president on Richard M. Nixon's ticket in 1968. Mandel became speaker anyway and was then elected by the assembly to replace Agnew, since Maryland had no lieutenant governor at that time. A deal, refused with such rectitude by Sickles, profoundly altered political history in Maryland and in the nation some might be inclined to say, and not for the better. Agnew left the vice presidency in disgrace, forced out amid charges of kickbacks arranged while he was still Baltimore County executive.

Peck

No crisis of conscience overtook the Schaefer campaign when the subject of election day cash—walking around money—was broached. You had to pay it, Venetoulis would reason later, not because you expected much work for your guy but to compete in an environment in which the money was expected. The picture of frenetic election day activity, with the little people jumping around the streets, led Young Tommy D'Alesandro to call it "flea money." If you didn't pay, your opponent would.

Flea money, Venetoulis said, "stayed in the city neighborhoods." Venetoulis thought the reformers had it all wrong when they talked about buying votes. Walking-around money was a lubricant of participatory democracy—relatively speaking, at least. It had a more salubrious impact than money paid to pollsters, consultants, focus groups, advertising agencies, and TV stations, which, in the electronic age, have largely displaced the precinct captains who used to move voters to the polls not by sound bite and attack ad but by main force. "If you gave the money to McGuirk or Staszak," Venetoulis said, "it went to Mrs. Stohowiak." He invented the name to represent someone who needed the bucks, came to expect them, and probably did get a few votes to the polling place.

The pulse of political money came at least once a year for three out of every four; a mayoral, presidential, or gubernatorial election was always underway. In 1971, a precinct executive had $100 to pass around to his troops, enough to put a few dozen workers on the street corners on election day. It might have been true, Venetoulis said, that some of the money "stuck to the hands of the precinct leaders" or even to the hands of the councilman or senator. Still, it was better than paying the pros, who carried it all out of town, win or lose.

Mrs. Stohowiak lived in 1971 in men like Peck Jones, who found himself drawn deeply into politics by life—and by death. He was a chauffeur, a truck driver for the Hecht Company, and a member of a club run by Julian "Fats" Carrick, who owned a bar in the Sixth District. In 1939, Peck's brother and sister-in-law, then in their twenties, were struck by a car and killed. They had an eighteen-month-old daughter. Peck and his new wife wanted to adopt her, but they were not sure how to proceed. They asked Fats. At one of the club's meetings, the restaurant man introduced him to Harry Caplan, a lawyer and a member of the club. "You take care of Peck Jones," said Fats to Caplan. The two men sat off to the side during the meeting, and Jones explained the situation. "We'll file it in court for you," Caplan said. Then he asked, "Can you get $50 together?"

"I can't get 50 cents together," said Jones, who then made $20 a week. "So they took care of that for me. No charge."

A man like Fats, let alone Judge Joseph Wyatt, who ran the Stonewall Club in those days, had resources. A job? City Hall and state government could reach into the "green bag," the list of annual patronage appointments by the governor, which was delivered to the assembly in a green cloth bag, and draw out a liquor inspector's post in time. Two hundred people were lined up for every job then, Jones said, so the man with a club connection vaulted ahead. A traffic citation? The club could get you "probation before verdict." A legal matter? The club had members who were lawyers, such as Harry Caplan. Those skills and talents attracted men like Jones, responsible, hardworking blue-collar workers who may have been pleased to think of themselves as precinct executives, treasurers, and members of a board of governors, titles that were not always available to them in the marketplace. Jones, whose mother had always called him "Peck's Bad Boy," was a tall, dignified, impeccably tailored man who remained deeply grateful for a lifetime.

On election day, Jones guaranteed the Democratic performance of those who lived on the streets radiating out from houses such as his on South Stricker Street. He took the Stonewall candidates door to door. On the Sunday morning before the Tuesday election, he picked up Stonewall's sample ballots, its list of endorsed candidates, clearly showing the citizen which lever to pull. Such Democratic road maps could be and were taken into the voting booth. On election day, Jones personally pushed a thousand of these documents through mail slots in the second and third precincts of the nineteenth Ward. Councilwoman Agnes Welch would say years later that the ballots put out by Stonewall, the Proven Democratic Organization, or the Bohemian Pleasure Clubs on the east side of the city or the Metro Democrats on the west side—these ballots *were* the issues. The proof was occasionally demonstrated: If a candidate was on one club's ballot but not so designated in the immediately adjacent territory, the falloff in his support could be breathtaking. Candidates were endorsed and their names entered on these voter guides in an ordered, often uncomplicated, though not very open way.

"We would have a private meeting, get all the issues and how well we could represent them to our people," Jones said. In the dank, smoky clubhouse inhabited by Stonewall, men named Bip, Harry, George, and Willie would go over one of the candidates' backgrounds. It came down to a three-letter word, said Peck Jones: "Could we *win* with the guy."

In time, Jones became a member of the governing circle of Stonewall and eventually its treasurer. The nineteenth ward had thirteen voting precincts, each with a captain as loyal and well versed in the chores of election day as Jones. Each captain had five or ten lieutenants. Lieutenants had help as well, so a ward organization could put hundreds of workers on the street, each armed with a dollar or two in walking-around money for enticing the reluctant to do their duty. Those funds were accumulated at bull roasts and oyster roasts or at the annual dance at the Emerson Hotel. Stonewall's members also paid dues of 25 cents a week, and Jones kept careful track of receipts and disbursements. All of this—the patronage, the dues, the kinship, the status as well as the money—made Stonewall supreme in its eight south side wards, the eighteenth through the twenty-fifth. Kovens would call McGuirk, Wyatt, or someone else on the board of governors. The conversation would go like this, according to the election boss, Gene Raynor: "We want Schaefer to win the election. What will it take down there—how much to win with Schaefer?" The response might be: We have seventy-six precincts at $100 a precinct and maybe $1,500 for the ballots. Each precinct executive got about $100, a considerable sum then, enough to fund the various runners. Presidential, mayoral, and gubernatorial races would come along one after another. A precinct captain would marshal his numbers and be graded the next day. If the guy didn't show up at headquarters, you knew he hadn't produced. The precinct-by-precinct scores would be laid out quickly for the boss to examine. Peck Jones was never afraid to show his numbers.

Nor was this phenomenon unique to Stonewall's domain. In the third precinct of Ward 3, the Little Italy streets controlled by the D'Alesandros, Schaefer took 377 votes to 18 for Russell and 11 for Mitchell. Young Tommy and his parents had trained the faithful well. No machine candidate for mayor had ever been as well prepared as William Donald Schaefer, but he might not have won without Kovens. Schaefer certainly believed that was so. Schaefer's vote roughly followed the outline of the white neighborhoods, though he did far better among blacks than many thought he could.

Schaefer won by three to two: 95,315 to 58,528 for Russell. Clarence

Mitchell received only about 6,000 votes, making him a non-factor. There was fearful talk of a black voting bloc in favor of Russell, as if that would have been a shocking distortion of democracy. In truth, whites were the impenetrable bloc. Blacks voted for white candidates, but the reverse was not true and would not be for another twelve years.

Willie Adams was not surprised about the showing of either Russell or Mitchell. "Clarence for some reason thought he could win, but there was no way in the world," he said. Adams, of course, had one of those annoying little conflicts that arise in politics: He was a promoter of his friend Russell and a political ally of Irv Kovens, who was with Schaefer. Between the two, Adams chose Kovens. Insiders assumed that this was the real alliance because Kovens was, of course, with Schaefer. Adams put it this way: "I didn't want George to run for office. He was a good lawyer—one of the best brains we had—and I didn't ever think he was cut out to politically run for office."

The Schaefer-Russell margins were relatively tight in the black districts, where turnout was light. In the white districts, where the vote was heavy, Schaefer won by larger spreads. To the extent that voters were exercising their own judgment, free of the machines, black voters were willing to act on their observation that Schaefer had paid his dues, knew the job, and attended to the needs of all neighborhoods, whereas Russell, though an accomplished and worthy candidate, had no similar background.

"My mother and father loved Don Schaefer," said Diane Hutchins, a lobbyist for the GBC who grew up in the city. "They respected him because he had done the work. He was a mature and deserving candidate in a race with two men who, though black, were not in his league. They thought it would have been unfair to vote for Russell or Mitchell simply because they were black. So they didn't."

Black voters in Baltimore were proud to think that they were voting for the best candidate, voting on merit—not a claim their white brothers and sisters could make, they were sure. Within a decade, the political complexion of the city would change even more dramatically with the presidential candidacy of the Reverend Jesse L. Jackson and the successful 1982 race for city state's attorney by Kurt L. Schmoke, a Harvard- and Yale-educated black lawyer who defeated a law-and-order white candidate, William L. Swisher. From that moment on, with University of Maryland Law School professor Larry Gibson managing the politics as jealously as Kovens or Pollack, black voters would take over.

Gene Raynor, who knew the city almost as intimately as Jones knew

Stricker Street, offered this district-by-district account of that year's voting:

First District: Greek Town, Canton, Highlandtown, Little Italy, the blue collar ethnic center of the city's east side, 90 percent white. Territory shared by D'Alesandro, Staszak, Mach, and others.

Russell: 3,433

Schaefer: 23,983

Mitchell: 518

Second District: A north central inner-city district including Bolton Hill, 60 percent white. Home of Orlinsky's New Democratic Coalition 2, a liberal club that joined with the East Side Democratic Organization of Councilman Clarence Du Burns.

Russell: 11,157

Schaefer: 8,596

Mitchell: 1,285

Third District: The northeast sector of the city, 70 percent white. The base of old boss Willie Curran, a political forebear of, though no relation to, the Currans of the later part of the century.

Russell: 5,411

Schaefer: 25,855

Mitchell: 541

Fourth District: North central area, 80 percent black. Once the domain of Jack Pollack, by 1971 completely in the hands of black organizations.

Russell: 18,803

Schaefer: 3,168

Mitchell: 1,963

Fifth District: Schaefer's west side base, though increasingly black, still heavily Jewish in the northern half. A war zone for Pollack, Kovens, and the Cardin family which gave the district a circuit court judge (Meyer) and a Congressman (Ben).

Russell: 13,622

Schaefer: 18,222

Mitchell: 1,411

Sixth District: South Baltimore, Federal Hill, Fort Avenue and Fort McHenry, Morrall Park, and Cherry Hill, 75 percent white. An assembly of neighborhoods, including Lithuanians, Italians, Irish, and, increasingly, African Americans.

Russell: 8,102

Schaefer: 15,972

Mitchell: 636

The *News American* editors thought about endorsing Russell but feared that they would lose 25,000 in circulation. Although Schaefer would charge later that the *Sun* found him no more than acceptable, the record refutes him. The *Evening Sun* endorsed him during the primary for his "transparent honesty, an appetite for municipal housekeeping and a disposition toward modest progressiveness. . . . There is scarcely a square foot of city terrain he personally does not know better than the inhabitants know it and no municipal tangle large or small, he has not dealt with before." Before the general election, the *Sun* found that, in a sense, the citizens had done what George Russell urged them to do: "Baltimore voters have now completed an election season which amounts overall to a call for change in the manner of municipal government. It is a change away from boss-built, boss-serving leadership and toward a more open politics where ordinary Baltimoreans can speak out from the bottom and expect to be heard at the top. . . . Mr. Schaefer is no flighty fire eater. He is a step-by-step man, pledged throughout his campaign to the proposition that progress is best made slowly and that 'magic solutions' solve nothing." The *Sun* knew well enough that Kovens managed every step of Schaefer's victory, but it hoped the new mayor would be an independent operator. And he would be. At the same time, he chose to see criticism of Kovens as repudiation of him—because it motivated him and because his sense of loyalty to Kovens would not allow him to accept plaudits from those who criticized his mentor.

Shaky and Big Chief

Schaefer's victory came on November 2, 1971, his fiftieth birthday. He had endured election night in a barely controlled fit of apprehension. He paced, he frowned, he predicted defeat—though his friend Raynor and others told him that the earliest returns made clear he would be a big winner. Even as the totals piled up in his favor and his lead became insurmountable, he fretted. Kovens must have wondered what it would take for the man from Edgewood Street to realize how much raw, street-level power and money were lined up behind him. Kovens couldn't have known how traumatic it had been for Schaefer to lose twice in the 1950s. In any event, a candidate for mayor might well have been uncertain about the outcome of his first election to that post, and Schaefer's anxiety served another purpose. He wanted to be winning on his merit, not solely because of Irv, though he never denied that Kovens's power had made him. What Kovens laughed at was also a habit of mind, a discipline. Schaefer would never allow anyone to call him mayor after he won that year's primary. Nor would he allow himself to think he had won until all the returns were in. He was too committed to the view that he had to work hard to overcome shortcomings—to make the honor roll. If he admitted that Kovens alone could make anything happen, he would be owned by Kovens. His speech about his terms and his later realization that his world and Kovens's were separated by a wide gulf of money were parts of that mental and psychological conditioning and awareness—if well camouflaged by nerves. Beyond that, if he moaned enough, his friends would want to console him, to praise and comfort him—always an objective, his many analysts said.

Meanwhile, Schaefer had a nickname for his mentor, an adoring one apparently: "Big Chief." He had the words embroidered on a cushion and presented it one day in Kovens's second-floor office on West Baltimore Street. Kovens showed it to visitors, tossing off a few lines about his power. He would have his private line to Schaefer's office, and he would have the best parking spots at Memorial Stadium. Schaefer could afford that. And he didn't care what Kovens said. He was now Mayor William Donald Schaefer.

"I don't promise what cannot be delivered," he had said when he announced his candidacy. "But I do promise the people that as mayor I will use all my knowledge and experience to bring Baltimore close to that ideal city which every citizen wants for himself and for future generations." Candidates always offered a new dawn . . . morning in America . . . a shining city on the hill. Almost no one thought this mayor of all mayors would come close to fulfilling his promise.

Charm City

Schaefer's Baltimore started at the corner of Howard and Lexington streets, a place of style and seasons, of rhythms as soothing and reliable as the raising and lowering of awnings on Edgewood Street. He grew up with the sounds of the trolleys, watching the drivers and their brakemen as he rode downtown to visit his father at Maryland Title, stopping off at the department stores—upscale O'Neill's and Hutzler's with its Fountain Shop. He felt the approach of the holidays on the sidewalk outside Stewart's big display windows, growing ever more excited as Thanksgiving and Christmas approached. "They kept the windows all covered up until Thanksgiving day and then they'd lift them to see who had the best windows." He peered in on Hochshild Kohn, its name rising like a five-story barber pole at the northeast corner of Lexington. He loved the aromas and the mildly giddy excitement of riding the escalators, visiting the tea rooms, and shopping. An aggressive bargain hunter, he relished moments locked in undeclared war with anonymous competitors, women usually, who he presumed were after the shirt, tie, or wallet he had spotted. He confessed to throwing a furtive elbow—all in good fun, of course—if others were pushing and shoving. This made a contact sport of shopping, but more than that, made him feel the life of the city all around him. He saw these stores as institutions, as civic as well as mercantile anchors, and as mayor, he spoke to the sales staff of each as if they were city employees. If necessary, he would demand to know why he'd had to wait so long— not because he was offended personally as a shopper, but because he knew that attitudes about his city were built on the smallest interactions. He was recruiting ambassadors, intervening on behalf of all shoppers from wherever: Why weren't the clerks more polite, more knowledgeable, more accommodating and more upbeat about their work—and their city?

Just down the street from Stewart's stood the Piccadilly. "They had an oyster bar." Across the street was Read's, a drug store that was part of a Baltimore chain that, he thought, did more volume than any other drug store in the United States. Lexington Street then was filled with fine shops for a clientele Schaefer called "the gentry." On Charles Street, moving east toward city hall, every day brought an even more elegant parade. "When you shopped there, you had money. These were nice stores for rich ladies who wore gloves." Some overwrought public relations type spoke of this corridor, extending to Mount Vernon, as Baltimore's Rue de la Paix, a reference to the famous shopping venue in Paris. It was at least that elegant, Schaefer thought. He could recite the lineup along Charles the way Steadman remembered the names of Orioles players: Fettig's, Almon and Workmeister, where his mother had worked—"a first class furrier," he reckoned; the Charles Restaurant and the Women's Industrial Exchange, where shoppers refreshed themselves amid the din of office workers and others, lunching on tomato aspic, chicken salad, and tangy lemon tart or perhaps charlotte russe. They might purchase a doll, a painting, a quilt, or a knitted hat, the handicrafts of women who were not anxious to have anyone know they needed money in days when it was shameful if a man's income did not suffice.

Best behavior was demanded at the Charles, where shoppers and lawyers and businessmen stopped for coffee. When Uncle Willie took his son there, it was a grand treat—"a big deal," Schaefer said. Donald would have a glass of milk while his father and his father's boss talked. The boy was always nervous; once, so determined was he to be on his best behavior, that predictably he spilled milk all over himself. He was certain his father was ashamed: "He could've killed me." Sixty years later, he still shuddered to think of the humiliation he felt, a klutz amid Baltimore's best, falling below his father's expectations.

Spilt milk aside, his memories were good ones, rich with the life and promise of his city. Schaefer went to the Thanksgiving Toytown Parade to see Mickey Mouse, Cinderella, Goldilocks, and Noah's Ark, a balloon menagerie floating down Charles Street to the strains of "Here Comes Santa Claus." That annual event began in the 1930s and ended in the 1960s, a victim of various forces.

It was altogether appropriate, given Baltimore's history, that its new mayor would have such a view of the city. Its business and civic patrimony had come down to him from merchants and bankers: Johns Hopkins, who had started as a grocer like Schaefer's grandfather; Enoch Pratt; and George Peabody, who once personally preserved the credit rating of the entire state when he pledged his personal fortune as collateral with London banks. In time, Schaefer would help to decide new transportation systems, subway stops, and the directing of light rail down Howard, the broad boulevard of his youth, once so vibrant, an idealized street scene that he yearned to recreate.

Like other Baltimoreans, Schaefer thought the waterfront was "dirty," even when it was a generator of jobs and commerce. "You didn't go there," he remembered, though the city's financial district was on its northern fringe, having located itself initially around shipping. Farm produce from the South, not to mention crabs, oysters, and fish from the Chesapeake Bay, arrived there, making the inner harbor piers critical. But trucking would steal the city's original reason for being. Decline would be more manifest later, blamed on other forces for the most part, but it started with trucks. They offered better and faster access to the nation's markets, so the piers became obsolete and fell into disrepair. Nearby housing was boarded up and surrounded by barbed wire. The city seemed unable to adjust to the new circumstance and turned its back on the water.

Through World War II, the port accounted for much of Baltimore's nonoffice commercial activity. It began to fail in the early 1950s as more modern facilities at Locust Point and the new Dundalk Marine Terminal began to attract more of the port business. Until then, at the corner of Pratt and Light streets were the Ericcson Line piers and the United Fruit steamers, which offloaded bananas. The ships' bows cast deep shadows across the cobblestoned streets. Ports could never be quiet or tidy: fruit bobbed in the harbor waters, steam whistles bellowed greetings and farewells, trucks rattled up and down the streets, and a train threaded its way through at night, delivering newsprint to the *News-American*, which was located on the city side of Pratt. The port's grimy air of adventure lingered far into its decline. The strong odor of coal smoke from ship's engines and an exotic counterpoint of spices under production wafted through the streets adjacent to the McCormick Spice Company's square yellow factory. As he did with the Block, Schaefer tried to keep the unique texture of McCormick long after manufacturing and shipping gave way to shopping. The yellow plant became a pleasing anomaly among glass-fronted hotels and the elegant pavilions of Harborplace. In 1986, McCormick joined the march to suburbia, taking up new quarters in Hunt Valley, fifteen miles to the north in Baltimore County.

Junk Cars, Junk City

By the time Schaefer made his first attempt to win public office in the early 1950s, his city offered a doleful first impression to visitors. Adjacent to Routes 1 and 40, along Washington Boulevard on the west and Pulaski Highway on the east, along the Baltimore-Washington Expressway and flanking approaches to the new harbor tunnel, travelers passed mile after mile of automobile junkyard: trucks, buses, taxis, cars, and even the occasional Army surplus tank. The more professional lots were arranged in junked car subdivisions, complete with cul de sacs for the spare parts harvesters who typically ran their businesses from decrepit trailers parked just inside fences encircling their estates. Compacted hunks were stacked neatly, grillwork grinning. Huge devices for crushing and shredding moved in nearby. A technology for reducing the discards to manageable forms evolved, producing mounds of shredded metal, which grew taller than the machines that reduced them. Cranes and lifts hovered over it all. On South Catherine Street, on Franklin, and on Mulberry, wherever a road entered or left the city, dead cars were Baltimore's signature, discarded and abandoned like the city itself, left to rot in the torpor of summer and rowhouse sameness. The famous marble steps, the steamed crabs, the diamondback terrapin, the romance of the port were unconfirmed reports of a Baltimore that travelers could not see. No one thought much about the abomination of visual pollution or about the discouraging vistas found at the city's portals—nobody until Schaefer.

Of course, a principal reason for actually going to Baltimore was not a public relations man's dream. The visitor was, in a word, ill and, in two words, terminally ill. If you were going to the Johns Hopkins Hospital, you were going to the best, but apparently you needed the best. You were beyond the hope of local doctors, maybe beyond hope itself. When that point was reached, people throughout the South would say, "They've taken him to Baltimore." The ominous report was an advance obituary and certainly not a recommendation to vacation.

The weather, too, was a culprit. Who could be energetic in the humid heat that drove people out of their houses on summer nights? Anesthesia gripped the spirit as well as the body of the city. "When you live in Baltimore, you don't think anything could ever happen," said Divine, a star of films by Baltimore's John Waters.

Things were more lively during World War II. Workers trooped into Baltimore to build ships, to make some decent money, and to be part of the nation's struggle against the evils of Hitler. Yet inevitably, some felt resentment at being separated from home and friends. An adopted city was unlikely to fare well by comparison, and Baltimore took a few round-house shots from its temporary citizens. One lonely laborer dashed off a dyspeptic ode to his host city and managed to get it published by the *Evening Sun:*

> You're dead and rotten; you think that you're alive
> You think you're a place; instead you're a dive.
> You're not worth this paper, you're not worth this ink,
> You can take it from us, Baltimore YOU STINK.

In a sense, wrote Francis B. Beirne in *The Amiable Baltimoreans,* "The city laughed as if it agreed. . . . Not a stone was hurled or a head broken." This was remarkable restraint, he noted, given Baltimore's history. In the middle of the nineteenth century, gangs known by such quaint names as Butt Enders, Plug Uglies, and Blood Tubs had the run of Baltimore. They were among its first image makers. Days of much religious ferment and economic competition helped to create the view that Baltimore was Mobtown. and for years it endured that name. By the end of World War II, though, much of the fight ebbed away. "Baltimoreans are quite accustomed to being left out or mentioned in a derogatory manner. In fact they take pride in being ignored by the outside world."

No Brazen Hussy

The city had done a splendid job of hiding its charms, but it did have its champions—even H. L. Mencken, the social critic, editor, and newspaper man, who was not usually known for promotion of anything. He wrote of Baltimore's "romantic waterfronts," "sinister alleys," and "pervasive rowdiness." He called it "unutterably charming" and "one of the most livable on earth."

"The old town will not give you the time of your life," he acknowledged. "It is not a brazen hussy among cities, blinding you with its zanthus curls, kicking up its legs, inviting you to exquisite deviltries. Not at all. It is, if the truth must come out, a Perfect Lady. But for all its resultant narrowness, its niceness, its air of merely playing at being a city, it has, at bottom, the one quality which, in cities as in women, shames and survives all the rest. And that is the impalpable, indefinable, irresistible quality of charm." Charm? The word might not have occurred to many, visitors or residents, as descriptive of Baltimore in the middle of the twentieth century. Baltimoreans themselves tended toward a hard-eyed view more in keeping with Mencken's customary skewering propensities. A sour question, which seemed to incorporate the observation that the nation had moved beyond Baltimore, summed up the dominant view. "If you're so great," people would ask, "why are you here?"

Mencken could be derisive as well. Baltimore, he said, featured "mile after mile of identical houses, all inhabited by people who regard Douglas Fairbanks as a greater man than Beethoven." Schaefer, whose taste ran to Englebert Humperdinck, the singer, and Hulk Hogan, the westler, would surely have been one of these—if he had known who Douglas Fairbanks was.

But in some cases, you were great and here. Mencken, for example, stayed on and on, proving that it was possible to prosper in Baltimore, even intellectually. The city had enjoyed its stars and its moments of glory, even its boom times, but somehow they slipped from collective memory and belief. Milton Wisniewski, Schaefer's Court Square pal, lived much of his life fearing that his immigrant background made him somewhat less worthy than Schaefer and his other colleagues. "I always felt . . . they couldn't say my name. . . . After a while they'd say 'You with the funny name.' I always thought they were so superior to me." Schaefer was in that "better" category in Milton's eyes. "Parts of West Baltimore then were a bit higher socially. East Side was blue collar. I always thought then that Don Schaefer would be somebody. Partly it was because I had so little esteem for myself. I thought he had more on the ball. I was a regimental sergeant major when the war ended. He was a lieutenant colonel. I knew he was more a man than I was in every way." A master of the law's most complicated skills, a reader of nineteenth century English letters and philosophy, and a painter, Wisniewski—like Baltimore and like Schaefer—harbored corrosive feelings of inferiority.

Mencken was different, but he saw the dynamic. "I grew up," he said, "entirely devoid of the usual immigrant's inferiority complex." The writer may well have been spared the perils of ethnic discrimination because he was relatively privileged and, as a German American, a member of the city's majority ethnic group. So was Schaefer, but the future mayor did not escape feelings of inadequacy, personal feelings having to do often with education or physical appearance, not rooted in a group experience. The inferiority to which Mencken refers is the kind foisted upon those whose names were difficult for Americans to pronounce (and who changed them to conform), who brought foreign-seeming food to school for lunch, or who practiced a different religion.

Some thought the city's geography, so advantageous in some respects, left it on a knife's edge of identity. Was it a Northern City or a Southern one? Whichever choice it might have made, the city found itself competing with other East Coast cities of greater size and importance. Philadelphia, New York, and Boston were all on the rise, pushing Baltimore down in comparison. And to the south, the distinctly southern national capital was beginning to look like the world capital it was. Until the election of John F. Kennedy in 1960, perhaps, Washington had seemed a backwater to an America that was not yet captivated by the star qualities of political figures. But the country would discover Washington's assets, lifting it beyond blue-collar Baltimore with its junk car parks, crabs, air pollution, famous hospital, and colorful mayors.

Chiseling

In truth, the residents of Baltimore sometimes had reason to wonder what malevolent star had crossed its firmament. The city's major employers insisted on demonstrating contempt for workers. Often, they were supported by political leaders. The city developed the municipal version of abused child syndrome, reacting violently for a time and then hunkering down to fend off the blows. Not stupid, of course, the angry still-here resident wondered why anyone who had a chance to leave would stay. Opportunity was elsewhere. One of the major culprits in the inculcation of worthlessness was the Baltimore & Ohio Railroad, whose president, John Work Garrett, managed handsome dividends for shareholders while cutting workers' wages. When the workers struck in July 1877, Garrett brutally put down their action with help from the national guard, ordered in by a governor who was willing to do the work of a man then regarded as the most powerful citizen, public or private, in the state. The Garrett ethic endured into the 1930s at least and was honored by mayors and governors who continued to do the bidding of those who thought government had no business helping the most deserving poor worker. Even during the Depression, a Democratic mayor, Howard Jackson, waved off help from the federal government, announcing that though thousands were out of work, he wanted to avoid undermining the work ethic. "All too often the federal government had to coerce the city into providing assistance for the needy," according to the historian Jo Ann Argersinger. Ten percent of the city's 804,874 residents were unemployed in 1933, and rickets, caused by declining milk consumption, was on the rise. The Baltimore Emergency Relief Commission bought milk in those days for 6 1/2 cents a quart and sold it to the poor for 11 cents. Between May 1 and June 1, 1936, relief rolls in the city were cut from 9,570 to 3,764, even as 3,000 new applicants showed up to apply every day. When Schaefer was in the city council, he frequently decried reliance on the dole, doubting that any deserving person would apply for it. That view was a common one, to be sure, but it was an attitude that was endorsed by the city's political and business elite.

When the National Industrial Recovery Act was passed and federal inspectors were dispatched to various cities to check on reports that employers were short-changing their workers, Baltimore was one of the worst offenders—and this at a time when workers were barely surviving. In early 1931, unemployment had reached 20 percent. The caseload of private charities doubled in one year. Nineteen breadlines were operated in the city. Governor Albert Ritchie urged business to recognize that it, not the state, had a problem, but private and public authority, working in league with each other, treated Baltimore as if it were a plantation. Under Mayor Howard Jackson, March 27, 1931, was designated "Self-Denial Day." "Summoned by church bells and firehouse whistles, citizens by the thousands carried purses, wallets and fists full of loose change to drop in boxes set up in stores, movie houses and libraries and even on street corners. . . . When the counting was done, the total came to $69,000, a measure both of personal generosity and political bankruptcy. Few other cities could dare raise Lenten sacrifice to the status of public policy, but it fairly typified official Baltimore's response to the Great Depression." Given that approach, it's no wonder that people with talent would leave, and it is even more remarkable that men like Hopkins, Pratt, and Walters and women like Miss Etta and Dr. Claribel Cone bequeathed it great treasures: books, paintings, sculpture, medical science, and higher learning. Perhaps it was guilt. Or perhaps it was just another product of the urban crucible, a vessel that could throw up a Garrett, a Babe Ruth, a Thurgood Marshall, a Eubie Blake, and Old and Young Tommy D'Alesandro.

Tommy

The era of Mayor Jackson gave way eventually to the progressive Republican Theodore Roosevelt McKeldin and then to an exuberantly machine-directed challenger named Thomas J. D'Alesandro Jr. (known as "Old Tommy" after his son and namesake was born), who gave himself and Baltimore a new sensibility as well as celebrity. The son of a laborer who had come to the city from the province of Abruzzi in central Italy, he was a man of sartorial panache, sporting a derby, spats, pinky rings, and breast pocket handkerchiefs; of sometimes hilarious profanity; and of deep devotion to Franklin Delano Roosevelt. D'Alesandro was a liberal, the absolute opposite of Jackson. D'Alesandro had named one of his six sons Franklin D. Roosevelt D'Alesandro and called him Roosie. Old Tommy served two terms in the Maryland House of Delegates, in which post he developed a pleasing populist style—demanding disclosure, for example, of those who had been allowed to withdraw their funds on the eve of a bank holiday that was kept secret from the rest of Maryland. Among the culprits was Archbishop Michael J. Curley, head of the Baltimore archdiocese, who withdrew $250,000. When Curley's name was read, D'Alesandro said, "I almost collapsed." He got back on his feet after he saw that Curley's Episcopal counterpart had taken $500,000.

With these secret withdrawals made public at his urging, D'Alesandro earned a dividend of public gratitude and political power. He parlayed that and his Little Italy strength into a seat in the U.S. Congress, where he instantly became a 100 percent supporter of Roosevelt. He endorsed the president's recovery programs, to be sure. D'Alesandro's affinity for Roosevelt was due in part to the president's leadership in opposing the barons who were coddled by Jackson and others and perhaps by Roosevelt's approachability. The president had personally arranged for D'Alesandro to fill twelve jobs in the Internal Revenue Service office in Baltimore after Tommy complained that U.S. Senator Millard Tydings, a Democrat but a diehard fiscal conservative who always voted against the New Deal, was getting all the patronage. D'Alesandro wrote to the president, stating his case, and was then invited to do so in person. By then, FDR knew the man called Tommy, having met him during campaign stops in Denton on the Eastern Shore and later in Baltimore. In the Oval Office, the son of an Italian immigrant and the patrician from New York got on famously, the president personally lighting Tommy's cigarette. "Wow, Mr. President,"

Tommy exclaimed, "if the boys in the old neighborhood could only see me now!"

D'Alesandro knew the value of honest enthusiasm openly expressed (a lesson that Schaefer learned surpassingly well). At a dinner for Maryland's congressional delegation at the Willard Hotel in Washington, D'Alesandro was asked to speak. A teetotaler, he'd been eating whiskey-soaked cocktail cherries and, without realizing it, lost whatever inhibitions he may have had. "I am very proud," he said, "to be seated next to one of your directors, my former employer of long, long ago, Mr. Charles P. McCormick [the spice maker] who paid me the handsome sum of 12 and a half cents an hour for picking fly shit out of pepper while wearing boxing gloves." Far from being offended, the businessmen loved to hear this joke told on one of their friends, and so D'Alesandro told it over and over.

His tenure as mayor was described by the *Sun* as usually balmy, often tempestuous, and nearly always educational. He endorsed the downtown merchants' request for a public-private partnership to tackle the renewal effort. He was a great raconteur with a very sensitive detector for bull. During an interview with a *Sun* reporter, D'Alesandro grew impatient with an unending stream of questions. Realizing that Tommy wanted the inquisition to end, the reporter resorted to a dodge. Blaming his "desk," meaning his editor and boss, he said, "My desk wants me to ask you one more question." Before the question was out, D'Alesandro leaned forward, put his ear to the papers stacked in front of him, and said, "My desk wants your desk to go f—itself." Old Tommy's days in elected office ended after his defeat in 1959, though he served for several years on the State Parole Commission. He also continued to hold court at his house on Albemarle Street, where he granted audiences to job seekers and political supplicants such as William Donald Schaefer, who loved Old Tommy's language, his colorful style, and his honesty.

Baltimore's Best

Schaefer worried about the flagging of Baltimore's spirit and began talking about it during his 1971 campaign, looking ahead to the time when he would be responsible for the civic soul. "There was a sense of depression, a feeling that Baltimore's not a nice place. When you said 'This is a good place to live,' people laughed at you. They had no basis for that feeling, but they had heard it and adopted it." He was determined to let them hear something more encouraging. The city was like Wisniewski: talented, ambitious, and fun loving but selling itself short. If Schaefer had a plan for his city in 1971, it amounted to triage: Find the strength of Baltimore neighborhoods, reinforce it, and hope for overflow. The outer city neighborhoods were his areas that could be shored up. They could share their healthy characteristics—attention to the schools, the sight of parents going to work, tidy alleys—with the areas that were in decline. You had to build from strength, he thought. Pouring huge sums of money into weak areas would fail; President Johnson's War on Poverty, its Model Cities cousin, and an array of other exertions had proved that in the 1960s. Schaefer wanted to stabilize pockets of strength and then build inward toward areas that needed rescue. Pigtown and Sandtown, Greektown and Highlandtown were places he knew in sometimes minute detail. On weekends, he canvassed Federal Hill, Bolton Hill, and Butchers Hill, looking for problems to solve and foundation stones to build on. Some of the areas that were thought of as blighted had been strong and colorful, as vibrant and idiosyncratic as the corner of Lexington and Howard streets. Greektown remained a port of entry for immigrants, a neighborhood bound together by churches, an area of small businesses with jobs for newcomers and politicians who could ease the newcomer's problems and of ethnic restaurants.

Along Pennsylvania Avenue in West Baltimore, jazz lovers could find vivid club and street life, "loud and cantankerous, pulsating with honking horns, droning voices and raucous laughter, and smelling of cigars, perfume and roasted peanuts . . . fast, brazen rhythms, its noon lights and taxicabs, its high heeled women and fancy cars," wrote Kweisi Mfume, the former congressman who became national president of the NAACP in 1995. "The black people here were as classy as any whites I'd ever seen . . . even on television. . . . They drove up in fancy fish-tail Cadillacs and handed them over to red-capped valets. The men stepped out sporting black Stetson hats, tailored sharkskin suits, bright silk ties, and shoes so shiny. . . . Their women were equally mesmerizing, preening glamorously in their pompadour hairdoes, sequined dresses and feather boas that swayed gently as their high heels clicked purposefully along the Avenue. Much like Harlem in the 1920s, Baltimore had this district of flourishing black business. At the Royal Theater, there were live stage shows and even livelier speakeasies covered the twelve block strip." People were ignorant of these neighborhoods when they called Baltimore "the armpit of the East." This sort of name calling would have Schaefer "chewing the carpet," to use Embry's phrase, or, worse, calling personally on the name caller to explain a few things.

Race

After World War II, black citizens migrated into many areas of the city from which they had been barred by custom and practice for generations. The movement of black Baltimoreans was change of the most logical, historically precedented kind in the sense that many ethnic groups had settled in identifiable parts of the city and then, following individual paths, moved beyond those welcoming places to be absorbed in other parts of Baltimore or beyond. As natural as this movement surely was, it had a far different significance when it was made by blacks. Institutionalized, legally required race discrimination, virtually a part of the city's charter (in which restrictive covenants, barred access to public accommodations, and voting restrictions had been enshrined and were rooted out slowly), left an increasing proportion of the populace with second-class status at best. "Three times before World War I, the city council passed ordinances forbidding blacks to live in white neighborhoods," according to *The Baltimore Book*, a social history of the city. In 1943, when Bethlehem Steel tried to train black workers, 7,000 whites went on strike. The Pratt Library closed its training to blacks and said, "most other staff members do not want to work with Negro librarians." For a time, the neighborhood of Roland Park had but one Jewish resident, whose household was boycotted by the milkman and other delivery services, which helped the gentry to convey their message of bigotry. Restrictive covenants, enforced by a network of collaborators—realtors, bankers, neighborhood associations—imposed a dispiriting apartheid, a series of dividing lines that must have been incorporated into the city's psychic makeup over time. *I can't live there. I can't work there. I can't shop there. I can't drink in this tavern.* These realities thrummed the message of inferiority, which was reinforced even more aggressively by real estate salesmen who directed black buyers to the county, where mortgages were easier to obtain. All of these forces and others led the city toward catastrophic, stunning change.

In 1950, when Baltimore's population peaked at 949,708, the year of Schaefer's first effort to enter politics, not a single census tract in West Baltimore had a black population in excess of 25 percent. When he was a boy, his own neighborhood and his own block of Edgewood Street reflected that circumstance: They were 100 percent white. Hilton Parkway on the east and Edmondson Avenue on the south were inviolate boundaries, Schaefer learned, and he did not cross them. Then came the shift:

Blacks moved into the white enclaves. Housing shortages and misconceived urban renewal policies based on clearance, racism, and blockbusting changed the complexion of the city almost literally overnight. Back from the war, shocked to find blacks on streets once all-white, a veteran quoted in *The Baltimore Book* said, "It wasn't integration, it was an evacuation." Rather than accommodate racial change, whites joined what some of them called "the exodus." "They saw a very secure world changing very drastically," said a former white city resident, "and they couldn't accept it. This was distasteful, and they felt they had no choice, I guess."

Blockbusting began on a given street with the purchase of a single house at an inflated price. A black family would be moved in, and then other houses would become available to speculators at deflated prices. The market would collapse, and realtors would make a killing. A collective existential nightmare ensued. Neighbors told neighbors, "Well, if I move, I'm not going to sell to blacks. I'm only going to sell to whites." Sometimes, they were lying. "Even my dear uncle," said one woman. "Guess when we found out he was moving? The day the moving van pulled up! This was right next door and he never told us one word about it." One group of Baltimoreans fled to escape another group, a corrosive and embittering spectacle for both. Schaefer recalls asking the pastor of St. Bernadine's Church just up the street from his house on Edgewood, whether he needed any help dealing with the fear and anger. The priest said no. Schaefer and his colleagues in the council offered antiblockbusting ordinances, but they did little good. This was part of the history that led to upheaval and protest in the 1960s, confrontation and direct action in the streets that did not seem justified to William Donald Schaefer. He cherished the Baltimore he had known as a child. When protestors marched to open Gwynn Oak Amusement Park, Schaefer saw unnecessary destruction of a shrine to the city's way of life—an affront to authority that he did not appreciate. As sympathetic as he had been with his votes, Schaefer was not a revolutionary, nor was he a supporter of those who thought discrimination and deprivation warranted direct action.

Radical Decline

Baltimore was in need of spiritual as well as economic renaissance—escape from industrial bosses (as much as from the political ones Rouse feared), from blockbusting, and from despair. The beginning of that effort may fairly be pinpointed in November 1952. During a meeting of the

Municipal Art Society, city leaders heard the sobering and unhappy forecast that Baltimore, no less than other U.S. cities, was in decline. Property values and therefore tax revenues were falling in parts of the city, the Commission on Government Efficiency and Economy concluded. It declared, "Unless radical action is taken, the municipal corporation will be bankrupt within a generation." That prospect was too grim to contemplate at first. Two years passed before any formal group was formed to fight back. Ted Wolfe, an executive at Baltimore Gas & Electric, spoke for many when he said, "Baltimore is not in bad enough shape yet to support that type of organization." But then in 1954, retail merchants and downtown property owners formed the Committee for Downtown. In January of the following year, formation of the Greater Baltimore Committee was agreed to by city business leaders at Jim Rouse's leadership—but did not get off the ground. He all but gave up before he realized finally that he could succeed if he relied on the authority of someone a bit closer to the establishment: a leading lawyer or businessman. He turned to Clarence W. Miles, a founding partner of the law firm Miles & Stockbridge. Just a year before, Miles had purchased the St. Louis Browns, brought them to Baltimore, and changed their name to the Orioles after a minor league team of the same name. Old Tommy would not hear of retaining "Browns" or permit a contest to pick a new name. Miles agreed to call a meeting of other city leaders at the Hotel Emerson and later at the ultraexclusive Elkridge Club—a serious venture, to be sure, since the eighty-three original members of the GBC agreed to pay annual dues of up to $5,000, sufficient to support a working director and staff of experts to study a wide range of city problems and to offer solutions. But another year passed. Then an Urban Renewal Study Board issued a report, and soon thereafter, the city established an urban renewal and housing agency.

"They saw that urban deterioration was insidious. It affected not only housing and community well being but also the city's commerce, industry, transportation, cultural life and support services. The rate of decay was outstripping efforts to reclaim blighted areas," Miles later wrote in his memoirs. "Many worthy projects were failing, not because opposition was strong, but because general support was woefully weak. Special interests had stronger voices than the majority who stood to benefit . . . plans met with indifference and then with failure. Influential civic leaders who cared about improvements were too few to break the stalemate. The business community was failing to provide the essential impetus for change. . . . It refused to look beyond its own limited, immediate concerns."

Miles was just the man Rouse needed. He got the city's attention and was joined by its topmost business leaders: Thomas B. Butler, president of Mercantile Safe Deposit & Trust Company, one of the most successful managers of estates in the country; Jerold C. Hoffberger, president of the National Brewing Company and later owner of the Orioles; and Daniel Lindley, president of the Canton Company, a major shipping firm. Board members included Charles P. Crane, president of the BG&E; Stephen C. Husted, sales manager of Bethlehem Steel Corporation; Albert D. Hutzler Jr., president of Hutzler Brothers; W. Wallace Lanahan, a stockbroker with Stein Brothers & Boyce; and Old Tommy's one-time boss, Charles P. McCormick, president of the spice-making company whose piquant products, manufactured in a plant hard by the harbor, seasoned the city air, an uplifting, almost defiant counterpoint to decline.

Miles became the GBC president, and he wanted Bill Boucher as the day-to-day director. Butler of the Mercantile objected. "My God, Clarence," he said, "he's a member of the Americans for Democratic Action. You really wouldn't want us to be tied in with that gang of wild liberals." Butler and his bank were powerful leaders, managing, as they did, the huge estates and trusts of extremely wealthy families. But Miles persisted, and Boucher was hired. In short order, it was the name Boucher that came to represent good civic works and the public-private partnership more prominently than any other, including Butler and Miles.

Rouse's concerns about the city were fully recognized, and a delegation of businessmen marched, without fanfare, to D'Alesandro's office to say that nothing could go forward without the city's involvement. The sums of money required and the condemnation powers, which were needed to dig up and reroute power and sewer lines, could not occur without city approval. Less than a month after downtown urban renewal ordinance #1210 was passed by the council, the first major step toward reclaiming the city was adopted. It was more generally known as the Charles Center Plan.

The idea was to become competitive with suburban shopping centers, as if ripping out old, decaying, and underused buildings and replacing them with new, modern, and more inviting structures could achieve that goal. Charles Center was to be "a great adventure in a city which normally abhors the new and adventurous," wrote Martin Millspaugh, one of the most important of the city's renewal leaders. A plan commissioned by the Greater Baltimore Committee's Planning Council was presented to Mayor D'Alesandro in 1958. New office space, new retail shops, a hotel, some housing, and parking were to be constructed on twenty-two acres of land, where all existing buildings were to be razed.

At first, all the work was to be underwritten by state and local funds. But when the rules changed, qualifying Baltimore's project for federal aid, the city fathers took it. Also in the fall of 1958, the citizens of the city narrowly approved city borrowing for the project. Some said that they were motivated by the Colts' dramatic 1958 world championship football victory over the New York Giants. Baltimore was ready to see its first major new construction in thirty-two years.

Charles Center was a design success, and in the beginning, it produced considerable new tax revenue. But still the suburbs grew and the city declined. Yet it was an essential step, a much larger success than one could measure by looking at new buildings, tax collections, and renewed commercial activity. Mark K. Joseph, Schaefer's physical development director and later his school board chairman, called Charles Center a bridge to the future renewal efforts of Schaefer and Baltimore. "It was the bridge to the Inner Harbor. No one would have believed in the harbor plans without Charles Center. It was a bridge spiritually as well as physically and commercially. Sure we were trying to save department stores. Nobody knew there weren't going to be department stores downtown. For its time, though, Charles Center was what you had to do." Almost every U.S. city learned the same lesson the same way. In a sense, Charles Center had to be built to prove that it was not the answer. When it did not immediately win back suburban shoppers, business leaders became dispirited. The city would need the strongest possible mayor to prop them up again, to find new Charles Centers, to keep searching for focus and foothold in the struggle.

A Nonracial Club

Physical renewal and its need for private financing brought the social change that had been held back in Baltimore. For years, the city had not a single "nonracial club," a place where Jews, blacks, and women could meet for lunch with friends and clients. Joseph Meyerhoff, one of the city's major property holders, art patrons and philanthropists, agreed to support the GBC and downtown development, but he wanted such a club to be included in the new amenities. Miles and Boucher were happy to be his allies, but their goal collided, as always, with what Miles and others called reality just as Henry Parks's open accommodations bill had been opposed by restaurateurs who said that business would be hurt. In this case, Miles feared he would be unable to attract enough members to make the club a going proposition. Miles wrote a memorandum to the club's board of governors: "The issue projected whether or not to permit colored persons to join the club is a very live and controversial one. The division of sentiment is sharp and obviously somewhat emotional. . . . I most earnestly submit that all efforts to obtain 200 additional members should be exhausted before the subject issue is decided," and that all members should be entitled to participate in the deliberations. If blacks were allowed in first, he reasoned, the needed dues-paying members might not be available.

But momentum was building quickly behind the physical aspects of the plan. The Federal Housing Act of 1959 was passed, making Charles Center eligible for big money from Washington. The federal Government Services Agency agreed to build on a site in the renewal area. In January 1961, an agreement was reached to demolish O'Neill's Department Store. Schaefer supported that decision, though not without a pang for the loss it represented. Triage demanded difficult decisions in the hope that a new day could be fashioned from decay. The businessman Morris Mechanic was granted authority to plan a theater on the south border of the Charles Center complex. Dozens of decisions were made in the months that followed, allowing BG&E and Hamburger's and Jacob Blaustein to begin new buildings.

"Ted"

Charles Center was under way, but by 1963, when McKeldin began his second term as mayor of Baltimore, Rouse saw new opportunities for the city. He sent McKeldin a memo suggesting a reborn waterfront, a move away from the decay, pollution, and vermin-infested streets that dominated the city's harbor district. McKeldin included the idea in his official address. Miles and McKeldin were joined, unofficially, by the Mercantile, which agreed to be assessed on the basis of the property it controlled to help pay for the improvements. The Merc, as it was known by some, "voted" land and buildings it held in trust for estates, the area of banking in which it specialized. Its participation represented critical leadership for businessmen who were not always ready to risk anything. A plan was to be drawn, but Miles and others thought that planning was a luxury, lest the "patient die on the operating table as the diagnosis was being made."

McKeldin had been one of Maryland's most active governors, and he had invested himself personally in the emergence of the city from years in which blacks and Jews were barred from so many aspects of city life. Like Old Tommy, McKeldin was an outrageously flamboyant man. He affected a Scottish brogue, loved grand entrances, claimed affiliation with a broad range of religious faiths, and presided over the construction of many roads and bridges, including the first Chesapeake Bay Bridge. With a wife named Honolulu and a chief political aide known as Sweetie Pie, McKeldin was a phenomenon. Though Democrats dominated Baltimore and thus the state, McKeldin insisted that Maryland had a two-party system: Out Democrats and In Democrats. His approach to Republican victory: Capture the "Out" party and hold its loyalties. Just as Kovens would do for William Donald Schaefer, Sweetie Pie kept the unions and the other interest groups at bay while McKeldin presided.

Every governor had a Sweetie, it seemed. Govenor Millard Tawes's was Hocker; Marvin Mandel had several, including Kovens. Schaefer found that these fixers and negotiators allowed the elected dummies and geniuses to go forward on big picture planning without the nettling distractions that might otherwise defeat them. McKeldin's man kept his law office open twenty-four hours day, sometimes falling asleep during phone calls. Asked what it was, precisely, he did for McKeldin, Adelson said with artful candor, "I represent points of view." If McKeldin was about to build something, start a big school construction program, for example, Adelson might ask the unions up for a bit of a confab. "What do you guys want," he'd ask early on in the conversation. "I want to take care of it so things don't get screwed up." McKeldin fretted about what Adelson did but never stopped it. Late one evening in city hall, McKeldin confessed some deep misgivings to Peter Marudas, a senior aide who later worked for Young Tommy and U.S. Senator Paul S. Sarbanes. "There are certain things you have to do to continue in politics that don't appear to be appropriate, the Adelson side of things. He justified it as the price of getting certain things done. In the macro sense, you couldn't fault him. The jobs he gave, the political deals, the people appointed to various posts."

Near the end of McKeldin's second term in Annapolis, the powerful Adelson went to Marvin Mandel for help. A certain judgeship needed the governor's approval so that the assembly could act on it. McKeldin was not moving, Adelson said. Could Marvin try to get it going? Marvin said he would try. "You know who's going to get it?" asked Sweetie. Mandel didn't know. It didn't matter. You helped with these things, and then you got help when you needed it. When Adelson said that he, Adelson, was to be the beneficiary, Mandel was astonished. He went to see McKeldin.

"You have to do this," he said.

McKeldin said he couldn't.

"Why not?," Mandel asked.

Because, McKeldin said, "The *Sun* will torture me if I do."

Mandel was shocked at such betrayal and hypocrisy. "What do you care? You're done. You're not going to run again. You owe this guy."

But McKeldin, who had confided much guilt about his reliance on Adelson, did not relent—shocking perfidy in Mandel's view.

When Adelson died, Spiro Agnew told a reporter, "Fagin is dead," a reference to the master thief in *Oliver Twist*.

Schaefer thought McKeldin was a bit of a fraud, a tall, broadly smiling man with a blond forelock who bestrode the city like some benevolent uncle. Schaefer put him in the "pretty boy" school of mayors. McKeldin liked to join groups and religions by asserting that his wife was already a member. "I don't belong to that group but my wife, Honolulu, does," he would say, whether she did or not. He liked to try out the construction equipment when cutting ribbons for his highway projects. When one union objected to having a nonmember at the controls, McKeldin asked for a union membership card. He had, said Marudas, "a feel for the history and texture of his times. He was a complicated and multifaceted individual who had to scramble to get where he was. He had made compromises."

McKeldin, like Rouse, thought Schaefer was a very narrow person. McKeldin's style, no doubt, annoyed and offended Schaefer, whose own political vaudeville act was yet to emerge. When Schaefer was mayor, he put McKeldin in charge of the city's zoning board of appeals, a post the older man filled with energy and appreciation. This pattern of fierce animosity replaced by close alliance and even friendship would become well-known to Schaefer's intimates.

While Schaefer was still in the council, throughout the 1960s, the march toward a new Baltimore skyline quietly gathered momentum. The newspapers were filled with reports of groundbreakings, a ceremonial topping out for buildings under construction, and architectural awards for those already completed. The projects seemed to be coming along on a production line: the Garmatz Federal Office Building (August 1963), the Sun Life Building (December 1963), the gas and electric company building (January 20, 1964), the "down under" garage (July 1964), a grand new and futuristically constructed theater built by Morris Mechanic (August 1964), the Maryland Academy of Sciences (October 1965), the Christ Lutheran Church complex (1965), the Statler Hilton Hotel (April 1966), a construction agreement for the United States Fidelity and Guaranty Building (September 1968), the opening of the office tower at Two Charles Center (March 1969). During this period, the council also approved an authority to develop the inner harbor. Schaefer, who always credited D'Alesandro and McKeldin for putting these projects on track, became the conductor of an urban renewal express. Dozens of projects were moving from idea to reality, though the movement was a bit subterranean, bureaucratic, and governmental. Few citizens seemed to sense the magnitude of Baltimore's makeover. Schaefer's job was to give it visibility, to create the necessary popular support for all that government spending, and, in the process, to demand even more projects. Despite the movement *he* could see, Schaefer knew that the city's business community and the profoundly doubting citizenry needed daily proof of progress. In time, he hoped, he would not have to explain or defend any project or plan because the benefits would be unfolding every day.

The pressure to deal with the city's growing poverty and its loss of taxpayers to the suburbs was intense and unrelenting. Much of the gentry had decamped long since for horse country in the Worthington Valley. It was followed by a mobile middle class that was certain it did not need the conveniences and synergies of city living and worried that no mayor could fix the schools, make the city safe, or arrest the physical decay. Greater Baltimore Committee leaders seemed ready to acknowledge defeat. These men, who had once been proudly determined to pay for the Charles Center project out of their own pockets, were dropping out of the work they had started so well. They were prepared to leave it to government, which they nevertheless distrusted and freely criticized. The task of providing a sense of constantly building momentum, of providing continuity and hope, fell to William Donald Schaefer. He knew it was a long haul and that he had to stay on schedule lest even scant traces of enthusiasm and confidence would vanish. Criticized often for having an "edifice complex," for being merely a bricks and mortar man, Schaefer worked in the realm of the intangible, trying to reignite the pride of the neighborhoods. His own quirky charisma, enforced by the organizational and financial strength of Irv Kovens, the genius of Rouse, and the zeal of his young city builders, would capture energy and high aspiration. Schaefer hated those who "downed" his city. As always, he tried to use their opposition, turning it to his advantage. Doubters, he said, using words that would have horrified Rouse and delighted Old Tommy, were "dumber than ape shit."

Caretaker

Schaefer knew city hall as well as he knew 620 Edgewood Street, but now he was seeing it whole for the first time. A forbidding and dusty warren of offices encircling a grand, five-story rotunda with marble balconies and wrought iron gratings oddly reminiscent of the French Quarter in New Orleans, the building was crowned by a gold-colored dome. All in all, it was a splendid symbol of government's power and majesty. Schaefer's office as president of the council had been on the fourth floor, so he had passed every employee in a hallway, had looked into every face in the building for years. He knew who was talented, who was reliable, who was smart—for the most part. Now he wanted to close any gaps. He knew he was a part of the building's culture and routine, idiosyncratic as he was: Crazy Don. A loon. Mean. Stay out of his way. He knew his reputation—ill-tempered, vindictive, maybe a bit "off"—and he knew that these cultivated attributes helped him. But now he had to disabuse a work force of the corrosive idea, eagerly whispered, that he was a one-termer, a man out of his depth, a mayor without qualifications.

The task of gaining respect confronts any new mayor, any new manager, governor, or president. People settled into their jobs and did them without energy unless they were motivated and loyal to someone or something. Schaefer convened a meeting in the Ceremonial Room, its floor to ceiling windows shuttered and heavily draped. New and old department heads listened to the new boss speak at first of what he would call cabinet meetings. He talked slowly, jabbing the air with the stubby forefinger of his right hand, scanning the faces and stopping when he was certain an individual was looking at him—giving what would be known soon enough as "the Stare."

"Anyone who does his job has nothing to fear from me," he said. "But don't ever cross me." If anyone had thoughts of joining some waiting-in-the-wings successor, Schaefer would address that possibility directly. "Never cross me." He repeated his warning as if he were some Chicago gangster, affecting visceral disgust for disloyalty and suggesting painful penalties. Several months earlier, during the campaign, he had promised a new day in city hall: "As an elected city official I have made the rounds of neighborhoods. . . . Many other top city officials do not. They become isolated from the urgency of our problems. They see matters in the abstract, surrounded by their rules and regulations. I plan systematic meetings in the field, taking government to the citizenry. I will attend. My department heads and bureau and division chiefs will attend. The purpose of these forums is not simply to talk. Rather, they will test the administration's policy and system for delivering services." Every administration tried something similar and tired of it almost as quickly as the workers. Schaefer fired an engineer in the public works department who had opposed his views on the Road. Bereska made sure everyone knew that man was gone and why.

Protecting the Dome

Schaefer saw the momentum and sensed the culture of his domain in everything he did. A special secretary was already in place, for example, a man who personified the staying power of the civil service worker. Walter Eric Beuchelt had served ten mayors of Baltimore over a half century, back through the D'Alesandros, the two terms of McKeldin, Jackson's five, Grady's truncated single term, and all the rest back to William F. Broening, the mayor who had first named Beuchelt to his post in 1920, a year before Schaefer was born. Thirteen municipal elections had come and gone in those fifty years and seven mayors, all but two of them Democrats. Beuchelt, a Republican, outserved them all. He was a lawyer by training, a former member of the Maryland House of Delegates, and, at eighty-one, a keeper of secrets imparted by man and building. Early on, the amiable Walter materialized in Schaefer's office, using a passageway that the new mayor was unaware of. Only Walter knew all the nooks, crannies, and doorways in this building. And no one knew Walter's actual duties except Walter. This was not necessarily to suggest that he had noth-

ing to do, although that could have been said and was said of some func-
tionaries. One such was Joe Bertorelli, a state senator who had been a
musician on the Block. His political talent was showing up in official and
politically useful pictures. When the assembly was not meeting, Bertorelli
presided over an immaculately clean desk situated prominently in the first-
floor lobby with its bas relief seal of the city inset in the beige marble floor.
A black telephone was the only item between the visiting citizen and the
good senator's cheerful greeting.

"What does Joe do?" Young Tommy was asked one day. The mayor's
expression grew somber, as if to give proper weight to the senator's job
description.

"He's to stay there at his post, and if the dome falls, he's to call me right
away," the mayor said.

In a sense, men like Bertorelli and Beuchelt did keep the dome in place.
Beuchelt was keeper of the Test Book, a hoary register of mayors' and
council members' signatures, each affirming his or her election, without
which no man was officially in office. Walter preserved other ceremonial
aspects of city life, the practical application of tradition and ritual. He
knew funerals, for example, those most basic of political events. Specifically, he knew how to drape public buildings, including, in 1968, Pennsylvania Station, which had to be prepared for the train-borne casket of
the slain Robert F. Kennedy as it passed through the city.

Walter also controlled important bits of patronage, though his power
fell far short of the iron-handed grip men like D'Alesandro and his patrons
were thought to have. There were still jobs outside the ambit of civil service then and a multitude of honorary positions to be filled on city boards
and commissions, all of them potentially prestigious to Schaefer's friends
and financial contributors. Joan Bereska wanted to know everything about
both categories. If someone were to report on the status of the dome under
William Donald Schaefer, Bereska wanted to say who it would be. She met
with Walter.

"What can I do for you?" he asked.

What is the status of this person? How long is his term? When does his
appointment end? What does this commission do?

"I don't know," Beuchelt said alarmingly often, showing some surprise
that the new crowd might care. Bereska cared. She did not wish to have
Beuchelt or a councilman exercising power that properly resided in the
mayor's office. If anyone were to confer a laborer's job, he would do so
after Bereska approved. Often over the next decade, she would need to

have something done for her boss, and she was anxious to know that whomever she might summon would come promptly, knowing that it was Schaefer who had granted the job and could take it away. An irony arose when Bereska found, at first, that many Baltimoreans were unwilling to serve their city, refusing the invitation of William Donald Schaefer, a man they thought of as a caretaker who would not last long in the job.

As she moved about the new universe of city government, Bereska realized that Walter Beuchelt lived in city hall literally. He was seen occasionally padding about in felt bedroom slippers — once having stepped out of D'Alesandro's private shower, a wet, stunning figure even for the worldly Tommy. Walter's public and private rooms were on the second floor. A refrigerator and a two-burner stove stood near the standard metal desk. Several beer steins given to him by McKeldin were displayed on the refrigerator. A phonograph and a large collection of records could provide music for 180 minutes, he happily reported.

Yet the hall was also a scene of tragedy in Beuchelt's life. In 1963, from the place he maintained for his family somewhere in the city, he brought his thirteen-year-old-son, Walter, Jr., to see Christmas lights being hung in the rotunda. The boy, whom he called "Walter child," watched the workmen for a while and then wandered off. When he had not been seen for some minutes, Beuchelt went looking for him. As he opened a door leading from the first floor to the basement, he found the boy hanging by his neck from a belt that somehow had snagged on a gate leading to the lower floor. Beuchelt screamed for help but was unable to revive his son. The boy had been cheerful that day, his father said, and they had stopped on the way in to buy his Christmas present, a pair of ice skates.

Beuchelt endured another decade in the relatively undemanding atmosphere that prevailed before Schaefer. What did he actually do? D'Alesandro could laugh at the question. Who cared? Schaefer cared, of course, so Bereska went after him. She stirred up so much dust in an actual housecleaning effort that Walter was forced to dine out. In this, he demonstrated the flexibility that had, no doubt, helped him to survive so many different mayors. "It's not good to eat alone anyway," he told a reporter. Bereska and the new mayor were asked to go easy on Walter, and they tried, but Walter knew by then that new administrations always exerted some pressure for change. Quickly enough, the pressure eased and life returned to its familiar rhythms. But one morning in January 1972, the phantom of city hall was found in a coma, head down on his desk, dressed as always in black suit, white shirt, and black tie at the post he had been destined to occupy until such a moment arrived. He was taken to nearby Mercy Hospital, where he died that same day.

Coins of the Realm

In a room off the mayor's suite, Bereska came upon a five-drawer file cabinet, locked. When keys could not be found, she ordered it hauled away. Three men came, but they were not up to the job. The cabinet could not be lifted, tilted, or budged. A torch was found, and the lock succumbed. The top drawer rolled out slowly, revealing a trove of transit authority bus tokens. Each of the other drawers was similarly loaded to the gunwales, totaling about $10,000 worth, it turned out. The federal Concentrated Employment and Training Act program then operating in most large U.S. cities—bringing $100 million a year to Baltimore—dispensed tokens to its students and trainees, so perhaps that explained why city government had so many on hand. But CETA headquarters were far from city hall, and a locked file cabinet was not a likely storage bin. Bereska wondered whether the tokens represented the abandoned scheme of some enterprising and larcenous soul. In the end, he or she had been too successful, accumulating more loot than could easily be removed. Or perhaps the stash was simply forgotten. Some thought Schaefer would fail because they knew that achieving forward movement was as difficult as moving a filing cabinet full of bus tokens or a building full of fifty-year men assigned to dome watching and hall draping. Schaefer never had enough money, but this cache of tokens was a symbol of times in which federal money flowed freely. By the end of his tenure, no drawer of file cabinet with even a few pennies went undetected.

Ten Votes

Baltimore's charter called for the strongest of strong mayoral governments. The council could only cut from, not add to, annual budgets. A simple majority of ten votes gave the executive whatever he wanted—and majorities were easily managed with alley paving, bus stop shelters, playgrounds, and the like. The mayor held the patronage reins as well, and the Board of Estimates, which handled the city's day-to-day business, was his instrument. He had an automatic majority of three votes there: his own and those of the public works director and solicitor, both of whom he appointed. Schaefer wanted to keep George Russell as solicitor and did for a time. Later, he said, Kovens helped him to get Benjamin L. Brown, a soft-spoken thoughtful man who left the bench to serve as top city lawyer for fifteen years. This sort of authority had been more than enough mayoral power for decades when mayors were almost ceremonial figures. James Michael Curley of Boston, Frank Hague in Jersey City, and the Pendergasts in St. Louis afforded themselves variously deep dips into the public trough or long vacations in Europe. In the 1960s, though, cities fell into a state of permanent fragility, subject to public employee strikes, summer riots, and a long list of other crises. A mayor could not be away for more than a weekend, if that. Schaefer relished the ceremonial aspect as much as or more than his predecessors did, and he took that facet of the job to unimagined heights, but he also knew every department head, their personalities, foibles, and ways of doing business—whom to confront and whom to finesse. Apprenticeship whetted his appetite—made it insatiable—and, over time, more than compensated for the disadvantages of an apolitical background.

"During the past years of racial and political transition," he wrote, in "Where I Stand," "the times may not have been ripe for 'management' matters to receive focus and priority. I believe now we are ready. Indeed, we have no choice. Most of Baltimore's citizens, black and white, have a stake in the system. They are demanding that it work for them. They are demanding a better, more efficient delivery of services. . . . We must seek ways of institutionalizing executive authority and accountability. City government is a big business with an annual budget of over 900 million dollars, nearly 40,000 employees and hundreds of operating departments and programs. Given this size and complexity, our chief executive must have the management tools and authority needed to direct and hold accountable constituent parts of a massive operation." To increase the flow of information—to him—he proposed the formation of a cabinet structure, a merger of smaller departments, and formation of policy councils on human and physical development. He wanted an office of neighborhood affairs to manage a series of mayor's stations and multipurpose centers, many of which came to cities via federal programs that Schaefer wanted to control. He also wanted an office of intergovernmental affairs, which would coordinate federal, state, and foundation aid to the city, influencing the terms, conditions, and uses of these grants to provide sufficient flexibility in applying rules made in Washington or Annapolis. What he promised was "vigorous management—my strength." As with most campaign documents, this unusually focused one went largely unread. Students of municipal government and of William Donald Schaefer would have found it a useful guide to what would unfold over the next fifteen years.

A Model City

Schaefer could claim an unusually proficient municipal team. Under Bob Embry's imaginative hand, Baltimore had built its own version of the Department of Housing and Urban Development, merging housing and development concerns in a single agency, the Department of Housing and Community Development. Its Charles Center project, twenty-two acres of downtown renewal, had become a national model. Unlike Washington's national HUD, Baltimore's was actually operating in a city, dealing with a city's problems every day. Embry presided over an operation that managed more low income housing units per capita than any other city in the country. As a result of intense management, public housing in Baltimore had virtually no vacancies—an unheard-of situation elsewhere in the nation. Schaefer organized rat and graffitti patrols. He feared the malignant power of the graffitto: Within twenty-four hours, like an abandoned car, it became invisible, part of the dreary landscape and acceptable without notice or question after a single day. Instant eradication was the answer, and Schaefer made public housing tenants responsible for surveillance along with his own managers. "We had a very benevolent, but strict system," Embry said, emphasizing "strict." Malefactors were asked to leave. Some 44,000 families were on the waiting lists, after all.

In the mini-HUD operation, Embry was the urban renewal commissioner, manager of low-income housing, and head of the Baltimore Development Corporation, the Off Street Parking Commission, and the Charles Center–Inner Harbor Management Office, which handled the two most glamorous renewal efforts. And Embry's shop was but one example of how city agencies had begun to operate: highly efficient, flexible, and responsive to the man who was running them. When Schaefer told federal officials that he knew what to do with the money, they knew from their increasingly frequent field trips to Baltimore that he was not exaggerating. Long before completion of his major building projects—the ones that gave him a national profile—Baltimore was becoming a laboratory for studying what the scholars called federalism, the interaction of state, federal, and local governments. Washington would occasionally use Baltimore to hold off critics who wished to kill programs outright. Schaefer's urban development engine—with cylinders labeled neighborhood im-

provement, downtown commercial, housing authority, and job training—
had to have the federal dollar as fuel.

The First "Do It Now"

A few weeks after taking office, Schaefer traveled to Indianapolis, where
he saw a spectacular Christmas display. An eager borrower of good ideas,
he returned to demand something similar—grander if possible—for Baltimore. He wanted big. He wanted bright and widely visible, a stir. What
about putting lights on the Washington monument? he suggested.

"On the monument? The Washington Monument?" Bereska asked.

Schaefer's face moved to that mocking expression, a menacing mien
preliminary to the dreaded Stare. He used it when people were being obtuse or asking what he thought was a dumb question—or questioning
him at all. By then, Bereska resonated deeply to the Boss's every demand,
took each as a challenge.

"The Washington Monument," she repeated to herself, as if to absorb it.

She called Stanley Zemansky, the city's purchasing agent, a humorless
suit, a lifer in the hall and as straight a shooter as any bureaucracy ever
created. Balding, slight of build, he spoke in clipped, impatient sentences
that seemed to flow directly from ordinances. It would not be possible, he
instructed, to buy the lights without first requesting bids. That would take
weeks, well beyond Christmas surely. Sorry, he said.

No, no, said Bereska, you don't understand. The mayor wants this and
we're going to do it, so please come to my office.

Perhaps, said Zemansky falling quickly back on his last defense, Bereska could take it up with Mr. Benton.

That might have been a good ploy. Schaefer's first instructions to all his
inner circle were never to offend or trifle with Benton. So Bereska, using
her well-recognized tone of aggravation, said, "Listen Stanley, come over
to my office. We don't have to call Mr. Benton."

Zemansky came as ordered, knowing that Benton might be unhappy
but Bereska and Schaefer would shout. Zemansky got the lights. Bereska
got the parks director, Doug Tawney, to summon his crew of foresters,
then essentially idled by winter, to hang them on the sacred obelisk (which
pre-dated the taller one in Washington, D.C.) at Mount Vernon Square—
and they were a great hit, an instant holiday tradition, complete in later
years with a ceremonial lighting, fireworks, speeches, sports celebrities,

hot cider, choral groups, and representatives of downtown stores hailing all for a bit of shopping after the cheer.

Zemansky's boss, Charles L. Benton, the city's powerful director of finance, said nothing. Though his demeanor approximated Zemansky's, Benton was not at all averse to ignoring rules when he wanted something done, and here he was feeling his way, trying to learn how he and the new mayor would coexist. He and Bereska were naturally antagonistic, not a good fit. He shut her out of meetings that she needed to attend on the mayor's behalf—of the city employee's credit union board, for example. Instead of a welcome to these councils, she received a food mixer and an apron. Instead of a thank you, she sent back a demand: Invite me to the meetings. No invitation came, so she began her own countercampaign. "What are they doing at those meetings?" she asked others on the board, "Watching blue movies?"

Still, Benton unnerved Bereska, causing her to trip over rugs and worrying that he would try to have her fired—and succeed. Schaefer seemed to love the insecurity it created in her. He invited her in to read a letter Benton had written, suggesting that very course of action. The new mayor had no intention of dismissing Bereska, but he was happy to have her work inspired by the prospect that he might. She was his point person, as imposing a figure as he—a tougher one in some ways because she could not bear the prospect of telling her boss that something couldn't be accomplished. He gave her responsibility and held her accountable in ways that were consuming, frightening, and exhilarating. In time, a brief time, she became known to reporters and bureaucrats alike as The Dragon Lady, a smart, creative, and resourceful operator who would work the hours and insist on the performance her principal demanded. A phone system in city hall automatically bumped calls to her on weekends, making her the duty officer, the person to be called first in an emergency.

Actual or Customary

Benton loomed larger than Walter Beuchelt, but he was just as eccentric and far more powerful. Schaefer knew that he was an indispensable power center, a brilliant man who could install his own plumbing, his own electrical wiring, his own masonry. His splendid hilltop house in College Park featured a driveway paved by Benton's own hand with Belgian block bought from the city, which, Benton said, had given him a very good price. In the hall, Benton communed with his books at a cloistered remove, working at a large desk illuminated by a green Tiffany-shaded lamp at the back of an otherwise dimly lit room. By the time Schaefer became mayor in 1971, Benton was a fearsome and mysterious figure. One night during Young Tommy's tenure, after a long budgeting session over dinner in Little Italy, Benton and the other numbers men returned to the hall to find themselves locked out of the mayoral suite. D'Alesandro did not give keys to anyone but his maid, and she had gone for the day. The mayor's men milled about, bemused by quantities of wine, only to hear locks suddenly turning and Benton emerging from within the mayoral office. He had gone into an adjacent office, climbed out a window, and, all six-feet-five of him, inched along one of the second-floor window ledges until he was outside the mayoral suite. There, he opened the window and climbed through. Benton could manage anything.

"We have to take care of him," Schaefer told Bereska, "and he will see us through." All the more reason for Bereska to tremble when Benton decided it would be best to fire her.

D'Alesandro found Schaefer hilariously unqualified as a politician—unsuited, unskilled, and without potential. "He was like an astronaut who doesn't like to fly," Young Tommy said mirthfully. But Schaefer knew who could help and who could fatally damage his mayoralty. Benton and D'Alesandro had not gotten on well together, a destabilizing factor in Young Tommy's administration and perhaps another reason for his early departure. The new mayor's scrutiny of the landscape identified potential hazards, including the finance director. Schaefer believed that he was working against every force in American urban life: poverty, brazen advocates for the poor, imperious bankers, a deadened city hall bureaucracy, sniping newspapers—everyone but those who had become, over sixteen years in city government, his deeply devoted partisans. He wanted Benton on his team, immediately. Benton could scale buildings and "find the money"—or not—for projects a mayor wanted. "Finding the money" and "making the numbers work" were phrases that would come into common usage in a Schaefer government that was determined to swing construction project deals in the private sector, deals that imparted momentum and made the city seem lively and hopeful. Benton conjured visions of a modern Archimedes, a man who could turn lead or anything else into gold. In a sense, he actually could. He knew city accounts the way Walter Beuchelt had known protocol. He could put his large hands into municipal pockets that were known only to him, or he could move sums between accounts in ways that left no fingerprints, and, sometimes, by cleverly investing federal dollars (a prohibited activity), he could actually produce money where none had been before.

Benton's career began at College Park, where University of Maryland President Harry C. H. ("Curley") Byrd protected him from those, including state legislators, who wanted to know what he did and how he did it. University accrediting boards were critical of the university in those days, but they found Benton's operation professional and efficient. Benton and Byrd refused to open their books for inspection by legislators, and for years, Byrd made the refusal stick. Testifying in tandem before legislative committees, they were always running into heavy flak—and always emerging with all they had requested. Everyone was in awe of Benton's capacity for work, his instant recall of issues and the detailed financial underpinning of each. He spoke in a high-pitched, raspy, yet rolling style that remained focused and terse, though impatience seemed present in virtually every presentation, as if he was a bit contemptuous of the innumeracy of his audiences—even as he took advantage of it.

After World War II, when Byrd needed money to complete work on a dozen new buildings, including Cole Field House, Benton learned from a colleague how to leverage more money from Washington. Under the law covering university expenses for the education of returning veterans, a claim could be filed for "usual and customary" costs or the university could figure out the actual cost of educating a soldier. College Park, the university system's main campus, had become almost a military camp in those days, covered with dormitory tents to house the many servicemen who swelled the campus population in 1946.

Benton guessed that the actual cost, if high enough, would put him far ahead, and he began to make the calculations. Within weeks in the fall of that year, he had secured about $5 million more for Byrd, permitting completion of Byrd Stadium, Cole Field House (then the largest basketball facility in the old Southern Conference), and the campus chapel. When state officials attempted to claim this found money for the general fund, Benton and others convened all-night sessions in Baltimore to "obligate"— spend, in effect—every nickel by signing a series of year end contracts with the firms that were engaged in constructing these buildings.

In 1956, a year after Schaefer was elected to the city council, Benton decided to leave the university. Byrd had run for governor, losing to McKeldin, and relinquished his post at the university to Wilson Elkins, who was not nearly the power player on campus or in Annapolis—and perhaps was a bit more finicky about rules and regulations. Benton saw less challenge and excitement and perhaps a curbing of his own freedoms. On the way to work one day, he heard McKeldin say on the radio that a job was open in the Baltimore comptroller's office. Benton took the civil service test, finishing first, and went to work for the city. In short order, nothing could be known about city government finance that Mr. Benton did not know first. Everything about money crossed his desk, usually before the mayor got a chance to see it. Benton managed all his projects, all his revolutions and power plays, while developing a reputation for heroic bouts with the bottle. He changed, and from that point, he was perhaps even more formidable. His drinking was replaced by deep devotion to the born-again Christian movement.

Mayors had power, to be sure, but often they were obliged to deal with wily bureaucratic competitors like Benton who could erect barriers that would quietly frustrate and bedevil their best plans. A good mayor had to be able to climb. Personalities and structures, if not recognized, managed, and neutralized, could eclipse the most stunning initiative. During a charter revision exercise in the 1960s, Benton convinced city lawyers and the charter commission to remove the office of finance director from the patronage lists and make it a permanent part of city government, answerable to no mayor. Since Benton was by then in that post, he became almost untouchable. Surely, he would not have succeeded in this coup under a mayor such as Schaefer, who would have demanded control of such an important post.

Benton's move protected him from the whims of headstrong mayors or the winds of new administrations. Schaefer knew that Benton could play it either way—as a helping force or a monumental hurdle. Benton was critical because Schaefer knew he had to get the budget under control first, and, of course, budgets were part of Benton's magic. A period of stabilization would have to come before pursuit of grander objectives. In these inaugural moments, Schaefer reaffirmed his personal approach to the power he had assumed: He would be a friend to no one. He might be close to some but he would always stop before an attachment clouded his judgment about the work they were doing. "I knew I had to be a mean sonofabitch. I couldn't afford to get close to anyone. I wouldn't have gotten anybody to do anything."

Because that decision denied him personal friendships, Schaefer's judgment about the price of public service was a hurtful one for him. He made the same decision about marriage, knowing that he could not be the sort of mayor he wanted to be and have a family. "You probably would have been divorced in no time," his friend and aide Lainy LeBow told him. Others said that he overdramatized his circumstances in life, insisting he was friendless—an orphan, he would claim later—to attract sympathy. Yet his only experience with managing large numbers of people was in the military where officers are taught that familiarity breeds contempt, an injunction against fraternizing with the troops. Schaefer thought that everyone was, sooner or later, a troop whose loyalty and commitment would be tested as if in a battle.

Team Baltimore

As its two hundredth birthday approached, Schaefer wanted a huge celebration for the Lexington Market. Nothing, except perhaps Hopkins or marble steps, defined the city more completely than its system of colorful public markets, where shoppers could watch rubber-gloved shuckers opening oysters and could swallow a dozen or so on the way to pick up whatever was needed for the week or weekend. Schaefer wanted a chorus of hosannas for these neighborhood institutions, and he planned to build a substantial addition to the Lexington Street facility—if surrounding businesses would let him. A cluster of bakeries and clothing shops and jewelers had been razed to allow completion of the subway, and this would mean more disruption.

Inevitably, a few businesses wouldn't leave and might have stopped the project because a taking under the power of eminent domain would have consumed a year or so. The shopkeepers had the leverage of time, but Benton applied extraordinary pressure to accelerate their departures. He and Schaefer's main man at the department of public works, Buddy Palughi, took over, informing these business owners that water main repairs in the middle of the street would require a considerable amount of digging. Heavy machinery moved in, creating dust and traffic jams—all designed to block customers, to provoke the merchants and force them out. Most of them got the message and agreed to negotiate a settlement.

When a few diehards showed no inclination to follow their neighbors, Palughi informed them that he had to dig up the sidewalk as well. One of the holdouts, an appliance firm called Lexco, got another building on Eutaw Street. "It was a superior site," Benton explained, well worth the additional cost to the city. He said that he had not told Schaefer what he had done, but Schaefer knew the story. Benton had done the same thing with a burlesque house on Gay Street—the Gay White Way, it was called.

In his Born Again incarnation, Benton became the avenging city hall angel, not necessarily something Schaefer endorsed. The Block had been preserved by Schaefer in an urban renewal ordinance as an attraction that defined Baltimore, a place to be saved for visitors to see, if not patronize. Benton, though, wanted the Gay White Way removed, and his knowledge of the federal tax code permitted him to construct an advantageous deal: The city bought the property, and the man sent Benton a basket of Christmas cheer every year for twenty years.

"Buddy"

Benton and Palughi were the sort of team that pleased Schaefer most. They were untroubled by laws, regulations, and accepted practices. They were swashbucklers, fun-loving and inventive; they were wicked and completely devoted to the man who made their escapades possible. Benton bought Palughi a crane one year, and Palughi promptly began demolishing a building that was still occupied, a fact that he discovered when the roof was removed with a man in bed just under it. Palughi was a type Schaefer remembered from his army days, the guy every commanding officer had to have. He was suspected over the years of making off with forklifts, and front-end loaders, and other pieces of heavy equipment, selling them where he could.

"He was my kind of guy," Schaefer said. "A little crude, like I am, and a guy who could absolutely get any job done for you." During Hurricane Agnes in 1972, Palughi and Schaefer visited a Sears store on North Avenue to borrow a few boats. As the mayor fretted that they might both be arrested, Palughi broke into the building, took the boats, and went back to managing the floods. Sears would be proud to help, Palughi predicted, and nothing the company did or said later suggests that he was wrong.

Palughi enjoyed remarkable access to the mayor of Baltimore. "He used to come into restaurants, into public places, and come right over and bite me on the ear," Schaefer said. Palughi would occasionally announce himself by shouting a derogatory word or two. Schaefer says he had no trouble with Palughi's profanity — enjoyed it, actually — apparently because it showed he was still one of the guys, not so high and mighty to reject the kind of language he indulged in himself. For Palughi, the exchanges certified a special relationship with the mayor of Baltimore — made it clear that Buddy was a big man. Finally, though, Palughi's language was offensive enough to draw Bereska's intervention.

"Knock it off," she told him during a private discussion she initiated. Bereska depended on Palughi as did Schaefer and Benton, but her job was always to anticipate something that could give the boss a problem. Schaefer said he was not surprised to hear that someone had tried to tone down Buddy's language. The public works man was becoming a character, a media star, so what he said mattered. At one point, Schaefer ordered him to stop getting his name in the paper. He says Palughi tried to comply. The two maintained their partnership, renewed every four years at least with a good-luck breakfast on Election Day mornings at Iggy's, a sandwich shop in Little Italy. Schaefer maintained that ritual long after Palughi died.

Big Dipper

Police Commissioner Donald Pomerleau's shadow fell across the new mayor's office too. As with Benton, Schaefer warned Bereska, and through her his staff, never to cross the police commissioner. The question arose naturally because Pomerleau's stock in trade then was, like J. Edgar Hoover's, the dossier of photographs or other incriminating materials available to be sprung for maximum advantage: to increase a budget, to win approval of some program, or, generally, to preserve the ability to do pretty much anything Pomerleau wanted. This mayor who loved to challenge almost anyone made clear that Pomerleau was a different matter. People failed to heed him at their peril. Schaefer's first driver, a heavy-drinking Irishman, according to Bereska, took to parking the mayoral car on the Block, inviting talk that the mayor hung out there—and, more perilously, inviting attention from Pomerleau, who enjoyed arresting people from city hall who wandered over there and then made sure their names were published in the *News American*. "They say he had a file on me. What did I care?" Schaefer said cavalierly. And he did not hesitate to challenge Pomerleau's authority when he had the backing he needed—from Kovens or, later, Governor Marvin Mandel.

Bereksa says that Schaefer was never a frequenter of the Block as mayor, though he went there often as a younger man. Now the whispering that might have arisen among those who saw and recognized the mayoral car was not acceptable. The driver, therefore, was "taken care of," meaning that another job was found for him. In addition to everything else, he had heard too many of what Bereska called "backseat conversations" on subjects ranging from the embarrassingly personal to the embarrassingly public. The police officers who chauffeured Schaefer could be trusted, but not if they drank and seemed unable to follow simple commands such as "Don't park the mayor's car on the Block."

Who would drive the mayor's car now that the tippling cop was gone? Bereska put out the word and was offered the services of Chuck Fawley, then assigned to the Public Works Department. Fawley reported for a two-week stint as chauffeur to the mayor, or so it was thought. Delayed in traffic one day and late for the next meeting, Schaefer began to shout at the twenty-two-year-old Fawley as if he were responsible for the snarl that was delaying His Honor. When the hectoring continued, Fawley pulled the car to the curb, got out, and said, "You drive the car." Schaefer looked up from the papers in his lap and said, "Okay, okay. Get back in. Let's go." Fawley completed his day's work and left, expecting to be fired or at least never to set foot in city hall again. But a few days later, Bereska called him back to her office.

"The mayor would like you to be his permanent driver. Is that all right?" she said. Fawley said sure. And the two motored around Maryland for the next twenty years, fixtures at virtually every fast-food joint in the state. At speaking engagements, Fawley was the timekeeper—as he was, more importantly, when Schaefer called on Tululu or Hilda Mae, after she became his steady date. Fawley necessarily knew Schaefer's daily schedule, but he never let either Hilda Mae or Mrs. Schaefer see it. If they knew that the mayor actually had nothing to do, he could not as easily beg off or get away. He wanted his freedom. "He was a visitor," Fawley discovered. "He wasn't a stayer." Fawley went along with Schaefer to Annapolis when he became governor, relinquishing his chauffeur's job to the state police, who always had that duty for governors. But Fawley was in the Schaefer family by then and was, at one point, thought of as the real lieutenant governor.

Bereska tried to deal with Pomerleau. She went to the Tuesday meetings of the city employee's credit union board as Schaefer's representative. But she was not invited to after-meeting dinners, lavish affairs at the best Baltimore restaurants, until she complained. The board was not alone in its discriminatory attitudes toward women. One of her friends reported that she made Benton and the other male board members uncomfortable. And as soon as she got into a meeting, trouble erupted. One of the board members said that he hoped the commissioner did not get into trouble for taking expenses twice for one trip. Bereska knew what he was talking about. At the Board of Estimates meeting that day, she had seen travel expenses paid for a police chiefs' conference, yet she also knew that a credit union check for $1,000 had been drawn and handed over to Pomerleau for a trip to Las Vegas. The meetings occurred at the same time. The next morning, as Bereska was completing some administrative chore, Joanna Sorenson, Schaefer's secretary, wheeled around the corner into Bereska's office as if someone were chasing her.

"He wants to see you and he's not happy," she said, as if Schaefer's rage had been directed at her.

Bereska walked into the mayor's office.

"Close the door," he said. She did. "God-damn it. Gooooooood-DAMN it. I don't want you to say a god-damned word. I told you never to get in Pomerleau's way and now he calls to tell me you've accused him of double-dipping. I want this thing taken care of by this afternoon or you can come back here and clean out your office."

She tried to speak. He held up his hand.

"I'd like to say something," she said anyway.

"Goddamnit. I don't want to hear anything."

She left the room.

Bereska had done little to provoke the commissioner beyond her participation in a dinner conversation. That was enough. Bereska and others on the credit union board had been anxious to head off a controversy, and they were titillated, no doubt, by an apparent financial peccadillo.

At Schaefer's command, his chief aide and other members of the board tried to soothe Pomerleau's anger, arranging to meet with him in his office that afternoon. He fumed and glowered, but when they left, he wrote a letter forgoing the extra expense money. The flare-up was precisely what Schaefer wanted to avoid, fearing that the commissioner could make his life miserable in one way or another. Bereska had thought she was protecting her boss in this case, hoping to head off a scandal. Schaefer knew this and, later, when he felt more secure, confronted Pomerleau himself, enlisting Mandel to enforce a budget cut the mayor had made.

Good Girl

Budget and personnel matters of the most dramatic—and mundane—variety occupied much of Schaefer's time, and many of the decisions he made in the first months of his administration in 1972 echoed into its final days. Venetoulis, the campaign manager, thought that Schaefer laid the foundation for much of his success in these early days. A public official had to have control over the bureaucracy, or even the greatest idea in the world would fail. Nothing was easy.

Very quickly, the new mayor and his city hall team began to operate like a family. He was the father, prodding, reminding, and encouraging an eager brood. He wanted ideas, demanded new approaches, and enticed teamwork by acting on the suggestions he received. The prospect that an idea would find its way into policy made his mostly young and female staff eager to please him. At the same time, his tone could be harsh. Bereska, who was first in line for his anger, meted out the mayor's punishments, saving him from that task—hence her unofficial title, "The Dragon Lady." Not that he would ever be reluctant to shout at someone who displeased him, but she was the operations manager, alter ego, and ramrod. He offered praise frequently as well, often writing notes that contained veiled apologies for his tirades. Over time, his little band of partisans developed their own intimate style of communicating, led by him often. He assigned nicknames and spoke or wrote to his coterie in near baby talk, a form he seems to have adopted as a means of softening some of his harsher communications. A brief undated thank you note to Bereska, on stationary embossed "From the Desk of His Honor, the Lord High Mayor of Baltimore" read:

Thanks
   You be good girl
      Take care of yourself
      take medicine
      stop working so hard
      go to "potee"
      eat moderately
      sleep well

The family theme was everywhere apparent. To chief assistant Daryl Plevy and her husband, he wrote a thank you for a birthday present: "You got my favorites!! You are good children for thinking of me."

A constant stream of notes and action memos began to flow from the Lord High Mayor's office to Plevy and others. Nothing was too minor or detailed for his personal attention. In regard to correspondence from his legislative task force, he wrote, "ONE person should be the point person to handle this. Mrs. Plevy will be the person." And she wrote him, "Mr. Mayor—Re appointment of department Heads. Please don't do them without me. Frank Kuchta and Judge Brown must be appointed after Jan. 1 or they won't get their raise. Daryl." Schaefer's response: "Yes SIR!!!" When a councilman and his constituents sued the city over Schaefer's decision to close a fire station, Plevy wrote, "Councilman DeBlasi said he'd like to work with you and the private sector in raising money to keep the fire station open if the court suit is not successful. He hopes you're not mad at him." Schaefer: "I'm mad at him." Impatience and sarcasm jump from every page. A long-in-coming analysis of how to market and reshape the school system's image was complete in January of 1984: "Good. Maybe we can implement beginning 1987."

Thank you notes were nearly a fetish. If Schaefer or anyone in city hall received a thank you, particularly one including more than the words "thank you," Bereska's team would send a thank you for the thank you. In short order, she came up with a series of forms, so great was the volume. She called them "Pick One," and they included sympathy, wedding anniversary, get well, and congratulations on your achievement/graduation/whatever. Schaefer looked them over and concluded, "Not enough messages. I don't think you have enough messages. You don't have anything for Club 90," a Schaefer invention that recognized Baltimoreans on their ninetieth birthdays. A card and a dozen roses were sent from city hall. At age 100, you got a personal visit from the mayor, who came to your door carrying *two* dozen long stems. Also he said, "Leave more space. I want to write here." He would write all over the cards and then on the back. He recognized the need for palpable connections with people who often felt estranged from government, who were more inclined to fight than to work with City Hall. Bereska facilitated Schaefer's impulse, gave it class.

Christmas cards, paid for personally by Schaefer, were at least as big a concern every year. A friend of the mayor's designed each year's card as her Christmas gift to him, providing a special communication for the thousands who made his list. The artist was not particularly sympathetic or sensitive, however, to social and political realities and was unwilling to accommodate them—until pushed hard by Bereska. One year, the crowd of carolers assembled by the artist in front of the Washington Monument had no black faces. Bereska sent the drawing back for revision. The artist balked. Bereska explained calmly that Schaefer could not send out such a card, did not wish to, and would not offend his constituents in such a way, intended or not. The artist then redid and returned the card, with most of the carolers facing east, their backs turned so that no one could tell whether the singers were black or white.

Hello Donnie

When he became mayor, Schaefer pushed for more legitimate theater in Baltimore, wooing the Mechanic family to get new productions to make

Baltimore a regular stop on their way to Washington or New York. Occasionally, a big star would arrive. Just before Christmas 1978, Carol Channing came to town with her famous production, "Hello, Dolly!" Schaefer's team got her down to city hall to meet the mayor, and, as often happened, the mayor and the actress became fast friends. Schaefer would have been delirious except for the scandal that arose when Channing's fur coat was stolen. She took it like a trouper, though, and agreed to show up at the mayor's outdoor New Year's gala at the harbor.

That event had been planned by Bailey Fine, one of Bereska's new hard drivers. Fine had been hoping to spend the first day of 1979 with her family, her time before that having been claimed by Schaefer for a program called Harbor Holidays. However, Schaefer had asked her to plan just one more project for him. Shortly after being assigned that mission, Fine found herself alone in the Ceremonial Room at city hall with Hilda Mae Snoops, Schaefer's largely anonymous escort and lady friend. Hilda Mae, who had grown up on the Hill, had by then become Schaefer's companion at public events. Except among insiders at city hall, though, she was not a well known feature of his life. Divorced and the mother of three children, Snoops worked at the Social Security Administration.

Hilda Mae all but grabbed Fine by the collar. "What are you doing with my man on New Year's Eve?" she asked.

"I'm not really doing anything with him," Fine replied. "He wanted this event, and I'm just putting it together, the way he asked me to."

"Oh sure," said Snoops, as if she didn't believe the story. "Let me tell you one thing. If his lips are not touching mine at midnight, you're in a lot of trouble."

Fine had arranged for a new clock to be on hand at the harbor and for the visiting star, Ms. Channing, to join the mayor on stage for the always dramatic countdown. When midnight came, the mayor of Baltimore's lips were touching Channing's. Snoops watched from off stage.

"Schaefer looked to me like he was having a pretty good time," Fine said. She and Snoops never spoke again.

Schaefer and Hilda Mae maintained a relationship for years but never married. The conventional view, that Snoops did not measure up to the standards set by Tululu Schaefer, was probably incorrect, but it persisted. "Mrs. Schaefer didn't like many women," said Schaefer's friend Mary Arabian. "She was afraid they were going to snag her boy. She had a biographical sketch of the kind of woman she thought he needed, a good obedient lady." Arabian said that she and Mrs. Schaefer got along well.

Coexistence was possible, she said, "as long as you weren't angling for her boy. She was a very bright lady," and very demanding in regard to her son. "If he had not succeeded in the way he did, she would have disowned him. She expected him to do well."

And he did, in part, because he was like her.

Not Wired for It

Before leaving office, Young Tommy and a panel of Baltimore citizens had hired a young Seattle administrator named Roland Patterson to run the Baltimore school system—to reorganize and modernize it. During an interview on the West Coast, the young Patterson had offered a clue, missed or accepted by the interviewers, to the orientation that would bring distress to Baltimore for the next five years. He said he thought that any number of young black men were being held as political prisoners in the nation's jails. He was not the only militant black American to hold such a view—one that was validated by some research in the years that followed—but it might have been an alarm signal for the leaders of Baltimore, who were, generally speaking, uncomfortable with those who were mounting the barricades of social reform. Patterson's style could not have been less compatible with Schaefer's—or with the style of Baltimore, itself. Patterson was in no mood to wait for promised progress, and he was determined to implement his ideas, whatever the cost to himself and others. He presided over implementation of a desegregation order issued by Washington, devising a plan that created enemies for him in the school department and in the community. Schaefer found him completely unmanageable and far too race conscious for the mayor's tastes. Schaefer accused Patterson of ruining public education in Baltimore, forcing things to a low common denominator.

"He saw his own alma mater, City College, deteriorating rapidly, and he began to develop a lack of confidence in the city school system," said Nancy L. Grasmick, Maryland's superintendent of schools when Schaefer was governor. "There was an arrogance about the Baltimore system: 'Don't touch my turf, we're the educators. We don't want any political interference, and we have our own agenda here.' He saw that the school system was such a predictor of the health of the city that he couldn't recoil from being involved." Involvement in the beginning meant dealing with Patterson, who had imposed a new organizational structure that wreaked havoc among black and white administrators. Animosity toward the new man reached across racial lines—and certainly into the mayor's office. Schaefer decided to get rid of him. It would take most of his first term. Schaefer would have to contend with Larry S. Gibson as well. A member of the school board appointed by Young Tommy, Gibson was a lawyer who shared Patterson's goals and intensity and who would leave the school board to become Patterson's lawyer. Schaefer and Gibson developed personal and political animosity that smoldered and flared through many chapters of the city's political life.

By then, the black establishment in Baltimore—its political, religious, and social wings included—had developed a proprietary interest in the city's school system. Control of the schools was given over to African Americans as their inviolate pool of patronage, recognition no doubt that black voters were many and might, in time, be a force in city elections. "There was a tacit agreement in the early 1970s that the school district would become the black agency of government," said Marion Orr, a professor of education at Duke University. At about this time, as blacks were finally moving into the ranks of teachers and education administrators, "a bond of personalism" developed in which supervisors were reluctant to fire or discipline poor performers. Teachers and others were moved about, to be sure, but this exercise became known as "the dance of the lemons." At the same time, the size of the education establishment grew as government in Baltimore became, unofficially, an employer of last resort for workers who had been shunned by white employers since Reconstruction. Jobs were seen as an antidote to summer rioting. Thus, the school department work force grew from 5,463 in 1950 to 10,622 in 1995, even as enrollment fell by 7 percent.

Seeing the larger role played by the schools, a prudent administrator might have been reluctant to interfere. Any effort to break the various codes, moreover, confronted Schaefer with two political dilemmas. He did not wish to alienate the emerging black electorate by interfering in one of the areas in which blacks had been successful, nor did he wish to violate the hands-off rule that had been asserted for generations by white Baltimore parents who feared that political domination would corrupt the classroom. He was caught between conflicting expectations: He was expected to stay out of—and to reform—a system that increasingly failed to prepare its students for productive lives. Few doubted that Patterson's real foe was the mayor of Baltimore. The school department had become, almost overnight, a nettle of bureaucratic, racial, and political complexity. "I think Schaefer felt more and more alienated from the system as there was this polarization around race and also there was a polarization about his desire to become more influential, recognizing the importance of education in everything that was going to happen," Grasmick said. The political significance of the schools could not have been overestimated. "He had to ask the General Assembly for additional funding," Grasmick said, "And he found it difficult to do that without having an ability to validate what was happening in the system." Finally, Baltimore's school system represented everything Schaefer disliked: It was the classic institutional aircraft carrier that does not easily turn at the captain's command.

As soon as he could, he named his friend and political helper, Norman Ramsey, to head the school board. Ramsey was there, everyone assumed, to fire Patterson. In early June 1975, after an eleven-day trial, the city school board voted seven to two to demand Patterson's resignation. An array of charges had been lodged against him almost a year earlier: Patterson was charged with failure to carry out school board policy, withholding information from the board, engaging in questionable management practices, and allowing standards to slip. The firing process that Ramsey and the school board adopted was an Alice in Wonderland affair, with the school board serving as judge, jury, and witness for the prosecution. Everyone believed that the verdict was in—decreed by Schaefer—well in advance. By then, Patterson had plenty of opposition, black and white, beyond city hall.

In a sense, neither Schaefer nor Patterson recovered from the ordeal. Patterson got a job in New York City, where he was put in charge of a large, poor, and underperforming system. And the assertive mayor uncharacteristically turned away from a task well before it was completed. He was burned out and unwilling to spend the time and energy that he saw would be required to turn the school system around. Among the many ironies was that Patterson's reorganization shook up the system in ways that, had he agreed with the goals, would have pleased Schaefer immensely. In later years, he wanted someone of Patterson's smash-the-crockery-if-you-must mentality to break the institutional code.

Looking back, Grasmick concluded that neither Patterson nor Schaefer had been the right man to deal with the schools. "Changing school systems, as you know, is tedious, long term," Grasmick said. "Schaefer's brain was not wired for that sort of job." Maybe no one's was. A future city administration would find itself with the same problems—and having no more success with them than Schaefer had. One of his last school board chairmen, the developer Mark K. Joseph, thought that Schaefer made a pragmatic decision about the schools: "He felt they were an area where he could spend unbelievable amounts of political capital, and he couldn't see much likelihood of success. It was not an area he knew much about, an area he had much feel for, an area where his experiences led him to know what do to. He instinctively made a judgment that he had to do what was reasonable. He couldn't tackle that the way he could tackle public works problems or inner harbor problems. It wasn't as tangible, and there were tremendous racial division issues, so he saw it as a divider, a loser even though he didn't question the importance of it." Schaefer's stewardship of the schools over the next ten years would be regarded as weak and ineffective, his greatest failure. This was all the more damning because he had done so much to change the culture and spirit of the city as a whole. His successor as mayor would encounter equal difficulty with virtually the same results, though the problem would be at least confronted as if to begin the long, arduous chore described by Grasmick.

Pioneers

Schaefer turned, with some relief, no doubt, to bricks and mortar—far more malleable than teachers and principals. With buildings, he could show immediate progress. He could make Baltimoreans proud, though he could not usually adopt the grand strategies of Rouse, obliged as he was to go step by step. Sometimes these steps were inadvertent, accidental, following no discernible plan. Things seemed into fall in place in part because he was constantly on top of them, adjusting on the fly, adapting and changing when the results unfolding in front of him compelled him to. Soon after he was elected, he changed his mind about something that would become a symbol of his renaissance: Stirling Street. He decided to save it. In the council, he had been driven to demolish, to tear down—the polar opposite of a politician's usual self-serving impulse: building. You cleared, and then you built. Both steps were Schaeferian: assertive, uncomplicated, and clean. But the *tabula rasa* of his mind could be filled in by a good idea energetically presented, and he would always reconsider a policy, as he did with the smashingly successful Stirling Street Renewal Area. Increasingly confident, he learned timing and taste, neither of which he had at the start. He had agreed to tear down a strip of rowhouses in the Shot Tower Industrial Renewal Area two blocks east of War Memorial Plaza. But state Senator Julian L. "Jack" Lapides interceded, opposing Schaefer and Councilman Robert Douglass, who called them "slave houses." Lapides knew that the street had actually been a model of integration, populated by artisans of the time, free blacks and whites, living together before the Civil War.

Schaefer changed his mind, and the project went ahead, though most of the prerenaissance residents were black and poor, and two out of three newcomers were white. What Schaefer saw was an opportunity to show Baltimore as safe and exciting for the people who were moving out of the city or not thinking about it as a place they could live and raise their families. Instead of demolition, then, the city offered the fifty or so houses for a dollar to anyone who could show the ability to rehabilitate and restore them. No one realized then that the posture and location of these houses would make them a dramatic, comfortable, and elegant foreground for the city center's skyline lying six blocks west. Some four hundred homesteaders applied to buy the Stirling Street houses. Later, houses in neighborhoods called Federal Hill, Otterbein, Butchers Hill, Ridgely's Delight, Pigtown, and Bolton Hill also began to find sweat equity and hard cash investors who were willing to take risks.

The mix of winning applicants on Stirling Street became a celebration of the city's potential for regeneration and growth. Writers began to speak of "urban pioneers" or "frontiersmen"—a new urban nomenclature, the language of a new folklore, a new excitement. Still, some of the talk along Stirling Street, surrounded by high-crime neighborhoods, was a bit daunting: "The good news is you can walk to work. The bad news is you might want to run." The really bad news was that poor, long-time residents were displaced. Among these was Mrs. Earlie Forest, a sixty-three-year-old woman, who was forced out. Had such a thing occurred in The Hill, neighborhood activist, vestryman, and later Councilman Schaefer would have been outraged. Here, he tolerated an individual injustice to pursue a greater good and felt that he could have explained his action satisfactorily—to himself if not to Mrs. Forest.

The Stirling homesteaders paid $1 for an 1830 house and $2 for two. In the first wave, twenty-five buyers took control of forty-two houses. They moved in with hammer and grit to reclaim a street that was located not far from the riot grounds of 1968, another symbolic aspect of the project. They were led by Ian Jewitt, a lacrosse player who was dean of students at the Gilman School. A young physician and an architect who bought two houses were also in the group. They spent between $16,000 and $36,000 to repair their homesteads. Among these pioneers were

Paul Gasparotti, a computer specialist at the Social Security Administration headquarters on the west side of the city, and his wife, Marjorie, a librarian. "If we didn't think it was making a comeback," she said, "we wouldn't have put so much money in it."

By mid-1972, this street bristled with people on ladders, painting window sills, loading and unloading trucks. Newspaper stories included the architectural details of these houses, palpable proof that the future would include elements of the past. But the bustle and the inherent risk taking were the message. A part of the city was alive, alluring, and challenging. The historic Federal era facades were preserved at the insistence of the city's planners. No one minded. The new owners installed expensive custom millwork. Some of the two-house units had up to six working fireplaces. They were as wide as a twenty-seven-foot house if you put two together, as several buyers did. Homesteaders haunted a storehouse of salvaged rowhouse relics harvested from restored houses and carted to a depot on Pratt Street for sorting and sifting by others: old doorknobs, bits of plumbing, embossed tin ceilings. An oak mantelpiece rescued from St. Mary's Seminary fit nicely on the second floor of one house.

A city loan fund of $689,750—$27,600 per house—made the projects work on family budgets. The money came from Section 312 of the Federal Housing Act. The actual work came more cheaply than it might have because the new owners did the laboring and rough carpentry. Fire had damaged six of the houses during a police strike that hit in the spring of 1972, but a pioneering ardor flared in spite of setbacks. Many other streets in many neighborhoods were becoming venues for illustration of the very same impulse to restore. On Federal Hill, procurement lawyer Scott Livingston spent weekends painting, plastering walls, and refinishing floors. He felt personally enlisted by Schaefer, a man he had never met. He felt part of something bigger than the Sheetrock panels he was nailing into place, bigger than the deck he installed overlooking the Inner Harbor. He had not become a member of Schaefer's Order of the Rose or of any other group concocted by City Hall, "But I wanted to be." And, of course, as the new spirit began to spread far beyond Schaefer's physical reach, he was.

II

Renaissance

CHAPTER 6

The Cheerleader Cometh

Schaefer had looked across the broad expanse of Pratt Street and, with some prompting from his friend Mary Arabian, thought it could be like San Francisco. But for years, it had been Baltimore, stagnant and sinister. Baltimore eyes had difficulty getting Schaefer's vision into focus. Bailey Fine, who grew up in Alexandria, Virginia, came to Baltimore after graduating from Skidmore College in 1969. She went to work for Bob Embry and remembers the reaction to Schaefer's outlandish suggestions: "We'd go to these civic breakfasts with him and he'd be the featured speaker. He'd talk about downtown and a revamped inner harbor . . . and tourism. People would turn and look at each other. Tourism? It was like working for a crazy person. We were embarrassed. I mean we loved the guy, but this was nuts. It just wasn't going to happen. But he said it over and over and over."

Schaefer's best lieutenants were newcomers like Fine who wanted to be part of the civic and political life of their adopted city, people who were willing to consider its potential and intrigued by the man at the helm. One of the doubters—a jaded outsider, in this case—was Mark L. Joseph, who had been hauled into the city by a family emergency, called away from studies at American University to tend an ailing family business. He found Baltimore a depressing place in the fall of 1972, a year into Schaefer's first term. Joseph dreaded his drive into the city every day from his family's home in Chevy Chase, the classy Washington suburb. He arrived via Route 40, Mulberry Street by name, turned onto Howard, with its strip of department stores to the south, and then up to Preston, where he turned right and into the center city. He passed the state office buildings and continued east to the company offices at Greenmount Avenue near the Greenmount Cemetery, resting place of John Wilkes Booth, Allen Dulles, a handful of Maryland governors, and Arunah S. Abell, founder of the Baltimore *Sun*. August personages all, they were nevertheless no help to the failing neighborhood where they rested. No one living was much help either, Joseph thought as he navigated a landscape that was as dark and dreary as any Edgar Allan Poe had conceived.

His father and grandfather owned the Yellow Cab franchise in Baltimore but it was a nearly worthless thing in a city that was famous for being in between and bypassed by families on their way to someplace else, by commerce, and by manufacturing. The city itself was quite clearly dying, Joseph thought, so why wouldn't a cab business die along with it? Washington had rebounded from the riots of the 1960s, but Baltimore seemed to be sliding further under. Yellow was going with it.

"For the first three years, we were certain we had to sell. We were so down we had to move into an even worse neighborhood—drug infested, terrible. We owned 100 cabs, 50 of which were not rolling. We were selling off assets to stay afloat, a prescription for bankruptcy." Desperate for something that might offer a way out, he and his father went to a meeting of business leaders the mayor had called at the Hilton Hotel. Joseph recalls that Schaefer, who had just returned from Atlanta, was talking even before everyone was seated: "'I got into a taxi cab and the driver said, 'Welcome to Atlan-Ta! When I got to the hotel, they said, 'Welcome to Atlan-Ta.' Everywhere I went, 'Welcome to Atlan-Ta. Atlan-Ta!' That's what we're going to do in Baltimore! But I need your help!'"

"Atlan-ta." No one pronounced it that way, but Schaefer wanted to build in some oomph. Joseph heard him say that the service industry—taxicabs, for example—made all the difference. Joseph's father and grandfather had never been asked to be part of anything in Baltimore. If they had been, they might remember their basic optimism, he thought. "In the service business, you have to be optimistic: The sun will come out tomorrow. Even in those days we had Preakness. We had a glimpse of what it could be like if we had conventions and hotels." Atlanta was not unlike Baltimore in terms of its sagging commercial center, so what Schaefer was saying did not seem so remote a possibility to the Josephs. He was talking to the right audience. "He wanted a chorus line of waitresses belting out, 'Hel-lo, Hon, Welcome to Baltimore!'" It was very democratic, very insightful of Schaefer to think he might get ahead by reviving a civic impulse, an instinct for community that had been submerged by ambient decline. Who else would have bothered to recruit the clerks, the cab drivers, the small business owners? In speeches to the Rotary Club, in limousines from Friendship Airport Baltimore (renamed Washington International in 1973), in the faces of newspaper reporters whose typewriters he wished to borrow, with sales clerks at the shirt counter of Hecht's, where he jostled for bargains, Schaefer began to instruct everyone that Baltimore was a business that demanded a work force as driven as its elected CEO. Suddenly, in the middle of that room, listening to the slightly manic mayor, Mark Joseph and his father, George, were looking at each other and realizing that they were thinking the same thing: "Maybe we can survive."

Someone Good

Hope was barely alive. But if anyone in the city continued to see Schaefer as nothing but a seat warmer, they were unable to persuade "someone good" to take up the difficult work that so energized him. Baltimore Democrats nominated "the dummy" for a second term by near acclamation. His vote exceeded the combined totals of his two Democratic primary rivals by eight to one. The caretaker had taken good care, indeed: His 89,196 votes put him far beyond Monroe Cornish, a perennial office seeker, who received 5,339. John D. Hubble, the third candidate, got 5,261.

Schaefer's move from stand-in to uniquely talented included a shift from bland to colorful, and both of these vectors could be observed at his second inaugural ceremony. A crowd of two thousand Baltimoreans, mostly schoolchildren and city officials, stood dutifully outside the new Maryland Science Center, then a solitary structure at the southwest corner of the expansive and largely undeveloped Inner Harbor. It was December 2, 1975, and the temperature was 42 degrees. Twenty uniformed Baltimore policemen stood at attention along a red carpet leading to the ceremonial platform, snapping off military salutes as the official party made its way up the steps. An honor guard from the Army's Ninety-second Field Hospital marched down the carpet, carrying the flags of the nation, the state, and the city. The Baltimore Boys Choir sang the national anthem. In his invocation, Archbishop William Borders thanked God for Baltimore neighborhoods, naming many of them: Washington Hill, Roland Park, South Baltimore, Violetville, Belair-Edison, Charles Village, Homewood, Little Italy, Bolton Hill, Reservoir Hill, Upton, and Hamilton. All of this was fitting, as Schaefer had come to renew his role as mayor of all the people. His mother, looking frail but thrilled, held the Bible as he took the oath. Schaefer then signed the Test Book, which had been so carefully guarded by Walter Beuchelt, using a pen and inkwell donated for the occasion by the Steiff Silver Company. Directly behind the city's 46th mayor sat his immediate predecessors, Judge J. Harold Grady, and Young Tommy, two enduring testaments to the power of the machine. Both had been given the job of mayor, and both had given it back. Now the job was in the hands of someone who really wanted it. Schaefer put his right hand over his heart, cocked his head back as if waiting for a military fly-by in his honor, and listened to the anthem. He had the bearing of command on this night, but he was still no one's rival in the world of the sound bite. It was Schaefer's day, but Tommy got the quote. "Grady and I are like Christmas bulbs," D'Alesandro told a *Sun* reporter. "They pack us away and then every four years they haul us out to sort of decorate the platform."

The reinstalled mayor read his speech without expression or drive. In time, Schaefer would learn that he could not read with much dramatic effect. He gave it up for good one Sunday when a child read Scripture flawlessly in church and began to ignore any prepared speech, just as he had tried to do when he was sworn in as council president. He tended to start every talk with some observation gleaned from his ride to work or from the radio, anything that might make a connection between the message and the audience. Sometimes the references were impossibly remote—names of tormenters in Annapolis in a Washington talk, for example—but he seemed to think that the world was tuned in to his life, watching its every turn. His spoken sentences did not scan, but Schaefer watchers discovered a remarkable thing: He was a communicator. The sum of the parts—body language, facial expression, hand gestures, costume, and quip—were adding up to a sharper image. The Chaplinesque shuffle, a well-timed dig at himself, his large head, his hats—all of these things were becoming as well known to Baltimoreans as FDR's cigarette holder and fedora with upturned brim had been to the nation.

On this December evening, Schaefer reaffirmed his devotion to making government serve the neighborhoods as if he were still campaigning, recapitulating his appeal for support. The speech, the ceremony, the trappings were there for his own glory—he had begun to demand them—but also to continue the pursuit of consensus. He was immediately governing, leading, and looking for the backing his projects would require from the residents of Pigtown, Ridgely's Delight, Mount Vernon and the rest. If he was to keep them enthused and voting "Yes" on multi-million-dollar borrowing questions posed on election ballots, he had to make them confident that he would never abandon them, or forget their needs. His only venture beyond the bread and butter of governing was his promise to make government and government programs open to all Baltimoreans, something a mayor had to affirm in those days, as if some segments might otherwise be ignored. He was standing outside the Science Center, a building whose wealthy sponsors had wanted substantial public support for their building and a rather exclusive and excluding approach to membership. Schaefer had said, "No, never." He loved to see the gentry, as he called them—ladies with their long gloves, men in dark suits—walking along Lexington Street. Their presence meant that an important part of the city lived, and he occasionally granted them special command of city resources and access to the public purse—but not for a public amenity designed to build public interest. The gentry always wanted to maintain a boundary between itself and the rest of the city. The mass of voters, though, were not stupid. They were watching from Patterson Park, Highlandtown, and Ashburton.

Schaefer's commitment to the neighborhoods, his covenant with the homeowners, made an easy ally of the council, whose members were always looking for ways to ingratiate themselves and be of service. Mary Pat Clarke of the Second District found ways to take advantage of Schaefer's focus, using her "elevator list." He used the elevator, too, she noticed, so naturally she would find herself riding with him on occasion. "I'd have one floor and I always had in my pocket one positive thing to say about what he was doing, and one request. It had to be a worthy project. I knew he was someone who heard nothing but demands: Help me, help me, do this, do that." She did not realize at first that she had to give him her votes, that her constituents would get his attention when he had her attention, and if she failed him, he would close the door and instruct others not to take her calls. On one occasion, frozen out for weeks, she stormed into his office, screaming about his *obligation* to the citizens of Baltimore—whatever he thought of her. A blow-up apparently was what he wanted—along with a few votes on his projects. Clarke was as driven and energetic as he, something he saw and responded to, but she was always in and out of his Siberia—opposing the Harborplace Project, for example. She hated being banished, but used the time to study his organization, his modern adaptation of the machine, a lovely dovetailing of the official and political. There were, she discovered, ninety-two neighborhood advisory committees. Each one would have a plan at the beginning of a year; they would target a blighting influence: vacant houses, drug corners, and the like. To accomplish it, they got a piece of the annual block grant money from Washington. "The next year we'd be back and we'd expect that to be done. What did they want next? It was a three-ring circus and neighborhoods were one of the three rings," Clarke said. "They were all going at the same time. There was always something happening in all these places." People saw that if they went to the advisory committee meetings, they had a share in the power.

Project by Project

While he was council president in the late 1960s, Schaefer had heard Jim Rouse speak of "the villages of Baltimore." What villages? Schaefer wondered with some exasperation. Baltimore was a city. At first, he had no idea what Rouse meant, but Schaefer always wanted to deal with manageable, smaller units; neighborhoods were his own basic building block. You found the strong ones, recruited the real leaders, demanding a tangible investment from them to establish a stake in whatever project was under consideration, and then you helped with money and city services. Baltimore was small enough, compared with Chicago, New York, or Los Angeles, to be a small-town place in which distinctly separate parts operated as a synergistic whole. In his speeches, Rouse thought aloud about the ideal-sized living place and wondered how to create it in the real world. He had many venues in mind, including the wilds of then-undeveloped Howard County, between Washington and Baltimore. But he also thought about the cities. "By building an image of the possible, we not only leap over a lot of roadblocks that would defeat us," Rouse said in a speech, "we also generate a whole new constituency of people who want to see that image realized." This was Schaefer's goal precisely, if more elegantly stated by the developer. "By creating the image of a rational potential of a city," Rouse said, "we generate the power to carry it forward. Without vision, there is no power. Piece by piece, project by project never harnesses the power that is available to the city."

Schaefer did not disagree, but necessarily, the two men took different routes. Rouse had latitude. He needed political backing to go forward with his most ambitious proposals, but if he failed, he could move on. He had done so, in fact, prospecting for the right waterside site in a number of cities—Norfolk, Boston, Baltimore, New York—before finding the right leadership and receptivity to his ideas. He could be even bolder. He could plan a "new city," to be called Columbia, and he could secretly buy large tracts of land in the woods of Howard County. No public official could be so daring legally, let alone politically. Schaefer was willing to take risks, but almost everything had to be aboveboard, and he knew that he ultimately had one shot on any initiative. He felt that he could not fail at anything. He had to have one victory after another, smallish ones if necessary, larger ones when possible, but absolutely no setbacks. Failure had a long afterlife. It left a "residue," to use his word, a psychological barrier that had to be surmounted—by government and by those who ran it. He needed momentum, a context for progress in which action meant something even when a particular initiative was questionable. He needed to work more methodically, sometimes holding back grand designs until the public saw the logic and gave its support. Otherwise, a handful of opponents could kill anything. Schaefer knew for years that he needed a new baseball stadium—and wanted it downtown—but felt that he could not say so. Unlike Rouse, he was required to take big ideas to the voters for approval, something he tried to avoid or delay until he was certain of success. At the same time, he hated to wait, and he suspected formal planning because he felt it used too much of a precious commodity: time.

"Time is not on our side," he would say, a pronouncement that seemed simultaneously hackneyed and vaguely Churchillian. People criticized Schaefer later for having no overall plan, for being episodic, for offering no continuity. But did he have time for a plan? How many terms would he be allowed to serve? What he was was entrepreneurial, thought Charlie Duff, director of Jubilee Baltimore, a neighborhood housing and jobs program in Butchers Hill, one of the successfully struggling city neighborhoods. Schaefer was a venture politician, canny at assessing the marketplace, seeing the underlying interplay between government, popular support, and business. He did not wish to throw money at neighborhoods that lacked intrinsic strengths, concluding that without some fundamental human or physical foundation, ladling on government money would be a pathetic waste. People had to care. People had to come forward with their own plans. "Can't you sew?" he would say. "Can't you make the curtains?"

Schaefer knew Baltimore neighborhoods and had a sense of each one—its individuality, its ethnic and religious bonds, though he would not have put it in those terms. In the 1960s, he saw that people tended to stay at home, to care about the appearance of their back alleyways, tiny backyards, and parks, boundaries and points of personal reference that had mattered to him and to his parents on the Hill. "When he became mayor, he really wasn't a downtown mayor. Downtown stuff was discredited. We'd done an enormous amount of it, and it actually hadn't solved the problem. So he got out in the neighborhoods, and those were the glory years of the Schaefer administration," the Harvard-educated Duff recalled. The romantic view enunciated later—that this man had married the city—was more accurate than anyone really knew. Neighborhoods were a little like a cousin's or an aunt's place he could visit for coffee and a chat, news of the kids, an admiring glance at the roses, a tour of the new basement family room, or a moment on the glider.

Schaefer thought he could achieve mass public approval by aggregating projects, starting one and then another and another until the vision was clear to all, a simultaneous promise and fulfillment—the little picture merging into the big, symbol becoming substance. Baltimoreans had to conclude when they voted for the Rouse projects that without them, the plan for the city's renaissance would be derailed. Of course, Schaefer wanted everything at once and refused to set priorities. He had to have a convention center, a high-class hotel, a subway system, an office building skyscraper, and a river of operating money. Before each general assembly session, Schaefer met with Ben Cardin, a young legislator and member of a leading political Baltimore family, and other state legislators from Baltimore on Saturday mornings. "We have to have four or five projects going all the time," he told Dennis McCoy, a Baltimore legislator and head of the city's contingent for several years, "or people will think we are doing nothing."

Convention City

Renovation of the old and construction of the absolutely new were made possible by Charles Benton in Baltimore and by Marvin Mandel and Janet Hoffman in Annapolis. Hoffman was Baltimore's lobbyist at the general assembly, an operator with the keenest understanding of arcane financial aid formulas, of legislative history, of personality, and of the political necessities. Without her, Schaefer said many times, the city's emergence from its cloud of despair and decline would have been impossible. After she had been a decade or so in her post, insiders called her the forty-eighth senator, a tribute to her ability to get votes for the projects Baltimore needed. This ability was so failsafe that she seemed to be there, voting herself on the very important bills.

As independent as she was, Hoffman knew that she needed Schaefer's clout, and often she got more of it than she expected. "We wanted money one year for a big improvement at Memorial Stadium and we needed votes. We had a weekend to get them. And I called the mayor and I told him the names of some of the people who had to be called. And then I told him that one way to do it was to have members of the Colts Corral (boosters of the team and its band) make calls. Well, you know, my husband had this woman who works for him who was active in that group, and the next thing I know, she had a call from Don Schaefer. He hadn't turned the job over to his staff or other people. He began making the calls himself. I wasn't assigning them for the mayor to make. But he did it."

Schaefer's prospects depended heavily on Hoffman's skills but also on friends in high places, particularly Kovens and Mandel. They promised bountiful patronage, but their own longevity had been threatened—by their own actions. Just a month before Schaefer's reelection victory in 1975, they were indicted, along with assorted other insurance men and demolition contractors, by a federal grand jury on mail fraud and racketeering, charges the newspapers shorthanded to "political corruption." Mandel, Kovens, and the others were accused of conspiring to increase the value of a racetrack by awarding it additional racing days. In the process of granting that rather small favor, these men walked into a long night of shame and censure. Schaefer insisted that neither Mandel nor Kovens ever did anything but help him and his city, and he never wavered for even a second in his support of both.

In the fall of 1976, Schaefer had gone to Annapolis to see Mandel about a convention center and various other projects. Marvin quickly said no. Mandel could make Schaefer do what he hated to do: set priorities, recognize what was achievable, and accept less than 100 percent. Maybe it was because they came from the same political clubhouse, Kovens's place in Northwest Baltimore, or perhaps it was Kovens himself who told Shaky to "Listen, God damn it!" Newspaper columnist and former Mandel press secretary Frank DeFilippo said that Edgar Silver would show up in Mandel's office regularly with instructions from Kovens: "Don needs a convention center. Don needs an aquarium. Don needs a subway. And Marvin would make it happen." And since Irv and Marvin almost always said yes, Schaefer almost always listened when Mandel spoke.

So before the 1976 General Assembly session began in January, Schaefer took a delegation of city business leaders to Mandel's office. "We want a convention center," he said. Schaefer thought he was obliged occasionally to remind Mandel where he, Mandel, was from, to reinstill the necessary level of parochialism. In this meeting, the needs of Baltimore fairly bristled, but Mandel, as doubting of Schaefer's vision as any Baltimorean, was saying no. "Why do you want a convention center? You don't even have a hotel. I can't support it. You haven't convinced me." He would go this far, Mandel said: Do your homework, come back later, and try again. In the meantime, he was telling the legislature and the wider world that a convention center was less than unlikely. In his annual state of the state address, the governor said the money wasn't there—end of story. And, of course, Mandel was under indictment by then, so it was hardly a propitious moment to be asking the assembly to spend huge sums of money for public works projects in his home city. Within weeks, though, armed with the requested studies, Schaefer and his people were back in Mandel's office, and by the time they left, Mandel was saying yes. At the same time, somehow, Schaefer was proposing to build a subway for Baltimore—an underground pyramid is the way Wally Orlinsky, the council president, described it, a monument to the pharoahs of Baltimore and Annapolis. So in the same year, two enormous public works projects for Baltimore were wheeled onto the legislative stage.

Hoffman got the convention center bill through the Senate with relative ease. The House of Delegates was another matter. The bill languished there. On the last night of the session, the convention center issue lay unresolved, with delegates from Montgomery County promising to kill it by speaking at length until the session ended at midnight. Schaefer sat in the balcony with Benton and Jeanne Mandel, the governor's ultraphotogenic wife. At about 11:25 P.M., Montgomery County delegate Charles A. Docter got the floor, as everyone in the chamber knew he had planned to do. Docter just happened to be running for Congress that year and saw a platform. Filibustering is not permitted under House rules, but with so little time remaining in the session, every maneuver has meaning and potentially fatal significance for pending bills. Schaefer sagged in his seat. On the floor, though, Ben Cardin stood. One of the youngest legislators in Maryland history and one of the most talented, Cardin made a prearranged signal to the presiding officer, House Speaker John Hanson Briscoe, who quickly ruled from the podium that House procedure did not permit extended debate and instructed Docter to take his seat. A tumult arose from the floor, with the delegate protesting and his colleagues from Montgomery County attempting to support him. A recess was called with less than thirty minutes remaining. The issue, Schaefer thought, was decided and dead. Minutes later, though, business resumed, a vote was called, and the bill passed.

"What happened? What happened?" the startled mayor asked, turning to Jeanne Mandel, the governor's wife, who was smiling her 1,000-kilowatt smile.

"That's your Convention Center bill," she said.

The next day, Mandel and Schaefer were photographed in silhouette near the window in the room where, months earlier, Maryland's governor had been saying the center couldn't be built and the mayor of Baltimore was reminding Mandel where he was from. Mandel had shown once again that difficulties with the law, such as charges of political corruption, did not necessarily result in a loss of political power. In 1976, a convention center and a subway were approved in a single year. The Baltimore juggernaut was rolling.

Schaefer found Speaker Briscoe in governor Harry Hughes's office on the last night of the legislative session several years later—to complain about the loss of some small bill the city wanted. Briscoe, who had never been thanked for the convention center victory, remembers hanging up on the mayor of Baltimore. Schaefer was in no way embarrassed. He needed everything, every year.

"A Bent Stick"

Schaefer wanted the big projects and pulled every trick he knew to get them. But he also had to run the city—had to have the trash picked up and potholes filled. He worried about these chores as much as he did about anything. "I knew the bridges would get built," he said. "I didn't know if the trees would get trimmed." At city hall, he presided in a beautiful but decrepit building, decades out of date. His secretary, Ruth Swann, found that she could not use her electric typewriter if the air conditioning was on. Offices were tiny, jammed together, irrationally placed throughout the building; passageways were blocked; false ceilings had been installed. Under its gilt dome, Baltimore City Hall was a frenzy of jury-rigged offices, as incoherent and inefficient as the worst government critic imagined. So in February 1974, the apparatus of government picked itself up and moved to the old USF&G two-building complex in the first block of South Calvert Street, there to deal with the city's needs until a $10 million rehabilitation of city hall was completed. Though it was overtaken quickly by other projects, the rehabbing of city hall had as much symbolic thrust as anything

Schaefer tackled. He wanted the building to look like the new as well as the old Baltimore when it was finished. It should stand out as a place of efficiency that would respond to citizen and businessperson alike. Schaefer had the solid and deserving citizens of his city in mind when he sought to give them a sparkling new seat of government, a classical-style building that would be as handsome on the inside as its wedding cake facade made it on the outside.

Citizens quickly found the temporary quarters. Inside, they found a different sort of leader. Schaefer wanted neighborhoods in his army more than anything, but he knew that they would not really be with him if he and the city acquiesced to everything they demanded. Government had been nearly paralyzed at times in Baltimore under McKeldin and D'Alesandro—or, at least, these two men felt beleaguered to the point of paralysis. McKeldin wrote to Lyndon Johnson, complaining that federal rules imposed on the antipoverty campaign seemed to ignore political reality. Richard Daley, the mayor of Chicago, was apoplectic. He called Johnson's aide, Bill Moyers, and shouted, "What in the hell are you people doing? Does the president realize he's putting M-O-N-E-Y in the hands of subversives?" Schaefer, who admired Daley, adopted a similarly political approach. He was not going to be nice about confrontations and "actions" aimed at him, and if people were coming to him with demands, he would set them back on their heels, demanding that neighborhood group A make curtains for their recreation center before he agreed to have it refurbished or that neighborhood group B hold a bake sale to buy a sliding board for their tot lot before he agreed to landscape it. He cut down the amount of time he spent in meetings with people who were more eager to shout than to act. The word got out that this mayor would be demanding partnerships, and if you hadn't thought through your own contribution, you might as well stay home. Daley had prevailed upon one of his congressional allies to propose legislation that would begin to cripple the participatory aspects of the poverty war. Schaefer was a softy compared to Daley. He began to develop what Baltimore lawyer Rick Berndt— one of Schaefer's cadre of civic soldiers—called a covenant with people, a standing agreement that City Hall would be there if the people, the businessmen, or the legislators were there with their share.

Schaefer's challenging tone was a challenge to the times, in a sense. He was not about to accept the idea that government was the enemy or that it could ever solve problems without the involvement of people. He scorned the liberals who seemed to think that money, a program, or a promise from Washington was all you needed. He was a liberal in the governmental sense, convinced that the people could aggregate tax resources and have some hope of solving big problems, but he was conservative in his view of human nature. In the civil rights cause, he thought there was a limit to what government could do for individuals. Affirmative action, set-asides in government contracts, and the like had limited utility, he thought, and he viewed them all with suspicion. His attitudes might have made him seem vulnerable to more than the usual degree of hostility, so the threat of some singular protest or violent act directed at him or some other symbol of the establishment remained in the air.

Those fears seemed more than well founded on April 13, 1976, when Charles A. Hopkins, a "bent stick of a man" walked into the temporary city hall with a paper bag in his hand—and a gun inside the bag. Joe Coale, one of Schaefer's aides, passed Hopkins as he was leaving the building at about 12:20 P.M. "What's he back for?" Coale wondered. The man had been angrily slouching through the building the day before, visiting Councilwoman Clarke and others with some grievance—not an unusual occurrence. Coale was on his way to arrange an interview for Schaefer on a local television station. Before he was two blocks away, "all hell broke loose" as police cruisers raced onto the sidewalks around the building.

Hopkins had gone directly to Schaefer's seventh floor office. He stepped off the elevator into a reception area connecting the two large bullpen rooms with desks for secretaries and other staff. Private offices, including Schaefer's, were connected to the larger suites. Kay Nolan sat at the receptionist's desk. Schaefer was in his office. Exhausted, he had "kicked the door shut," Coale recalled, hoping to have a short nap, something he needed that day, in a rare concession to long hours. He had been up late the night before, watching the General Assembly pass his convention center bill.

Nolan found the man's manner alarming even as he was pushing toward the bullpen. "I'm sorry, but you're not allowed here," she said. "What is your name?"

"I'll show you who I am," Hopkins said, pulling the gun from his bag and firing a shot that hit her in the neck.

Joanne McQuade, attending to something in one of the back offices, heard the shot and knew exactly what it was. A target shooter and gun collector then, she found the sound unmistakable if hard to absorb in the environment of a downtown office building. A Schaefer worker recruited by Bereska from the Girl Scouts, McQuade had come to think of her job as "that which shall be assigned from day to day." A willing and conscientious soldier, she accepted these assignments, some of them quite exacting and large in scale, as they came. Here was another. She was the first to reach the wounded receptionist, though later she thought ruefully, "I advanced when I should have retreated."

"Oh, Joey, he shot me," Nolan said. Hopkins seemed to have vanished as McQuade rushed to a phone with an automatic dial button connecting to the city hall operator. Before anyone answered, she sensed someone standing behind her.

"Hang up the phone or I'll blow your head off," Hopkins commanded. "Where's Schaefer?"

"He's in Annapolis," McQuade said. The automatic secretarial lie came easily and believably. "Let me help you get out of here," she said then, hoping to divert him. He wasn't buying. "He had a hand on my collar and the gun up to my ear. He pushed me along in front of him. We went across the walkway to the other building where the council offices were. He knew exactly where he was going. He wanted a councilman."

Within minutes, they were standing outside Councilman Dominic Leone's office. A waist-high gate separated the outer office from his secretary's desk and the door to Leone's private room. The councilman was talking with someone, but he saw Hopkins vault over the fence, still holding McQuade's collar. "He was pulling but I wasn't coming, so he let go," McQuade said later.

Leone stood. "Whoa, fella, what's the problem?" the councilman said.

Hopkins answered by firing his weapon twice, hitting Leone in the chest and stomach. McQuade bolted for a nearby stairwell. Councilman Joe Curran looked out his nearby office door, and Hopkins, by then back in the hall, shot at him. Then the shooter moved on, entering Orlinsky's office, where he found Councilman Carroll Fitzgerald and shot him. By now, police were racing into the building. One of them, Patrolman Thomas Gaither, confronted Hopkins and shot him six times before being wounded himself.

Schaefer came out of his office when he heard the commotion.

"Boss, I've been shot," Nolan said. "The bullet's over there on the windowsill."

Schaefer walked toward the adjoining building to see what was happening. He saw Fitzgerald, blood seeping from his wound, waiting for help. And he saw Joe Curran sitting at the bottom of a flight of stairs, his head in his hands. Police were racing into the council floor, guns drawn. A helicopter hovered over the building.

Leone was rushed to nearby Mercy Hospital, but his wounds were fatal. He had risen from his chair with the confidence of the athlete he had been as a youth, only to be summarily executed. At the age of fifty, he had been overwhelmingly elected to a fourth term the year before, along with Schaefer. A colorful, friendly man whom some thought of as a shrewd council strategist, Leone enjoyed playing the horses and would occasionally take out dice for a game of craps in his office. On that day in 1976, he was facing trial for bribe taking. Death relieved him of that ordeal at least.

A police caption led the shaken Schaefer from the building. McQuade and Curran were taken to police headquarters.

"He killed Dom," Curran told McQuade, sobbing, confirming her fears.

McQuade knew the cop who interviewed her. During demonstrations in City Hall Plaza, he had been assigned to take pictures of the demonstrators from the mayor's second floor office windows.

"Was he holding a weapon?" the cop asked.

"Yes," she replied, "a .38 snub nosed."

"How do you know?"

"I own one," she said.

Images of these moments—of the shooting, of the surprise on Leone's face, of Curran's anguish—remained in McQuade's mind. "I had a tremendous amount of guilt over Dom's death. Maybe I could have done something." She had saved Schaefer by convincing Hopkins that his quarry was out of the building and then leading him away from Schaefer's office. But there was nothing she could have done for Leone.

Within a year, Curran was dead of a heart ailment that doctors said was exacerbated by the shock of the rampage and Leone's death. Curran had been a somewhat unheralded fighter in the civil rights wars, one of the few white public officials who were sympathetic to the anger of the disenfranchised but, like Schaefer, unwilling to give up his authority.

Charles Hopkins had no known connection to the great social movements of the time. People at city hall knew him by then, suspected that he was unstable, and half expected him to run amok. But what could anyone do? Public officials were obliged to live with their fears or risk political damage by appearing to oppose some perfectly innocent citizen's search for redress of a legitimate grievance.

Hopkins had arrived in city hall that day with the .38 that McQuade recognized: a $50 Titan Tiger—a fairly high-quality Saturday night special, so called because such guns are so easy to obtain and so often involved in weekend shootings. A jury found Hopkins not guilty by reason of insanity, a verdict that was widely criticized. After years of treatment, the shooter was deemed no longer a threat and released.

Schaefer held vivid images of Fitzgerald and Curran in his mind, just as McQuade did. Fifteen years later, as governor, he and Councilman Curran's son, Attorney General J. Joseph Curran, successfully challenged the National Rifle Association by imposing limits on the types of handgun that could be sold in Maryland—then a politically risky endeavor but one in which Schaefer had a personal stake.

Shoring Up the Dome

With its elegant classical style, Baltimore City Hall stood on the cusp of its one hundredth birthday at a moment that would come near the nation's two hundredth anniversary. Schaefer hoped that a more efficient and comfortable building, having been treated to a $10 million upgrade and expansion, would be ready at about the same time. To get the work approved, he had fought off another of those recurrent know-nothing uprisings, this one of people who thought the building should be torn down and replaced by a modern structure. East Baltimore's Joe Bonvegna, a state senator, had called the old building "a piece of junk." Schaefer simply became more committed, though he understood the point of view. He'd been a knock-em-down guy himself in the beginning. Historical interests backed him with reminders to the city that architecture was symbolic—in this case of the city's history and the strength of its governing system. What the mayor was doing, they said, would preserve the symbol while recreating the function of a structure that had been built when Baltimore had but 300,000 citizens, a third of its size a century later.

The General Assembly approved an $8 million loan to complete the work, and Schaefer set aside about $1.5 million to repair the dome, which, Young Tommy's quip notwithstanding, was in danger of falling if it was not shored up. The glass eye of the rotunda was to be cleaned, restored, and backlit, and the entire atriumlike entryway was to be reopened to resemble the space intended by the architect, George R. Frederick, whose building opened in 1875. Most ingeniously, the restoration would take advantage of room left between the original floors to provide new offices on mezzanine decks. With these spaces inserted, the building's square footage would almost double. No changes would be made to the mayor's grand ceremonial room or to the council's chambers, but both would be restored to their original luster. At the same time, the workmen were inventorying those special elements that have played an important part in the design of the original building. Cabinets, display cases, fireplaces, paintings, full-length mirrors, hinges and special lighting fixtures—to be refinished or relocated and included with the final design plan. Schaefer's own quarters were almost completely made over with the oversight of Benton, who saw to the comfort of his own offices as well. He had his agents, one of whom brought to him a stunning array of things, including gold-colored spigots for his private lav. Chandeliers were sent out to be reconditioned and converted from gas-powered to electric.

A $25,000 carpet was bought for the Ceremonial Room. The decorator, Rita St. Claire, had insisted upon it, and Schaefer had succumbed. Bereska said that, once installed, it became a case of the Emperor's new clothes: The politically correct observers lavished it with praise, not to speak of the impeccable taste of the mayor and his advisers. Others whispered that it was unimpressive. There was a bit of a scandal when newspapers found out how much it cost, but the controversy turned out to be a brief one.

Schaefer saw a mantelpiece he thought would be nice, circa 1890, within which a nice gas or electric fire could be lit when needed. "I like that," said the mayor, and cold evenings thereafter, the chauffeurs would turn it on. "He'd put his feet up and watch the movie *Patton* for the 7,000th time," Bereska recalled. He found proper spots for his African violets and, though Bereska thinned them out a bit from time to time, his stuffed animals. Bernie Trueschler, a gas company executive, says that he visited with Schaefer once in these accommodations and found the mayor in fuzzy pink slippers. Some people were struck by Schaefer's devotion to the rowhouse on Edgewood, but Bereska thought he had moved, psychically at least, to 100 North Holliday Street, the official address of Baltimore City Hall.

"Police Aid"

A year after the double triumph on subway and convention center, Hoffman cut a deal that gave Schaefer the sort of cash assistance that kept his city going while the public works big projects were being built. Even with repair work on buildings, sewers, and the like deferred indefinitely,

Schaefer's annual budget problems were acute. As businesses and city residents pulled out, the property tax rate being double that of surrounding jurisdictions, the city's tax revenues fell year after year. Schaefer needed dollars from Washington and Annapolis, or he needed Annapolis to take over the support of some heretofore locally supported function: the community college for example, and later the jail. One year, with Schaefer's blessing, Janet "made" a senate president and gained a $32 million grant for Baltimore. First she recruited Councilman Joe Curran, whose son Joe, Jr., was in the state senate, to round up votes for Steny Hoyer, a young Prince George's County legislator who was then competing for the post of senate president. The chore was made somewhat awkward by the fact that young Curran had already committed his vote to Senator Jim Clark of Howard County. Hoyer was elected, though, and the next summer, Hoffman was given extraordinary standing for a mere lobbyist: Hoyer named her to a committee with Lieutenant Governor Blair Lee III to discuss various issues, including aid to Baltimore. They came up with a plan under which "police aid" would be distributed to the various jurisdictions and settled on a formula that advantaged Baltimore. This sounded fine to Hoyer, who helped to pass the new program.

Hoffman, Schaefer, and Cardin worked together for years to keep the money flowing, often employing official-sounding names such as "police aid," which were nothing more than fig leaves to cover the sort of payoff that is commanded by a jurisdiction like Baltimore that had much poverty but enough political power to address it. Hoffman argued that this assistance was justified historically, a position that was not widely accepted by those who saw the city carrying off truckloads of loot every year. She and Schaefer were almost too successful. In time, the critics caught up with her and grew resentful and even bitter because, even knowing and seeing the game year after year, they were helpless to end it.

Senators such as John Coolahan of Baltimore County began to lie in wait for Schaefer during hearings at the Senate Committee on Budget and Taxation. "Where's Willie Don the Con?" Coolahan would ask with a shake of his wavy blond hair. Strong and just as daring as Schaefer, he was called the Lion of Halethorpe in honor of his hair and his home district. He was that imposing. Coolahan said he and Jack Cade, a proud Republican from Anne Arundel County, would take bets on how long Schaefer would remain in the witness chair before walking out on the committee and its tough, knowledgeable questioning. Schaefer's insatiable pursuit of state money, his unwillingness to set priorities, and the huge public works projects that he took home turned even his natural allies sour. Montgomery County's Margaret Schweinhaut gave Baltimore a new name: "the city of greed." In the war of images, need did not compete with greed. Schaefer didn't care what they called him and understood their need to decry what he was doing. As Schweinhaut talked that year, the mayor of Baltimore sat with Hoffman in the balcony, head in hands. The picture of him so despairing, so dejected, so much at the mercy of Schweinhaut and the others ran in the newspapers. Even when he lost—and he lost infrequently—his dejection seemed so pitiable and so personal yet he seemed always to be lamenting the damage done to Baltimore.

One-Man Band

Schaefer drove on as Baltimore's super development chief, the access point to everything in his city, the control freak with no compunction about enforcing his freakiness. He was Citizen One, a man who represented the people before the bureaucracy—a home owner who was determined to have a street lamp replaced, a zoning infraction redressed, a barking dog muzzled. And he was not obliged to take the word of some anonymous clerk that the matter would be taken care of. He brought an entire city's complaints to experts who could solve them and stood there impatiently, hammer in hand, to make sure solutions came along quickly.

"He never understood any program," Embry thought. "He'd go out and find problems. What he understood was alleys. He came in on Monday morning with twenty-five or thirty things he wanted done."

Embry was a one-man urban development band. He was the renewal commissioner, supervisor of the Inner Harbor projects, builder of low-income housing, head of the Baltimore Development Corporation, and czar of off-street parking. "We had more low-income housing per capita than any other place in the country. We never tore down a house that I didn't go out and see it first. We never rehabilitated a vacant house that I didn't see first. I didn't want to tear down something that should be fixed up or fix up something that should be torn down." Embry always went to look at neighborhoods before issuing a Section 8 certificate that allows a tenant to rent for less with a federal subsidy: How strong was the neighborhood? What impact would the reduced rent have on that street's residents? Schaefer gave himself credit for Embry and the other whiz kids on his staff. "The genius is not the mayor," he said. "Genius is getting the talent. Embry would have been offended if our public housing was a shambles."

Embry's work gained some currency in national urban affairs circles. In the summer of 1975, presidential candidate Jimmy Carter came to see Baltimore, to learn about urban programs that worked and to talk about his own commitment to cities. He had one problem: no political host. Mandel and Kovens were antagonistic to him; Mandel was backing California Governor Jerry Brown simply to spite Carter. Schaefer was uncommitted. So one of Carter's advance men asked Embry whether he would take the candidate around the city. Embry said he would. "And, oh, if a reporter asks, would you mind saying you're for Carter?" Embry said he hadn't really focused on the race, but he was not for Brown. Carter, he knew, would have an urban policy, and he had been a good governor, so Embry said sure, and he did.

When Carter was elected, Embry figured in the usual speculation about who from Maryland might be in the Carter cabinet. He actually was in contention and flew to Atlanta to meet with Carter. "I'd like you to be the HUD secretary," Carter said according to Embry, "but I can't offer it to you now because I made a commitment to have two blacks and two women." In the end, he picked Pat Harris, a black woman. But Harris picked Embry to be her assistant.

His Kingdom for a Hotel

When Embry left for Washington in February 1976, the Inner Harbor remained a lovely, undeveloped plain. Much hidden infrastructural work was under way around the shoreline: playing fields on the south, a home-steading program in the Old Otterbein neighborhood (which Schaefer pronounced "autobahn," as if it were a highway), dredging work at the harbor entrance, construction of finger piers, a contract signed for construction of a clipper ship to be called the *Pride of Baltimore,* approval of a $30 million bond issue for financing of houses at Inner Harbor West, and an upgrading of the city's bond rating by the investment house Moody's—which meant the city could borrow at lower rates—based on the potential at the Inner Harbor. What was needed was a new hotel, preferably built by or for one of the national chains—a final endorsement of lowly Baltimore's potential as a tourist destination. Finally, Ackerman & Company of Atlanta agreed to build an office tower and a hotel at

Constellation Place, roughly at the corner of Pratt and Light streets, within sight of the harbor. The Chesapeake & Potomac Telephone Company would relocate there, joining the insurance giant, USF&G, which had its textured beige tower on the north corner of that same intersection. Just across Light was the IBM Building. Big names were moving in, spending big money, endorsing Schaefer's confidence. In the spring of 1977, though, Ackerman bailed out, saying that the hotel wouldn't work and the company couldn't get the financing. But it had signed an agreement to pay certain damages if it chose not to exercise its option. So Jay Brodie, who had taken over from Embry, told the builder a release could be worked out—for a price.

"We'll negotiate what you owe us," Brodie said.

"I don't owe you anything," said Charles Ackerman. "I tried. It wasn't my fault." But he agreed to meet at Brodie's offices on Saratoga Street, two blocks from city hall. Brodie began by saying he was certain a fine company like Ackerman's did not wish to have a failure in Baltimore sullying its reputation when it tried to do work here again or in other cities. At some point, Baltimore's team suggested that Ackerman could leave with the city's blessing if he wrote a check for $2 million. The figure came from nowhere. It was not specified anywhere in the agreement, but Brodie called it "reasonable"—enough to cover the difficulty of finding another developer and the lost time and opportunity. Gene Feinblatt, still the housing authority's lawyer, told Ackerman the figure was not negotiable. A wonderful bluff, thought Brodie, who had no wish to be tied up in court if suing the developer proved the only option. After about an hour, Ackerman said, "We'll do it." The money was deposited in a city account and used later to pay for the overstreet walkways that would connect the hoped-for new hotel, the phone company, and other buildings to the harbor. A year or so later, Ackerman was back in town to bid on another Baltimore project. When he came into Brodie's office, the director had forgotten the earlier negotiations. "Charlie," said Brodie, "I don't know if you've been here before."

"I've been here," Ackerman said. "I left $2 million here."

A. N.

But still there was no new hotel, no profession of faith in Baltimore's future. Hope lay then with the Hyatt chain. Its marketing experts were studying Baltimore to determine whether a hotel could be profitable in such a city. Would people really want to stay in Baltimore, a place passed through without pause for generations? Hyatt's men did not think so. They said no. Sorry, "the numbers" just didn't work. But somehow Schaefer managed to get a phone call through to A. N. Pritzker, patriarch of the family that owned Hyatt. Would Mr. Pritzker please come to Baltimore? He came with his wife and her mink coat. "It took three guys just to lift it," Schaefer marveled. The two men—everyone called Pritzker A. N.— toured the city in the afternoon with dinner to follow at the Chambord, a restaurant at the corner of Charles and Madison streets. Bankers, bureaucrats, businessmen, city officials, and others were there to make sure A. N. got the flavor. He'd brought some of his own experts along as well, and one of them was explaining after dinner how their project worked in Louisville, running through the numbers and how they added up to "go" in that project. One needed various chunks of money: city, state, Hyatt, federal, and loans were all part of the equation.

Schaefer noticed that Pritzker was not happy. "He was having lamb chops and he really didn't want lamb chops. He'd had lamb chops the night before. He didn't really like lamb chops," Schaefer recalled, embellishing the hotelier's unhappiness. What he meant was that A. N. was out of sorts and a little distracted. But Pritzker had discovered something, beyond the numbers: Schaefer, who called everyone "Mister," and had a talented team Pritzker referred to as "the fellas." Brodie kept a letter A. N. had written to them on a Saturday. It started "Dear Fellas" and at the bottom said: "Typed by ANP." At seventy-eight, Pritzker worked weekends when typists weren't around, just as the mayor of Baltimore did.

Schaefer thought he had earned the older man's trust by showing him performance, dynamism, and unrealized potential. "He saw a moving city, a city that was determined. He liked that."

Schaefer watched A. N. that night at dinner with some alarm, but then an amazing thing happened as the Hyatt's numbers man talked about how much money his team had in the Louisville deal—a million dollars, Brodie thought.

"No, no, no," Pritzker said, standing up and waving off the presentation of his man from Louisville. "It was $500,000." Here's how it worked, he said, and quickly stated the numbers accurately. Bankers had gotten involved in Kentucky, he said, and they were a critical part of the deal.

Sensing an opportunity, Schaefer stood to make the case for Baltimore's money men. Pritzker, he said, would be risking his money on our city, on our Inner Harbor. He was hoping someone would take the hint and say, "Count us in. For the good of the city, and so on."

Instead, there was silence.

"Nobody was going to write a check for anything, not a quarter," Brodie said. And why was anyone surprised? "Tell me when these guys ever stepped up for a big Baltimore project because I can't remember one." Twenty years earlier, the business elite of Baltimore had proudly prepared to accomplish the twenty-two-acre Charles Center redevelopment plan without federal money. Under the rules then, renewal projects were eligible for federal money only if a project included housing. Until revised, Charles Center did not, but, more than that, the Baltimore leaders were proud as always to be doing their deal without the federal government. When the rules changed making Baltimore eligible for the money, the Charles Center leaders were challenged—they had made such a noise about self-sufficiency. In the end, of course, they succumbed, and the federal money began to roll into Baltimore for project after project, hundreds of millions dollars to underwrite a parade of new buildings and projects leaping out of the tired old urban landscape. The atmosphere had changed radically, and the business community was more than happy to see government carry the weight and the risk. Its leaders were on the dole, their work ethic undermined by Washington's largesse.

All pretense of independence having vanished by that night at the Chambord, Schaefer quickly found himself in the hands of his old housing commissioner, Embry. And Embry had an idea: a program that was quickly dubbed UDAG, for Urban Development Action Grant. Embry had seen so many worthy efforts fail for lack of the gap financing—the space left when anticipated revenues failed to cover costs. His idea was to lend the money to solid projects, get the repayments, and loan the money again. If the cities and the federal government could be partners on such developments, the Ackermans and Pritzkers of the world would see that someone else was taking risks along with them. In this case, HUD gave Baltimore a $10 million UDAG, and Benton figured out how the city could finance construction of the parking garage that the hotel would need. They also employed several other new wrinkles in what increasingly was referred to as "creative financing." A deal was to be signed, finally, but then Brodie got a phone call from New York. Equitable Bank would not finance the deal. Its board, having agreed to put up the money, suddenly concluded that it had too many hotels in its accounts. The deal was off. Brodie went to Schaefer's office.

"Who are these people in New York?" Schaefer asked. "I'm going to get them on the phone, I'm going to give them a piece of my mind. Couldn't be worse, right?"

"When's the last time you've been to Baltimore?" he asked the banker. Fifteen years or so ago, the man said.

"You don't know the city, then. You don't know what we're doing here. I want you to come down. Maybe you'll make the same decision, but I doubt it. I want you to give me a day."

Like Pritzker, this man found Baltimore and its mayor irresistible. The financing got back on track.

In this version of the development art, the Hyatt Corporation agreed to make the city a shareholding partner, and in time, the hotel produced $2.4 million a year for the city, net. In its first year, the Baltimore Hyatt did better than any hotel in the chain. Old Man Pritzker knew what he was doing. Walter Sondheim learned that the real definition of "developer" during these days was a three-letter acronym OPM—for other people's money. The Hyatt men, he observed, would have a $30 million project, but only $500,000 would be Hyatt money. The rest would be borrowed or would be granted or loaned by the government. Baltimore and Washington were putting up the millions, buying Pritzker's acumen and buying his Hyatt name to hold high in Baltimore as another symbol of the city's arrival as a newly revitalized urban center, one with a future.

Hyatt's profits didn't bother the pragmatic mayor of Baltimore.

"The more money he made, the more I made. If Pritzker was successful, if Pritzker drove a hard bargain with us, and we benefited by it, nothing wrong with that," he said.

Sundays in the Park with Don

Image was everything, as long as it grew from substance: jobs, tourism, tax receipts, stores that could survive, his own election and reelection. "People don't want to live in a lousy Cleveland, a lousy Pittsburgh, a lousy Baltimore. They want to be proud of their city," he thought. So he had worked "like an absolute animal" to get Hyatt into town. People in Baltimore and beyond knew that Hyatt didn't set up shop in just any little backwater. And he knew that men like Pritzker would respond to the leadership they found in cities where they prospected for projects. So Schaefer continued to work at a pace that vaporized most of the people—businessmen and others—who moved toward his orbit. He needed to keep convincing Baltimoreans even as he was wooing New York bankers. With no family obligations, he could show up at work on Saturdays or Sundays. City officials began to recognize that Schaefer might call on them at any time unannounced, and if they weren't there, he'd leave them a note. He became a defender of public art, knowing that even if it was controversial and provocative, it was stimulating and further proof of municipal life.

Arnold Lehman, director of the Baltimore Museum of Art, remembers a cold Sunday afternoon when a museum guard called to say that the mayor had come and wanted to see him. He wanted to see how the museum's new outdoor sculpture garden was progressing. So for the next hour or so, Lehman and the mayor of Baltimore slogged around in the snow and mud just east of the BMA's main building adjacent to the Johns Hopkins University's main campus in north central Baltimore. The city's museum had been founded with the incomparable generosity and, ultimately, faith in the city of Dr. Claribel and Miss Etta Cone. These sisters, patrons of Henri Matisse and others, left their collection to Baltimore on the condition that the city would cherish and sustain it after their deaths.

Though his name was etched into a bas relief medallion and implanted on the museum's marble floor in gratitude for his support of art and architecture in Baltimore, Schaefer insisted that he knew nothing of the Cones or their bequest. This was an act, his friends said, to protect him politically from any appearance of interest in art. It was like ordering Perrier. He preferred to ask for fizzy water. Perrier was just too fancy for him or for the people he always knew were listening over his shoulder.

The gardens, the arts academy, a sailing ship called the *Pride*, the World Trade Center, and the vision of its architect—all were demonstrations of a city's creative power, even a city such as Baltimore. In deference to his voters, Schaefer saved his public expressions of cultural enthusiasm for Hulk Hogan, the TV wrestler, for African violets, and for model trains.

Schaefer had discovered by then that he liked art. At the BMA one day with an arts patron whose name was Hooper, Schaefer came upon a canvas, all white with a single red dot in the center.

"That is a beautiful painting," the woman said.

Schaefer said, "It is? Geez, I could do that. Throw some white paint on it."

A lecture ensued from Mrs. Hooper.

"I learned from her, so I got to where I liked it. I don't like it," he corrected himself, "but I liked it."

"He knew nothing about art as far as I know, " said Bailey Fine. "But he knew people cared about it, that it was part of the city's cultural life, part of what made a city worth saving." As a member of the city council, Schaefer had learned of a commitment in the city of Philadelphia to set aside 1 percent of the annual budget for art. In what might have been the first hint of his eclectic style of governing, Schaefer proposed a similar bill. McKeldin vetoed it, possibly one reason why the two men were enemies in the beginning.

Schaefer knew monuments, of course, and, looking ahead to his own memorializing, wanted a statue of Tommy the Elder. He ordered two poses: one standing and the other sitting nearby on a bench, both overlooking Hopkins Square, where the city's Charles Center rebirth had begun in the late 1950s. Schaefer also paid for an installation of Civil War soldiers on Centre Street and sanctioned the spending of millions to save the facade of a historic building on Bolton Hill called the Beethoven in honor of the builder's favorite composer. Each of these works, wrought in granite or iron and steel, was placed unprotected for the public's enjoyment. Schaefer loved it when his arts director, Jody Albright, converted the old Bromo Seltzer tower, modeled after the Palazzo Vecchio in Florence, into the city's arts center. During one of his many promotional interludes, he would be photographed with arms raised with the ballet dancers at his new Baltimore High School for the Arts, another "frill" that he absolutely insisted upon.

The Wild Man of Edgewood Street was in league now with the Cones and Mrs. Hooper. They were codependent and flourishing in one moment of time. People would call that moment a renaissance—too grand a term for Schaefer, though he lived with it. "People said I was a crazy man, putting sculpture out in public. They said folks in the ghetto will tear it all up, smash it to pieces. They didn't. Not only that, they watched it to be sure nothing happened to it. There was less than 5 percent damage to any piece of sculpture. They understood it."

Even if he didn't.

Wild Man

When Schaefer took office in 1971, one in four Baltimore families lived on an income that fell below the federal government's poverty line. A full 65,000 families were unable to afford decent housing; the growing problem of vacant houses continued to erode neighborhoods; 25 percent or more of inner-city residents were jobless; drug addiction, it was estimated, drove Baltimoreans to steal as much as $300 million worth of their fellow citizens' property each year; and the tax base, the segment of residential and commercial property that provided the city with operating capital, continued to shrink. In the 1950s, some city businesspeople had wondered whether matters were sufficiently dire to require a business-government alliance committed to finding remedies. No one denied the trend twenty years later, but still the response was spotty. Baltimore had diminishing capacity to save itself, so Schaefer grabbed at any federal or state lifeline. Model Cities and the Community Action Agency—what remained of Lyndon Johnson's War on Poverty—had sent $40 million to Baltimore in 1970. Schaefer thought the money needed far better management.

The federal Department of Housing and Urban Development offered programs—or had offered them until just before Schaefer was elected. The man who was then in charge of the vast bureaucracy of HUD in Washington was George Romney, a former American Motors executive and former governor of Michigan who had been appointed by Richard M. Nixon. The Republican president's approach to the nation's cities, to racial tension, and to the poor was almost liberal, reflecting stubborn fears of urban rioting and a political decision to ease conditions that might cause it. One of Nixon's policies, in fact, was a daring departure from the policies of his

Democratic predecessors. In the domestic equivalent of his decision to recognize China, Nixon proposed a guaranteed annual income for poor families—tantamount almost to a communistic solution—which he called the Family Assistance Plan. The proposal went so astonishingly far beyond the canons of Republicanism that committed poverty warriors were certain they could not live with it, challenged its motives, and killed it. A Marylander named George Wiley, head of the National Welfare Rights Organization, fought successfully against the program on Capitol Hill, arguing that just as his subordinates were making the current welfare system work, the larger system wanted to "reform" it. Thirty years later, Republicans and Democrats combined forces to dismantle the system Wiley had saved, turning it into a time-limited, job-based program that included none of the entitlement elements Nixon's proposal had contained. Here, no doubt, welfare advocates were too strong for their own good.

During Schaefer's first weeks in office, Secretary Romney came to Baltimore to explain another of Nixon's decisions: to impound HUD program funds, a tactic to defeat the spendthrift, program-happy Democrats. Embry and his deputy, Jay Brodie, took the HUD Secretary on a tour of vacant lots and suggested that they would stay vacant as long as Washington clung to Nixon's rules. Embry and Brodie threw him together with angry neighborhood leaders who had been counting on HUD follow-through to rebuild. HUD was concerned that the new urban renewal projects, including the new housing that was to be built, were resegregating urban neighborhoods—"as if," Brodie said with anger and sarcasm, "America was prepared to do anything else—move black families into suburban neighborhoods, for example." Cities would build where they demolished, Brodie thought, or not at all, since scattering the refugees of demolition was politically hazardous. With a stroke of the federal policy pen, Nixon and Romney cut off all these housing programs in "areas of concentration," which included large portions of Baltimore.

Romney might have been congratulated for leaving his comfortable office to come to the city, but his hosts wanted to convince him that he had erred, and they did not mute their disagreement. The secretary spoke briefly with Lucille Gorham, a neighborhood activist who urged him to reconsider.

Gorham had experience Romney could not fully appreciate. She knew urban renewal from the street: It had decimated three of the neighborhoods where she had lived with her eight children, all born before she was 30. Her neighborhoods were worth preserving, she thought—even though

Washington saw them as segregated: "My grandmother lived next door, my aunts lived across the street, all the neighbors knew each other. My grandmother held keys for all the kids in the neighborhood. You lose those people when you move. You have to make new friends. By the fourth move, the emphasis on community had gone. We had to keep our own keys." If the government thought blowing up these places was a good idea, Gorham was ready to suggest a different approach and she was not shy about confronting the HUD secretary.

Brodie followed up immediately: "I have to tell you Mr. Secretary, as a result of your policy, these lots are going to be sitting there vacant forever, and these people have been promised housing through the whole renewal process, and we're in a situation of breaking this promise."

"A very unbalanced presentation, Mr. Brodie," said Romney as he turned to leave Baltimore.

Six out of Six

A few weeks later, Schaefer and two of his aides drove to Washington for a meeting with the secretary. Mayors could command such an audience in those days of riot mania, but Romney was no cream puff. A man with carefully combed gray hair and a ruler-straight jawline, he gave the impression of meaning whatever he said. He was waiting when Schaefer arrived with Bob Embry, Mark Joseph, and Republican Senator Charles "Mac" Mathias. Joseph was the young Baltimore lawyer and developer who had helped Schaefer to write his platform paper, "Where I Stand." Mathias was one of the most liberal Republicans in Congress, a man who had made stands of his own against discrimination in parts of Maryland where that was not regarded as heroic.

The secretary spoke first. He had reviewed Baltimore's pending grant applications, six in all. "You can expect to get two," he said, smiling as if this would be welcome news at a time when some cities faced the prospect of no help at all.

The mayor of Baltimore responded with a torrent of abuse. "You know, Mr. Secretary, you don't understand anything about cities. Nothing. You don't understand how people begin to depend on things and how difficult it is to have things changed around after you've been working on them for years. Who the hell are you to say we can't have these programs?"

"What do you mean?" said Romney indignantly. "I'm the secretary. I've been around." His project evaluators were not impressed with some of Baltimore's ideas, Romney said, and there had been scandals in Detroit involving similar proposals.

"I'm not the mayor of Detroit," said Schaefer, leaning across the table, unleashing the Stare. His look said, Don't lay the sins of other mayors on Baltimore.

From this point, the encounter grew even more intense and loud, the mayor and the cabinet secretary shouting at each other like schoolboys. Joseph, Embry, and Mathias were almost literally diving under the table.

"It was fantastic," Joseph recalled. "They would have literally thrown blows at each other if the conference table had not been separating them. Neither would let the other have the last word." The shouting went on for twenty minutes or so. "We'll never see another dollar from these guys," Joseph thought as he walked out. "Why did you do that?" he asked Schaefer as they drove back to Baltimore.

"I didn't see where I had anything to lose," Schaefer said years later. "What he wanted to do was absolutely wrong. He was stunned. No mayor talked like that. We had a rough ride, but he saw that I was serious — not just busting his balls for the hell of it."

Here was a basic Schaefer ploy: a shocking frontal assault on whoever was standing in his way, an assault as well upon the standards of decorum, flinging them aside in a way that was in itself shocking. Most people, including cabinet secretaries, fell back when faced with a seemingly unrestrained force that was willing to inflict embarrassment and pain. Schaefer himself was never embarrassed by his performances, allowing them their fullest dimensions. He had the supreme advantage of conviction: He was not pushing something for ulterior, personal, or corrupt motives. He was pushing for people and for a city. He had the moral high ground in his mind even as he behaved like a kindergarten child intent on having all the blocks.

"A lot of people are used to working for people who will accept something less than perfection," said Schaefer's friend and adviser Walter Sondheim, who was school board president under Old Tommy and the head of Charles Center Inner Harbor under Schaefer. "He cannot bring himself to do that."

And why should he when his approach worked so well?

"We got all the projects," Joseph said.

Twenty-five years later, the principals could not remember specifically what projects Schaefer had insisted upon. It hardly mattered. The nature of the initiatives was not the point. If something was even marginally useful, it had to be continued, tried, supported. Baltimore was desperate and could not afford to lose any bit of help that might have been available. If Lucille Gorham and the others were coming out of their houses to confront a cabinet secretary in Baltimore, Schaefer would do the same in Washington. He saw his job as fighting the fiercest, most aggressive, most demanding fight he could imagine. If Romney couldn't see that, he truly didn't know what cities—Baltimore, at least—were all about.

What the HUD secretary endured that day in Washington was the essence of Schaefer's leadership style: the City College "Wild Man," rough edges bared, sent in now by Schaefer himself to "smash things up," startle, and subdue. Impatience, anger, and despair were part of the demanding persona that was now working on behalf of an entire city, not just a high school sports team. At times, his antics made him seem nothing so much as a case of arrested development—and frighteningly consistent. "If his antagonists had *died*," said Sondheim, "he'd keep pursuing them."

To be sure, some people thought that Schaefer's manias were outrageous and unacceptable, possibly even clinical. "He needs professional attention" became a common observation, not just among enemies and critics but among intimates as well. Though useful to him, temper obscured his complexity, his zeal for progress, his tenderness, and his ability to change and adjust. His moods could be frightening, verging on silent vacant catatonia: manic-depressive illness, said the amateur psychoanalysts. How long could he endure his self-inflicted bouts of depression and rage? People expected him to have a stroke or to be carried away in restraints. He did not protest those characterizations.

"It's called get them to a frenzy, an absolute frenzy," said Bereska, who had seen the act perfected. Anger was only a part of it, and it was not reserved for cabinet secretaries. Step One in the process, Bereska said, went like this: "Moan and say, 'We're not going to solve this problem, we're not going to get this or that grant.'" Then, unable to bear the gloom descending around him, unwilling to disappoint him, the "ragged little army" from the ragged little city would march at double time to find a way. Schaefer hated setbacks and relished them at the same time because he knew they gave him leverage.

"We would support him like few mayors in this country were supported," said Joseph R. L. Sterne, the *Sun*'s editorial page editor, "but he knew better than to thank us and say 'Whoopdeedo!' or 'I appreciate your support!' He would look for anything that was critical and call up and bitch and shout, and his favorite line with me was, 'Well you've succeeded.

You've destroyed me. The Baltimore *Sun* has destroyed me. I hope you're happy. There's nothing I can do any more because you have ruined everything I wanted to do.' It was a wonderful technique."

The frenzy was deliberate and calculated for the most part. "I'd call people periodically," Schaefer said, "just to ride their ass a little. The bureaucracy will move as slowly as you allow it to move."

There were times, Joseph said much later, when the screamer and his victim might have stopped and laughed at the absurdity of it, when the gambit was so transparent it might have collapsed of its own preposterous weight. The contract between citizen and mayor, between leader and partisans kept it in place. Had anyone else done to Schaefer what Schaefer did to Romney and many others, he would have put that person in Siberia for life. He hated confrontation directed at him—the whole political tone of the 1960s offended his sensibilities—but he knew it worked and employed it himself throughout the decades ahead.

"Outrageous" was just another word for nothing left to lose.

Too Nice

Driving by the Inner Harbor one weekend well into his second term—he was always driving by something on weekends—Schaefer saw bare dirt, emptiness, the perpetual aftermath of demolition that characterized urban renewal efforts in many U.S. cities. "Bombscapes," they were called, left to burn impressions of abandonment and futility into the consciousness of the poor and taxpayers alike. Do something with that, he demanded as soon as he got to his office on Monday morning. By then, well into his second term, managers of the municipal apparatus sprang into action at the very sound of his voice. Charles Center/Inner Harbor Management, the Public Works Department, and the department of parks did something. They planted grass. They planted flowers. They planted bushes. They planned parks and esplanades between the water and Federal Hill on the south side of the harbor. They began to stage festivals—Sunny Sundays—an ice cream stick ship regatta, picnics, spaghetti dinners and the like. At first, no one came. Then almost everyone did.

Schaefer was horrified by the landscaping done at his command. "No, no, not that nice! Don't make it beautiful!" he moaned. "People will fall in love with it, and we'll have a hell of a time putting anything else down there."

He was right, of course, but his warnings came too late. Baltimoreans had already fallen in love with the harbor, now that they could see it, and walk safely next to it and in the open parklike setting around it. Cities needed open space for people, and this seemed ideal to many. The affection that Schaefer sensed was not an immediate problem, since no one had any idea what would go in that space.

Schaefer was not happy with any of the ideas that were advanced for development of this land—nor did he receive many. Advertisements were placed in national newspapers requesting ideas, bids, proposals, anything at all for development along the harbor piers. There were no responses.

Finally, though, as Schaefer had been negotiating with Hyatt, Jim Rouse was opening a complex of buildings at Faneuil Hall and Quincy markets, warehouses in Boston that were refurbished for installation of upscale boutiques and food stalls enlivened by musicians and other entertainers. Inside and outside spaces flowed together, working on a human scale, and blending elegantly into the historic surroundings of Boston. The buildings, extending from city hall to the Boston harbor, were far less inviting for a developer than the open spaces of Baltimore, and Rouse was convinced that his home city, the one he had always hoped to reshape, could have its own version of Faneuil Hall. He asked Embry, Brodie, and then Schaefer whether he could make a proposal. When Schaefer heard that Rouse was interested, he smiled to himself.

Rouse would return now to be a key player in the renaissance he had started twenty-seven years earlier, in 1952, with the Greater Baltimore Committee. He had built malls all over the country, gotten the new town of Columbia under way, and become a national figure in the process, so Schaefer was eager to have him back. He was convinced he could rely on Rouse's vision, integrity, and competence to make something of this most prime city real estate. As with much of what happened in these years, Schaefer and his team had no concrete idea what to do. No one had been willing to risk time, money, and reputation on Baltimore. People were still laughing to think the city could ever prosper as a tourist destination.

In the beginning, lot lines, plots, and numbered areas were arid demarcations on dizzying architectural drawings, one of them showing commercial property on the west side of the harbor only. Rouse, Embry, and the others soon realized that they could arrange the buildings to symmetrical effect at the corner, one along Pratt Street and one along Light, in an L-shaped configuration that would be connected by a broad, sloping esplanade that moved gradually down to the water. The buildings would have outside eating areas, verandas—the city's front porch, as it were.

From their cars, visitors could see the historic USS *Constellation*, the Civil War vintage ship that had been rescued and relocated in Baltimore. Schaefer insisted the market buildings stand somewhat lower than the top of the *Constellation*'s mast, a point of contention with Rouse, who resisted, relented, and then rejoiced in what he called Schaefer's more instinctively sensitive eye. The ship had a captivating majesty, a touch of authenticity that put history on the skyline and held it above the commercialism of kite shops, cookie vendors, and trendy restaurants such as Hooters, which came later, featuring waitresses in short shorts and tight T-shirts.

At Brodie's urging, Rouse spent $30,000 to build a splendid scale model of the project he would build. A speaker's bureau was established to sell the project throughout the city. Rouse was a galvanizing speaker, but he was not among the project's public advocates: He was a developer, the devil incarnate, a man who had come to despoil the natural beauty of the harbor for profit: Thus did opponents hammer at him with great initial success.

His Rouse

As Schaefer had predicted, Rouse's plan met ferocious opposition from those who had grown to love the harbor's newly opened vistas. The city had bonded with the new view and the new activities—the music, games, and festivals. They didn't need an in-city shopping mall. Nor did the restaurant owners in surrounding Federal Hill and Little Italy. With the help of businesses and Councilman George Della, an organization formed to defy Schaefer and Rouse, to kill the project on the planning board.

The gentrifying neighborhoods of Federal Hill, regarding the harborside park as their very own piece of the city, were led in battle by then councilman (later state senator) Della, a crafty practitioner whose Stonewall team had helped to elect Schaefer in 1971 and 1975 and who was working for him again in 1979—but would oppose the Rouse proposal. One day in the spring, with the project's approval very much in doubt, Della and Schaefer talked on the phone. As the conversation continued, others in the room knew that the topic was the Rouse project and the referendum. Schaefer, phone to ear, migrated toward the window in the way he sometimes did when anger was welling up in him. As a Lenten sacrifice, he had promised to deny himself the relief he got from unregulated swearing. But now he was fully provoked, and he was seething into the phone. "George . . . George . . . Get off my, my . . . Get off my Rouse!

Get off my Rouse, George!" Joan Bereska remembers him shouting.

Not for the last time, Schaefer was hampered by his success. His opponents were defending and loving the city as he had urged them to do. Many estimable Baltimoreans joined Della in active or philosophical opposition. Among them were the progressive councilwoman Mary Pat Clarke, Mercantile Bank president H. Furlong Baldwin, and State Archivist Ed Papenfuse, a Roland Park resident.

"Why are you wasting your time on that?" Baldwin asked Rick Berndt, a downtown lawyer and member of his bank's board of directors. "The last thing we need down there is another shopping center."

Goldilocks and the German General

Berndt, though, was as competitive as the ferociously patrician Baldwin, and he knew what needed to be done to save the project. He had worked in election campaigns for Barbara Mikulski and for U.S. Senator Paul S. Sarbanes whenever they needed him, and he quickly conceptualized the Harborplace issue as, in effect, a candidate that needed the same sort of organizational effort as a senator or mayor. Berndt had organized the successful attempt three years earlier to convince Baltimoreans that they should spend $7 million to build the new aquarium. He was also removed enough from the early efforts to promote the Rouse project to be an objective critic. His worrying represented a dimension of Schaefer's grip on the imagination of the city; its dynamic young leaders were thinking along with him about how to move the redevelopment ball.

The effort was complicated because voters had to be doubly educated: They had to vote *against* Della's proposal and *for* Schaefer's. Della had gotten his anti-Rouse question on the ballot by collecting signatures on Sunday afternoons at harborside. The city council passed an ordinance authorizing a second ballot question allowing voters to limit development there, allotting 3.1 of the available thirty acres, leaving plenty of open space. Baltimore could have it both ways, in other words: new revenue, new jobs, and a wonderful harbor view. Various city and Rouse officials would later claim credit for suggesting that, as a matter of strategy, the city's plan needed to give the voters a positive choice—something to be for. (Harborplace turned out to be one of those successes with a thousand fathers.) Here was another exercise in ballot tailoring, the sort of pre-election planning that had elected Baltimore mayors and comptrollers, though this one was a bit more complicated than most.

Schaefer crackled and fumed, taking the matter personally as if people did not have a right to oppose him or his plan. He seemed to be ordering the entire city to get off his Rouse. The genteel, visionary developer was a perfect target for the opponents who found a South Baltimore secretary, Louise Alder—attractive, articulate, and very Baltimore—to be their spokesperson. Her theme: "We finally have something beautiful in this city and now they want to take it away from us. No one elected him King, did they?" Here was personification of the "Poor Me" Baltimore militant, suspecting the worst. Schaefer called her "Goldilocks," a term of respect, if not endearment, since she seemed to win every encounter on television.

For most of the summer and early fall of 1979, Goldilocks was eating all the porridge. She and her supporters rode a wave of anti–City Hall sentiment, which grew partly from unhappiness with Schaefer's manner and partly from a propensity of Americans to fight city hall. In Baltimore, citizens had turned back a proposed downtown sports complex in 1974, rejecting the Camden Yards railway yards as the location, and of course Mikulski and her neighborhood cohorts had defeated Schaefer on "the Road." Now many citizens felt that they, not Rouse or the mayor, had rediscovered the wonders of their city's harbor, and they became its fierce defenders. Their protests resulted in the imposition of height restrictions on Rouse's marketplace-style buildings and preservation of more open space, but they were not satisfied. The people's crusade gathered momentum throughout the summer.

Then, imperceptibly, the political center of gravity began to shift. At one of his regular Sunday morning basketball games that June, Berndt started muttering the worry that was on the minds of all the players, including Mark Joseph, by then Schaefer's physical development director; Nick Schloeder, a lover of politics who coached at the Gilman School; and Bob Hillman, another young lawyer. All of them were official or unofficial members of Schaefer's organization.

"We could lose this thing. It's getting worse and worse," said Berndt, who had worked on enough campaigns to develop the instinct and antennae of ward leaders. "We're losing all the elevator polls." When he heard people talk about the Inner Harbor ballot question, they weren't speaking favorably. "We have to get the mayor and Rouse out of this," Berndt offered, to unanimous nods. "People love him, but they will not mind teaching him a lesson." At the same time, he said, Schaefer's power and credibility would be cemented forever if the project were approved.

Berndt prepared a balance sheet of strengths and weaknesses. Under

"Strengths" he wrote: Schaefer and Rouse. Under "Weaknesses," he wrote: Schaefer and Rouse. Then he took it to both of them. Rouse understood instantly. Schaefer squinted and scowled and privately questioned Berndt's loyalty, Berndt heard later.

"He's a Sarbanes and Mikulski guy," Schaefer said, offering the ultimate bit of evidence: "He must be a Harvard grad." Berndt, who did not take the mayor's grumbling personally, had actually gone to Villanova and the University of Maryland Law School.

But Schaefer could see as well as anyone that the other side was ahead, and he knew better than anyone that Berndt was part of his invisible machine, an organization of young strivers who were as committed to the city as he. Schaefer knew because he constantly recruited new members, reveled in their talents, and gave them uncommon authority—all of which intensified their loyalty to him. Schaefer had an organization that was larger and more representative than any Kovens had cobbled together. Still, he had to be convinced to cede so much power on such a pivotal issue.

"Will you hear me out?" Berndt asked.

"Okay, Junior," Schaefer said, "but you'd better listen to me a little, too. You don't know everything."

He began to call Berndt "the German General." At first, Schaefer didn't buy the conclusion that his anger made the other side stronger and that the pro-referendum forces were in the wrong hands. He knew Berndt was right, though, about getting the campaign into the neighborhoods. He agreed to step back—but not out of the campaign.

"Stay in touch with me," Schaefer said.

Berndt scrawled a campaign plan on a dozen sheets of yellow legal paper and began methodically assembling a team, ordering the requisite T-shirts and balloons, arranging to print pamphlets, and rounding up volunteers. They met on Sunday afternoons and during the week, meetings that were limited to two hours. Typically, banners were stretched across Baltimore streets at election time asking voters to "Approve All Ballot Questions." Usually, but not always, these requests for borrowing were approved by a citizenry that knew streets had to be repaved and the like. They could be trusted to vote "Yes," needing no introduction to the realities of keeping the city going. But that approach appeared disastrous for the issue of 1979. Berndt made sure the mayor's planning area committees were advocates of the plan. He contacted all 123 neighborhood associations and as many as 50 political clubs.

Berndt got Bill Boucher and the GBC to raise a campaign fund, knowing he would need money. This was the ultimate issue election, though Berndt knew it would be won or lost in many of the usual ways. He would need sample ballots, if nothing else. Goldilocks had been saying there were no "real people" who wanted to see the project go forward. Berndt ordered a slide show to present at neighborhood meetings. The first version featured men in dark blue blazers, gold buttons, and the like. "This will kill us," Berndt declared. It had to be redone. The final version showed kids on bikes, women from Highlandtown, and black people; it fairly screamed its message: "What are we, Martians?" Ten copies were ordered, and ten projectors were purchased. Vinnie Quayle of St. Ambrose Housing, and the Reverend Vernon Dobson, an influential black minister, were the featured speakers. At the same time, Berndt worked the opponents, meeting with the restaurant owners in Little Italy, hoping to be persuasive enough to reduce their ardor for spending money on the campaign at least. In the end, they put $4,000 behind their appeal, far less than the $85,000 spent by Berndt and the GBC.

The General targeted black opinion leaders such as Congressman Parran Mitchell. He made a pitch to the Inter-denominational Ministerial Alliance, a group of inner-city ministers, most of them black, who could influence the thinking of thousands. This group, which had sued Schaefer for failing to promote blacks in city government, agreed to distribute pamphlets in neighborhoods and in their houses of worship—60,000 on the Sunday before the election. Berndt prepared a brazen script for them: "We want you to vote for this project, but more importantly, God wants you to do it." The ministers wrote a rousing letter, which was rewritten by Congressman Mitchell and published in the *Afro-American*.

After a few weeks of this new campaign, Goldilocks showed up on the television news one night with an implicit acknowledgment that the tide was turning away from her. "We're in some sort of professional campaign here," she said.

"You bet your ass you are!" Berndt shouted back at the screen. At the same time, he was careful to avoid confirming her charge, as true as it was. He had money, a citywide coalition, and experience that dwarfed the forces of Goldilocks.

Schaefer was at least as shaky that November election night in 1979 as he had ever been. He won easily against the usually weak Republican opposition, the former McKeldin aide and state legislator, Samuel A. Culotta. The Rouse project was approved by a vote of roughly 59,000 to 43,000. Schaefer's own popularity, the faith Baltimore was developing in his leadership, and the German General's work accounted for the margin—a comfortable one, given how the early elevator polls had gone. Baltimoreans reelected their mayor and gave themselves a new Main Street.

Pin Money

Schaefer did not mind dueling with Goldilocks, but taking on any segment of the business community was painful for him. He thought of himself as a corporate executive, even as the businessmen he dealt with as mayor—in the beginning, at least—regarded him as an accident of democracy, pretty much as he suspected. The GBC activists, organized and led by Rouse, did well with Charles Center, but then their passion waned. Where once Rouse and the GBC had petitioned Old Tommy and shown him the way, the Schaefer-era GBCers seemed weary or unwilling to be permanent directors of what were, after all, city affairs.

Schaefer saw this weakness, but he was simultaneously in awe of the business community. His mental image of the city father was almost as dated as his image of downtown, that freeze-frame picture of retail energy pulsing on city streets. He thought of his father's pin-striped bosses, of Vernon Eney, the esteemed Piper and Marbury lawyer who, like Sondheim, epitomized high-level civic involvment. Schaefer had respect for Walter and Mr. Eney (he could never, despite constant exhortations, think of calling the man "Vernon"), but he was uncertain with the money guys.

"Rich people intimidated him. People in industry blew him away. He felt very much out of his element," thought Bailey Fine. At the same time, she said, he overcame his awe. "He didn't care how much he was intimidated. And he never showed it—an actor even then. He'd get edgy when he had a meeting with GBC guys or if he was invited to a dinner with a power player. But once he found out they could be manipulated as much as anyone else, he was better at it than they were. They thought they could use him, but in the end they got used—and loved every minute of it." The best of them did, anyway. Some went on disrespecting him even as he showed fortitude they would never display.

Young Tommy saw it, too. "He really had no success in the private sector, but in politics he was suddenly equal to, if not surpassing, some of the most successful businessmen in the community. That made him feel good. Businessmen saw that, and they catered to him. They helped him. They had a fine working relationship." As far as it went.

"He didn't know what business needed," Bernie Trueschler said. The man from BG&E worked with the mayor, but liked to hold him at arm's length.

"He was in perpetual turmoil, head-in-hands turmoil," Trueschler said. At times, he would observe the mayor of Baltimore leaning back, looking at the ceiling for long periods of time as if to say, "I'm tired of this. How long will this last?" Trueschler seemed to think Schaefer's moods were entirely involuntary, evidence of a troubled mind—certainly not a calculated strategy. The gas man seems to have missed or simply dismissed the possibility that Schaefer understood perfectly what business wanted much of the time and simply chose to provide it on his terms.

Trueschler was right, no doubt, that Schaefer's approach to running the city was project by project—another way of saying entrepreneurial. Others called it spasmodic or episodic, a stump-to-stump trip through the swamp of urban life in the 1970s and 1980s. Schaefer's approach could not be found in Wharton School textbooks, but it had the advantage of creating urgency and drama. He opposed the renewal projects in the beginning because he "thought poor," from modest origins, and didn't see at first the potential he could amass. In some respects, Baltimore business thought Schaefer deserved his inferiority complex and seemed willing to enforce it. Trueschler insisted that he made Schaefer come to him, but in time, since the mayor could deny rights of way and access to streets where their utility lines were buried, many responded to his whims excitedly. They were essentially his people, unofficial department heads equivalent to Frank Kuchta in Public Works or Marion Pines at Manpower. In Baltimore government as redefined by William Donald Schaefer, the boundary between public and private was not always easy to see. He wanted it that way.

Schaefer could rely on Baltimore businesspeople for the odd $25,000 or even $75,000 for something he was doing. He would often call someone like Trueschler, who would call a few others, and money would be found. Schaefer had the advantage then, Trueschler thought, of being broke. "Everyone knew the city had no money, so they couldn't refuse him." Not on the small stuff, at least. Trueschler could rely on competition between the corporate boardrooms, a feeling that company X or Y ought not go unrepresented in some civic endeavor. That plus the oft-spoken corporate ethic, the solemn view that business owed something to the city where it did business, made Trueschler an effective fund raiser. Yet the sums his colleagues surrendered were usually not heroic. The idea of civic responsibility expressed in this way makes one understand the meaning of the street term "chump change." Trueschler called these contributions "pin money," withdrawals from petty cash—nickels and dimes cast upon the muncipal landscape to buy peace from the cranky man in city hall. If the city's needs were larger, as when bankers were needed to invest in a hotel or to hang onto the city's baseball team, the doors were often closed. They would rally to save the Baltimore Symphony Orchestra but Schaefer knew he could not count on Baltimore businesspeople or Baltimore banks to risk real money on the pivotal projects of his renaissance.

Schaefer liked to bring businessmen into his Ceremonial Room for lunch, make them pay for it, and then step back while Embry, Frank Kuchta, or Janet Hoffman talked about their jobs, the projects they were working on, and often how those projects helped business. C&P Telephone's Hank Butta, a Baltimore boy who had gone to school with Young Tommy, reacted the way Schaefer hoped he would. Butta had assumed no one in the city government could hold his or her own in private business. But Schaefer's people knew what they were doing.

"We asked them some nasty questions," Butta recalled. "They had the answers. They were interested in productivity. They were interested in saving money. They were interested in being under budget. Everything we were interested in." Many of these luncheon guests were also interested in having their companies involved in civic projects. C&P's Butta took care of that involvement himself, becoming one of Schaefer's most reliable volunteers and his liaison with business. A favorite of Schaefer's staff, Hank took any job Schaefer gave him, wanting to beg off but never able to say no.

"People asked me all the time, 'How can you be loyal to this guy? He loses his temper. He does the damnedest things. Why do you put up with it?' I've known the man for thirteen years. He never asks me for anything for himself. He's always asking for others—for kids, for people out of work, for high school dropouts. He never asked me for a favor. And he always had something going on in his head. Things we did were not always born in his head, but they were always stimulated by him. He wanted us to cut high school dropouts from 15,000 to 10,000 in a year. 'Don't tell me you can't. You can. You just haven't thought of how yet.'"

A Few Tough Men

The Inner Harbor efforts moved along in full public view while Schaefer struggled with the daily problems of running a city that was ever vul-

184 / WILLIAM DONALD SCHAEFER

nerable to the vicissitudes of modern life. The schools, housing construction and demolition, public safety, and solid waste disposal demanded his attention constantly. Landfill space was running out even as waste paper was becoming America's number one product. The decade saw barges dispatched from New York or New Jersey with huge cargoes of refuse looking for a place to offload.

In Baltimore, entrepreneurs, con men, and necromancers appeared at Board of Estimates meetings for the purpose of showing city officials how to deal with trash, suggesting that they could make it vanish. One of these drummers came with a vial of chemicals that, when shaken, seemed to dissolve a small bit of refuse. This could be done by the ton, he promised. Such men pressed for million-dollar city contracts, and one or two were successful. Mayors were desperate, willing to try virtually anything to rid their cities of the plastic, Styrofoam, and paper that drifted in alleyways, choked streets, overflowed street corner garbage barrels, and submerged the dumps. Schaefer threw in with an idea posited by the Monsanto Corporation, and together they built something called a pyrolysis plant just south of the city. Pyrolysis was thought to be an advance over incinerators, capable of generating power via steam, but it turned out to have serious shortcomings—and a huge price tag, not to mention embarrassment, for Schaefer and the city.

Meanwhile, the pursuit of land for dumping continued. Schaefer found himself in negotiation with Henry J. Knott, a red-haired Baltimore bricklayer who had built himself and his family into a construction dynasty. Knott spent much of his later life in great acts of philanthropy, an avocation that he never confused with business. Knott owned land in Baltimore and Anne Arundel County, just over the city line, that Baltimore thought might be used for a landfill if the necessary permits could be obtained. Benton began negotiations to buy the property. Knott wanted $16,000 an acre, a steep price for otherwise useless land—a quarry—whose highest and best use then seemed to be as a repository for trash.

"I can't get anywhere with him," Benton told Schaefer. "Why don't you go and talk to him." A luncheon was arranged.

"How about giving me a break on this," Schaefer said.

"My price is $16,000," said Knott.

"Henry," said Schaefer, "how 'bout making me look a little bit good, like I've worked on this."

"My price is $16,000."

"How about coming down $1,000."

Silence from Knott.

"How about coming down a nickel," said the mayor.

"$16,000 an acre. Take it or leave it."

"Okay, Henry, we've got to have the property. Whatever you're price is. We've got to pay it."

Benton believes that the city could not have done better by taking Knott to court, and the paper-choked city could not wait for a lengthy trial. Baltimore paid $2.2 million for the land. Schaefer had hoped that his friend, Anne Arundel County Executive Robert Pascal, would be able to help rezone the property so that it could be used for a landfill, but that never happened. A few weeks after the purchase, though, Knott and Schaefer talked again. Wasn't Schaefer at work on a charity of some sort, a city project that needed private financial support? Knott asked. How was the fund raising going? Schaefer said he was short of his goal, whereupon, Schaefer said later, "He goes in his pocket and comes out and hands me a check for $25,000." This was a curious, if not inappropriate, exchange between a businessman and a public official—and certainly a bargain for Knott. If it was designed to salve the businessman's conscience or to make Schaefer feel less plundered, it might have worked. The unspoken deal was this: The city will pay through the nose, and I will be a benefactor down the road; you won't look good in the first instance, but later you will. In this case, if Schaefer's recollection is accurate, Knott made a huge killing in the first instance, selling Baltimore land it had to have and could not use.

Schaefer was often at the mercy of his businessmen partners in those days. He went for some high-tech solutions that blew up in his face. Benton had recommended against Monsanto's pyrolysis plant because it didn't have sufficient redundancy: If one belt shut down, the whole plant shut down. And every few months, the operation had to stop altogether to clear away the barnaclelike formations of a rock-hard substance formed by the burning. It fell to Schaefer to make a judgment about the risk. Listen to the hard-driving Berndt? Listen to the engineers from Monsanto? Go with the brilliant Benton? Schaefer had the power and peril of choosing in each case. Benton might be right about the pyrolysis technology. But what difference did that make? Maybe the process would work, and Baltimore would solve an immediate problem that was central to the city's day-to-day functioning. In this case, there was the mayor of Baltimore with a huge failure on his hands, an experiment that, however laudable, stood along the parkway as a major symbol of municipal folly and failure, the sort of stumble that reduces a leader to a laughingstock. Businessman and builder Willard Hackerman remembers a morning meeting at which Schaefer was explaining matters to the GBC.

"Monsanto had promised the world, Schaefer said. 'They're saying, "If you'll give us some more money, we'll get it started." But they couldn't get it started.' Schaefer was so down." But once again, his mood was a lever. He knew he was talking to a group of men with money and a stake in what he was doing at City Hall. Schaefer's appeals came in many forms, sometimes indirect, sometimes overt.

Hackerman took him aside after the meeting. "Look I don't know what I can do, but if I can be helpful, I'll do what I can. I don't like to see you this way."

Schaefer nodded glumly.

Hackerman sent his engineers to the plant. They got it started, but they came to the same conclusion as Benton: "They had a model as big as a coffee table, and they jumped from that to a tremendous thing. It hadn't been tested at anywhere near that size. We ran it for a year. Then it proceeded to fall apart. It was just awful."

Schaefer, though, felt that he had found a resource useful at other problem sites. He realized Hackerman could run the city's Pulaski Highway incinerator better than the city could.

The initial deal was for seven years—good for Hackerman and good for the city, Benton reckoned. Later, Hackerman wanted to add a fifth burn line at a cost of $10 million and extend the contract for thirty years. Benton advised against that one because he thought the price of dealing with trash would fall, leaving the city locked into an inflated price, but Schaefer went ahead anyway. Hackerman says he paid for the new line in the end and, he believes, provided trash disposal efficiently and at a price the city could not have matched if it had run the incinerator over that same period. Money would have been budgeted for the purpose, after all.

Hackerman, too, got out of the incinerator business in time, a fact suggesting that Benton's forecast was accurate. "It's not practical now. Landfills now are so inexpensive," Hackerman said. Neighbors thought the burning obnoxious, possibly carcinogenic, and took up the cudgels against Hackerman for years. Hackerman fought on and then, suddenly, pulled out, closing the incinerator in 1994 and eventually giving the property to the neighborhood for cleanup and redevelopment.

The Big Picture Mayor

Schaefer was certain now that he understood the bigger picture and would have been able to convince people who thought of themselves as victims of City Hall that he, William Donald Schaefer, would never abuse them unless it was necessary for the greater good. Increasingly, he was certain he knew his plans embodied that utilitarian ideal, and he never failed to assert his convictions. He was not looking for consensus. He could become the force he was in part because he had no competition, public or private. Unlike many U.S. cities, Baltimore had no jealous and overbearing private power structure, no group of entrenched CEOs who wanted to run the city from offstage. With the exception, perhaps, of Mercantile Bank's Baldwin, no one wanted to bother with politics. So when cities stopped having quite the function they had early in the century, Baltimore lacked institutional stability and purpose even more than most.

"The establishment of Baltimore has been — not weak — but it just hasn't cared much," said Charlie Duff, the scholarly neighborhood development professional at Jubilee Baltimore. "Even the GBC, which led on Charles Center, was not so much a Baltimore establishment group as it was a center city neighborhood organization oddly in keeping with Schaefer's view of Baltimore. Tommy the Elder saw the potential of the Charles Center effort and Walter Sondheim held it together."

What Baltimore had as structure in the last half of the twentieth century was Jewish philanthropy, a corps of bright young doers, and men like the saintly Sondheim, who had become a lifelong dollar-a-year man, a bridge between the cantankerous Schaefer and the men of business who looked down on the field of battle, involving themselves timidly or not at all. No wonder, then, that Schaefer revered Kovens, who was always there to solve problems, to raise money for his campaigns, and to whip private or public opponents into shape behind him. Rouse lamented the power of the machines, with justification. But in a sense, the clubhouses, the men and women of the neighborhoods, were the only power structure the city had — yet another reason for Schaefer to honor their needs.

After he was defeated by Mikulski and the other anti-Road warriors, the proud mayor of Baltimore agreed to make peace with Mikulski and all of his opponents, including Duff's father, who was then president of the Fells Point–Federal Hill Improvement Association. They all met at the foot of Broadway to bury the hatchet. A boy then, Duff came with a gold-plated Boy Scout hatchet and happily covered it with dirt.

"He became a friend of those neighborhoods. He was ruthlessly pragmatic in the sense that he would subordinate his own ego. They were neighborhoods that might do something to help him, so he wanted to make peace," Duff said.

Perpetual Turmoil

This was not to say that the managerial class did not participate in civic affairs. Top leaders in the phone company, the gas and electric company, and the banks were involved in many aspects of city life. None were more involved than the men at Baltimore Gas & Electric. One of its chairmen, Charles P. Crane, had been chairman of the Association of Commerce, a precursor of the GBC, which he also chaired for a time, and head of the Convention Bureau. Known as Skipper, he was a promoter of the Port of Baltimore, having produced several studies of how it could be reclaimed. He had a profound influence on the life of the city, not just because his company supplied power, light, and heat to its residents but also because he felt that his business demanded active participation in governmental and civic affairs. He saw no difference between the two aspects of his life.

One year, when Mandel was governor, he called Crane for help with the democratic process: repairing the voting machines, to be precise. "Gentlemen," said Crane, "I have a new job, and therefore you have a new job. It's to repair and put back on the street and rebuild the reputation of the board of supervisors of elections before the next election." The machines were back in working order between the September primary and November general election day.

Of course, the company benefited from being so involved. When their nuclear reactors at Calvert Cliffs fell under scrutiny from regulators in Washington, it helped BGE to look like a pillar of the Maryland community. When their men neglected to hook up meters at state office buildings, essentially giving the state free power for five years—past the statute of limitations for claiming payment—all the civic good works were bankable: Schaefer and the legislature paid the $3 million BGE would have collected had someone not erred. Others would be out of luck, but the gas men had clout.

The relationship was mutually beneficial. "When we had a real need to see him, an electric or a gas emergency, we were able to see him. And he had us involved in his projects up to our eyeballs. He was a firehose of ideas. If he needed help, Trueschler would send him help," said George Gephardt, then a junior executive with the company.

BGE sent Schaefer an expert on warehousing, and when the city's water billing system failed, the people who went down to straighten it out were from BGE's collection and credit department. The water-metering system that Baltimore knows now is a creation of those volunteers.

But the city's business leaders were as timid as any Baltimorean in these days, unwilling to risk real money on anything—the Orioles, for example.

Mr. Williams

In early 1979, Jerry Hoffberger, a beer baron and owner of Baltimore's excellent baseball team, decided to sell the O's. Schaefer and others instantly worried that it would go out of local ownership—and out of the city.

Schaefer appointed two stockbrokers, F. Barton Harvey and W. Wallace Lanahan, to head a committee that would seek local investors to buy the team. They failed. Some said it was because they, themselves, did not invest significantly. Others said there was a squabble over control. In the end, the Baltimore money men weren't willing to take a risk, didn't see much future in baseball and more than "pin money" was needed to save the team. These men and others like them often raised millions for the symphony—but for baseball they didn't see the same urgency or potential.

In time, though, a buyer for the Orioles was found: the famous Washington lawyer Edward Bennett Williams, then a part owner of the Washington Redskins and a man who loved the sporting life. Williams had developed his own credo from the playing fields of Holy Cross, his alma mater, and RFK Stadium: He thought of everything he did as "competitive living." Every day brought a game to win or to lose but always to relish.

When Williams called it competitive living and when he came to Baltimore, Schaefer was absolutely certain he would take the O's to Washington, which had no baseball team. A man like Williams would want to add something his adopted home city wanted desperately: major league baseball. How could the nation's capital be without it?

Williams insisted that he would stay as long as the team was supported by the city and its fans. When he arrived, that condition was a worrisome one that might well have allowed him to leave in short order. Baltimore had failed to support the Orioles even when the team was the best in baseball, winning pennant after pennant, boasting the game's best talent, and playing before sparse crowds.

Williams had played to Schaefer's strength. The mayor made sure the new owner wasn't disappointed. He fired up a classic Schaeferian assault team, calling it the Designated Hitters. It consisted of business men and women who were dispatched to sell season ticket packages just as they had sold the City Fair and one hundred other city projects. Admissions and season ticket sales spiked upward.

Schaefer knew that he could not count on Williams. He knew he would have to handle the owner with extreme care and sensitivity. The two men had begun their relationship by directing every bit of their talents toward controlling each other. Williams started agitating for concessions from the very first moment after he bought the team: Fans from Washington couldn't find the park on 33rd Street, he complained. It took too long to get out of the city.

Support would have to include a new stadium, he began to suggest. To show his determination to get one, he insisted on a series of short-term leases for venerable old Memorial Stadium, leaving Schaefer and his impoverished city to wonder how a new one could be paid for. This was Baltimore, after all. Williams was making a brilliant bargain, one he couldn't lose. He would get a new stadium at no cost to him or be free to relocate and be a hero in D.C. Schaefer was sure which outcome Williams wanted more. "There wasn't any question in my mind, and I don't think there was any question in his mind, that he was going to move the team to Washington," Schaefer said.

Everyone knew that Ed Williams was dying. He had liver cancer. Surgeons kept him going, and by force of his legendary will, he made himself seem unaffected by the disease. Still, his health left Baltimore's team in jeopardy. An urgency based on the sure knowledge that his cancer would not stay in remission forever drove every move. Williams himself seemed to rise above the prerogatives of his disease, bending it to his competitive living credo. He was an imperious, Babe Ruthian figure in the town where Ruth had been born, and he was just as likely to leave for a bigger show.

"I WILL NEVER LEAVE BALTIMORE as long as the fans support the team," Williams would say, virtually whispering the qualifier. "He always had a club," Schaefer said. Williams insisted he would "NEVER LEAVE" even if he didn't get a new stadium. The promises became something of a joke, according to Larry Lucchino, Williams' protege and law partner.

Williams put on a veil once at a political function he attended with Schaefer, looked at the mayor, and said, "What else do I need to do? I'm proposing marriage." It was the sort of public theater that Schaefer himself excelled at. Married they were, but the union had to be sealed with a new ballpark.

Williams knew his partner well, recognizing in Schaefer another colorful public actor, a man you could deal with. "Ed never did anything without thinking it through," says his biographer Evan Thomas, author of *The Man to See*. "He used to joke about rehearsing a spontaneous joke." Williams probably chuckled to his friends about the stadium coup he was engineering. Yet, Thomas said, it would be too simple to imagine that he had only a new ballpark in mind. "He was full of mixed motives. He did care about the city of Baltimore. He probably did feel sentimental about it. What was contradictory in others was consistent with Williams."

He could insist that he would be ever-faithful while refusing to sign a long-term lease, for example. "Basically," says Thomas, "Ed was trying to shake a stadium out of the state of Maryland. That's the way Ed thought."

In Baltimore, a few mannered movements always preceded any agreement on lease negotiations. Lucchino would arrive as Williams's setup man, softening the ground.

"Larry knew how to smash things up," said Schaefer. "He was the destroyer. He'd smash the silverware. He'd smash the windows. Every year, the same thing. He'd say, 'You're not giving us enough.' And when we got to a certain point, total impasse, Mr. Williams would call me. He'd say, 'Donald, meet me at the Tremont.'"

The Tremont Hotel is one of Baltimore's smaller, perched on a steep hill just down the street from the Women's Industrial Exchange, several blocks north of the Inner Harbor. It was a place to meet in privacy.

"I'd go up there. He'd go in one way. I'd go in another. We'd meet in the penthouse. We'd always have a nice dinner. Then he'd say, 'We're not getting anywhere, and it's your fault.'"

The first time Williams did this, Schaefer was rapt. He was alone in a room with a lion of the law, a famous man who had been reduced to pacing and wringing his hands, appealing to him, Don Schaefer.

"Williams would say something like 'Look at all I've done for Baltimore, and you want to take it away from me.'

"Then he said, 'This is what I want to do.'

"I said, 'Yes, sir.'
"'I want this.'
"'Yes.'
"'And this.'
"'Yes.'
"'This.'
"'Yes.'"

The mayor of Baltimore gave in on almost everything every year. As long as Baltimore had the team, its mayor would accede to the owner's demands. He did say "No," though, when Williams wanted the city to turn over a 10 percent tax on tickets.

"Can't do that," the mayor told him. "I can't. Have to have that money to maintain the place." If he couldn't keep Memorial Stadium tidy, at least, he would be unable to keep the fans—and unable to meet Williams's demand for fan support.

Schaefer began to sense when the owner's dinner invitation would come and then to wait for accusations about what Schaefer was doing to the great Williams. "I'd be sitting there trying to keep from laughing." He had little to bargain with, but he had learned something about these wealthy and powerful men, these Knotts, Pritzkers, and Williamses. They had their pride, their concepts of themselves, and Schaefer could use that if he was patient. Since his reputation was all about irrationality, impatience, and fast action, his willingness to see Edward Bennett Williams as a sort of national-level Vernon Eney allowed him to think of the famous litigator as a gentleman who would realize that Baltimore was a great place to own a team. Williams said later he found Schaefer a bit obsequious but he stayed in Schaefer's city.

Shades of Progress

Williams was a threat, but he did not drive Schaefer away from the day-to-day toil of pushing Baltimore out of its doldrums, of maintaining a sense of forward movement by the accomplishment of a thousand projects. If graffiti were the scourge of any urban landscape, Schaefer would scrub it off—and put up something in its place. He challenged, goaded, and ridiculed department heads if they couldn't find something he had found—abandoned cars, for example. He got most such derelicts off the street one summer by observing pointedly that he had seen one on the way to work—and just wondering whether anyone else had seen it. He did the same thing later with panhandlers: "Anyone know what that man or woman needs? That panhandler?" If anyone asked him which panhandler, he stared back as if to say, "All of them. Find out if we can help." Some people, he concluded, wanted to be on the street and homeless, but he wanted to ask each one for an accounting.

Cabinet members and department heads scrambled personally and recruited their minions to address his incessant, "impossible" demands. One of these diligent workers was Randy Evans, a refulgently mustachioed middle manager in the housing department in the late 1970s. Evans came to Schaefer's attention because a dilapidated house on Lancaster Street in the trendy old port district called Fells Point languished without the attention it needed in Schaefer's view. After driving by that house—he was always driving by something—Schaefer had Fawley stop at a pay phone. He called Evans.

"I want that house fixed by morning," the mayor said.

Evans sat for a moment and thought—not what a jerk he was working for but "What am I going to do?"

Low-level panic led him to an answer, lame as it may have seemed. He went to the Sears store on North Avenue and bought curtains, curtain rods, and shades. And he ordered a sign that read, "Renovations by William Donald Schaefer and the Citizens of Baltimore." The next morning at 7:00 A.M. he and another housing department worker went to the house to put up the curtains. On the second floor, one man stood on the other's shoulders to reach the windows because the floorboards beneath them were rotted through. When they finished, they propped up the sign and left. Schaefer called an hour later.

"Nice work," said the mayor.

"That," said Evans, "is when I became one of those people who heard what he said, knew it was unreasonable, and went and did something anyway."

Nothing may have symbolized the nature of the struggle more completely than Evans's gambit on Lancaster Street. The entire city was standing on someone's shoulders, it seemed. Schaefer conceded later that much of what was done in these early years relied on sleight of hand, camouflage, and facades of change when real change was not possible immediately. He needed holding actions while he arranged real accomplishments. If these were Emperor Schaefer's clothes, he expected his own troops to pretend that his city looked splendid—not because it did, but because any other attitude would have been too depressing to bear.

Reinventing Main Street

On July 1, 1980, Schaefer and Rouse stood on a special platform like generals reviewing troops. Cannons boomed, trumpets blared, anthems soared, and bagpipes skirled in honor of Harborplace on its opening day. The *Sun* called it a day of jubilation for Rouse and Schaefer "whose joint confidence in Baltimore's vitality was so vividly expressed in the spectacular marketplace." Scanning a horizon that was filling up with renaissance projects, the writer observed that "one change has led to another and another until anything and everything is possible in the upward surge of Baltimore renewal." For this new beginning, Baltimore had turned back to the water, the source of its original strength. Robbed by trucks and airplanes of its reason for being—seaports having been largely supplanted by airports—Baltimore had repackaged itself against all odds. Rouse's Harborplace would now become not just a new tile in the commercial mosaic, but the center of the mosaic, a new Main Street for visitors from the surrounding counties and for a nation of conventioneers in search of space to display their products.

Some said that Harborplace guaranteed the death of the old center, the Lexington and Howard axis so revered by the mayor. He hoped to go back to that corner in time with a developer and a plan that would confer rebirth there as well. As much as Schaefer saw the limits of renewal in Charles Center, he wanted to try something like it along Lexington Street. The new subway stop, the new Social Security complex, and other efforts could bring it back, he thought, and forge a link with the new harbor attraction. The undertow of suburbia continued to pull residents away, of course, mocking everything he and Rouse did to restore the glory of downtown. Yet, on this day, they were a glorious union of government and private enterprise, of idea and action, vision and will, style and substance. They had imagined this place, willed it into existence, teased and coaxed and wheedled it to life. As always, the mayor thanked his predecessors, the Tommies and McKeldin. In other moments, he pointed to the German General and to neighborhood activists like Frank Novak of Harbel and Lucille Gorham of the East Side.

Harborplace was the pinnacle of Schaefer's furious pace, his project-driven, fifteen-year mayoralty. The Rouse Company's two shedlike buildings at the harbor's edge with their soft green roofs invited the city and its guests to sit for a moment over a cookie or an iced tea, to relax and let the watery foreground wash away their cares. When pressed later about priorities, about putting all the public money into this single project, Schaefer sometimes argued that Harborplace was, after all, just another city neighborhood. This was too glib, of course, yet the place did have a relaxed feel to it—like Baltimore.

Back in city hall after this day of adulation, much of it carefully orchestrated by his staff, Schaefer heard more congratulation than he could stand. "You must feel fantastic," Lainy LeBow said to him. He didn't. Praise made him anxious. It led to complacency, to a reduced sense of urgency. He had seen what had happened after completion of Charles Center, a splendid achievement that almost instantly had become an abstraction beyond the planners, developers, and city officials who had made it happen, a label for something most Baltimoreans could not define or describe. Some twenty-two downtown acres had been razed and rebuilt, a triumph of planning and design, a smashing victory of renewal over blight, according to the experts who lavished awards on its architects. As if a description would make it reality, they called it an integrated, "people-friendly" creation that would bring apartment dwellers and suburbanites to shop-filled streets. But in time, Charles Center demonstrated the difference between physical renewal and real-life renewal. New did not always mean lively. The women who wore gloves while they shopped at Stewarts did not return. Charles Center had been planned for the Baltimore of the 1950s. That city could not be reclaimed. Now the city had Harborplace, but Schaefer knew that the new pavilions would not be enough. He was competing with decay and with other cities that had plans for their own waterfronts.

He cocked his head and contorted his face into a hard, disapproving scowl. "That's done. It's old news. Every city will have something just like it. What're we going to do now?"

The Golden Age of Cities

Democrats and fear of riots had won billions for Baltimore and other U.S. cities in revenue-sharing dollars, manpower development funds, community development block grants, and the like. Baltimore did better than some cities because it marketed itself in Washington as a laboratory for HUD and other agencies. Policy makers, if so disposed, could travel thirty-five miles north to Baltimore to see how their ideas were working. "We knew how to spend the money," Schaefer said, as if spending well could ever again be seen as a virtue. At one point, he and his green eyeshade guys were caught arbitraging with federal money, putting it in the bank and earning enough interest to manage a few small projects—or big ones, if the practice had been allowed to continue.

He was right about his management and spending proficiency. He had one of the best public housing administrations in the nation. He had a model manpower program under Marion Pines, one of the many whiz kids who were thoroughly devoted to him. Federal, state, and local governments worked together in a textbook demonstration of federalism, a term that become obsolescent in the 1990s as Washington turned responsibilities over to the states. Though federalism sometimes seemed inefficient and disjointed at the time, it worked as well as might ever have been possible in a system that doles out control in four-year increments. It was McKeldin who had first proposed tearing out the old piers, evicting the rats, and building something new, but he had had only four years to supervise that work and envision the future, and those were his declining years. Schaefer arrived, thanks to the dreaded scalawags, with precisely the right talents to complete the work of McKeldin and the Tommies.

The Shadow

But there were limits to the magic that Rouse and Benton and even government treasuries could work. Benton and Schaefer bridled at the parsimony of Baltimore business and the shrinking federal presence. For a few years, they had received millions of federal dollars for housing, for job training, and for general purposes, but the city's taxable property base, after showing some signs of growth, was narrowing. At $6 per $100 of value, Baltimore taxpayers were giving about as much as they could be asked for—double the rate paid by homeowners in surrounding counties. Yet Schaefer was constantly in need of money to do the projects that trundled along tantalizingly before him. Even when he could justify asking the citizens to approve a huge loan, he first had to get the matter approved by the city council, put it on the election ballot, and sometimes wage a high-intensity campaign for passage. These bond issues had to be presented to the voters at a political remove, lest the mayor appear to be thrusting his hand into the taxpayers' pockets even more aggressively and often.

In time, though, Benton came to Schaefer with a method by which the city could virtually create money: What if the city could create tax savings? These would be of no direct value to the city, which, of course, paid no taxes. But if deals were structured adroitly, federal tax savings could make them work. For every glittering project like the World Trade Center, Schaefer had a dozen smaller ones that were ready to be launched if only the money could be found. (When Schaefer's fifteen-year-stay in city hall ended, his staff filled 1,400 large packing boxes with the records of projects undertaken, projects proposed, and rejected.) Benton could find it. Not everything was UDAG-worthy or UDAG-scale and the local banks continued to play their game conservatively, so Schaefer and Benton, venturing out onto the ledge of creative financing, formed their own bank. Jacques Schlenger, a partner in one of the city's most esteemed law firms, Venable, Baetjer and Howard, provided some of the thinking that framed up the banking house of Benton and Schaefer. Learning of Benton's new role, savvy local lawyers came to him with ideas for financing projects. Benton and the city's treasurer, Larry Daley, pursuant to legal agreements written by the city's law department, transformed themselves into the equivalent of bankers as the need arose. They became trustees of the Loan and Guarantee Fund and, later, simply the trustees. At the same time, simultaneously, no doubt, the two found opportunities for making deals using a constellation of quasi-public bodies—obscure city agencies that could be public or private as financial circumstances and the law dictated. The city could do things that private entities could not and vice versa. The trustees and their agencies began to make marginal or high-risk projects, projects the banks would not touch, seem doable. With the proper agreements drafted, Benton and Daley gave Schaefer things he coveted: new money, speed and flexibility, advantages that would not be available to them if they confined themselves to activities that were strictly in conformity with the city's charter.

The trustees and agencies and the agreements were insinuated into the daily and weekly business of the city, introduced without fanfare or definition via the turgid and mechanical actions of the five-member Board of Estimates, which wrote the contracts and paid the bills for city business. With at least three of the votes on this board in his pocket, Schaefer *was* the Board of Estimates. In time, Benton and Daley were managing loans totaling more $100 million. Daley once made a study of the projects he was responsible for and recoiled at their scope and complexity.

They learned that they could sell city property and then lease it back under terms that essentially changed nothing as to real ownership. The agreements held that when the lease expired, the city regained full ownership of the building. Using one or more half-city, half-public agencies, the trustees borrowed the value of the building and paid back the loan-purchase price at terms profitable for the buyer, who could use the tax advantages of owning the building—advantages the city had essentially transferred to him.

Baltimore's new bankers were far more daring and creative than the average man or woman in a chalk-striped suit. With Schaefer's blessing, they took money that had been borrowed to provide low- and moderate-income mortgages and started Coldspring, a new town in town that became one of the signature renaissance projects. The city was bringing in Moshe Safdie, an Israeli architect fresh from well-chronicled success at the World's Fair in Montreal, to design the hill-hanging buildings in the northwest quadrant of the city. For Schaefer, it was another project to demonstrate the city's vibrancy.

What amounted to diversion of public money—raised for one purpose and diverted to another—occurred out of the general public view, even though it was included on the Board of Estimates agenda. These maneuvers were often handled in what amounted to secrecy. Here was Schaefer following Richard Daley's directions: Do it and then let them try to get the money back. The city's purchase of the dump site from Henry Knott illustrated the convoluted processes that Benton devised and managed. To buy the land for $2.1 million, the city handed over a $1 million down payment and agreed to installments of $8,755 a month over thirty years, making the real cost of the land $4,151,800. Benton said that the city paid Knott $16,000 an acre because an adjoining landowner had won a judgment of $25,000 an acre. In time, the city would appeal that judgment and prevail, paying $8,000 an acre, half what was paid to Knott, who insisted not only on his price but on selling the entire piece of land on the theory that the remaining piece in Anne Arundel County would be of no value if a dump were actually situated just over the city line. In this case, speed and flexibility may have led to a loss of taxpayer money—and unnecessary enrichment of the already wealthy Knott. If the city was truly in desperate straits, it had every obligation to be certain that the land it was buying would help to solve its problem. But Schaefer did not believe he needed to answer any of the questions about process that might be raised by transactions such as this one. He was an honest man. Period. People who insisted on process were enemies of progress.

"Henry Knott," Schaefer said, "is a truly philanthropic individual. . . . But he is truly the toughest businessman I have ever met. He fights for every penny. You'd think he didn't have a penny to his name." It was after this event that Knott arrived in Schaefer's office with the $25,000 check for one of Schaefer's projects. For his part, Knott said of the land in 1980: "They condemned it. I wish to hell they hadn't. I'd take it back tomorrow if they want to sell."

Creative financing was also at work in the incinerator deal worked out by Willard Hackerman. "They were trying to get more money for the kitty—for the phantom, the Shadow, that kitty they had," Hackerman said, "so they offered to sell me the Pulaski Highway incinerator." Here, Benton and Schaefer accomplished two goals. They found money for projects, and they shifted responsibility for trash to Hackerman. Benton says that the city transferred the incinerator under a sale-and-leaseback agreement, a financing arrangement in which the city got immediate cash and then, via fees and lease payments, bought back the municipal property it had sold. Hackerman thought of it as a sale, period.

Even before the Baltimore *Sun* wrote an eight-day, twenty-two-article series in April 1980, to describe the scope of hidden trustee operations, calling them "the Shadow Government," Schaefer's old housing mentor and founder of CPHA, Frances Froelicher, began to notice changes in his method of governing. He had grown more comfortable with operating in secret, she thought, avoiding formation of committees that would give citizens a say in public policy making. "Schaefer believes that he does not particularly need advisory commissions because he has been a member of the city council and in government for many years. . . . I think he feels he doesn't want to be bothered with citizens' committees because he has listened to all that in the past. He is in power right now and he wants to accomplish what he has wanted to accomplish all these years."

Schaefer's style by then had diverged markedly—and lamentably, Froelicher thought—from the CPHA's philosophy. "It does not strengthen democracy," she said. He had abolished the Mayor's Advisory Committee on Equal Rights in Education, a panel her husband had served on. "Schaefer really didn't want that kind of input. I think with all of his experience, he thinks he knows what's best for us. We're very fortunate to have him, but it's a different philosophy."

Riposte

Schaefer wailed about the newspaper stories, accusing reporters of calling him a thief. No such accusation was made, but Schaefer was engaging in an old political ruse: Erect a straw man—a false charge—and prove it untrue, ignoring the real issue if possible. Since the world thought honesty a hallmark of Schaefer's public life, he could win the day as long as no one focused on the cost of loose and undemocratic operations in city hall, on the favoritism in contract awards that went along with secret operations, or on the hard bargaining of businesspeople. Yet he could not deny that a central feature of his 1971 "Where I Stand" blueprint had been housing assistance for the middle class, money he had provided as promised and then diverted to the construction of Coldspring. This is what Froelicher had in mind: the actions of a man who had decided he no longer always needed the advice and consent of the governed.

A day or so after the final story in the *Sun* series was published, Schaefer attended the GBC's annual meeting but delayed his appearance until the end. All of a sudden, he emerged from a curtain behind the speaker's lectern in a flowing black cape and wide-brimmed black hat, the Shadow Government personified. He stood silently as the crowd slowly got the point. Then, with a flourish of his right arm, he swept the cape up and over his eyes. His audience was laughing uproariously by now, partly at his stunt and partly because businesspeople too hated to find their operations unfurled for public view. If any of them had been disadvantaged by the trustees' operations, they knew they had little to gain by complaining. If they stayed quiet, on the other hand, they too might have a turn at the trustees' bank.

Schaefer had allowed his demand for speed to authorize expenditure of money he might not have spent had he been more patient and if his

staff had been as good as he always said it was. Asked whether he had
any concern about the size of the city's development bank or the way it
was managed, Schaefer said he didn't—and wanted no part of a charter
reform movement either. The charter might then have become a strait-
jacket; as it was, it granted him tremendous power, and he did not wish
to see that diluted in any way. What he wanted was more power, as he
had from the start. His defense, given full display in the final day of the
Sun series, was persuasive as far as it went:

> "Yeah," he said, "we could bring the trustees under the charter and
> then we're right back where we were. We can hold up movement.
> As far as the first part of the question, undemocratic? No matter
> what you do, you're wrong. If you sit still and you come up with an
> innovative idea, the innovative idea is wrong. If you come up with
> an innovative idea that didn't work, you're wrong. If you come up
> with an innovative idea that does work, it's the wrong process. So,
> you never can win. You just can't win. No matter what you do, in
> trying to do anything, there's always somebody who says it should-
> n't be done that way.
>
> "And you know you gotta look and ask Have we made any prog-
> ress? And, you know, we've made progress in the last eight years,
> ten years. And it wasn't sitting, waiting for the world to come to us
> and hand it to us. Because I've seen other cities who've sat and cried
> and never came up with an idea in their lives. I could sit here and
> say, 'Oh, no. We've got to make sure that we don't do any thing
> unusual.' Stay absolutely within the pattern and we would still have,
> down at the Inner Harbor, a nice rat-infested place, the neighbor-
> hoods would be the way they were fifteen years ago."

The press, he said, was on his case with extraordinary resources. "No
other industry in the United States is watched like the city of Baltimore
and the state of Maryland and the federal government. No other industry is watched the way we're watched. We've got three dailies, twelve or
fifteen radios, three television stations, all watching us to see that we
don't do anything wrong."

When it was suggested that his was not an industry but a government,
Schaefer said, "Oh, we're an industry. Don't fool yourself. We're as much
of an industry as you are. We're as much of an industry and we're a corporation the way you are. Only, our clients are you." Schaefer continued
to rail about the Shadow Government stories and occasionally signed his

notes "The Shadow." He conceded privately to Jeff Valentine, an *Evening Sun* reporter, that his operation had gotten a bit out of control, but he was pleased when the National League of Cities put out a booklet for other mayors, showing how they could form their own shadow governments.

Willard

While he and his wife were at the beach in the summer of 1984, Willard Hackerman read a newspaper article about a plan to buy one of the mansions on Mount Vernon and turn it into a bed and breakfast. Schaefer and Marion Pines, who was by then head of the city's housing department, opposed that idea. They wanted to preserve the square as a historic and artistic—not a commercial or tourist center. Pines had gone so far as to stop an application for federal assistance with the conversion. Hackerman called Pines and said, "I think my wife and I will buy the mansion and give it to the city."

"I think I'm going to faint," Pines said.

A few weeks later, Hackerman walked into Schaefer's office and asked him whether he still wanted the building. Sure, said the mayor. Hackerman handed him "one of those big goddamned keys." He had paid $1 million for the house, which Schaefer eventually conveyed to the Walters Art Gallery, which supervised its conversion to a restaurant and offices connected to the gallery.

Hackerman's generosity was, to some extent, a product of Schaefer's. His company, which was fabulously successful all over the United States, had built the Convention Center at a Schaeferian pace. "He told me the Sons of Italy convention was going to be there when it was finished. I was concerned we might not be done in time, so I wrote '168' in large numerals on one of the walls. The construction manager said, 'What is that?' I said it's the number of hours in a week. As far as I'm concerned you can work every hour. Just get finished for the Sons of Italy."

Hackerman also built Harborplace, the National Aquarium, and other renaissance buildings. And in April, 1991, he sold the state a warehouse it needed for Camden Yards. "They condemned it. We challenged the award [the price the state wanted to pay for taking the property]. We settled:" for $11 million. He and a partner had paid $4.6 million in 1983.

Critics say that Hackerman made a killing. He said he didn't remember how much he'd made. "They couldn't have finished the project without the building, and they made marvelous use of it," he said. He shared that success with the city. One year he mediated a labor dispute between the Baltimore Symphony and its musicians, throwing in a few dollars of his own to make the agreement work. As with Treuschler, Pines or Schaefer could call Hackerman with virtually any request, and he would say yes.

When Schaefer became governor, Hackerman went to see him about money for a new oncology center at the Johns Hopkins Hospital, where the contractor was a member of the board. "We needed $100 million. Schaefer said, 'Okay, I'll give you $33 million.' Then the recession hit, and he said 'I can only give you $16 million. That's all I've got. That's all I can give you. I just don't have the money.' I guess I was a little persistent, so he walked out of his office and left me standing there. 'I just don't have the money,' he said as he went by me. 'If you don't believe me, ask Charlie.' I went over and talked to Benton. He said some of the capital projects were coming in a little cheaper because of the competition during the recession. So at the next cabinet meeting, Schaefer said, 'I told Hackerman we didn't have any money and you said we did.' The state's share went up to $30 million from $16 million."

Hackerman was helping out too. He took Henry Knott to lunch, and the two of them outspent the state of Maryland. "We got our contribution number up to $40.5 million," Hackerman said.

Rain Forest

Without Benton, Schaefer might have run aground on the financial shoals early on. Benton's handiwork lay within the ledgers of every city project, and perhaps no one but he had a real idea of how heavy his hand had been. "I think," said one of his contemporaries, "that anything Charlie left was okay, clean and proper. I also think that often, before he left, things were not in order." If he finagled the books, taking money that had been voted for one purpose and washing it bureaucratically for use in another project, or engaged in minor league arbitraging, investing federal government money and taking the interest for local uses, a prohibited practice, he knew how to retrace his steps or how to have those steps blessed by Schaefer and the Board of Estimates. After the city's accountant, Daniel Paul, discovered these practices and brought them to the attention of federal officials, Daniel Paul became the ex–city accountant. After another deal with Henry Knott, in which the city made valuable financial concessions, Benton insisted that all of what he and Knott had done was approved by the authorities. Benton was unrepentant. "I avoid the Board of Estimates," he said, "like the plague."

Schaefer depended on—and watched closely—his man with a green eyeshade. If Benton gave him a stack of papers to sign, Schaefer said once, he signed them carefully, reading each document as it came to the top of the pile, just to make sure. For the most part, though, Benton was seeing him through, as Schaefer had predicted in 1971, and seeing him through the most important projects, the ones that led to the term "renaissance."

In early 1980, with the aquarium headed toward completion, reality threatened yet again to undermine vision. Money was almost always a problem in any publicly financed job as costs in the marketplace tended to creep past prices established by competitive bidding. If a building turned out drab and uninspiring, the fault could often be traced to lack of money for a more adventurous design. Schaefer knew this dynamic as well as anyone, but he was determined to give his aquarium a crowning innovation. It would feature not only an angular geometric design of glassed-in shark tanks and aquatic habitat, but also a roof-level exhibition of tropical vegetation and exotic birds: a rain forest in Baltimore. Other cities had aquariums, after all. Hadn't he borrowed the idea from Kevin White in Boston? So even if Baltimore's was bigger, better, and newer, it needed something special to make it unique. As frequently happened, Schaefer argued with his own team to keep the project alive in its original form.

"I want a rain forest more than anything else. It's going to be spectacular. We have to be imaginative. I'd almost rather have that rain forest up there and nothing underneath it," he told his aides. But shortly after construction started, the usual reports of cost overruns began to arrive. The aquarium's board of directors, the architects, and the construction bosses came to Schaefer's door.

"I know what you're going to say," he told them. "You're going to say we can't have the rain forest. I don't give a damn."

"But we don't have enough money. We have to cut back on something," they told him.

Fine, he said, but he left them with a cautionary prediction: "I'll tell you what you're going to cut back on. You're going to cut back on the rain forest."

They came back with precisely that recommendation.

"Well, you can go soak your head in shit," he told them, "because you're not going to cut that rain forest." It was part of the momentum he needed.

The aquarium had to be spectacular, exciting. A Roman circus, people began to say. Yes, Schaefer would have shouted in reply. Yes! We do absolutely want to entertain the citizens — distract them from whatever bad feelings they have about their city.

Benton helped to save the rain forest by finding another way to pay for seats in the building's auditorium. The project's numbers were working, and although the building would be late in opening, that would become an advantage.

The Man in the Seal Pool

Schaefer had cavorted with goofy hats — or made regular hats seem goofy — for so long that Baltimoreans stopped thinking it was odd. He wore a pith helmet and held a raven to celebrate Baltimore's claim that Edgar Allan Poe, who died in the city, was a native son. He put flowers with flowing ribbons on his head during the annual Mount Vernon Flower Mart. He wore straw boaters and baseball hats, snap-brims and fedoras, even a tank commander's hat with earflaps. He peered from the turret of a tank and managed to look military — or at least not silly. When Governor Michael Dukakis, running for president in 1988, allowed himself to be photographed in the same headgear, he looked like *Mad* magazine's cartoon character Alfred E. Neuman. A columnist newly arrived at the Baltimore *Sun* from Chicago remarked with awe and admiration that Schaefer was violating — and prospering by violating — a cardinal rule of politics: Never wear silly hats.

The hats were not all goofy by themselves, but paired with his head and his facial expressions, they gave him the appearance of the deadpan comic Bert Lahr or a more manic version of Charlie Chaplin. The effect went beyond high jinks for the cameras. Joanne McQuade, the master of chores who may have saved his life during the city hall shooting in 1976, said that Schaefer was a "great changer of hat" — a man whose moods, mannerisms, and expressions were changing along with his hats, all to his great political benefit. He reached the apex of his acting and hat-wearing talents during the inauguration of Baltimore's new aquarium.

In the frigid days of January 1981, Schaefer had sentenced himself to a public dunking. At a morning meeting with reporters, ignoring the advice of his handlers, he had hurled another of his surprise declarations. Referring to the aquarium, he said, "If that goddamned thing is not open on time, I'll jump in the shark tank." "Shark" would be amended to "seal" in time, but at first the promise was just a joke anyway. Everything with Schaefer was instinct, opportunity, and action. The National Aquarium in Baltimore was to open on July 1 of that year, a deadline with real significance: As soon as the fish went on display, the city would begin to collect admission fees of at least $250,000 a month, money it desperately needed. But Schaefer insisted that the attraction had to be "first class, first day." The people movers had to work perfectly, and the filtration system had to be flawless to avoid the humiliation—and bad PR—of visitors marooned between exhibits, fish dead in their shimmering new habitats.

Schedule and quality inevitably came into conflict, and when news organizations began to ask whether Schaefer would follow through on his promise, certain opportunities occurred to the mayor and his city hall team of idea generators, promoters, and flacks. In late May, his press secretary, Chris Hartman, told a reporter he didn't know whether the mayor was still committed to the swim. "I can't confirm it," he said, "but I have noticed him looking through swimwear catalogues." The mayor's driver picked up a selection of bathing suits from a theatrical costumer near City Hall. Schaefer spread them out on a table in his office. "We chose the most outrageous one," Hartman said. People started sending things to Schaefer: a straw hat, a cane, some bathtub toys. Hilda Mae threw in another ducky. Also, Hartman said, Schaefer had been seen padding around his private city hall office in beach clogs.

How refreshing it was, the *Washington Post* editorialized as the event approached, that some politicians were willing to keep their word even if they might look foolish in doing so. Calls came from curious reporters in Los Angeles, Detroit, Phoenix, Washington, New York. Some thousands of dollars in free publicity were about to offset lost aquarium gate receipts and promote this new Baltimore attraction for tourists and convention planners throughout the country. Schaefer was using failure—even faking failure—to make a splash.

An eloquent statement of Schaefer's strength and of Bereska's brilliant, compulsive staffwork lay just below the water's surface. "How will the mayor get in the water?" she alone had asked. "Will he dive? Will he jump? Will he sit down and ease his little tushy into the water?" Steps, she thought, hidden steps. That was the answer. Here was the majordomo thinking ahead, as she always did, about how the boss would actually do the things he did. At her direction, a city policeman built some steps.

So at midday on July 15, 1981, not far from Baltimore's business district, while bankers and clerks, cops and construction workers paused for lunch, Schaefer stepped into the bright summer sunlight wearing a bathrobe and a straw hat. In his right hand, he carried a plastic ducky; in his left, a white walking cane. The city's about-to-be-opened National Aquarium, its World Trade Center, and the sparkling pavilions of Harborplace rose all around him at the city's Inner Harbor. Blinking a bit against the glare, the mayor pulled several more duckies from the pockets of his zebra-striped robe. Then he tottered down a red carpet to the edge of the Aquarium's outdoor seal pool and dropped his toys into the water. He stepped out of the robe, and there he stood, resplendent in a red-and-yellow striped Victorian swimsuit, featuring elbow-length sleeves and trunks reaching nearly to his shins.

He had come to swim with the seals, to help them inaugurate their new surroundings, and to keep his promise. He paused for a moment at the edge. No blade-thin youth, the fifty-nine-year-old swimmer nevertheless betrayed no hidden girth or knobby knees. He was a bit rakish, in fact, in his straw skimmer with its two-inch black band tilted slightly forward.

"I'm just a little fish in a big pond," Schaefer murmured as he dipped a toe in the water, testing the temperature. Then he began his descent. Down and down he went following Bereska's steps, continuing until he was completely submerged, leaving the skimmer floating above him on the surface. He bobbed quickly back into view, retrieved the hat, and set it back on his head.

"I'm a man of my word," he said as he swam toward a long-haired blonde on the rocks. "It would have been beneath my dignity to make a promise and not keep it." Dignity, indeed. He was playing it broadly now, recoiling in horror at the sight of his face reflected back from the surface of the pool. But his splashing and floundering ended as he turned toward the mermaid. He stopped to gaze blankly over his left shoulder as if to ask, Can you believe how lucky I got? Would you mind leaving while this young lady and I talk? He hoisted himself onto the rock beside her and demurely accepted a kiss on the cheek.

Then the seals, held in abeyance off stage, came waddling down the runway from the aquarium. "Over here," Schaefer hollered, as if they needed direction. "How are ya? How're ya feeling?"

With sunlight flickering off their mirrorlike black skin, they flopped into the water with the mayor of Baltimore, sliding around and under his legs, popping back to the surface, and looking at him quizzically. He confided in the crowd, brought it deftly into the act: One of the animals was the official mayor's seal—a little joke here—given to him personally by officials at the New England Aquarium in Boston. Schaefer could, of course, speak to the animals. "We had a long conversation when I was in Boston, and he couldn't wait to get here for the swim," the mayor said. "He told me our aquarium is a great one, the best one he's ever seen."

City Hall had not actually ordered the seals' participation. "Christ, these are wild animals," Hartman marveled later. "He didn't know they were coming." But Schaefer was never upstaged by man or beast, and Bereska knew that such moments, unscripted, brought out the best of the improvisational in him. You planned everything, but maybe you didn't tell him exactly what was coming. Then you got spontaneity. She had seen it work many times, exciting audiences and pleasing Schaefer. He hated the expected, the shopworn, and the tired. He wanted new—demanded it—and there were bitter recriminations when the spectacle did not please him.

Several hundred spectators, led enthusiastically by members of the city council, crowded onto a narrow adjacent pier as if drawn by the handlers of a diving mule or an escape artist who was trussed and padlocked and about to be thrown into the water like the Great Houdini. What they saw was a crowning moment in the history of American boosterism and of political leadership. Here was Schaefer selling his product, Baltimore, projecting its virtues onto national and international screens. Nearly every place in America had a man devoted to the selling of his city or town, but none was quite like Schaefer. Even in a city that was known for producing colorful leaders, he was an eclipsing figure who reinvented the public office closest to the people. Schaefer was the politician as conjurer, willful and insistent, a man whose antics and successes set him apart. At the same time, he was nearly a man out of time, as though he actually hailed from an era in which his outfit would not have seemed so quaintly zany. He was a throwback forging toward a future that some could not imagine or accept.

More Baltimoreans might have turned out for the big dip if they had not become so accustomed to such performances. The usual claque of local reporters came, of course, and they were joined by network camera crews, including one from *Good Morning America,* and someone from the international photo service Gamma. Two national magazines dispatched writers.

What the outside media saw was high purpose and near-buffoonery in exquisite balance as Schaefer reached the zenith of his public acting career. Everything else had been but a prologue for this grand moment.

He had posed as a ballet dancer and as H. L. Mencken and Edgar Allan Poe (sons of Baltimore, like himself). He had allowed a baseball team's mascot, the San Diego Padres' chicken, to put its spatula-shaped lips around his balding head. He had swaddled himself in a diaper to promote child care. It was water this time, but Schaefer took his parts where he found them. Almost no one would have cast him in the roles he chose, but he seemed able to make any part plausible, any venue hospitable. He could swim with seals, with pols, with the wealthy and well-born, with intellectuals and ward bosses and presidents. He was shy and awkward but playing the lead. If he could risk ridicule and maintain his dignity, if he was married to Baltimore as people had begun to say, maybe there was something to his claim that Baltimore was best.

Out of the water finally and back in his business suit, the mayor of Baltimore walked in his odd, Chaplinesque way toward city hall, receiving the plaudits of his people, most of whom knew of the dip.

"Did you go swimming today?" asked a worker in a yellow hard hat.

"Yep," said the mayor.

"Did you go skinny dipping?"

"Nooo." There was a limit even for this mayor, though the people of his city were never sure just what it was.

This was odd, of course, for a man so preternaturally shy and unsure of himself.

"He felt pretty good about it," Hartman says. "You know when you've hit a home run." But was the performance a little too good? Schaefer worried immediately, as always. What sort of legacy was he creating for himself? He knew he was precariously balanced between a promotional push that would send him toward greater eminence or into a zone of vulnerability, unprotected by the popular view that his efforts, however loony, were put forth in the public interest. In July 1981 and for years afterward, nothing but plaudits reached his ears. He had made a splash heard 'round the world. He had generated publicity for his city. His newspaper-clipping service sent along accounts of his plunge from China, Japan, Romania, Bulgaria, Italy, and many other countries.

Some enterprising soul took one of the photos and made a poster out of it, using a picture of Schaefer descending into the water. He didn't much like it and predicted that no one else would either. He was wrong, of course, but his misjudgment might have been caused by his hope that the image would have a limited life span. That year, Schaefer was president of the Maryland Association of Counties, and he took 250 copies of the poster with him to the association's annual summer meeting. "No one's going to want 'em," he said. He was wrong. Everyone wanted them and his autograph too. "Christ, they were lined up out the door," Hartman says. For years, dozens of seal pool posters were signed and mailed out every week. Replicas of the duckie were hot items, too, requested by civic and charitable groups, which used them as grand prizes in a drawing, as a door prize, or in an auction. His instinctive worry, though, was well founded. Years later, in his second term as governor of Maryland, his most inspired public moment was recycled and recast as he had feared. His picture in the red-and-yellow striped bathing costume showed up on the cover of The National Inquirer, a supermarket tabloid under the headline, "America's Wackiest Governor."

Enemies List

Schaefer kept a desk calendar, a daily register of thoughts, events, and notations on people who he felt had crossed him. He might write something like: "Trueschler promised $15,000 for X and came up with $10,000! What a pig." And every day he saw the letters from complainers and whiners who accused him of having an "edifice complex," building things for his own glory. Such correspondents nettled him from the start. Robert Crooks, a citizen of the business world, wrote to complain about what he regarded as antibusiness policies that Baltimore had pursued for decades. "Sir," he began, "Twenty-seven years ago, Baltimore had a fat-head for a mayor. He was causing many businesses firms to leave the city. He put some kind of stupid inventory tax on them. One business who was in Baltimore for 100 years at that time left for greener pastures. Since that time, many businesses moved out. Some companies who wanted to come here and build never did because some other state gave them better deals.

"Here it is 27 years later and a business that grossed 80 million a year is moving out which means lost of revenue for the city, jobs, etc.

"Nothing really has changed has it? But who expects any difference."
Schaefer wrote back instantly:
"Dear Sir?
"Twenty seven years ago we had a great mayor—'Old Tommy!'
"Twenty seven years ago you were a young fat-head. That's the only change. You're an older Fat-head.
"Regards, W. D. Schaefer."
Here was Schaefer's inviolate loyalty wrapped into a tight, acidic pack-

age: Old Tommy had indeed imposed an inventory tax, which had been opposed by at least one city councilman, the same W. D. Schaefer, until the tax was repealed. But that did not mean Schaefer would side with any self-appointed critic.

For a time, he wrote these epistolary rockets, held them, and then destroyed them. But he let a few of them go. "Dear Edit-turd," opened a missive to the *Sun*'s editor John Carroll. Accustomed to the occasional criticism, Carroll chuckled and remarked on the language only privately. In later years, correspondents were not so indulgent with Schaefer's splenetic outbursts, and the outrage he generated engulfed him.

Schaefer thrived on controversy. He fought constantly with a succession of political figures—Council President Orlinsky, Governor Harry Hughes, anyone who he thought had crossed him. "There were mornings," said Paul Schurick, one of his most faithful aides, "when I could tell someone was going to lose a life. You knew someone was going to get their head chopped off. It had less to do with them than being in the wrong place at the wrong time. Sometimes it was me." The convergence of perceived slights, time, and place created an anger and impatience in Schaefer that erupted against whoever was nearby, much as a parent, distracted by a work matter, flares at a son or daughter out of all proportion to the infraction.

The syndrome kept the Schaefer family on edge. Provocations were constant: Aggrieved citizens were always ready to hammer someone like Schurick, who worked for Marion Pines in the manpower office but whom Schaefer regarded as one of his own personal family. Citizen Jones (his actual name is lost to memory) wanted a trash pickup that day. The mild-mannered Schurick explained the trash pickup procedure and schedule, told the man whom to call, and started to hang up. The citizen was not through. Why was the city so delinquent? Why were city employees such dolts? Why should *he* have to call anyone? Didn't Schurick know anything? A gentle man, as calm and unflappable as he was tall, the six-foot seven-inch Schurick paused. He said he would be happy to do whatever the man wanted done. What the man wanted was to scream at a city official. So he screamed. Though the mayor vented bile when it pleased him, his minions were to offer themselves to the citizens as doormats. But on this day, Schurick did not feel like being further abused and hung up. Less than ten minutes later, Schaefer was on the phone to Pines, having just heard from Citizen Jones.

"I want Schurick fired," said the mayor. "I don't care what the man said. We don't hang up on our citizens. We're city employees. We're here to be abused. Fire him."

Pines got off the phone and walked from her office to city hall.

"You can fire me, but I'm not going to let him go," she told Schaefer. "He's one of the most committed people you have in city government, and you ought to recognize it." Schurick stayed.

Schaefer's treatment of people often did not measure up to his own standards, but it was his prerogative, he thought, to upbraid those who were most devoted to him. And they seemed to love him for it, to forgive him, and to explain his lapses to anyone who asked. "He's a very complicated person," they would say. These devotees came to be known in the early 1980s as "Koolaid drinkers," a reference to the flock of religious zealots who, in 1978 in Jonestown, Guyana, had drunk cyanide-laced punch and died in service to the paranoid delusions of their leader. Some of Schaefer's most talented staff members did drink deeply of the boss's brew, and although they did not actually die, their lives were profoundly affected by their immersion in his harsh aura.

But the abusive strain did not escape notice or mention by everyone in the Schaefer circle. While many were willing to indulge him in almost any trespass against kindness and consideration, Randy Evans, the housing development specialist and one of Schaefer's most trusted aides, was not. Schaefer slammed him for some infraction one day, and Evans called the mayor on it, saying that he would leave if it ever happened again. Mark Joseph observed the tantrums with similar disapproval and vowed to react in the same way should the abuse turn his way. It never did. Schaefer raised his voice to the sainted Sondheim once, and, like Evans, Walter brought the matter to his attention. While he and the mayor were flying to Germany, Sondheim decided to broach the subject of ill treatment—*bullying* was the correct word, he thought.

"You know," he said, "you ought to think more about the way you treat people. You really do abuse people, and often they're the most devoted to you."

"Oh," Schaefer said, head snapping around. "Name someone."

Sondheim did.

Schaefer went into a long silence. Halfway across the Atlantic Ocean, though, he turned to his traveling companion again. "Name some one else," he said.

"Why don't you just get the Baltimore phone book," Sondheim said.

His Family

But the ill treatment continued and perhaps intensified as the years wore on. Schaefer ordered a session with an antiburnout expert. He wasn't good at articulating what he sensed in his staff, so he laid on a group session in which people would honestly discuss their problems and search for solutions until they were so exhausted that they told the truth about their feelings, regardless of the consequences. Exercises of this sort were sometimes called encounters and with good reason. People would get tired and begin telling the truth about how they felt—something that could be ruinous as well as therapeutic. The problem, Bailey Fine and others knew, was Schaefer: his pace, his demands, and his expectations. "You had to keep running to catch up and knew when you got there it'd be kind of neat," she said. People ran as if they were being urged on by their fathers. After about two hours, the group leader stopped and said, "You don't need burnout therapy. You need family therapy."

"Of course," Fine thought. "The staff was his family. He called the boys son, the women little girl or mother. He had no family." One of his favorite "little girls" was Daryl Plevy, who came to him as a twenty-seven-year-old law clerk from Schaefer's old partner, Mary Arabian. He gave Plevy a seat in his office, literally, at his desk so that they were bumping each other's papers off the crowded surface, almost competing for the phone. Plevy knew almost nothing of government and nothing at all of Schaefer. He assigned her to negotiate with the Esskay meat-packing company to keep it from leaving the city. She helped to forestall that departure for a time. He gave her the title of "Follow Up Officer." Everyone was responsible for follow-up in their own bailiwick, of course, except that follow-up is something people in general, and governments in particular, routinely fail to do. So Schaefer tried to institutionalize and give structure to a function that too often got set aside. One day he had Plevy call Pines, who was considerably older and far more experienced, to ask whether some newly decorated trash barrels emblazoned with the logo of yet another Schaefer cleanup effort had been deployed. "The mayor asked me to call," Plevy said. She could feel Pines seething through the phone line.

"No they're not out there yet, but they'll be out when I said they'd be out and I don't need you calling me to check up on me."

"Oh," said Plevy, "the mayor knows you don't need checking up on.

He's just so excited about this project that he wanted to know if it had happened yet."

Schaefer was sitting next to her and almost cheered. Plevy and others thought that he enjoyed creating the conflict and the collision as much as the creative tension he was using. What was happening amounted to hazing, "an initiation," Plevy thought. "He did set me up, but the fact that I passed the test motivated me to pass more tests. I got more and more responsibility."

Mary Arabian had warned her. "He made them compete with each other. It was a constant struggle to outdo one another. It was brutal. But they knew it. And they kept doing it."

Plevy began to chafe under her working conditions. Schaefer was, of course, the ultimate follow-up officer, and he was watching her every moment. "Can I have my own office?" she asked him after several months. Ah hah! he seemed to say. "I was wondering when you'd ask me that." And he led her down the hall to a place he had picked out for her weeks before. Another test had been passed.

"He was proud of me for asking finally," Plevy said. The lesson? It's all right to be assertive, okay to ask for something, to take the initiative. It was a bit unorthodox—and totally manipulative, as well. Plevy loved it.

It was a good thing she did, because Schaefer's agenda called for even more difficult chores. He needed someone tough, smart, and competent to do the next job: beginning to ease Bereska out of her dominant role in city hall. He gave Plevy the boards and commissions, the first major responsibility that Bereska had handled twelve years earlier, wrested from mysterious Walter Beuchelt. This job was so central to the mayor's well-being that its transfer to Plevy was recognized as the start of Bereska's decline and fall, a development owing to her emergence as a near-rival, her evolution as his enforcer, and the power of rivals who were replacing her as Girl Friday. In time, Schaefer moved Bereska out of his immediate, daily line of sight, giving her a less prominent office. While he was waiting to give Plevy more responsibility and a new office near him, he was working out ways to divorce himself from Bereska.

Plevy had some insight into the psychological motivations that her new boss employed, but Bereska knew only that she had to keep running. She was responsible for doing, for ideas, for everything. In the same way that Plevy took care of following up, Bereska was charged with looking ahead—and with giving definition and snap to the projects he demanded. She saw Schaefer's talent and political instinct and helped him to realize his potential in the way he shaped himself and his city. He had wanted something to say when he met with community groups that would impart the concern he felt for involvement and follow-through and activism. He wanted to urge his neighborhood operators to act immediately on any good idea. "Start" was his one-word rule, enunciated to Plevy and others. Don't fret or delay or even plan too long. Start. Bereska thought about it and suggested that he tell them to "Do it now." Those three words, offered to him in a memo, became the most famous of the bromides, in Schaefer's lexicon of leadership. Things did not just happen and he knew it. They were built on guilt, fear, genius, and personal motivation—his own and his circle's. He prided himself on choosing talented, committed, and even driven people, and he never chose better than Bereska.

She was, by all accounts, brilliant, creative, and a good political analyst—tough enough to ram his policies into place. She was probably too good at what she did—particularly at being his enforcer. She ordered people around as peremptorily as he did. In the beginning, when many thought he was a short-termer, she was an unchallenged presence. Over time, new adherents moved in, though, all of them anxious for his favor—and unhappy with her style. He watched the friction with some enjoyment, imagining, too, that it would produce even harder work for him. Bereska's role in City Hall caught the attention of many outside the inner circle, including newspaper reporters who more than occasionally wrote about her. Wouldn't she make a good mayor, a few of them said. All of it together began to work against her in the political bureaucratic chemistry.

For years, though, Bereska attended to Schaefer's every public and personal need. After he stopped even his rather moderate social drinking, Bereska was deputized to make sure that nothing interrupted his abstinence. She thought it was a magnificent thing that he had stopped, another personal sacrifice he had made to the demands of his job. Her responsibility was to keep his hand filled at social events with a glass of ginger ale. If she was not there, she was to deputize someone to perform the function in her stead. Once while she was on vacation, a glass of bourbon was handed to the teetotaling mayor, and he took a big gulp before realizing what he was holding, Bereska heard about that. She was not there but it was her fault.

Did he realize how much power he had over people? Marion Pines asked him once. Bereska with his permanent duty officer, for example, installing a phone system that "rang down" to her house on weekends if there was anything that needed the mayor's attention. Weekends in the sense of work-free days did not exist. The devotion went much further. Did Schaefer know, Pines asked, that women were delaying marriage, delaying pregnancy, delaying a second child—out of deference to him? He looked at her blankly. A confirmed only child could be blind to the toll he took or expect it as his due. A writer once referred to Schaefer's talented, faithful women as "the all-girl gestapo"—and they were an awesome band. "I think intuitively he trusted women," said Sandy Hillman, who because his tourism director. She thought she understood the mutual attraction: "Women are better team players than men. Women make all the concessions. We would have followed him anywhere." Years later when he was asked what happened to Bereska, Schaefer insisted he had never abandoned her, never lost faith in her. He thought she had simply been eaten up by the growing band of Schaefer women.

Lainy LeBow replaced her. Lainy was a far less important character in city hall than Bereska. Lainy was not a generator of project ideas, not an enforcer, not a part of the renaissance apparatus. She was adoring and uncritical and, finally, someone to care for Schaefer. Even in the life of a man who was so wedded to his job, emotional needs remained. Lainy met them. She jollied him into better moods, and she understood and challenged his pouts, his self-pity. But she modulated what she understood about his psychology and did not throw it in his face, and she protected him in a more personal way than Bereska had. "She was like a blankie, a kid's blankie. A very comforting figure, just what he needed with people like his mother, Hilda Mae, and Bereska around him," one of the other women in his life said.

Trashball

He needed comforting around the clock—and got it often from strong, imaginative, and loyal followers even when he abused them. The business management guru Tom Peters, a big Schaefer fan, observed that Baltimore's leader had an ability to infuse others with his own passion. People began to see him as a human counterforce against welfare dependency, dysfunctional families, poorly performing schools, and even the American Dream, the magnet pull of single family detached houses in the suburbs. Embry and others thought Schaefer didn't understand any particular program. They also began to see that it didn't matter. *He* was the program, the common element in everything that happened.

He wanted a continual campaign against litter, and, hokey as it seemed sometimes, he pursued cleanliness the way he pursued his other enemies. He raved about how kids in particular seemed to have no idea that they created trash.

"Figure this out," he said to Bailey Fine one day at a cabinet meeting. She imagined some sort of broad-scale communication would be needed to hammer home the antitrash message. She went to friends at the Ad Council, an organization of local advertising companies. Someone suggested she try VanSant Dugdale, one of the city's largest ad firms. Dan Loden, a young account executive, was assigned to the project. Together, they concluded that they could transmute refuse into basketballs bouncing loose through the streets of Baltimore, bounding over marble steps like multicolored tumbleweeds to be scooped up and swished into trashcans remade with mesh sides to resemble basketball nets. If detritus could be dunked, hooked, and shot into these receptacles, it would never become litter. They would call their game Trashball.

Around this somewhat airy and fanciful concept, they commissioned an antitrash ditty and went to New York to have it recorded. A film was made to give the whole thing maximum exposure. Local sports figures were enlisted to be the stars. A collegian named Marvin Webster of Baltimore's Morgan State Bears basketball team agreed to participate—a very useful thing, because Webster's shot-blocking ability had given him the perfect nickname: the Eraser. In this situation, Marvin "The Eraser" Webster would be swatting away trash. The Orioles pitched in too: Al Bumbry, the fleet outfielder; Earl Weaver, the fiery manager; and Jim Palmer, the cerebral pitcher, were among them. They did the Trashball thing in person all over the city from the Inner Harbor to Bolton Hill. They talked earnestly about an element of blight everyone could control. Kids should play this game because The Eraser, Al, Earl, and Jim wanted them to. At some of these events, the dunking, hooking, and shooting went on as the Morgan State Band played in the background.

Schaefer loved it. He went to New York City to see the movie and, when he got back to Baltimore, arranged to have a load of trash dumped at City Hall Plaza so he and other city officials could hone their Trashball skills. He posed beneath the Shot Tower with a huge push broom. Similar events, often starring the ballplayers, were done in neighborhoods throughout the city. The Trashball movie was shown in local theaters. It worked, Fine thought later, because even when people air-mailed their Twinkie wrappers onto the sidewalk, they saw that Schaefer and his crew were working overtime, pumping out ideas, risking their dignity—challenging Baltimoreans to do the right thing. Habits would not change overnight, but the effort had to be made. A willing suspension of disbelief was necessary to pull this off, and people were increasingly happy to oblige.

Fine's only regret was buying into an idea that limited the impact of her campaign: Why not charge other cities for what Baltimore was doing, someone said? But, of course, other cities were as strapped for cash as Baltimore was, and few takers appeared. Had the idea been available for the asking, Trashball would have drawn more attention to Schaefer's city. Nevertheless Fine's idea became the standard by which other ideas were judged, motivating the City Hall team to think deeply—too deeply, some thought—about other ways to gain the boss's favor.

One of the ideas born of this fervor later was called "Pink Positive Day in Baltimore," an effort to further lift the city's spirit by adding splashes of pink to sidewalks and the like. Here, it seemed, the idea machine had ginned up a turkey. No one noticed. High spirits and confidence were good objectives, of course, and they no doubt led Schaefer to buy in. But "Pink Positive" seemed to have no concrete purpose. By now, though, Schaefer's City Hall had developed a reputation for such PR high jinks: Trashball, the Baltimore's Best/Baltimore Is Best bumper stickers, City Fair, and a hundred other campaigns that were elements of the civic Baltimore under Schaefer. In a sense, it was a grown-up version of kids with a blanket thrown over the clothesline coming out to perform for their parents after a cookout. Every enterprise, large or small, was a part of Schaefer's effort to hang on until real help arrived: a convention center, an aquarium, a world trade center, a shiny new hotel with a fancy name—all designed to attract tourists and their money.

Retreat. Schaefer's father and mother in the doorway of the family's "Shore," a summer cottage on Marley Creek, just off the Furnace Branch in Anne Arundel County, in the 1930s. Schaefer Family albums in the Maryland State Archives.

Camera Shy. Though he would be one of the most photographed Marylanders of all time, the young Schaefer hung on the edge of a picture taken in the late 1920s by his neighbor on Edgewood Street, Betty Lonergan. Years later, Mrs. Lonergan sent it to Schaefer's mother with a note reminding her that young Donald had always resisted having his picture taken. Family album, Maryland State Archives.

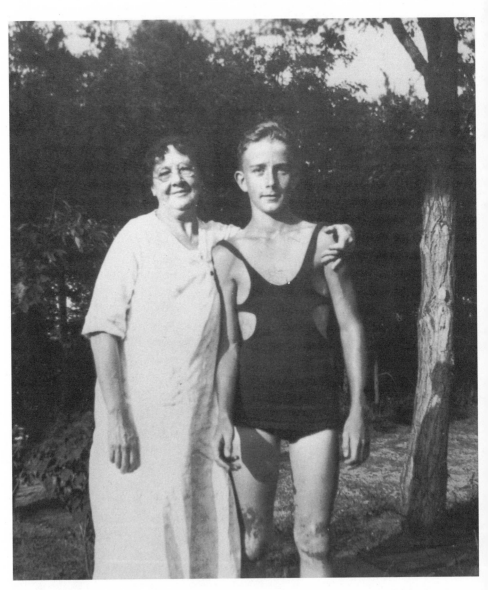

Beautiful Swimmer. When he took his famous seal pool dip, Schaefer looked quite comfortable in an orange-and-red striped Victorian bathing costume. Well he might have. He had worn a similar suit as a young man at his family's summer vacation retreat. Here he poses with his maternal grandmother, Clara Skipper, in the mid-1930s. Family album, Maryland State Archives.

Constant Companion. You needed someone to talk to, Schaefer said later of Lolita B. Cook, and he must have talked with her frequently in those stressful war years. Her picture shows up twenty or thirty times in two albums, more than any other person by far. Family album, Maryland State Archives.

Dapper Don. With his mother at Atlantic City, circa 1946. Schaefer cut a dashing figure in those days, right down to the two-tone wingtips. Family album, Maryland State Archives.

CITY COUNCIL
5th DISTRICT

JACOB J.
EDELMAN

Lawyer, Federal Labor Referee, 1935-1939. Incumbent Member City Council since 1939.

MICHAEL J.
HANKIN

Lawyer, former Assistant City Solicitor. Sixteen years experience as a Public Servant.

LEON A.
RUBENSTEIN

Lawyer. Served with distinction for eight years in Maryland Legislature.

WM. DONALD
SCHAEFER

Lawyer, Lt. Col. United States Army Reserve. Active in civic and community affairs.

Voter's Guide. The palm card from Schaefer's successful 1955 run for the Baltimore City Council. Such aids could be taken into the polling place, and candidates in Baltimore always printed plenty. Maryland State Archives.

Neighborhood Man. Schaefer as council vice president meets with residents of South Pulaski Street in 1965 to discuss the soot that was then invading their houses from a nearby factory. Fred G. Kraft, Jr., for the *News American*.

Front Porch. With his mother on the Schaefer's front porch at 620 Edgewood Street in 1971. His shingle still hung from the railing, but Schaefer hardly practiced law at all after becoming a councilman. Ellis J. Malashuk for the *Sun*.

Line of Succession. Here was a rare gathering of Baltimore's colorful mayors in November 1972. *Left to right*: Thomas J. D'Alesandro, Jr.; Theodore R. McKeldin; Phillip H. Goodman; Thomas J. D'Alesandro III; J. Harold Grady; and Schaefer. James F. Lally for the *News American*.

Job Search. In 1973, with Congressman Parren J. Mitchell (*seated*) and Alton R. Williams of the Rouse Company, Schaefer makes the first in a series of calls to line up 2,200 summer jobs.

Monumental Christmas, 1973. The artist Betty Wells did a drawing for Schaefer's holiday greeting every year. He insisted on having each of several thousand cards addressed by hand. He took a batch to the beach every year to do his share. Volunteers from the Hibernians did most of the work, though, bringing bag lunches to City Hall and spending a day to get the work done. Betty Wells.

The Stare. Schaefer's staff knew that this pose meant the two-way phase of the discussion had ended. Chin tucked, forefinger poised, eyes more sharply focused, Schaefer's determination to be heard was respected by all who wished to avoid exile. August 1973. John Davis for the *News American*.

Pride of Baltimore. If you said it often enough, he thought, and put it on the back bumper of enough automobiles, maybe it was true. 1976. James Kelmartin for the *News American*.

"Shaky" and "The Big Chief." Schaefer and his mentor, Irvin Kovens, aka "The Furniture Man," who named governors and mayors from his store on West Baltimore Street. Kovens called Schaefer "Shaky" in part because the mayor was never confident of victory. June 1979. Irving Phillips for the *Sun*.

FACING PAGE (*top*): On his Toes. He could always find the right pose. Here he dances with Congresswoman Barbara A. Mikulski in 1980 at the city's new School for the Arts. His own tastes ran to Engelbert Humperdinck and Hulk Hogan, the professional wrestler, but Schaefer knew that the city was a haven for the arts, a strength he wanted to build even as he gave opportunities to talented young people. Ted Kirschbaum for the *Sun*.

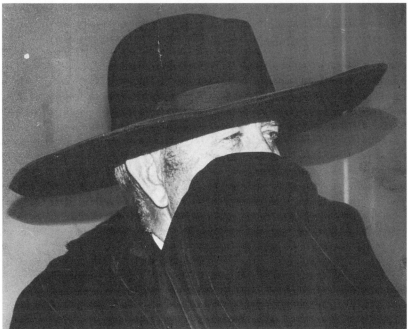

The Shadow. Schaefer posing as Lamont Cranston, "the Shadow" of radio fame, after the *Sun*'s eight-day, twenty-two-article series on his off-book banking operation, which was designed to avoid slowdowns caused by the rules of government. November 1980. J. Pat Carter for the *Sun*.

Greeting Godzilla. Schaefer mugged with the best of them. He did these things because he enjoyed them—but also to draw the attention of a busy city to matters its citizens might not otherwise have the time or inclination to notice. He demanded a river of ideas, used them with élan, and put himself at center stage. He meets the monster here during the City Fair in 1981, one of the earliest efforts to revive faith in the city. John Davis for the *News American*.

Baltimore's Best. Schaefer, Jim Rouse, and Clarence M. Mitchell, Jr., legislative architect of the Voting Rights Act of 1964, comparing notes in February 1982. *News American* photo courtesy of the Maryland Collection, University of Maryland Library.

Point of View. Schaefer shows President Ronald Reagan his city from the observation deck of the World Trade Center. Reagan, then striving to reduce government's role in urban renewal and other endeavors, called Baltimore a shining example of the American free enterprise system, conveniently forgetting how much federal money had gone into the landscape he surveyed. July 1982. Paul T. Whyte for the *News American*.

Debate. Schaefer won a fourth term in 1983, defeating former judge Billy Murphy. Though he thought Murphy might be the African American to energize Baltimore's majority black electorate, Schaefer would have won a fourth term even if only blacks had voted. *News American* photo courtesy of the Maryland Collection, University of Maryland Library.

Thumbs Up. Schaefer and Edward Bennett Williams, owner of the Orioles, ride in parade after the Os' 1983 world championship victory. Schaefer managed to keep Williams in Baltimore until he could, as governor, provide the stadium every team owner demanded. *News American* photo courtesy of the Maryland Collection, University of Maryland Library.

FACING PAGE (*top*): Jilted. Schaefer did everything but publicly beg Robert Irsay to leave the Colts in Baltimore. Irsay's response was to toy with the mayor, the city, and the Colts' fans, thus supplying *Sun* editorial cartoonist Mike Lane material for this stinging commentary. When Irsay stole away with the team in the middle of the night, he dealt Schaefer one of the worst setbacks of his career.

Rare Defeat. Mayor Schaefer and his lobbyist in Annapolis, Janet Hoffman, watching the state Senate cut $5 million in education aid for the city on March 22, 1984. Robert K. Hamilton for the *Sun*.

America's Mayor. Schaefer and Senator Paul Sarbanes pose with cover of *Esquire* magazine's September 1983 issue, which named Schaefer America's best mayor. *News American* photo courtesy of the Maryland Collection, University of Maryland Library.

Remembering H. L. Mencken. Schaefer as the Bard of Baltimore at the opening of Mencken's house in Union Square as a tourist attraction in June 1984. When Schaefer saw this picture, he was shocked, seeing in himself, even behind the costume, a striking resemblance to his father. Paul Hutchins for the *Sun*.

Above: On a Roll. Schaefer pitches in to rid a city of the stream of trash dumped by unthinking citizens. Cleanup campaigns like this one in 1984 sometimes seemed contrived, but Schaefer felt that the city would drown in trash without them. He and his staff—and the neighborhood leaders— enjoyed these moments as much as they did the more elaborate ceremonies of City Hall. Delmar Aylor for the *News American*.

Left: Chicken Men. Schaefer and Frank Perdue, the Eastern Shore poultry mag- nate, have a bite during a 1984 tour of Baltimore City Market stalls set up at the Convention Center. Clarence Gar- rett for the *Evening Sun*.

Power Trio. Pam Kelly, who handled political chores; Floraine Applefeld, Schaefer's chief of volunteers; and Joan Bereska, his chief of staff. Women were the heart of Schaefer's operation at a time when women's talents were seldom recognized or employed at high levels of government. *News American* photo courtesy of the Maryland Collection, University of Maryland Library.

The Magnificent Seven. Of the Inner Harbor's many parents, these were the most important: Martin Millspaugh, Walter Sondheim, Jim Rouse, Bob Embry, Bill Boucher, and William Donald Schaefer, all on horseback. Standing is Sandy Hillman, Schaefer's tourism boss. May 1985. Fred G. Kraft, Jr., for the *News American*.

The Admiral. Schaefer and Hilda Mae Snoops, emerging from a wooden crate marked "Baltimore's Gift to the State." Looking altogether confident and prepared to steer the ship of state, Schaefer knew that he had rough seas to travel. In Annapolis, he sometimes seemed to be fomenting a mutiny. November 1986. Walter F. McCardell for the *Sun*.

Biologist. Learning from a student at Hilton Elementary School in Baltimore. Schaefer had no family, so he made every kid in Baltimore, and later Maryland, his kid. November 19, 1991. Richard Tomlinson, Governor's Press Office.

Perfectly Schaefer. When a majority of voters on the Eastern Shore voted against him in 1990, he referred to their part of the state as an outhouse and began to write bitter letters. He then suffered the sting of cartooning delivered by KAL of the *Sun,* who wondered whether the governor had lost his bearings. February 8, 1991. KAL.

Leaders of the Free World. Schaefer hosts President George Bush and Russian President Boris Yeltsin along with an unidentified Secret Service agent on the *Maryland Independence,* the state yacht. Richard Tomlinson, Governor's Press Office.

Kaptain Keno. Schaefer turned to another gambling source to fill budget gaps caused by a national economic recession in the early 1990s. Schaefer fumed indignantly to editors at the *Sun* when these drawings appeared. "They're not funny!" he insisted. January 30, 1993. KAL cartoon by Kevin Kallaugher for the *Sun*.

The Pose. Schaefer addresses the Maryland General Assembly, emphasizing his point in his trademark way. 1994. Richard Tomlinson, Governor's Press Office.

He Built It and They Came. With Cal Ripken and Peter Angelos on opening day, 1995. Schaefer, looking good in an Orioles jacket, knew that Cal was a Baltimore treasure and called Orioles principal owner "Peter the Great." Richard Tomlinson, Governor's Press Office.

McDon. Schaefer and friends celebrate his sixty-ninth birthday at a favorite haunt, McDonald's, this one in Hagerstown. Schaefer became a recognizable face in fast-food joints all over Maryland. He also liked the calamari at Connolly's on the waterfront, the mashed potatoes at Bohager's, and everything at the Sip 'N Bite. Lainy Lebow-Sachs is at his left. To her left is U.S. Senator Paul Sarbanes, and to his left is Mark Wasserman, Schaefer's economic development secretary. Richard Tomlinson, Governor's Press Office.

New Contract. Always anxious to promote business development, Schaefer wants three cheers for Martin Marietta, the aircraft manufacturer. Richard Tomlinson, Governor's Press Office.

CHAPTER 9

"The Best Damned City"

They called it the Hyatt Regency, a name that seemed too rich by half for dowdy old Baltimore. But slowly, the city was growing into its renaissance airs. A. N. Pritzker and his wife were the honored, unofficial first-night guests at Baltimore's new Inner Harbor hotel. They spent the night of October 5, 1981, in a suite overlooking Baltimore's new main attraction and the next morning rode to city hall in a lush orange-and-black version of the original Yellow Cab, something out of a Dick Tracy comic strip, which called for them at the hotel's half-circular front drive. Purchased and restored by Yellow Cab's Mark Joseph with this very day in mind, the 1937 car usually stood in the lobby of Yellow Cab's new art deco headquarters on Howard Street, far from the Greenmount Avenue desolation that had so dispirited young Joseph when he had come to sit at the bedside of his family's dying company. Now his boffo cab was carrying A. N. and serving as another symbol of a resplendent, reborn Baltimore.

Ten years into Schaefer's tenure, Yellow was rolling five hundred cabs every day, five times the total at the time Schaefer made his "Atlan-ta" speech. Later, when the Hyatt and the convention business hit full stride, Yellow added more. And cabs represented only a fraction of the operation. Joseph had diversified, adding a limousine service, health care vans, school buses, and the like. He and his father had been half right: They not only could survive, they could prosper in the new Baltimore.

The city's free fall had been broken, generally, according to Marc Levine, an urban scholar who has spent more than fifteen years studying Schaefer's Baltimore, before and after his tenure as mayor. "Looking at overall economic health, retail sales, service receipts, Baltimore's trajectory was downward with business activity slowing down during the 1970s, but by the mid-80s the increase of poverty had slowed and ran the same through the 1980s. Instead of hitting bottom, it started to creep up. Per capita income picked up a bit. The tax base actually grew until the real estate crash of the late 1980s." By 1983, taxes from the downtown area were up to $12 million, a twelvefold jump from 1963, when the same city blocks had produced only $1 million. Property values "skyrocketed," Levine said, "and provided a margin for maneuvering within constraints of the chronic budget problems. The bottom line is that as difficult as things are—with the overarching forces of decay and outmigration—Baltimore did not become Camden, Detroit or Newark." And in its first year, the new Hyatt did better than any other hotel in A. N.'s chain.

Schaefer's enthusiasm had drawn Yellow Cab's Mark Joseph into various City Hall enterprises: He was appointed to the Convention Bureau Advisory Committee. He enlisted his company in a program called Metro Crime Stoppers, making his cab fleet—a vast mobile communications system—available to police. He helped on an antivandalism campaign. He had been in many audiences over the years since the Atlanta speech, and he admitted that he got a special thrill when Schaefer mentioned his name, offering it as an example of ideal businessman-citizen involvement. With Schaefer's help, he got an exclusive contract to serve the new hotel. Florists, caterers, restaurants, bars, airlines, and other hotels did better, too. Some 15,000 new jobs were claimed as a result of Harborplace, and the chain of new construction continued with a total of 10,000 new or rehabilitated housing units coming into use. Neighborhood organizations continued to hammer Schaefer for policies that enriched businesspeople while offering the workers jobs selling balloons and big cookies, cleaning toilets, and carrying suitcases. Embry and Brodie responded by pointing out that many Americans had begun in the labor force with jobs of low pay and no glory. Brodie's own father-in-law, Phillip, had started as a bellhop and ended his career as a maitre d'hotel at the Mayflower Hotel in Washington, where presidents called him by his first name. The case studies did little to quiet the critics, but no one could say what alternatives existed for a city that was losing employers in virtually every sector, led most conspicuously by Bethelem Steel, where jobs dwindled from a high of 35,000 in the late 1970s to fewer than 10,000 by the time the new Hyatt opened.

Over this period, the transformation of William Donald Schaefer continued apace. Not the least enthusiastic of the converted was Jim Rouse, who now regularly extolled the virtues of Baltimore's mayor, calling him "a special force" whose courage, wisdom, good judgment, PR flair, and passion for his city gave hope to cities everywhere. This was the man who had ridiculed Schaefer as a mere title search lawyer, a creature of the bosses, a petulant child of no talent whose election doomed Baltimore to continuing decline. "I have come to meet and know and work with many mayors. . . . I have never seen the equal of Schaefer," Rouse wrote in the *Evening Sun* in 1983.

Two Baltimores

But amid the glowing praise, so many awards, and so much promise, Schaefer found himself the target of angry and bitter recrimination. He was, the critics declared, a "bricks and mortar man," a caterer to capitalists who sacrificed the needs of the needy and the neighborhoods. Harborplace was diminished as an avenue of excess, an ego-driven, business-favoring indulgence. Even some businesspeople groused that he had abandoned them along Lexington, Charles, and St. Paul streets to wither and die as the new money flowed toward the water. So he knew early what sort of reelection campaign he would face in 1983 against Judge William G. "Billy" Murphy.

The son of an influential Baltimore family, founders and operators of the *Afro-American* newspaper, Murphy was a canny denizen of Court House Square, a man whose ironic grin was a constant rebuke to white Baltimore. He had won a judgeship and the reputation for fast-talking, race-conscious public speaking that was designed to politicize the city's powerful but passive black electorate. Murphy was perhaps too good on the attack—too good for two reasons. First, Baltimore's black electorate was not prepared to abandon reason and objectivity for a purely black-based political appeal. Historically, according to the state legislator Pete Rawlings, black Baltimoreans resented the suggestion, made from within and without, that they would choose skin color over merit and qualification. So Murphy's candidacy raised caution flags among blacks as well as whites. The stance he took was dangerous also because its tone of superiority left him even more vulnerable to attacks on his own record.

Schaefer worried that Murphy could be the man who would awaken what people called "the sleeping giant" of black political consciousness. He would never be optimistic about an election, enjoying his achievements.

He would know the work yet to be done better than any critic. Nevertheless, Schaefer was at the top of his game in 1983 and getting stronger. His political managers did their polling, which showed him with an astronomically high 72 percent approval rating, and prepared to waltz him toward four more years. Schaefer led the challenger by prodigious figures among blacks as well as whites. No opponent had threatened him at all since he vanquished George Russell twelve years earlier, but Murphy might have been a different story. He was by far the best opponent since Russell. Still, had he seen Schaefer's polling numbers, Murphy would have recognized that he had no realistic hope of an upset either. In that year, though, a year before the Reverend Jesse L. Jackson's 1984 campaign for president energized black urban voting blocks across the country, Murphy had to hope that he would have a measure of the new electoral magic.

Schaefer did see the poll numbers and, of course, refused to find comfort in them.

Murphy came at him with the accumulated criticisms of twelve years, years in which opponents had wanted resources directed at other municipal enemies from poverty in general to education and drug abuse treatment. So important to the spiritual revival of Baltimore, the Inner Harbor was used by Murphy as a symbol of the subjugation and neglect of what he called "the outer harbor." (Ironically, Schaefer had used a similar term when he ran in 1971.) What was happening, the challenger argued, was enhancement of the Inner Harbor at the expense of the poor neighborhoods. There were, he said, borrowing from the *Sun*, two Baltimores: one large, poor and disadvantaged, the other far smaller and privileged.

"We were all very idealistic," says Marc Steiner, a talk show host on WJHU radio and a one-time youth gang organizer, who had grown up in Baltimore and saw Murphy as a man who could lead the city's disadvantaged black majority out of its electoral doldrums. Baltimore had been, for blacks, an even more quiescent and downtrodden place psychologically than many U.S. cities, Steiner thought. Many had adopted what he called the attitude of the "handkerchief head," the subservient person waiting for orders from white people. The argument for Murphy's electability, though, necessarily applied that term to lower-class whites as well—"the Hon crowd," which had been held in thrall by the clubhouse pols just as much as blacks had. This was the same group that Russell had scolded in his speech about dummies and ascension by divine right of the bosses. Steiner and others inside the Murphy camp thought they could put the Hons together with progressive whites and the awakening black masses to create a force large enough to defeat anyone. "We all thought the time had come and that we had in Billy Murphy a man who members of the white middle class, the working class, and the black middle class would come out and get behind." Outsiders thought they saw change coming in Baltimore, too. Political operatives from Atlanta, a cadre of strategists loyal to former Atlanta mayor Andrew Young, held important positions in Murphy's campaign.

Steiner tried to suppress in this thinking what he knew was missing, but he couldn't. "Your brother, your brother, your brother," people fairly chanted at Billy, wondering where Arthur Murphy was in the Billy Murphy campaign. Widely respected as a pollster and strategist, Arthur Murphy had said no. He wasn't available, had other commitments, sorry. The problem was this: If Art was not on board, why should anyone else be? The blue smoke, the mirrors, the symbols, the who's with you and who isn't of politics did not add up to victory if your very politically astute brother was not on your team.

Soon stories broke in the Baltimore newspapers about tax problems Murphy had with Washington. Finally, Murphy wanted the wave of history and demography to do all the work. "We could have done a lot better, but he would not campaign," Steiner said. "He wouldn't go door to door." With the prospects of victory falling off the table, the campaign encountered a number of other severe internal problems and began to implode. "It was a disaster from Jump Street," said Steiner.

Awakening

Shaky as ever, Schaefer was certain he would lose. His concerns sprang not just from the arrival of a fire-spitting opponent, but from the change he could see and feel in Baltimore as a political place. In his early years, Richard Lidinsky of the Young Men's Bohemian Club and Peck Jones of Stonewall could bring in the votes he needed. Often, they didn't bother to work the black precincts. Turnout was always low there, and the politicians did not put much of their money on streets where results were not predictable. This voting malaise was lifting, though, and Schaefer knew it when, in 1984, a young Harvard graduate and Rhodes Scholar, Kurt L. Schmoke, took the city prosecutor's office away from William L. Swisher, the last of Jack Pollack's candidates. Swisher had won by appealing to crime- and race-based anxieties. Now came Schmoke, another young man who looked good in a suit, but a man who had been to fancy colleges —

who had paid, in Schaefer's view, no dues to the community—and was about to be hand-carried into the halls of high office. Schaefer resented the hell out of this and feared for his own political future. In spite of his commanding lead in the polls, Schaefer went to Larry Gibson, by then Schmoke's chief political strategist, to find out whether Schmoke might be willing to endorse him.

"Why would we do that?" Gibson wondered. "I have only one objective, and that's to get Kurt Schmoke elected mayor. I don't see how endorsing you would help in that regard."

Schaefer strongly intimated to Gibson that 1983 would be his last race for mayor. He would be out of the way for Schmoke. Here was the brutal, fear-driven, ego-sacrificing pragmatism of Schaefer looking for a deal in the most unlikely place. From the days of Roland Patterson, Gibson had been one of Schaefer's most despised adversaries. No one knew this better than Gibson, who was a bit amused by Schaefer's overture. Gibson said he would probably not work in the Murphy campaign, partly because he had his own concerns about Billy and partly because he was planning a skin-diving trip to the Greek islands that summer. He was taking himself out of the picture, in effect, but Schaefer wanted more. The wily Gibson says that he didn't realize what the mayor of Baltimore wanted until much later. If Schaefer might ever have had the ability to ally himself personally or politically with Schmoke, the possibility vanished then and there, and Schaefer made Schmoke a mortal enemy. It was not yet time for a black man to be mayor, but that time was nearly at hand, and Schaefer knew it.

The Soul of His New Machine

Schaefer was in no immediate danger. He could rely on another of his creations. He could mobilize volunteers at virtually every level of the city: Berndt, Embry, the Mark Josephs, Sandy and Bob Hillman, and Sally Michel. These men and women represented a generation of leaders who were ready to take over from Vernon Eney, Rouse, and Clarence Miles. In the neighborhoods, Schaefer had established Mayor's Stations and staffed them with loyal supporters who could be paid from federal funds. He had a grid of area advisory committees to decide (up to a point) how grants should be spent, and the neighborhoods saw the money flow. And he had Floraine.

Floraine Applefeld, head of Schaefer's volunteerism office, was an interchangeable part in the political and governmental machines. She and her team did promotional works in the off years and campaign work on election years. In reality, she was doing political work in every year. She opened and staffed a campaign office, stocking it with the criss-cross address directories of voters. "We'd get volunteers to sit on the phones, talk to people about the candidates, find out if they're going to vote for them. You do your polls that way. We gave out all the literature. When people wanted literature, I had men that went out with their cars, gave out their signs—all the lawn signs, window signs, and the bumper stickers. I had people that came and got a hold of a machine to make buttons. We made our own buttons. It was fun."

The connection between city hall work and campaign work was seamless. "They were the same thing," Applefeld said. "I used the same people . . . the people who worked for my projects and the people that volunteered to help me in the campaign office. They loved the work, and they loved the candidate."

No one loved the work and the candidate more than Applefeld herself. She bought the requisite "Schaefer for Mayor" T-shirts for volunteers one year and, while picking them up, totaled her new car on the beltway. "Lights on the beltway construction blinded me, and I went into a truck, great big truck. The next thing I knew, I was in an ambulance. I had really messed up one of my legs badly, my knee and everything."

As rescue workers were prying her out of the car, she kept instructing them: "Get the T-shirts. Get the T-shirts."

"What do you mean 'Get the T-shirts?'" a cop said.

"I grabbed his hand, and here I am probably unconscious and said, 'Please, get the box of T-shirts.' They got the boxes of T-shirts, put them in the cop car and followed the ambulance to the hospital. And there's my cousin standing next to me when the policeman walked in and said 'Where do you want us to put the boxes of T-shirts?'" Floraine kept working through her injuries because she had internalized Schaefer's credo: "If you stand still, you're dead. He didn't believe that line about if it ain't broke don't fix it. If it wasn't broke, it could *get* broke."

Applefeld had significant control over they city's spirit. The logo for her office was "Baltimore's Best/Baltimore Is Best," a bumper sticker and all-purpose declaration addressing the city and its individual residents. Schaefer was constantly looking for ways to make his point about the importance of good self-image. One of the major annual tools was the summer ethnic festival. Applefeld was one of the directors.

The festivals were a reflection of Rouse's idealized conception of city life, inviting expressions of ethnic pride, folk art, civic unity, and a celebration of all the city's many communities. They brought out the richness of Baltimore for everyone to enjoy, even people who lived outside the celebrated neighborhoods. Festival-goers danced, ate stuffed grape leaves or kaloupkis, displayed painted Ukrainian Easter eggs, talked—and repopulated downtown. When it came time for an election, people voted their new confidence in and hope for the city and their belief that, while Schaefer might have been building monuments to something, he was not forgetting them.

Schaefer fought back most ferociously over Murphy's "two Baltimores" charge. The big money from Washington, he said, had gone to the neighborhoods, by and large. He invited everyone to examine the ledgers. No one did, of course, but by now it mattered little. The symbols of progress— of splendid phoenixlike renewal at the water's edge—carried the winning message. All the money spent on job training, public housing, streetscape improvements, parks, and the like was invisible and unquantifiable. In the neighborhoods, though, people knew that they had been well treated and responded accordingly.

Schaefer won that year with something like 72 percent of the vote, a number approximating his standing in the early polls. Even without his wide victory margins in predominantly white precincts, Schaefer would have won. He defeated Murphy in every neighborhood of the city, including the predominantly black precincts. In fact, he would have won in the black districts alone without the huge majorities he accumulated in white precincts. Murphy was not the breakthrough candidate after all.

Tululu Irene

Two days after her son's fourth mayoral triumph, on November 11, 1983, Tululu Schaefer died. Schaefer hurried to the hospital when he learned that his mother was fading. His friend Sister Mary Thomas, president of Mercy Hospital, and Joanna Sorenson, the mayor's secretary, were with him. Tululu's parish priest, the Reverand William N. McKeachie, rector of Old St. Paul's Episcopal Church, said he had not known that his parishioner was hospitalized until after the September primary. One of his associates apologized to her, and she returned the apology: "I'm so sorry. But Donald has been very busy lately."

McKeachie had once asked her whether she wasn't an extremely proud mother. "Well," she said, "the political thing is not important to me. I'm glad he's a faithful son and believes in the right things."

It was a day Schaefer's city hall family dreaded. Tululu was his family, the person for whom he seemed to have given up marriage and children. Now, at eighty-nine, she was gone. She had struggled to live on, fighting cataracts and other ailments. Schaefer's staff insisted that he had visited with his mother as much as possible, but as Tululu said, he'd been busy, and he was not good at staying in touch with people who were close to him and dying. He would visit them in the hospital, and sometimes he would call, but often he temporized and lamented later that he had not called before someone died. He agonized when friends or their husbands or wives died. And now who did he have?

He had three cousins on his mother's family's side: Anita Keinzle, her sister Jeri, and Anna Mae Gaigler. Anita and Anna Mae lived in Maryland, Jeri in Florida. Anita in particular stayed in close touch with Schaefer and Jeri had been a soulmate when they were youngsters and through the early years of his law career. But when he spoke of family, a rarity, Schaefer never mentioned the cousins, though they wrote to him regularly and had him out to dinner or a picnic at least once a year. The cousins knew a good deal about Schaefer's parents and paternal grandparents, having grown up in the same West Baltimore neighborhood. Schaefer had been completely faithful to his mother, a good son who believed in the right things.

But Anita thought something was missing between mother and son: the most basic expressions of affection. "I'd love to hug him," Tululu told her niece, "but I think he'd faint." Somehow, as close as they were, as committed to her as he had been, this mother and her son did not always connect. They seemed to have spent a lifetime hoping to bridge an emotional chasm that turned out to be too wide. One thing seems clear: If Don Schaefer missed his mother's embrace, as many of his friends speculated later, she missed it at least as much.

On the day of the funeral, Schaefer sat at the front of the church with Hilda Mae. Janet Hoffman managed the seating of dignitaries, including Governor Hughes, Congresswoman Mikulski, and U.S. Senator Sarbanes. Members of the City Council served as pallbearers. Irv Kovens rode in the hearse with the mayor and Ms. Snoops to Western Cemetery, just a few blocks east of the house on Edgewood.

He was bereft as his friends had feared. He felt orphaned, alone. Some of his critics complained about the formal arrangements, the official cast to the ceremonies—police escorts and the like. A public man, even one so devoted to his job, should have been able to bury his mother in peace. Or was the reaction based on antipathy for the ceremonial nature of almost everything that happened in Baltimore under Schaefer?

Yet the dreaded moment of anguish and loss reintroduced him to at least one of his many opponents. "I went to the funeral service and then on to the grave site," wrote Kweisi Mfume, then a member of the city council. He and Schaefer had warred over a dozen issues, including Mfume's quest to make Martin Luther King Jr.'s birthday a holiday in the city. "I knew what it was like to lose your mother, no matter what your age or station in life. . . . Standing there at the end of that grave, I saw a side of him I'd never seen before. He wept uncontrollably before the flower-draped coffin as it rested on the struts over the freshly dug hole. My mind, for an instant, darted backward in time, to when I stood where he stood. Although long since closed, that chapter of pain was now unfolding its pages before me. I discovered we had come from similar backgrounds, with mothers who had been strong influences in our lives. His personal sense of loss was now reminding me of my own. Although we occasionally clashed in the council after that, the level of our anger was never the same. That day in the cemetery something intangible had changed between us and brought with it a mutual respect."

Again, an enemy had become an ally, and Schaefer would become one of Mfume's strongest supporters, applauding his service in the U.S. Congress, where he represented the Seventh Congressional District for ten years and later his ascension to the presidency of the NAACP. In 1999 Schaefer backed Mfume as a candidate for mayor of Baltimore, undoubtedly the highest compliment he could have paid his old adversary.

If a man like Schaefer could launch himself more ferociously into work as a place to hide his grief, the opportunity was there for him. And, to the relief of his friends, he seemed to rebound reasonably well. He had to, in a sense. His city was bristling with new buildings, proposed new buildings, contracts for new buildings. The new subway, approved by the state in 1976 along with the convention center, connecting the corridor that extends from Owings Mills in Baltimore County to Lexington Market and other center city stops, opened on November 19, 1983. Redwood Tower Associates announced a plan to develop 175,000 square feet of office building space above the Water Street Garage a few blocks north of Harborplace on Redwood Street. A few weeks after that, garage construction was announced or begun by Days Inn, the Sheraton Hotel, and the Rusty

Scupper. A ribbon was cut for the opening of One Center Plaza, and another office tower and the Space Telescope Building on the Johns Hopkins University campus opened. On March 25, the city celebrated the twenty-fifth anniversary of the Charles Center Plan's adoption. Five days later, on March 30, the Brookshire Hotel opened—to the laughter of city officials who had decided a garage could be converted to a hotel despite ceilings that would be only about 7 feet high. "A hotel for midgets," one critic sneered. But in renaissance Baltimore, where every hotel room was needed, developers of the Brookshire were undeterred by mere headroom and pressed ahead. The garage-to-hotel transformation was completed expeditiously and fared well among visitors of varying heights.

Proposals were entertained for conversion of the old BG&E power plant on the harbor just east of the aquarium and for the old Fish Market a few blocks north. The Six Flags entertainment company planned to tackle the brick power-generating hulk and would become one of many enterprises hoping to turn the location into something lucrative despite the industrial trappings symbolized by massive smokestacks on the roof.

Schaefer met with many of these developers, welcoming them all and thinking carefully about the timing of each project the city blessed. Rouse was anxious to develop a new shopping venue on the north side of Pratt Street—a street-width's distance from Harborplace—but Schaefer held him back. Walter Sondheim marveled at the mayor's timing instincts in such matters. Rouse's Gallery opened in 1985 to as many raves as his famous waterside pavilions.

Others, as always, marveled at Schaefer's nerve. With help from Benton's sharp mind and Embry's federal action grants, he had coaxed A. N. Pritzker to overrule experts who said a Hyatt Hotel would not work in Baltimore. And he was hoping he could find someone to redevelop substantial sections of the failing commercial district radiating out from the new subway stop at Lexington Market. He had breakfast one day with a developer from California, Robert Murdock, whose man Friday was Bob Haldeman, former chief of staff for President Richard Nixon up to and including the Watergate scandal. As had many of the Watergate survivors, Haldeman turned out to be a commodity in demand, a government operator whose presumed high-level government access, no doubt, made them marketable. Murdock wanted to build a hotel at the Inner Harbor in about the same spot as the old McCormick spice plant. Schaefer had tried to get his nemesis, Henry Knott, Sr., the man who sold him the dumpsite, to build the hotel, but Knott couldn't see much promise in it. According to Tom

Biddison, one of Knott's lawyers at the firm of Gallagher, Evelius and Jones, Knott always tried to invest in must-succeed ventures—shopping centers where growth was certain and housing in places where buyers were plentiful and had few choices. He could build what they needed at the right price and have some reasonable hope of making money.

Harbor Court was going to be the highest-end lodging, a product for the rich, who, Knott thought, had too many options. They could stay where they were or move any place they chose. He didn't see why anyone would want to live at the Inner Harbor and turned Schaefer down—again.

Murdock, on the other hand, was eager.

"What would I have to do to show you how much I want to build that hotel?" he asked over breakfast.

Schaefer was looking out the window of the Sheraton's coffee shop when the question came.

"See that building?" he said, pointing at the corner of West Baltimore and Park. "Buy that building right there. It's a nice, important, historic building. Buy it and fix it up. Then we'll see what we can do."

Murdock turned to Haldeman. "Buy that building," he commanded.

"Okay," said Haldeman, smiling.

"Right now," said Murdock. "Go and buy it right now."

Haldeman excused himself, wondering no doubt how one bought such a building in Baltimore all in one day. He found out. Soon enough, Murdock owned the requisite good faith building, fixed it up, and eventually won the Harbor Court contract. Many notable rich people did choose to stay in the very sumptuous hotel rooms, and a few others bought condominiums overlooking the harbor. Old Henry was wrong on this one.

Blue Chip-In

Schaefer didn't care for James Earl Carter, but Carter was the last president with a fully articulated urban policy. UDAGs, revenue sharing, housing programs, and the 1973 Comprehensive Employment and Training Act (CETA) were all fonts of money for mayors when Carter was in office. Schaefer used them all, shaping them to his political and policy needs. Revenue sharing, which pumped millions into the city's collapsing fiscal arteries with no restrictions on its use, was manna from federal heaven. But the program called CETA was among the most important for Schaefer, who managed to mold it into a public works program that was fully integrated with his neighborhood development effort. At its peak, CETA spent as much as $200 million a year in the five-county metropolitan region to train the undereducated and skill-deficient inner-city participants. Work experience, training, child care stipends, and a host of other attributes made CETA an ideal tool for mayors. Schaefer's program had even turned the much maligned Public Service Employment program—leaf raking, pure and simple—into an efficient way for the hard-core unemployed to enter and remain in the work force at higher and higher levels of pay. Laura Morlock, a public health researcher at the Johns Hopkins University, found that PSE graduates, people who were taught the importance of showing up for work, stayed in the work force and improved themselves financially with each year they remained. The program died ultimately at the hands of those who considered it part of the Democrats' "coast to coast breadline," a derisive observation by then congressman Jack Kemp, a New York Republican. But in Baltimore, under the follow-up ferocity of Plevy and Schaefer, the program had been a distinct success.

The architect was Marion Pines, a manpower specialist whose skills and energy were nationally recognized by scholars such as Sar Levitan, who sent federal bureaucrats and policy makers to Baltimore for a glimpse of federal programs that were working well.

But these programs went on the block in the 1980s and Schaefer realized that he would have to save them. As Ronald Reagan's administration began to chip away at CETA, revenue sharing, and all the housing programs, Schaefer took his case to Capitol Hill. He appeared before any committee that would have him, beginning with the House Ways and Means Committee. He was a hit. His passion and the reputation and image of his city—not to speak of the O's and the Colts—got him through the door, with plenty of attention once he was there. But his presentations did little to hold the federal dollars.

The largest percentage of Washington money, particularly the community development block grant funds, went directly into the neighborhoods, though some was used to prepare infrastructure, such as piers, riprap, and shoring up at the Inner Harbor. Orlinsky battled with Schaefer constantly in those days over every possible policy question, but he thought Schaefer was right to complain that people did not appreciate how much money was going to the neighborhoods.

The PSEs were bread and butter for Schaefer's City Hall team. These workers built walls, put up community signs, rehabbed child care centers, did parks maintenance—whatever needed to be done. Baltimore's mayor was attempting his own synergy: Use the jobs program to get people employed, yes, but do it in a way that augmented your public works effort, saving a dollar or two, perhaps, and making the city more livable. "They weren't building bridges," said Paul Schurick, "but they were making a contribution. Kids saw what it was like to have a job." Leaf rakers were learning to show up for work—a new experience for many—and were making their neighborhoods look good in the process. Everything would build on itself.

"There was value in erecting a sign that said Welcome To Hampden," Schurick said—to the city and to the workers. Reagan would visit Baltimore later and declare its glistening new skyline a tribute to the free market. Others thought it was a hymn to government pump priming.

As Reagan's team dismantled or starved the jobs program, Schaefer asked the free marketeers to bail him out. His prospects were not great. If government thought it was wasteful, what must the generally antigovernment business guys think? Schaefer, as always, went to Butta, the phone company honcho and solid Baltimore boy, a kid who had come up the way Schaefer had. Butta's parish priest got him a football scholarship at Loyola, one of the city's best parochial high schools. The priest told the coach that Butta was a kicker, though he had never kicked a football in his life. He looked good in his tryout and the coach said, "Okay." How long had he been playing football? "About a week," Butta said. The priest pretended not to hear, and he hoped the coach wouldn't have second thoughts. The scholarship held.

Butta, who mastered every job in the phone company from lineman to CEO, never forgot the opportunity he'd been given. He knew the value of the PSEs, and he was always ready to take Schaefer's case to the business community. When he came to his colleagues, they said, "Oh God he's back for more money."

"It's not money I want," he told them.

Like Schaefer, he saw local businesses stepping into the employment breach left by Washington as "a fundamental piece of what we were trying to do in Baltimore." By the early 1980s, Butta thought Baltimore had finally developed—under Schaefer's goading—a core of reliable CEOs: USF&G's Jack Moseley, BGE's Trueschler and George McGowan, banker H. Stephenson Peck, Mercantile's Baldwin, Crown Central Petroleum's

Henry Rosenberg, and Monumental Insurance's Leslie Disharoon. Despite Butta's optimism, Schaefer as usual fomented a "donnybrook," Butta recalled.

"He called us to his office and he said, 'Reagan is pulling a lot of my programs away. I don't have money to open swimming pools, to teach fire safety in the schools, to insulate homes — all this stuff is going unless you guys help.' We listened. But no one said anything. He got up and walked out of the room. But the next day he asked us to come back, and he just reamed us a new one."

"You weren't listening," Schaefer said. "You don't have any idea what I was talking about. Do you think I asked you over here for a free coke?"

A few of his guests got a bit heated and started to give it back to him.

Butta intervened. "Excuse me, Mr. Mayor. Are you asking us to raise money for things that previously were paid for with tax dollars?"

"Well," Schaefer said, "we've got a genius on the premises."

"Well," Butta said, "what you're asking is kind of foreign to what we believe in."

Schaefer had tried to annex corporations, to fuse them in some way to his municipal apparatus, to make Butta, Baldwin, and the rest unofficial department heads. What he was seeking now was a new and thoroughgoing partnership between public and private resources. Without that, he was saying, all would be lost.

"Have Marion Pines make a list of these projects, cost them out, we'll see which ones we can support. We'll try to raise money for the ones we agree with," Butta said.

Pines and her team went to work, producing a booklet with sixty-eight projects crisply defined and budgeted one by one. They called the whole thing Blue Chip-In. The business guys looked it over.

"We won't do the golf courses. Let the golfers pay for that," Butta said. But BGE loaned the city a manager who took over the courses and turned them into a thriving business, giving Baltimore one of the least costly and best-run systems of municipal courses in the nation, with low greens fees and well-cared-for courses.

Butta, Trueschler, and Moseley personally worked a bank of phones arranged by the phone guy, Butta. They asked an insurance company to run a program that taught fire safety. The company pledged $100,000 to the effort. Trueschler and BGE took the home insulation program. Butta took the old Mount Clare Mansion and employed seventy-five kids to work the grounds for the summer. In a single afternoon, they raised $675,000. Then Pines and Butta barged into offices all over the city until businesses had covered most of the projects. They found jobs for 1,200 kids whose salaries had been paid previously by the federal government. A year after that, they lined up more jobs than they could fill.

Schaefer never let up on them. Every time he saw them, Butta said, he jabbed at some chore they hadn't attended to—or at least not to his satisfaction.

"How long can you look at that filth outside your office?" he asked Butta one day.

"What're you talking about. My building is spotless."

"The tree grates are full of cigarette butts," Schaefer said, referring to the metal coverings over the tree wells, installed to keep the sidewalks level and protect the roots.

"My people aren't out there," Butta said.

Schaefer stared at him, saying nothing.

"So I cleaned the tree boxes."

Moseley, whose office was across the street from Butta's, said that Schaefer wasn't the mayor: He was the head janitor, the police chief, the job development manager, and the sanitation chief.

Absentee

Schaefer chose not to attend the 1984 Democratic Convention in San Francisco. Instead, he went to San Diego to see that city's zoo. He had endorsed Walter F. Mondale that year, but he was not overly fond of him. And he hated conventions of all kinds, annual meetings, and conclaves of the sort that were designed to get people out of their home cities and into a thinly veiled vacation. He never wanted to leave Baltimore, but in this case, he was anxious to see the famous zoo. His absence was observed by Maryland's assembled Democratic team, but he was hardly missed. Hyman Pressman was on hand at the convention to represent Baltimore, along with many other office holders, including Governor Hughes and Attorney General Sachs.

Near the end of the four-day nominating session, Hughes and Sachs arrived at the convention hall a bit early and were sitting on folding chairs waiting for the program to begin. Hughes had picked up a complimentary copy of the San Francisco *Chronicle*. After a moment, he turned and held out the newspaper so that Sachs could see the banner headline:

"MADMAN KILLS FOUR CHILDREN AT MCDONALD'S." Someone with an automatic rifle had run amok in San Diego.

After a second, Hughes said, "Schaefer's in San Diego, isn't he?"

Sachs winced and then howled with laughter.

Mayflower Day

His father said, "The Colts are going to win today," so they went to Memorial Stadium even though his grandfather, his father's father, lay near death. The end came a few days later. . . . My aunt asked me if I missed him and I felt like saying I didn't know, he'd just died, but I said yes while trying to bear the image of the corpse by thinking about the Colts. They'd beaten Green Bay 41-21. It was their only victory that year.

William Gildea, When the Colts Belonged to Baltimore

Schaefer felt that he should love the Colts the way his city, or most of his city, loved them. He didn't. He was too preoccupied with a thousand other things to sit for so long at any entertainment. He went to games, of course, but found ways to leave after making his appearances. If the team fell behind, the mayor could plead high anxiety and clear out to avoid the pain. He knew he needed an all-purpose cover story because at Memorial Stadium, Baltimoreans were doing what he always urged them to do: cheering for the city, in effect, taking pride in its greatness, standing and sitting together.

Baltimore might fairly have burst with pride from its role in bringing the National Football League into the modern era. The city had gained a measure of status from men like John Unitas, Alan Ameche, Raymond Berry, Don Shula, Bubba Smith, and Artie Donovan—all players on the 1958 team that won a sudden-death championship game in the last minute against the New York Giants. That game spawned a generation of Sunday afternoon couch potatoes and gave the NFL a fabulous TV market. Players' salaries and owners' profits accelerated, and the team became, unbeknownst to civic leaders, an important amenity, an urban institution that was as critical to a city's image as a good library, school system, or symphony. Baltimoreans knew more about themselves and the nation knew more about Baltimore as the result of football, a game that was very like the gritty industrial city in which the team flourished. Baseball did not fare nearly as well. The stadium seldom sold out even when the Orioles were in the World Series. The Colts games always sold out, though the park had not been built for football. It was a make-do venue but an altogether fitting one. A bit angular and demanding some effort from the spectator, the park was obscure and anonymous in comparison with Yankee Stadium, the Superdome, or Joe Robbie Stadium in Miami.

Unitas, the quarterback, was a young man from Pennsylvania's coal mining and steel-making area and therefore a fitting hero for the men and women of Bethlehem Steel. Workers from the Point were in the stands on Sunday to watch the sometimes surly Unitas, as bandy-legged and swaggering as William Donald Schaefer himself, willing victory with a cast of talented and determined teammates—like Schaefer's. The steelworkers sat in the seats next to bankers, stockbrokers, and pharmacists, who cared just as deeply about football and the Colts and would convince themselves that it was okay to leave a sick relative's bedside to see the team play.

For Schaefer, particularly after the championship year, the team was Baltimore's symbolic claim to greatness. So in 1976, when the team's new owner began to make clear his interest in moving to another city, Schaefer's anxiety reached new levels. Could the city hang on to its momentum, his progress, and its NFL team? Could it nurture and retain its sporting birthright? If it couldn't, how could it claim to be a great city? Schaefer thought of the Colts as a handhold on the slippery slope of decline, despair, and low self-esteem. He knew the city's grasp was slipping.

Robert Irsay, a red-faced, white-haired industrial air conditioning contractor, bought the team from Carroll Rosenbloom in 1972, a year after Schaefer became mayor. Rosenbloom had purchased the team in 1953 and built it into a champion. Irsay moved the franchise in the other direction. Like some other owners, Irsay thought he knew enough to intervene in team decisions. And as early as March 1976, he flirted openly with other cities that were anxious to put themselves on the NFL map. Phoenix was the first of these suitors; representatives of that city met with Irsay in Chicago and made what was described as an "attractive offer" for the Baltimore team. From that point on, newspaper stories were regularly written about Irsay in one city or another meeting with city officials and exploring some deal even as, in Baltimore, the owner and his agents were demanding improvements at Memorial Stadium, a new training facility, and improvements in the lease deal. When ground was broken for the training facility, Irsay made clear his modus operandi: "I had to go to California to get this going," he said. In August 1979, he met with officials in Jacksonville and 45,000 fans who were determined to win his heart and his team. Later that month, he handed Governor Harry Hughes a $25 million wish list during a meeting at the state fairgrounds in Timonium. It was not a matter of *if* he would move the team, he said then and there, but *when*. Two months later, at a meeting of NFL team owners, Irsay seemed to relent, saying that of course he and Baltimore could reach an understanding. Irsay was always brutally frank about whatever position he happened to occupy on a given day. In 1979, he said he had shopped the team around only to improve the stadium. Maybe it was only better seating and concession stands he had in mind, or maybe it really was just a matter of when he would leave.

Schaefer knew: Irsay was leaving. "If it rained on Tuesday and he didn't like rain on Tuesday in Baltimore, he was going. It didn't make any difference what we did." Affecting full-blown optimism in public, Schaefer tried to mimic the mind-set of other Baltimoreans: "You didn't think about them not being here." He thought about it all the time, of course. He worked the irascible Irsay constantly and spoke glowingly of him to reporters, probing all the while for an accommodation—a long-term lease, perhaps, name the terms. Irsay said he saw no problem with signing such a lease, but shortly afterward, the team played an exhibition game with the Atlanta Falcons in Phoenix, and another shopping expedition ensued. Irsay met with officials in New York to discuss a move to Shea Stadium to replace the departed Jets. Schaefer tried not to notice. He tried to establish a personal relationship with the owner, meeting with him periodically at the new practice facility. Irsay would be accompanied by his wife, who always brought her hairdresser on the team owner's jet, and by a priest, who Schaefer assumed was on hand to pray for victory or perhaps happy landings. Irsay's son, Jimmy, would be somewhat ostentatiously walking around the facility lifting weights.

Schaefer found Irsay a decent and reasonable man—until lunchtime. "Nine o'clock, he was fine. Ten o'clock, fine. Eleven o'clock he was fine. Then we'd go to lunch at a place called Francis Scott Key across from WCBM, and as we walked in the door someone handed him a double vodka, and when we sat down someone gave him another. Then he had the third during lunch. And he was an entirely different personality."

Irsay and Schaefer might well have hit it off. "I'm known to like odd people," Schaefer said. "I liked him at first. We got along pretty good. I guess it was because anything he wanted I did for him." But Schaefer's assessment of Irsay's psyche was not encouraging for the long run: "It was absolutely essential that he be better than the next guy. If you had a cup of coffee, he had to have a larger cup. If you had an airplane, he had to have a larger airplane." If another team owner had a stadium with sky-boxes, Irsay would have to have them.

Schaefer spent years trying to sell Bob Irsay on a stadium that could never have skyboxes. Here was Schaefer, who had changed the face of a city, bending to the will of a single man with nothing on his mind, it seemed, beyond a bigger and better sandbox for his highly paid athletes. In a sense, the urban history of the late 1980s and 1990s in America had to do not with public education, highways, or teen pregnancy, but with luxury suites at football and baseball stadiums where the wealthy owners could make big profits and the corporate community could entertain. The boxes brought prestige and money. The people paid for ballparks that many of them could not afford to use.

Asked once during these months of negotiations what he might do to keep Irsay, Schaefer said, "I guess I could buy him a pound of chocolates. I don't know what else I could do. We negotiated with him, agreeing to everything, but he was a double-crosser. He lied. He flew into BWI one night, I met him. We were going to have dinner." Irsay appeared to be drunk. Schaefer babysat him, pretending Irsay was as sober as Vernon Eney, desperately hoping he could deal with this man as if he really did care about Baltimore. Irsay, meanwhile, had been flying around the country dangling his team in front of cities like Jacksonville and Memphis. But he had told Schaefer he would call before he did anything. The two men talked in a private airport lounge. When they emerged, Irsay taunted the waiting reporters. Schaefer tried to keep him cool, but the reporters were goading him without meaning to, thinking they were asking him proper and appropriate questions.

"Why don't you spend your own money to renovate the stadium?" one of them asked.

Irsay said he didn't have that kind of money and pulled out his wallet.

"Here. Here's all the money I have in the world." He took a handful of bills out of his pocket and handed it to Bill Glauber of the *Sun*.

"Go ahead, count it."

Glauber, stunned, did what the owner asked as the group moved down a hallway. The reporter walked along with Irsay's $1,200 in cash, wondering how to give it back to a man who seemed, at that moment, unconcerned about getting it back. Schaefer watched in silent horror. But nothing more than theater transpired before, after forty minutes, Irsay got back on his plane and left. He promised to call Schaefer to report on his decision.

Schaefer had given up on Irsay and turned to other measures. Irsay, he knew, had been looking for an excuse to leave. "He was doing everything to discourage people, throwing good players out. But he was still getting 40,000 for the games. He wanted skyboxes. But we couldn't do it unless we tore down the stadium and rebuilt it." Having done everything but beg publicly, Schaefer allowed city legislators to file a bill in the state legislature that would have frozen the team in Baltimore by taking it as a public amenity under some version of eminent domain. The timing was not propitious, though Irsay wasn't, in any case, open to a rational argument for staying—or even to a very good deal. By now, the matter had descended to the level of decimal points: the percentage rates on the $15 million or $20 million loans Irsay needed. Who would offer the lowest rate for the football team owner's borrowing?

At the same time, Maryland sweetened its deal. Schaefer had said earlier that a new stadium could not be built, but he and Governor Hughes promised to free up $7.5 million already offered to spruce up Memorial Stadium and agreed to a $15 million low-interest loan Irsay needed for the note then coming due for his original purchase of the team. The deal also included the $4.4 million purchase offer for the team's Owings Mills training facility and the state's guarantee that 43,000 seats would be sold in the next season. Frank J. De Francis, the governor's economic developer, told Hughes he thought Irsay's demands had finally been met. But the owner's almost daily meetings with governors and mayors continued from Bakersfield to Jacksonville and one point in between, Indianapolis. Schaefer and Baltimore's state legislators were certain he was using the city to get the best deal elsewhere. When the 1984 legislative session opened in Annapolis, a bill was filed that would allow Baltimore to use its eminent domain power to seize the team. If the measure passed, Schaefer could take the Colts the way he took buildings for urban renewal, asserting some overriding public need. This was the ultimate weapon, proof that Baltimore had lost the game. Since the gambit was provocative and almost certainly would have failed, it showed the city's utter desperation. On March 27, the state Senate passed the eminent domain bill, and when Irsay read about it the next day, he called his lawyer, Michael Chernoff. That's it, he said in effect, we're moving. Instantly. If the Colts were headed for court, they wanted it to be an Indiana court, imagining that Hoosier judges would find that the equities lay on the side of football in their state. Irsay figured he had to move before the bill passed the House and was signed by the governor. Unbeknownst to Schaefer, the deal was all but done.

On the table in Indianapolis was the promise of a brand-new $80 million domed stadium, a twenty-year lease giving Irsay all the revenue from tickets (except for taxes), and half the income from skybox rentals. Indianapolis guaranteed the sale of about 40,000 tickets—equivalent to about $7 million a year, according to Jon Morgan, author of *Glory for Sale,* which chronicles how owners use America's love for sports to pry huge payoffs from public treasuries. The team had been promised $25,000 for moving expenses—though Mayflower Van Lines, headquartered outside Indianapolis, took care of the move without charge. (Irsay kept the moving allowance anyway.)

On Wednesday evening, only hours after Irsay learned of the state senate's vote, Mayflower trucks pulled up to the team's training facility in Owings Mills. Their first mission was to grab the team's financial records, on the theory they had the most legal significance. Shoulder pads and blocking sleds could come later. Employees had not been told of the planned evacuation in an effort to keep it secret for as long as possible. One of them called local media, and television cameras showed up to record for posterity what Morgan calls "the ignoble scene of an NFL franchise sneaking out of its hometown." John Steadman, the sports columnist, also got a call and immediately phoned Hank Butta.

"Did you know the Colts are leaving?" he asked. Butta said no. "Well, the vans are pulling out right now," Steadman said. A wet spring snow fell as the green and yellow trucks headed out of town. Schaefer feared that the image of their departure would hang the tag "loser" across the profile of his overachieving city. He'd had a bit of a premonition and turned on his bedside radio just before midnight. He listened without moving as an announcer described the result of what he regarded as an inevitability. He did not sprint for the phone or his car, he said later, concluding that it was too late, short of a highway blockade. Indiana State Police cruisers met the vans as they crossed the state line, making complete the appearance of one state hijacking another's sports team.

Governor Hughes later blamed Schaefer, asserting that De Francis had the matter in hand when the desperation move for expanded eminent domain rights went into the legislative process. Schaefer respected De Francis, but he also knew that Irsay had been waiting for the right deal and the right provocation. Baltimore had been doomed—by its prudent unwillingness to build a new stadium, by the nationwide seller's market for NFL teams, and by Irsay's guileful determination to leave for a greener ballyard. The owner was right about one thing: The team was valuable. In its first year of playing away from Baltimore, the Colts' revenues grew 35 percent—from $19.5 million to $26.3 million.

Crumbs

The city was left with almost nothing of its proud football heritage— no memorabilia of its championship seasons, no trophies or jerseys or labeled game balls with the scores of big wins, nothing. Not even the name Colts. No sign remained that Unitas, Berry, or Ameche had ever trodden the field adjacent to 33rd Street. The day of the Indianapolis ruling or a day later, Baltimore County Executive Ted Venetoulis got a phone call from the Colts' lawyer, Michael Chernoff. "I don't know who to talk to in the city. I think everyone in that town hates us," he told Venetoulis. "We were wondering if Baltimore was going to appeal. He had called Venetoulis because they had worked together on securing the Colts' training facility in Owings Mills. "We'd like to end this thing now," Chernoff said. "We'd be willing to negotiate some things if he doesn't appeal. You're going to lose the appeal. It's just going to cost us all money."

Venetoulis called Schaefer to report the call and to ask if and how he should proceed.

"See what they have in mind," Schaefer said. Venetoulis and Chernoff, anxious to be out of view or earshot of any Baltimorean, met at the Hay-Adams Hotel in Washington, a block from the White House. Venetoulis drove back to Baltimore with the sense that Chernoff and Irsay were looking for something as yet unstated. "We ought to ask for more," he told Schaefer. "We ought to go back and ask for a vote if Baltimore's name ever came up for an expansion franchise."

They decided that they would also ask for the training facility. "They wanted $5 million in cash for it," said Ventoulis. "We had paid $3.5 million." Venetoulis and Chernoff met again, this time at a motel in Chicago. Venetoulis did not want to blow money on an appeal, so he sought an opportunity to salvage something—even if that something was rightfully Baltimore's to begin with. "The mayor's got to have the name of the team and an agreement that Irsay will vote for Baltimore." They wrangled over that for hours, touching also on the city's demand for payment of its legal fees.

Irsay wanted cash. He was in the middle of a divorce.

"If you want a deal," Chernoff said, "We have to do something about the property. There's no sense in us holding on to it."

"I'm not sure the mayor wants it," Venetoulis said.

No decision was reached, but they met again a few days later at the Hay-Adams. Chernoff reported that Irsay wanted $5 million and suggested the city get an appraisal.

Venetoulis reported to Schaefer once again: "I'll pay the appraised value and not a penny more. I have to get it through the council," Schaefer said. "I'm sure they'll go along with buying it, but we can't pay an inflated figure."

Negotiations resumed, this time concentrating on the name. Baltimore said that it wanted a promise for restoration of the name if the city got a team within ten years. Three, said Chernoff.

"We ended up at five," said Venetoulis. "We could have the name automatically if we got a team. After that we could negotiate, but we'd have to pay. Schaefer showed his ineffable pragmatism by calling Irsay to ask for his vote when Baltimore was eventually in line for an expansion team. The vote had been promised but was denied when the time came. There was a point where ownership of the name really did change."

Irsay agreed to take $3.5 million for the training facility. Unwilling to part with actual money, he would not pay legal fees. The city had already spent $600,000 on lawyers and wanted to cut its losses without appearing to miss any opportunity of winning. They were fighting over the crumbs, but Schaefer was pleased to get something out of the deal. It was not much: a few Jerseys and game balls. Most important, he thought, was Irsay's agreement to vote for Baltimore and return the name if a team came to the city in five years.

Schaefer refused to attend the meeting at which the deal was to be signed. He participated by phone. Irsay was also on the phone. At a signal from their seconds, they signed simultaneously—one man in Baltimore, the other in Chicago.

At that time, Chernoff was still insisting that without the eminent domain bill, things could have worked out differently. Schaefer said later that he agreed only reluctantly to try to seize the team, knowing that it wouldn't work but afraid not to make every possible effort to keep the team. He was less concerned with appearing to fail personally than with the blow the city's fragile psyche would have to absorb, setting back all the work he had done in neighborhoods and with the Aquarium, the Convention

Center, and the Inner Harbor. Schaefer was often accused of focusing on bricks and mortar, and he did, but he saw construction as a spur to the imagination. And he knew that losing the football team would work the other way.

"We had gotten past that inferiority thing," he said. "We had the best damned city in the United States. Part of it was smoke and mirrors. . . . There was always something else we were doing."

In the Baltimore years, he would never have conceded for one moment that anything he did fell short of concrete reality; the concept of smoke and mirrors was not one he could live with. But now some of the most substantial smoke had wafted away toward Indiana. Schaefer had been weakened by the willingness of another mayor to provide the skyboxes.

In those years, Schaefer had been unwilling to divert so much political and financial capital to the chore of keeping a football team. The power of the owners was no more than an abstraction to him or anyone in Maryland. Priorities were, in order, the renaissance, education, and then the sporting psyche. He and Butta had rejected a proposal to simply pay Irsay $7 million a year to stay. But the mayor of Indianapolis then, William Hudnut, was fully involved in the bidding for Bob Irsay, his priest, his wife's hairdresser, and the whole retinue of sporting extortion.

"He was a good man," Schaefer said of Hudnut. "He had to do what he had to do."

And so did the mayor of Baltimore. Schaefer's idea women and men came to a meeting shortly after the team's departure to hear the cheerleader without a team. He was hurt but still confident in the partisans, the men and women of zeal who stood at the opposite end of the spectrum from Irsay. "They could never rest. They never rested one minute. They always knew if we rested, the city would start on its way down," he said. "Even if they didn't rest, even if they worked nonstop, the setback was always waiting for you." He was talking about himself, of course.

Moving On

Media images of white-haired, pink-faced Bob Irsay and his night-riding Mayflower vans helped to keep the city's last remaining major league sports team, the Orioles, in Baltimore. Owner Ed Williams wanted to move the O's over to Washington, Schaefer was certain, but Williams, who consorted with Supreme Court justices and even presidents, did not wish to think of himself as a knave or sneak like Irsay.

By now, sports were the major preoccupation of Schaefer's public life. Young Tommy and McKeldin had faced the demands of poor people and black militants, who had made legitimate claims for power and a share of government's favor. Schaefer and time had all-but neutralized protest. But he had to contend with sometimes sociopathic, self-important, and greedy club owners who were willing to plunder public treasuries state by state, using the popular love of sport as a mighty lever. Though Irsay could be dismissed as a drunken oaf, a man to be rid of, his departure left a stain on Schaefer's renaissance tapestry. Classy as he was by comparison, Williams might have left another. Chicanery was everywhere.

Cleveland Browns owner Art Modell was offering hope and redemption on the NFL side. A man with the league-founding stature of Chicago's George Halas, Modell promised to be Schaefer's ally at NFL ownership councils, to help him get an expansion franchise or even, eventually—could he be serious?—bring the Browns to Baltimore. Modell and Schaefer met secretly at Martin State Airport east of Baltimore in 1985 within a year after the Colts' departure. There, they discussed various incarnations of owner and franchise in Baltimore: bringing Cleveland's team or selling it with the sure knowledge that a man such as Modell could have from his fellow owners what he wanted when he wanted it. Who else would have a better shot at winning an expansion franchise? Publicly, Modell talked about Irsay's perfidy as a public relations disaster for the league, a destabilizing and almost criminal assault on the NFL's capital: its fan base. He voiced his outrage even as he talked about moving his own team. For his part, Schaefer said that Baltimore's policy would be to reject any deal that resembled what Irsay had done. Neither Schaefer nor Modell appeared entirely forthcoming about their intentions. Whether Schaefer would have taken the Browns in those days is unclear, but he needed someone at the NFL table to represent Baltimore. Modell's promises of help notwithstanding, Baltimore never seemed to have a faithful ally. When Modell abandoned Baltimore in a 1993 vote that might have restored the city's franchise, Schaefer felt victimized and misled. Some would think later that Schaefer was naive and that Modell was acting to preserve an option for himself, denying Baltimore's bid and leaving himself in a position to take what people were beginning to realize was a more than generous offer. It would only get more delicious as years passed.

Pothole Princess

Meanwhile, Schaefer had a city to run. There were ribbons to cut, festivals to plan, and new renewal areas to target. In the fall of 1982 Schaefer told Bereska, while driving back to city hall, that he wanted something done about potholes and he wanted it done immediately. Something dramatic, visible, and compelling was needed to get the pitted surfaces of Baltimore streets repaired and to show drivers that their city and its mayor wanted them to have a smooth ride.

"Oh, Boss," Bereska said, "Don't you think we should let Christmas go by first, wait for spring. You've got your other Christmas stuff going. It's cold." As usual, she knew she'd spoken too soon even before she was finished.

Schaefer turned in his seat. "Okay, Mouth," he snapped, using one of his terms for his chief aide, "I want it done now, and you are going to do it."

Humiliated and feeling somehow responsible for his anger, she went to work, filled again with the infuriating and irresistible need to please him. As soon as they got back to city hall she went to the bathroom, put the toilet seat up, and sat on the bare, cold porcelain hoping to jolt an idea—

a good idea—into her quavering brain. In a short time, she had it: Why not ennoble the inelegant pothole by harnessing it to love and the coming Valentine's Day celebration?

The swains of Charm City could make a public declaration of commitment to their ladies—and their city—by subsidizing the cost of road tar to be dolloped into the jolting erosions. A sign would be erected right on the street, naming the giver and the recipient of this public expression of care and concern. For $5, advertisements explained, one could be "Sweet to Your Street and Also to Your Sweetie." Interested subscribers could call in their pledges on a special city hall "Heart Line." Alliteration and rhyme, not to speak of euphemism, were integral. A "Pothole Princess" could be crowned at the site of "roadway irregularities."

Bereska met with public works crews to encourage their heartfelt participation—no simple task, since many of them thought the promotion ridiculous and not in their job descriptions. She stood in the public works department main yard one morning and told them they damned well would put on the heart-shaped shirts she had designed and preside at the pouring of the tar—or leave. She reminded them that she had arranged many of their jobs in the first place. It was for moments such as this that she had quizzed Walter Beuchelt so thoroughly.

Signs were set up at the location of every work site. One read as follows:

> Friends are Special Valentines,
> Deserving of a special treat.
> So filling potholes in a road,
> Is friendship to a street.
> We really think you're wonderful,
> So just in honor of you.
> We've filled that pothole at 2810 Pulaski Highway
> With love and asphalt too.
>   (signed) Citizen X and the City of Baltimore.

People rushed to have one of their own, selecting a favorite verse to go with it. The willing suspension of Baltimore's legendary cynicism showed again how fully the citizens had embraced the antics of their mayor. No one hooted. Jim Rouse sent $300. Thirty fourth graders at the Margaret Brent Elementary School pooled their funds to patch a $2-sized hole in honor of their teacher. The idea developed an instant national following as well. United Press International put a story about the project on its wire, and the CBS news department filmed the work of filling and designating a hole on 27th Street east of St. Paul. The *Wall Street Journal* ran a feature story. The cities of Lubbock (Texas), San Francisco, and Palm Beach, among others, announced that they would follow the Baltimore lead.

Schaefer's occasionally abusive manner could work supremely well, as exhibited by this caper. If he sent two people out to do the same chore, knowingly put them into explosively conflicted situations, or verbally abused them, he usually got the results he wanted and, over time, persuaded many that his nastiness was well meant, challenging, an opportunity to excel. And he almost always recognized the work that emerged, a kindness that was not always sufficient to make up for the bullying that preceded it. "Thanks," he wrote Bereska. "And do not just throw this in the 'can.' You worked hard & it was a success. It's as simple as that. Thanks, D." "How could I do without you?" he wrote her after another success. People felt hounded, harassed, abused—and indispensable. His treatment eventually sent Bereska to a therapist's couch, but she kept those notes and many others like them in a series of scrapbooks.

Pride, Gained and Lost

If resident citizens and visitors might now drive with greater ease, they remained unhappy about parking. Schaefer's team decided that the real problem was lack of knowledge. Baltimore had plenty of parking spaces, but some were not as convenient as others. The solution was to reeducate the motorist. Over four months in early 1986, a team of parking map mavens plotted out the location of every single spot in every single lot in Baltimore. The idea rested on the same assumption that informed some of Schaefer's approach to the schools: The problem wasn't lack of performance by teacher and student, he suggested, it was all the "negative" high-profile reporting in the newspapers. The problem could be cured by convincing the papers not to keep publishing the system's dismal test results. In the parking lot war, the idea was to aggregate parking slots on maps drawn to show how a citizen, turned away and frustrated by a "SORRY FULL" or "MONTHLY PARKERS ONLY" sign outside his or her favorite garage, might find another, equally commodious place nearby. The rationale became the theme for this effort, which contained a statement of the problem as well as its solution: "Parking," the signs said, "is not a zoo." If you'd been feeling like a rat in a maze, lost and unhappy, City Hall would show you how to get out.

Very large animal-shaped balloons indicating garages or lots with unused space were hoisted above the city early on the morning of May 14, 1986. The plan was for Baltimoreans to awaken to find another effort at making their lives a little less stressful. Instead, though, the big balloons were quickly lowered, deflated, and put away that same morning and never used again—not because someone thought the idea loony but because another of Schaefer's efforts at spirit building had run into ultimate disaster. Few Baltimoreans ever knew of the balloons, because the *Pride of Baltimore,* a sailing ship whose name was the crystallization of all that Schaefer wanted for the marketing of his city, had been lost that night along with its captain in the fury of a sudden Caribbean storm.

The parking zoo press conference was canceled as a pall descended over City Hall. Schaefer knew the perils of sailing as well as he knew the dangers of firefighting and policing, and he gave the *Pride*'s men and women the same level of respect. He knew them all and held them as close in his informal family as he did those he worked with every day. He had wanted the *Pride* to be a replica of the ships that had sailed from Baltimore during an earlier time, a handsome vessel that would glide majestically into U.S. and foreign ports flying the city's flag. He had shrugged off complaints about misplaced priorities, arguing that the elegant and hearty vessel would make the city look young and vital even as it bathed itself in past glories. The rugged captain and dedicated crew had hosted parties for convention bureau bookers and others who had an interest in Baltimore, including the folks in Detroit on Lake Michigan who had come aboard the ship the night before Schaefer's famous seal pool swim. In Liverpool, in London, and in Baltimore, Ireland, the *Pride* had set its angular profile on the landscape to be marveled at and remembered as the romantic emissary of a city sailing toward a more promising future. Baltimore's mayor admired the know-how of the *Pride*'s crew, and he thought Baltimore had no better representatives anywhere. Now, as if he had sent them into mortal combat, he mourned their loss. Schaefer and his close aides, Pam Kelly and Lainy LeBow, met that morning without speaking. They feared that one sound would provoke unrestrained tears. They knew one thing: He would have a memorial—and a new ship. The *Pride* could not be lost.

Rhodes Scholar

Schaefer had been a good manager of opportunities—real and imagined—as his career unfolded. He had avoided fatal mistakes, first of all—

his decision to avoid the race against Paul Dorf for state senate, for example, and his careful milking of speculation that he would run for governor. He had moved up in the political firmament, not only by doing his job well, but by a studied denial that politics had anything at all to do with his decisions, personal or public. He refused to engage in virtually any political insider talk that usually provides common ground between reporters and politicians. He refused to acknowledge that politics was part of any equation—partly to keep the discussion on project and policy but also to avoid any suggestion that he knew what Kovens and the boys were doing. If he never talked about any of it, he had what the intelligence community in Washington called plausible deniability. At the same time, he was fiercely loyal to Kovens.

The Big Chief had steadied him on the slippery ladder of machine-blessed ascendancy so mournfully deplored by Russell in 1971. Kovens was with him when no one knew he wasn't a dummy. Schaefer felt he owed everything to the Furniture Man, so in 1985, when Irv and Edgar Silver began to push him toward Annapolis, toward a run for governor, he knew his usual temporizing would have to end. He did not wish to leave City Hall, though he had encouraged speculation about such a step for years, entertained it in his own mind, turned it over and considered it, compared it to the job he had and rejected it. Publicly, he left the whole question dangling—much to his personal amusement and political advantage. As long as he looked like a winner in such a race, he was accorded a different dimension of respect in the power-driven councils of the state assembly. Individual legislators gave great weight to anything a governor or even a likely governor said or did—the better to avoid damage or to enhance the legislator's standing. It was a coy deflecting of a candidacy he did not really want, and a power game Schaefer could play to the advantage of his city. But now the Big Chief was coming to him, urging him to run to block Steve Sachs, the attorney general who Kovens saw as a representative of those Justice Department lawyers who put him in jail. Sachs had not been involved in the case, but he was a former assistant U.S. attorney—and therefore one of the enemy. So Kovens was, fifteen years after he put Schaefer in the mayor's office, asking his charge to repay the debt. Kovens was claiming the favor he knew he might need some day. He'd asked Schaefer for precious little—hadn't needed to ask for much—and, besides, during the four years that elapsed between his indictment and conviction, he was in too much trouble to intrude on the multi-million-dollar redevelopment deals Schaefer was making all over the city. As early as 1973—in the middle of Schaefer's first term—Irv had been a target of federal investigators, nailed into place by public scrutiny and an army of lawyers determined to get him. He had been convicted, imprisoned, and released. Now, though, he could use Schaefer to club the legal establishment that had put him in jail. He could do this by denying Sachs a step up on that ladder he'd owned for so long. Kovens had come out of retirement to elect Schaefer mayor, and he had solved all the tough little problems in city council and elsewhere, problems that distract or unhinge or preoccupy a mayoralty—as demonstrators had done with McKeldin and D'Alesandro. As much as he pledged undying loyalty to Kovens, Schaefer had played him—ignoring him, catering to him, and using him—but never abandoned him. This time, though, Kovens had the force of political and social history on his side. Baltimore had a majority black population whose dream of political control had been deferred—denied—by Kovens and Schaefer. Schaefer had seen the future at least three years earlier, in 1982, when Kurt Schmoke was elected Baltimore State's Attorney, piling up a huge plurality over Bill Swisher.

Schmoke paid a courtesy call on the mayor shortly after that election. The 36-year-old Harvard Law School and Oxford-educated Rhodes Scholar sat in the dark mahogany paneled ceremonial room in City Hall, waiting for Schaefer to appear. The mayor came in eventually, sat down, and said nothing. The mayor of Baltimore sat and stared his stare. Then he said, "So you're the guy who got 100,000 votes." The figure actually was 102,403. Schmoke had done in 1982 what Russell had failed to do in 1971: He had become the first black candidate to win a citywide race for anything other than a judgeship and the first candidate other than Hyman Pressman to get more than 100,000 votes. Better than 93 percent of blacks voted, virtually all of them for Schmoke. The numbers heralded a new era, one in which Schaefer could not depend, if he ever might have, on the weaknesses of the opposition. It meant, perversely, that he might not be able to win a fifth mayoral term on the strength of his record of urban uplift. He was a figure of some statewide and national renown but was increasingly vulnerable at home. History, so long deferred, was now at hand, and Schaefer was staring at its personification, another guy who looked good in a suit. Schaefer had known then that his days in city hall were coming to a close. He would openly resent Schmoke's ascendancy, certain that the young aspirant had paid no dues. What it all meant for Schaefer, though, was difficult to miss: He might have to think seriously about a job with the state of Maryland.

"Governor Sachs"

All politics is local: *House Speaker Thomas P. "Tip" O'Neill*
All politics is parochial: *William Donald Schaefer*

Polls taken in 1985 showed that the mayor of Baltimore was the most popular public official in Maryland. No one else came close. His approval ratings—the percentage of respondents who gave him good marks for his job performance—were above 70 percent. He was "godlike," thought Bethesda-based polltaker and political consultant Keith Haller. Writers began calling Schaefer "the Colossus of state politics," a man whose success at rebuilding a forlorn and decrepit port city made him seem like a miracle worker. During the 1980 All Star Game at Memorial Stadium, the sportscaster Howard Cosell called Schaefer "the genius mayor." No mayor had embodied the soul of his citizens with Schaefer's skill since Fiorello LaGuardia in New York, said columnist George Will. He was good, too, at ducking the daily questions about his intentions. Any time he left Baltimore, he must surely be out campaigning, reporters assumed. "Why did you go to Dundalk yesterday?" he was asked one morning.

"I went to Dundalk," he said, as if the answer were self-evident, "to see the Dundalkians."

But Kovens wanted to know what he was doing there as well. So the Big Chief and the reluctant candidate met for breakfast with Edgar Silver at the Hyatt once a week to take Schaefer's political temperature. Kovens was not subtle. "You bastard, you better run," he snarled.

Schaefer wanted Maryland House Speaker Ben Cardin to run. "Ben can beat 'im, Ben can beat 'im," Schaefer would say, attempting vainly to convince anyone, including himself, that Cardin had a shot.

Polls showed Sachs to be a prohibitive front runner in a race with Cardin. Edgar handicapped the race if Schaefer were to jump in, going over precinct maps county by county across the state, showing the candidate and Kovens how the race could be won. At the end of the fifth such meeting, with Schaefer still refusing to commit himself, Silver said, "I have to get to court. I'm leaving if you're not going to get in." The two men walked back toward Court House Square and city hall, past Harborplace, past the Legg Mason tower and the USF&G building. Schaefer was turning toward city hall when Silver said, "I'll tell you this, you'll do well as mayor with Governor Sachs."

"Governor Sachs!" Schaefer exclaimed, fairly vomiting out the words as if that title and its significance were only then acquiring some reality for him.

"Goddamn right," said Silver. "I love Ben Cardin, but there's no way he's going to beat Sachs." Then Silver made his final pitch: "I really think you can win. You'll enjoy it. And we'll take care of it all." Schaefer's candidacy would fill the heads of politicians and businessmen with visions of their own Inner Harbor, the judge said.

Coupons

Schaefer had a state full of excited, devoted campaign managers by then, men like Bobby Joe DiPietro, who had been mayor of Laurel at the age of twenty-four. He wrote Schaefer a letter saying, "Look, you seem to be doing everything right, so I'd like to have the opportunity to talk to you." One day, Schaefer showed up, unannounced. Said DiPietro later, "He pulled my letter out of his pocket and said he thought he'd drop by. He started right in with these probing questions: What were our best attributes? What were our worst problems? He said we had to solve our worst problems first while nailing down the positives. We couldn't do one or the other, he said. We had to do both at the same time. Had to keep up with the daily stuff as we were trying to do something flashy."

DiPietro remembers spending the first twenty minutes of the visit in awe, but he had an idea that he wanted Schaefer to hear. He saw his city of 12,000 as the hub of a metropolitan region that needed social and cultural relationships with places such as Baltimore, and he thought that other counties needed similar connections. "I had to let my citizens know what he had to offer. They had to know about the zoo, the Inner Harbor, the B&O Museum, the Peabody Conservatory, but I had to be able to get them to the city. The trains were running as a commuter line but not on weekends. I said we ought to run these trains all the time, a unified government approach so you could leave Laurel and come back on a Sunday afternoon. Schaefer just thought that was a phenomenal idea." So they wrote a joint letter to Governor Hughes, asking for a midday train on Sundays so that a Laurelite could, for example, ride into Baltimore to have a crab cake at Phillips Harborplace.

DiPietro figured he had met the consummate salesman. "If he got one more person to the city, his day was complete. He saw my letter as an opportunity. He was practicing the advice he gave to others: You take your assets and you work 'em. He was working me. He was hot, and he had a live one. He taught me more in the first couple of years I was mayor than the rest of the time I was there. He was received in Laurel like a king. A majority of Laurelites came from the city. Everybody had this tie to Baltimore. A lot of my activists had this direct connection with him. They could talk old neighborhoods with him. 'My mom and dad lived on such and such street in Baltimore City.' He could go on about the history of that street, who lived in the alley that ran behind it, the name of the guy who lived on the corner. He hadn't come to Laurel because he was running for governor. He came to Laurel because I asked him to. He loved being mayor. That's what was important to him."

DiPietro signed on. He got to know Schaefer better as the days of that summer wore on. In Salisbury one day, they pulled into a Roy Rogers for lunch. Schaefer loved fast food. "We go in there, and he pulls out his coupons. I went into hysterics. He carried them all the time. He had 'em for a small fries, a medium coke, et cetera. He got that sheepish grin on his face and said, 'Don't you have your coupons?'" Later, when Schaefer was in retirement, a friend called him one day, interrupting his attempt to dry-clean his own clothes. He had not been touched by the Depression, but he was not a spendthrift.

Square Peg

Mark Wasserman, who had been Schaefer's personal representative on numerous development projects, would manage the campaign from Baltimore, with DiPietro and many others eager to follow his lead. Irv Kovens would be marginalized. The Furniture Man had called the tune, but now Wasserman, LeBow, and Berndt would devote themselves to making Kovens a political wallflower. Schaefer knew that this was necessary as well as he knew how to get to his office in the morning. Yet, when they weren't looking—or even when they were—he brought his mentor onto the floor. He followed his own rules of loyalty with reckless fidelity, accepting Irv's help and refusing to disavow his involvement.

Within weeks, Schaefer was in and Cardin was out. Sachs looked at Schaefer's standing in the polls and marveled at them. He had been certain that Schaefer would not get in, so now he pretended to relish the idea of whittling the temperamental mayor down to life size. He told a reporter that he expected see his own standing versus Schaefer's climb steadily in the months leading to the Democratic primary election, just before which, in the late summer of 1986, his popularity line would cross Schaefer's, which would be moving down by then. Sachs chose Larry Gibson and Blair Lee IV of Montgomery County as his co-campaign chairmen, knowing that both would nettle Schaefer and hoping to provoke the volatile mayor into attacking him.

Sachs also knew that he was up against deep feelings of admiration and respect for a man so driven to serve. He knew because he'd felt the same admiration. Sachs remembered the first time he saw Schaefer, in 1978, when he was running for attorney general. "I went to a thing, a neighborhood thing in Patterson Park, and I was standing alone in the audience, praying that the mayor would acknowledge my presence, and sure enough he did. 'Here's this young man . . . he's running for attorney general.' I was so pleased that he recognized me." But the two men were rivals—never close politically or personally. Shortly after Sachs's first election victory in 1978, Baltimore was hit by a paralyzing snowstorm. "There was a little looting. I got to the office, and the mayor is calling. He wanted me to say the state would do something about insurance, that it would insure shop owners against looting. I couldn't tell him what he wanted to hear. The law didn't permit it. I was enough of a pol not to say, 'Don go shit in your hat.' But I couldn't give him the right answer."

"One Maryland" was Sachs's campaign theme, a not-so-subtle allusion to Schaefer's well-publicized marriage to Baltimore. If elected governor, Sachs was saying, Schaefer would be the governor of Baltimore alone. The rest of the state would have to fend for itself. Sachs began referring to Schaefer as "petulant and parochial," a man who acted like a baby and who had no compunction about serving his city to the exclusion of all the other twenty-three municipalities. Sachs devised a campaign commercial that showed a board game in which a pair of hands tried to force square pegs into round holes.

Some thought the thrust of all this was a bit harsh. It was "prosecutorial," warned Joel Rozner, a lawyer and astute organizer who had moved to Maryland from Boston, where politics seeped into one's bones before birth. The combative Lee, as confrontational as Schaefer, saw it in more dramatic and personal terms: "I had written about these guys, Kovens and the rest of them, in my college thesis. We were fighting against the restoration of Kovens, Marvin, and the rest of the bad guys." Lee had his own ax to grind: He had managed his father's campaign for governor in 1978, the year Hughes had flashed out of the pack to win on a reform platform that had swept the patrician Blair Lee III off the political board.

Once begun, the 1986 race for governor of Maryland became a bitter personal war between the ostensible forces of light and the supposedly malevolent Darth Vaders of the Baltimore machine: Irv Kovens and the scalawags that Jim Rouse had so reviled. They were poised to have their way once again, working this time against people on their own side of the struggle such as Berndt, Wasserman, and LeBow. Not at all ready to cede the moral high ground to Sachs, these Schaefer loyalists found themselves arguing with their candidate. He would not step away from Irv—insisted on standing next to him, in fact. The Big Chief had never asked him to do anything nefarious, Schaefer proclaimed, to the point of protesting too much. Kovens had never done anything but help him, he said and had, in fact, been the difference between success and failure at every step along the political way. The candidate moaned about how vulnerable he was to Sachs's charisma, but he was certain he had maintained a distance in the voters' eyes between his performance in office and the crimes alleged against his mentors Kovens and Mandel. His record was his shield even against the dramatic downfall of his pals. Everyone, it seemed, had forgotten Schaefer's debt to these men—everyone but Schaefer. So Irv could raise money as always and make certain the clubhouse lieutenants knew the drill. He did it, undoubtedly, because he wanted to make something of a comeback personally, showing that his involvement was not a kiss of death, and to stuff Sachs into retirement.

In Crisfield that July for the annual crab feast, one of the main political events of every year, Schaefer verbally accosted *Evening Sun* reporter Doug Birch. In that day's paper, Birch had quoted the mayor of Baltimore on the subject of his rival.

"He's a bunch of shit with the environment," Schaefer had reportedly said. "He doesn't know what the hell the environment is all about." Schaefer was quoted as saying, sarcastically, that he hoped Sachs was elected "and does all the things he's talking about. The dumb asshole. I hope he's tough on the environment and drives goddamned industry out of the state." When a throng of reporters asked him about these comments Schaefer denied having made them. When Birch heard this he went looking for Schaefer.

"Look me in the eye," Schaefer said when they met. "I never said it."

"Look me in the eye," said Birch, "I have it on tape."

"I said it," said Schaefer, "but it was off the record." Whatever he had said or not said, on or off the record, Schaefer ended his part of the conversation by declaring that "Steve Sachs couldn't touch my big toe."

Sachs said that Schaefer "doesn't know the difference between an outhouse and the state house." He thought Schaefer would inevitably fire off a few shots just like this one, revealing himself to be unfit for Maryland's highest elective office. The opposite might have occurred, once again: The more intemperate and colorful Schaefer seemed to get, the more parochial and petulant, the more people liked him.

Poll Cats

Nothing moved Sachs up in the polls, and Schaefer headed into the summer with an enormous lead. The attorney general, whose career had seemed so promising, tried to save himself with a bit of ticket magic of his own, reaching out to Parran J. Mitchell to run with him for lieutenant governor. Mitchell might well have been a draw in the black precincts, overwhelmingly Democrat, in heavily black Baltimore and Prince George's County. But ticket mates seldom help much, and even the dignified and fiery Mitchell, a one time '60s poverty warrior, brought little more than a day's headline for the Sachs campaign.

If Mitchell was to be helpful, the political world would see it in poll results. But when the Baltimore *Sun* took its next sampling of voter sentiment, its question about preferences in the race for governor did not include Mitchell's name along with Sachs's. The results were largely unchanged from earlier measures, showing Schaefer with an undiminished lead. Called for a reaction to these results, the Schaefer camp was exultant and paraded the figures throughout a convention of local Maryland officials in Ocean City. The Sachs forces were campaigning there as well, and they erupted when a reporter called them. In a testament to the power of polls, Sachs and Lee ordered up a small airplane for a trip to Baltimore to protest in person. Lee was certain the *Sun* had sandbagged his man on purpose. The real culprit, though, was ineptitude. No one had thought about how the questions should be posed. The newspaper's managing editor, Jim Houck, made matters worse by suggesting that a similar survey done by the *Washington Post* had also failed to include Mitchell in the questions. Lee managed to get someone at the *Post* to find the questionnaire and read him the gubernatorial preference question, and sure enough, the *Post* had asked its sample of 800 or so voters whether they preferred the Schaefer-Steinberg ticket or the Sachs-Mitchell team. Houck ordered the poll story held while the poll was redone, and it showed a slight improvement in the standing of the underdog attorney general—very slight.

It might not have been the newspaper's finest hour, but the impact on the outcome of the 1986 race was probably minimal. "The difference between 32 percent and 28 percent was not monumental," Sachs readily conceded, but the importance then was movement; even a point up in a stagnant campaign was a sign of life. And they were having to struggle to show even that small bump in their standing.

When the *Sun*'s poll did not run as scheduled on that Sunday, the *Post* wrote a story further embarrassing its competitor in Baltimore. The new, improved numbers were published a few days later with the right question. Lee's view was that, just as in 1978, when his father was running for governor against the *Sun*'s chosen candidate, the fix was in. The *Evening Sun* had run a page one editorial, endorsing Harry R. Hughes in that year along with a poll that showed Hughes on the rise, a signal to Marylanders that a vote for Hughes would not be a meaningless protest. Before that newspaper push, Hughes had seemed to be what Baltimore Senator Harry McGuirk had called him "a ball lost in high grass." Sachs now faced the same fate, though he had no newspaper to find him and no opponent as sullied (by association) as were Hughes's in 1978.

More important were the stature of the two men and the issues. Schaefer called Sachs antibusiness, largely because he had enforced environmental pollution laws so unbendingly against the Fairchild Corporation in western Maryland that Fairchild had decamped for Virginia. Sachs was perfectly happy then to be the bad guy, hoping that people would think him a hero for defending the groundwater, allegedly polluted by careless Fairchild dumping. But Schaefer also remembered moments when, as attorney general, he thought Sachs had not been sufficiently protective of bank-run credit card operations, betting that they would never follow through on threats to leave Maryland for Delaware. But they did leave. Again, Sachs hoped to make that a populist plus for his candidacy. Truth to tell, according to some Baltimore businessmen, Schaefer was hardly more business friendly than his rival. He wanted to be, but some thought that his style and approach could never fit with the business crowd. Even his friend and ally Trueschler found something less than probusiness in Schaefer's approach. "He was pro-project. He wasn't organized enough to be anything like what business wanted." Schaefer's real problem was this: He wanted business to do well, but he could not admit there was a problem, so he never made anything like a systematic effort to find a comprehensive solution.

The attorney general knew that he needed a bold stroke and offered one in the arena of education: a one-cent increase in the sales tax to be committed solely to the classroom. Some commentators declared the race over and done with at that very moment, as dead on arrival as Walter F. Mondale's similar thrust had been when he had run for president two years earlier.

"It was not aimed at Schaefer," Lee said. "It was not an anti-Schaefer thing. We were saying, 'He's going to raise taxes, but he won't tell you. I'm going to raise taxes, and I'm telling you now.' It was a pro-Sachs thing, defining who and what Sachs was. But it wasn't Sachs's era. People didn't want to hear about taxes."

They fought also over stadiums: whether to build a new one for baseball and where. Even before Schaefer got into the race, Sachs had taken a position on the best location for a new baseball park. Sachs thought of himself as the real father of Oriole Park at Camden Yards, the baseball stadium that was eventually built. He had picked it from one of the studies while Schaefer was still insisting that Memorial Stadium could be salvaged, whether he really believed that or not. Later, Sachs appeared to favor a site in the beltway community of Lansdowne, just outside the city in a community closer to Washington with sufficient space to build the necessary parking. "We were saying there should be a new stadium, Schaefer was saying B.S. Never mind where. Where came later." Schaefer had to disagree politically because he had to have the initiative and couldn't appear to be following Sachs. Lee wrote fourteen drafts of an article about government and sports stadia for the op-ed page of the *Sun,* and finally it was printed. Tom Flannery, the *Sun*'s gentle cartoonist, drew a picture of Sachs in a box at the new ballpark as Schaefer and Hughes arrived: Sachs was saying to them "Tickets Please." When Schaefer got aboard the stadium train, he, too, said the stadium had to be in the city.

Sachs continued to hope that Marylanders would see that Schaefer and Annapolis would be a bad fit. Debates, he hoped, would provide the format, but Schaefer and bad luck trumped that strategy. At first, Schaefer refused to debate at all. Why should he? He was far ahead and could only hurt himself in the sort of battle he knew Sachs excelled at. So he declined virtually every invitation. Then, without notice, he showed up at radio station WBAL unannounced in mid-debate, to the utter consternation of all, including Sachs, who protested that Schaefer was making up the rules to suit himself and should not be allowed on the air—a seeming contradiction of his earlier lament about the people's right to hear just how parochial and petulant the mayor could be. Schaefer stayed and held his own.

Schaefer's team leaders remembered the remarkable 1983 television debate with Billy Murphy, but they knew they might not be so lucky in the Sachs race. Marion Pines and Sandy Hillman tried to prepare Schaefer, grilling and quizzing him on a range of issues. Imagining that Sachs would raise questions about the Shadow Government, one of them asked Schaefer where the trustees, Benton and Daley, got their money.

"Damned if I know," Schaefer said. "Better call Benton."

Pines and Hillman didn't know whether to laugh or cry. They need not have worried. On the night of the event, Billy Murphy and Schaefer were joined by Lawrence Freeman, the candidate of Lyndon LaRouche's minions, and by Monroe Cornish, the perennial candidate who had run against Schaefer in the 1975 mayor's race. Cornish gave the idea of "wild man" a new definition, talking at length about the assassination of John F. Kennedy, about how he, Monroe Cornish, was not allowed to make his points in most forums, and about how much of what was being said by the leading candidates was a "bunch of garbage." Each time he was allowed, under the debate's format, to make a presentation or to comment on someone else's point, Cornish railed against the "garbage." When the program ended, Pines took a call. "How much did you pay that guy?" her son asked her before nearly collapsing in laughter. Against the manic pose struck by Cornish, the volatile Schaefer was demure and tranquil.

Four years later though, as in 1983, debates were fine stitches on a tapestry completed much earlier in a single moment—the one when Schaefer declared his candidacy. Sachs carried on bravely, wondering whether lightning might not strike, wondering whether Schaefer might have the stroke that many predicted would surely overtake such a manic personality. Lee, too, had known what was in store very early. He had gotten a phone call from a friend in the Schaefer camp shortly after one of those meetings between the mayor, Wasserman, and the rest of the City Hall gang.

"Schaefer's in," Lee's informant said. That's it, then, Lee said to himself. He had seen the poll numbers, the trial runs between Sachs and Schaefer, Sachs and Cardin—all the potential match-ups. Schaefer beat everyone—badly. In their hearts, Sachs and Lee knew they had almost no chance.

Family Feud

From the beginning, Schaefer's campaigns were run by Kovens on one wing and reformers on the other, all of them using the tried and essential tools of Baltimore campaigns: money for literature drops, money for cab fare, money for one's share of the ballot printing costs, money for whatever. They called it walking-around money, and it was the one tangible bit of grease the reformers hated most, a real perversion of democracy, they thought: buying votes. The machine might be dead, but its withered appendages pulsed back to life on election day if the money was there to provide the spark. Schaefer ran with the knowledge that he had plenty of money for advertising. Some of it came from obscure little accounts like the one he turned over to his friend DiPietro. The mayor of Baltimore had installed the mayor of Laurel in a most delicate position: Between the Good-Government Hatfields and the Darth Vader McCoys, Schaefer established DiPietro and ordered him to hold his ground. As always, the candidate knew that there would be friction, relished it, and found a way to use it. He wanted and knew that he needed what the Big Chief could still give him, no matter what Wasserman and the others said, so he asked DiPietro to meet with Kovens and Mandel one morning at the Hyatt Regency Hotel and then showed up in the middle of the scrambled eggs with LeBow, Wasserman, Berndt—to show them that he was still in charge.

The good guys fumed. Schaefer snickered. Mandel and Kovens kept eating. "All the rest of the day I got yelled at," DiPietro said.

The clash reached a crescendo during a meeting that night in a second floor dining room of a restaurant in Little Italy owned by Frankie Babusci, Buddy Palughi's partner and one of Bereska's most reliable soldiers. The good guys wanted DiPietro to surrender all the money that had been collected in the small campaign account Marylanders for Schaefer, which DiPietro had started. He refused. Schaefer had instructed him to do just that: "Don't give 'em the money. We'll need it. We need some money laid back for last-minute things." This open and heated discussion of saving up sums of money to be used for "last-minute things" left the moralists very nearly hysterical.

When Schaefer arrived, he ordered quiet, and then he lit into DiPietro. "Give Mark that money. We can't have this. We have to win this campaign," he barked.

DiPietro walked out after the meeting chastened. He was walking toward his car alone, ready to quit, when a Cadillac pulled up beside him. The window in the back passenger seat slid down, and DiPietro glanced from the sidewalk into the grinning visage of Baltimore's mayor.

"Screw 'em, junior," he said, "Don't give 'em a nickel. . . . You heard me." Then he said, "How much've we got, $100,000?"

"Maybe $200,000," DiPietro said.

"Don't give 'em a dime!" Schaefer commanded, and the car pulled away.

Siss Boom Ba

Schaefer and Kovens had trumped Sachs's choice of a running mate by picking Melvin A. "Mickey" Steinberg, a state senator from the Democratic strongholds of Baltimore County. Steinberg was a seasoned Annapolis player who brought Schaefer the legislative dimension he lacked. Jewish like Sachs, he hurt the attorney general in his base. The forces of light—Berndt and company—favored Delegate Nancy Kopp, also Jewish but from heavily Democratic Montgomery County, younger and more intellectual than Steinberg but not one of the boys. She might have helped Schaefer in Montgomery County, which he had all but written off with his suit for school aid equalization. "What language do they speak over there?" Schaefer asked one day during the campaign. In a government in which redistribution of income is the state government's reason for being, Montgomery voters were more and more conscious that "their" money was flowing to Baltimore. Schaefer and a host of liberal legislators from Montgomery County had made certain of that for decades. In the end, Montgomery and Prince George's counties were the only two out of twenty-four that went for Sachs.

The poll lines remained essentially constant throughout the campaign, never crossing as Sachs had predicted, never really moving toward each other at all. Like Adlai Stevenson, a talented man who had had the ill fortune to be running against the national war hero Dwight Eisenhower, Sachs could not compete with Schaefer, who was seen as a savior of Maryland's only real city, its center of culture and jobs, its historic port—and the former residence of many who were then living and voting in the counties. Schaefer had been a monumental success, putting himself and his city on the national billboards, television, and magazines. He was an activist mayor, a genuine character who was the most can-do leader anyone had seen in Maryland, a man of flair and energy and of impeccable honesty who might just be able to do for Maryland what he had done for Baltimore.

Schaefer defeated Sachs in the primary by better than 3 to 2, a decisive victory by a mayor over a tough campaigner who had already won two statewide races and who might have been able to reveal Schaefer's weaknesses as liabilities for a governor. Mayors do not often fare well when they attempt to move up, but Schaefer had done it long before the 1986 race, attaining the rank of miracle worker who would bring his manic turns now to Annapolis.

Lee admired the political effectiveness of Schaefer's blunt, open style, though he found plenty of P. T. Barnum bluster and buffoonery in it as well. Sachs had been the thinking man in a time that was ill suited for his résumé. Lee was bitter: "People basically wanted to get bullshitted and they had the ultimate bullshitter" he said years later. "They had the ultimate bullshitter running, so it all worked. This was the era that Schaefer was born for. Happy days are here. Siss boom ba. City is great. We're great."

Sachs was far more philosophical, mellow even. "No one could have beaten Don Schaefer this year," he told the faithful as he conceded defeat. "I could have beaten anyone else, I think. I guess I was first among mortals." Sachs knew the old line about how "the people have spoken, the bastards," but he didn't use it. Like Russell, who made big money in the practice of law, Sachs left politics. He joined the Washington firm of Wilmer, Cutler and Pickering, where he represented such major national firms as McDonald's, one of Schaefer's fast-food favorites.

Six weeks after the primary victory, the Democratic nominee defeated his Republican opponent, Thomas J. Mooney of Prince George's County, with 82 percent of the vote, a record victory margin.

Rot and Glitter

Soon after Schaefer's election, as if a cloud of hype had lifted, the Goldseker Foundation released a study of the city's prospects called "Baltimore 2000," a stocktaking of the previous twenty-five years with an analysis of implications for the future. One of the city fathers, nameless in the report, provided its most often quoted observation. There was, he declared, "rot beneath the glitter." The critics who called Schaefer the master of bread and circuses had been right, this man said. The city was smaller in population and thus in political power and was weaker financially. It was buffeted by changes in the national and worldwide marketplace and changes in the social compact, forces no mayor in the country could resist. The task was monumental and overwhelming: Between 1960 and 1985 Baltimore's white population, which tended to be its most affluent, dropped from 611,000 to 298,000—more than 50 percent. The city's median household income in 1985 was $16,700, while in the surrounding counties, the figure was $31,000, almost twice as high. Twenty-four percent of city residents had incomes below the federal government's official poverty line, up 20 percent from the day in 1971 when Schaefer and Mark Joseph wrote his mayoral platform paper, "Where I Stand." Among suburbanites, only 12 percent were officially poor. Thirty percent of the region's manufacturing jobs had been lost, and while that figure was offset by a 30 percent increase in technology-related employment, the likelihood that city residents were competent to fill these jobs was pitiably low. The schools were performing so miserably as providers of industrial workers for the 1990s that Goldseker's Baltimore advisers predicted that few companies could afford to think of moving their operations to the city. The failure of Baltimore's system of public education—a failure that was duplicated in almost every other U.S. city—foreclosed a prosperous future.

A few years later, David Rusk, a respected scholar and one-time mayor of Albuquerque, New Mexico, said that Baltimore had simply gone "beyond the point of no return" unless some way was found to dramatically alter the fundamental structure of government in Maryland. There would have to be collaboration between Baltimore and the surrounding counties, whose residents wanted nothing to do with the city. Baltimore had to have major infusions of money because it had become the repository of the urban poor and elderly. It still offered many jobs, but many workplaces were leaving the city as well. Rusk thought that leaders in Maryland should think about dispersing the poor into areas of relative affluence where they could be absorbed and allowed to prosper in ways the inner city would never permit. His ideas were scarcely noticed, much less debated.

Historically, said Professor Haywood Harrar, a Baltimore native who left to find a teaching job at Virginia Polytechnic Institute, the burghers of Baltimore withheld education from blacks and whites, blocking the city from participation in the age of technology. In the 1930s, he said, the city had declined to educate blacks because that would upset labor markets: Jobs requiring skills should go to whites and whites only. The University of Maryland Law School in Baltimore excluded blacks until 1935 and then admitted only a few. "By the time black folks had an opportunity to take over the education system, by the time the barriers were lowered, there were not enough of us to take advantage of it. Because of the historic stifling and crippling of the black leadership elite, things began to fall apart. When we got the opportunity, there were not enough of us to take advantage. It's one of the reasons we have the problem we have today with schools and crime. Baltimore is reaping the whirlwind, the seeds of discrimination and oppression sowed for 100 years."

Some of this gap could have been filled by an innovative and imaginative school system that found ways to attract young people, despite their economic deprivation, into the classroom. Whether Schaefer could have pulled this off is doubtful, but he did not try, choosing instead to put his considerable energies elsewhere. His successor, Kurt Schmoke, put himself into the effort without stint but failed too. But Schmoke at least started, and if his successors find ways to deal with the issue, he will be seen as the man who had the courage to say that education is the key. Politically, it seems fair to conclude that Schaefer saw his opportunities more clearly with the businessmen and downtown renewal, since he was, far more than Schmoke could have been, a downtown man of the 1950s who felt comfortable with lawyers, businessmen, and utility company managers. Schaefer's talents were more efficiently addressed to this aspect of the city's future, and the results there probably justify his particular decisions about the complex triage he was asked to perform. Some of the patients died, but, he judged, he probably could not have saved them. He was probably right.

The Straw

Despite Schaefer's success over fifteen years in the mayor's office, many residents of the neighborhoods that he cherished had moved to the surrounding counties, leaving Baltimore's population at 753,000, some 20.7 percent below its 1950 peak. (One of the markers of a city that is past the point of no return is population loss of 20 percent or more from the peak.) Once composing 30 percent of the state's population, Baltimore now made up only 17 percent. Political power waned correspondingly, threatening the city's ability to help itself by means of its representatives' leveraging funds from the general assembly. As ominous as these measurements surely were, the most remarkable aspect of "Baltimore 2000" was the report's very existence. Had Schaefer been mayor, he would have found a way to block its publication or undermine its deadly forecast. He had managed—by force of will, by yet another flurry of exciting projects, by urging people to believe that a negative view was too corrosive to consider—to raise an illusion of progress, superimposing his own conception of a better future before that future could be achieved. He had held back reality, in a sense. The public relations impulse had its down side: Rage against feelings of inferiority could slide over into denial, which could block efforts at solution. But Schaefer never failed to recognize how bad things were even as he demanded positive thinking, proclaimed renewal, and midwifed rebirth. He hoped that rot would retreat in the face of commitment. More than that, he knew that if he even acknowledged the struggle, weaker souls would give up.

Goldseker found Schaefer's allies on the business side every bit the pikers and dropouts they had seemed to be, company men who wouldn't or couldn't step up to buy the Orioles in 1979 or to invest in the Hyatt Regency in 1980. The absence of a capitalist presence that was able and willing to go beyond the pin money granted at Trueschler's request left Baltimore an even more impoverished place than many cities with high percentages of poor residents. Of the *Fortune* 500 companies that year, only one was actually based in Baltimore. The "concentrated energy and influence" of such businesses were not available to Schaefer or his city, Goldseker's report found. The enclave of grand baronial mansions flanking the Washington Monument at Mount Vernon Square were largely vacant. (Hackerman House was a magnificent exception.) "Deep roots and unquestioned power" of wealthy families were not a sufficiently large part of Baltimore's heritage. In Atlanta, Boston, Cleveland, Dallas–Fort Worth, Minneapolis–Saint Paul, San Francisco–Oakland, and Washington, charitable foundations gave $37 per capita each year, compared with $9 per capita in Baltimore.

"It seems fair to conclude," the "Baltimore 2000" report held, "that while single issues and particular institutions have been able to generate corporate or private philanthropy, active and continuous concern for the city as a whole has not been characteristic of broad segments of either corporate leadership or private wealth." Perversely, some said, the long tenure of William Donald Schaefer had "further weakened private civic initiative, especially in the business community, by allowing it little scope." That observation was laughable; Schaefer allowed whatever scope was requested. Private civic initiative had had one big push within its capacity, Charles Center, and when that was completed, the civic initiative—even the GBC's initiative—fell somnolent. The CEOs threw in their summer jobs and their pin money—to keep him off their backs or to satisfy whatever remained of their boardroom noblesse oblige. But often they could not save themselves, much less the city. More and more of their businesses, particularly the banks, were bought up by larger national operations, hauled into mergers, or left to fail: "a massive decampment," banker Baldwin called it.

Business was leaving along with the populace even as Schaefer completed his makeover, transforming Baltimore into a tourist destination and giving it a reason to continue. Whatever tenuous grip was achieved on the sheer rock face of decline was provided and nurtured by Schaefer, by government, and by a few men like Hackerman and Meyerhoff. Schaefer liked to call himself a CEO, and by the end of his tenure in city hall, he was about as close to an economic force as Baltimore could boast. "The magnet of the Inner Harbor, the redeveloped downtown, the strong neighborhood life, the relatively low cost of living in proximity to the Bay, an effective government, strong cultural institutions, a good transportation network, a growing stock of new and renovated middle and upper income housing and a recovered sense of municipal pride: These make a potent combination," the report conceded. It was a short list of Schaefer's accomplishments.

He'd had an unusually long run. He had elbowed and punched and swore his way across the urban landscape as much as he had danced and smiled and mugged for the cameras. This man whose political skills were disparaged had been elected mayor four times, had avoided scandal, and had built an exciting skyline in the least likely of U.S. cities. He and the other "messiah mayors" proved that cities were governable—if not salvageable. He provided a leadership ideal, as well: the image of a man willing to sacrifice himself personally for the greater good of his vision for the city. When would any city see such a leader again? New eyes, new talents, and new approaches would be needed to find a sustaining new reason for Baltimore to go into the twenty-first century. The ingredients of progress had been in place when he was elected, as he had insisted in the face of Russell's sneer that he was a dumb Pollyanna. Like baseball's Reggie Jackson, Schaefer had been the straw that stirred the drink, the one indispensable resource offering the city hope, a new industry, a new Main Street. He'd been a great mayor, thought Mark Joseph, because he'd been thoroughly transparent, a modest man of uncommon leadership talents, an instinctive political genius who eschewed politics, a man who insisted upon underestimating himself without ever succumbing to crippling insecurity, a man of passion who drove people to and beyond their abilities — willingly and without remorse, usually — if they could help him to sell his city. Schaefer transcended his own salesmanship. He sold so hard, spun so hard, fought so fiercely to assert his view of reality that reporters and others sometimes concluded that PR was all he had going for him. The truth was profoundly ironic: Hype and glitter were sometimes necessary, but they were also blinding at times, obscuring rather than illuminating the substance of the man and his accomplishments.

Schaefer had evolved into a nearly perfect representation of his city. Mark Joseph, the developer, thought he shared its every joy and pain — a fact given flesh and bone reality when his wristwatch was stolen one morning while he sat, arm out of the window, in the mayoral limousine waiting for a traffic light to change. The thief just pulled at the band and ran with the mayoral timepiece. Schaefer touched people and they touched him. He seemed to understand how they felt, what they were thinking in an array of personal circumstances. By facial expression or body language, he began to reflect those feelings back to them via television or newspaper photographs. He was not a good speaker in a classic sense, but he was a communicator. By pantomime, by truncated language — sentences without subjects or verbs — by petulance, by impatience, and by a wide spectrum of other evocations, he bonded with his city. His various acting roles and the public theater he demanded seemed transforming. He moved into a different psychic dimension, away from his insecurities and awkward responses. Public moments turned out to be the ones in which he seemed most comfortable and confident, a zone in which all his fears of inadequacy slipped away. Now he was slipping away — not without the usual fanfare, of course — to another stage, wondering if his covenant with Baltimoreans could be broadened to include an entire state.

III

Exile

A Gift

Before taking up his new post, Schaefer made one last mayoral circuit of the city, visiting favorite spots and people, winding up finally with Mrs. Snoops at the Inner Harbor. For a moment, they disappeared while he changed into a white admiral's uniform with fringed, gold-colored shoulder boards, which turned out to be part of his final PR stunt. The couple was then spirited into a large shipping crate decorated with a giant bow and hoisted onto the deck of a ship moored at Harborplace. The big wooden box was labeled, preposterously, "Baltimore's Gift to the State." Such a presumption was a full step too far, unnecessary and essentially pointless. He'd won. If he was to be a gift, he would have to demonstrate that over time. Bands played and people cheered, but a man in the front row held up a small sign that said, "Farewell, you pompous clown."

A few days later, Schaefer took the oath of office as Maryland's fifty-eighth governor in the state senate chamber with Hilda Mae holding the Bible, waiting for him to raise his right hand. For only the second time in his public career, his mother was not with him for one of these moments of affirmation. His cousins Anita and Jeri came but were virtually anonymous and certainly not part of the official First Family. Jim Rouse offered the day's principal remarks, encouraging Marylanders to be proud of their selection of a new governor and urging them to recognize what a fine choice they had made, a better one than they might realize. Schaefer was governor now, but people still felt the need to vouch for him. In contrast to his defiant mood in the first days of his mayoralty, he had no confidence that he was the best-qualified governor. Mark Joseph, the developer, thought that Schaefer had accumulated so much experience and assimilated so much information that he had almost the equivalent of insight and intuition. His mind was not wired for a job that would demand generalizing, but generalizing would be needed, since a state was so much larger than a city. He remained unsure of himself, focusing as always on what he didn't and couldn't know. He had been divorced from his first governmental wife—Baltimore—and was now forced to take a second by arranged political union. Maryland was too big for him to marry even in a symbolic way, and he knew that he must not be the governor of Baltimore alone.

Schaefer could not slide into power without opposition or challenge. People had marked his success at shaking the Annapolis money tree and gathering up the ripest plums for Baltimore, whatever the implications for the rest of the state, and some of those he had bested resented it. They remembered Schaefer's Shadow Government exploits and the remarks of Charlie Benton, who had sworn to avoid the board of estimates "like the plague." Senate President Thomas V. "Mike" Miller, Jr., handed Schaefer a framed copy of the state constitution as nothing less than a warning: In Annapolis, the senator was saying, power is shared; the assembly fraternity guards its prerogatives jealously and would never be as malleable as the city council of Baltimore.

As he had done in his first meeting with city department heads fifteen years earlier, Schaefer asserted himself wherever he could. David Iannucci, a ranking legislative craftsman who would be asked to pass Schaefer's legislative agenda, spoke for many, staff and legislator alike: "I had the impression of a man who was very, very temperamental, prone to mood swings, but someone who could cut through the nonsense." Iannucci remembered the first staff meeting. Alan Rifkin, a Steinberg protégé and the new administration's chief legislative officer, was explaining at length a series of bills, leading Schaefer to imagine that Rifkin fancied himself a man of power. "Wait a minute," said the new governor, "How much do you make?"

Rifkin answered.

"And how much do I make?" the governor asked.

Rifkin answered.

"Why does he think he has to do this with us?" Iannucci wondered to himself.

Rifkin knew. "He was making a point and making it early: 'Don't ever forget I'm the governor and you're the staff. Don't ever forget it.'" And, he might have added, Don't cross me, or Here are my terms, or You don't know everything. After four terms as mayor, after smashing electoral victories made him Maryland's governor, Schaefer was again drawing lines in the playground sand. Either anxious for a way to assert authority or certain that one had to do that constantly no matter how much authority one gained, Schaefer made his point, however petty it might have seemed. Years later, when his secretary of juvenile services, Linda Rossi, left a meeting early to meet with Baltimore County senators who were angry about a reform school in their district, she slipped him a note to that effect.

"Okay," he scribbled back, "if you'd rather be with them than with the governor."

Thinking that he was kidding, she left. By the time she got back to her office, a note had arrived; her presence at future cabinet meetings would not be required. She immediately called a party store, ordered a bouquet of balloons, and had them delivered to the governor with a note that said, "Please take me back!" He did, of course. Together, they closed several juvenile detention centers, sending some of the young offenders back into the community, a risky thing politically, but Schaefer agreed with Rossi that conditions at these facilities were beyond fixing. No serious political or crime problems arose as a result of their action.

Like Iannucci, many in the assembly were excited by the prospect of working with a man of such drive, despite what they had heard of his idiosyncrasies. His first public power move came instantly in the matter of selecting a new state treasurer. The new governor wanted his own man, Walter Sondheim. But the post of treasurer, as he well knew, had to be filled by a vote of the general assembly, one of the state constitution's ways of ensuring a balance of power. The treasurer sat on the board of public works, which let all the state's contracts; it was the state's version of Baltimore's board of estimates. So Schaefer wanted his friend with him—and he wanted to be sure of having a majority on the board. But here he encountered a difference between executive power in City Hall and the authority of a Maryland governor. Schaefer had been elected with a record-setting 82 percent of the vote, so he thought his choice should be accepted if that choice were the well-regarded Sondheim. The state's gift to him, as it were. But Schaefer was entering a political arena that was ruled not solely by the governor, but also by the house speaker and the senate president. Speaker R. Clayton Mitchell of the Eastern Shore and Senate President Miller of Prince George's County, both as new in their jobs as Schaefer was, were determined to show independence, particularly if the headstrong new governor tried to roll over them. To make matters worse, Mitchell was still smarting over Schaefer's decision during the campaign to bypass him as a running mate in favor of Steinberg. Though an early Schaefer supporter, Senator Miller loved the parry and thrust of politics; he would sometimes provoke a fight for its own sake. He and Mitchell respected Sondheim and would have accepted him in another circumstance, but they turned instead to Lucille Maurer, a former Montgomery County legislator who had helped to devise financial aid formulas for distributing state money to local jurisdictions, particularly for eduation. In addition to being brilliant, Maurer was widely respected for fairness. Very soft spoken and very liberal in the best sense of Montgomery County's then liberal tradition, Maurer would be the easiest possible sell in both houses. Schaefer lost in his first outing, and Sondheim was the casualty.

At about this time, fortuitously, the Magna Carta came to Maryland on loan, and the state archivist, Dr. Edward Papenfuse, made a presentation—with Schaefer in mind. "The whole import of that document and of the inconsequential talk I gave was the sharing of power that King John had to learn to do in relationship to the barons. There was no way for me to be explicit about this and its relationship to King William Donald, who had not been able to really work out the vehicle by which he could literally share power gracefully with people over whom he simply didn't have control." Had he learned the lesson, Papenfuse thought, Schaefer's introduction to Annapolis would have been easier and his eight years there less painful. Annapolis did not immediately get Schaefer's message either, Papenfuse thought. Schaefer, Miller, and Mitchell were in for some difficult days and months.

Snowman

Mark Joseph watched this transition from Baltimore as Schaefer's fears and insecurities, never entirely dismissed, arose anew. Joseph thought he understood what was happening in the mind of his friend and former boss—what the new governor was adjusting to and what he was guarding against. Schaefer knew, Joseph thought, that "when you have limos, bodyguards, a deeper patina of power, you're removed from being a man of the people and maybe you even act more imperious. . . . There's a jarring element to it." In Baltimore, Schaefer's passion and integrity came through to people in powerful identifiers that were simple, direct, and unadorned: swimming with seals, wearing silly hats, throwing a temper tantrum in the newspaper, having his watch stolen while his car was stopped at a traffic light in the city center. Schaefer knew that intimacy could fade as soon as he drove across the city line. Sachs's campaign commercial about the square peg hadn't worked in the campaign—had backfired, in fact—yet even Schaefer knew that it was on the mark.

But he did know how to run a government and how to get people's attention. He knew how to take charge. Days after the inauguration, Marylanders found themselves imprisoned by snow. From the mountains to the shore, roads were clogged and dangerous. Schaefer ordered implementation of the snow emergency plan. What snow emergency plan? he was asked. He called his cabinet into early morning session. New or old, state government officials could not recall any sort of plan for dealing with a big snow. Local officials at the county, city, or village level handled that. No more, said Schaefer. He would have a plan for the state—and he would have it in two hours. When the chastened bureaucrats returned to present their ideas, Schaefer wanted to know what the planners were doing for the farmers. What about the livestock? Were any cows caught out in the pastures? Did they have enough feed? What other problems did farmers have? The planners looked at each other, and one of them suggested a brief recess while they addressed the governor's questions.

In Baltimore, after snow immobilized the city in 1979, leading to a bout of vandalism and looting, Schaefer had purchased four-wheel drive vehicles and sent his team scurrying to prepare for any further accumulation. Now, he didn't have Buddy Palughi to help him "borrow" from a Sears store. Still, command posts were established. Hourly updates were prepared for reporters, whether they wanted hourly reports or not. Schaefer was happy for the kind of emergency that demanded a big logistical exercise. For years, he had maintained bomb shelters in a civil defense network throughout Baltimore, making sure water, canned foods, and medical supplies were up to date, usable, and sufficient. "I thought it was my responsibility to protect the city," said the man of two wars: World War II and the Cold War. Such enterprises lent him the aura of command and allowed him to appear in front of TV cameras in outdoor gear, surveying his armada of plows. A blizzard was a chance for him to show how he and government could do something tangible for citizens. In the coming years, he might well have prayed for a flood as an antidote to the more abstract problems that would confront him.

Two Stadium Two-Step

Snow was perhaps the only thing Schaefer hadn't planned for. Long before the inauguration, he and his staff were laying out their 1987 legislative agenda. He would use his mandate immediately. By the time his Baltimore team arrived in Annapolis, he was ready to go. "We did in six or seven weeks what we usually spent six or seven months doing," Iannucci recalled. Schaefer managed it all in the same way. "He'd scream and yell about some answer that was wrong in his mind and begin to taunt the poor victim. He'd get so mad there was no right answer," Iannucci said. "After a while I learned to recognize when we had passed into the no-win zone. You'd just stop and wait for another day." Iannucci realized that the game with Schaefer was not to win, but to avoid the outbursts of anger that got in the way of action.

Schaefer's personal transition from city hall to state house lasted overly long because he did not fully trust anyone who was in Annapolis before he got there—including, it turned out, Lieutenant Governor Steinberg and Rifkin. In short order, Charlie Benton came down to help as budget secretary and was quickly branded "the svengali of numbers," a man who had so much of the governor's trust he could play political games with legislators and deflect the blame. Once, Benton leaked word that new taxes were under consideration, and Schaefer blamed Iannucci, who quickly ended up in Siberia. It took him months to recover. Finally, they got the evidence that Benton was the culprit, and Steinberg went in to explain it to the governor. "Sometimes I hear things," Schaefer said at the next cabinet meeting, "and I overreact. People shouldn't take it to heart." His people in Annapolis should give him as much slack as his staff had learned to do in Baltimore, he was saying.

Iannucci needed his own personal introduction to his new boss, because he was about to begin a major project: passage of a bill that would permit the construction of two massive sports stadiums in Baltimore at the old railroad facility known as Camden Yards. The commercial desires and whims of sports team owners continued to command Schaefer's attention, providing the enduring subtheme of his political life. Sachs had stolen his thunder a bit on Camden Yards, but that site had always been Schaefer's preference. For fifteen years he had known that it was the place to put baseball and football. To keep the Orioles and major league baseball in Baltimore and to replace the Colts, he needed state-of-the-art facilities. A dual-purpose park might work, but whatever route was chosen, the state would have to commit an enormous sum of public money.

Schaefer's stadium man would be the Baltimore lawyer Herbert Belgrad. Belgrad was a meticulous worker whom Harry Hughes had chosen to head the Maryland Sports Authority, which he had formed in the final year of his second term, a year before Schaefer was elected. Years earlier, while he was an assistant city solicitor in Baltimore, Belgrad had worked with Schaefer on housing programs and had traveled with him once to New York City to inspect a program Schaefer wanted to see started in Baltimore. Belgrad had not been a political figure except in the bar association, but he had campaigned for Paul S. Sarbanes when Sarbanes was a candidate for the Maryland House of Delegates. Along with Benjamin Civiletti, later U.S. attorney general under President Jimmy Carter, he had knocked on doors in precincts along Belair Road in East Baltimore.

Belgrad called on Schaefer in Baltimore right after the 1986 primary and was alarmed to find a man who looked beaten. Schaefer regaled his visitor with bitter recriminations against those who had been disloyal during the campaign, people he thought were friends who had worked for Sachs. It was a long list, phone book long. "Son," he said to the fifty-five-year-old Belgrad, "I always thought you were my friend. I know you've not been part of my political team, but I heard things that upset me. Lawn signs and bumper stickers for Sachs?"

"On my wife's car," Belgrad interrupted. "You're not married, so it may be difficult for you to understand, but my wife is her own person. She's not under my control."

Belgrad found Schaefer's mood worrisome. "You've made remarks that put a cloud over me and the authority," Belgrad said after listening for a time. "This stadium thing is not something I sought, so if you don't appoint me it won't be a problem. We'll still be friends."

But the governor-elect was just venting, looking for a way to rid himself of his usual bout of postelection blues. Shaky before the votes were counted, he could be morose afterward if the totals were not to his liking. Why hadn't everyone voted for him? Why had his margin been so slim? Finally he said, "I wanted to clear the air, and you've done it." He asked Belgrad to continue in his post. Hanging onto Belgrad saved precious time, and the pragmatic Schaefer knew that he was keeping an extraordinarily efficient and methodical man to do a complicated job.

Belgrad assembled a finance committee made up of every good lawyer and finance person available in Baltimore. They gave him cram courses on municipal and state finance, including general obligation and revenue bonds, both of which might be used to build the stadiums. Civiletti and Jerry Sachs, president of the Capital Center in Landover, were also on Belgrad's team. They concluded that more power was needed immediately. The initial sports authority bill that had been proposed by Hughes and passed in 1986 included no means to raise money for construction, no condemnation power to allow the taking of land—none of the real tools that were needed.

The law required the authority to hold hearings in whatever community it chose for the stadiums. Schaefer, Hughes, and other parties had prepared three separate studies, each with different recommendations and a different site. To sort through them, Belgrad hired the consulting firm of Peat Marwick. His first lesson was that the state could build two stadiums for just a little more than the cost of a single, dual-purpose venue, and none of the experts he consulted thought dual-purpose facilities worked well. Since the assembly had ordered a single stadium, though, its views would have to be reshaped, and the enabling legislation would have to be amended to permit what appeared to be the best solution. So all the new governor needed to do was overturn the year-old decision of a wary assembly while convincing it to spend $280 million to woo the barons of professional sports—to submit, some legislators said immediately, to the extortion of men like Irsay. Schaefer anticipated all of this, but he still needed big money: $70 million for baseball, $85 million for football, and $125 million for land acquisition.

Iannucci, Rifkin, and Belgrad drafted a bill designating Camden Yards as Site Option One and proposing to buy eighty-five acres, including various buildings, one of them owned by Schaefer's friend Willard Hackerman. Rifkin was to marshal the votes. As they talked, Rifkin said to himself silently, "How in the hell are we going to make two stadiums fly? How in the hell can we make *one* fly?" The general assembly of Maryland liked to warm up gradually to big spending programs, big change in the laws of the state—anything big. Often, it took years for the 47 senators and 141 delegates to digest big projects, complicated legislation, or a controversial change. Schaefer had challenged the assembly's prerogatives with the Sondheim nomination and had been rejected, but, undeterred as always, he prepared to challenge the legislators on a half-dozen major legislative fronts. He thought that you had to keep moving, had to do everything at once. His new administration proposed an agenda that year of immense scope and magnitude:

Tort reform would adjust the way Marylanders' and their lawyers went to court to win damage suits against each other.

Workers' compensation reform was designed to make Maryland a more business-friendly state.

APEX was a new distribution formula for education aid that was certain to be controversial for a governor who in 1979 had sued Montgomery County, the state's richest, to get his hands on more of its money.

A new cabinet-level Department of Environment was proposed to be charged with land use regulation, air and water pollution control, and primarily rescuing the Chesapeake Bay from ruinous chemical runoff.

But the stadium bills drove everything. The big question was how to pay for them. Schaefer could not use the basic government borrowing device: general obligation bonds sold to investors and guaranteed by the state's treasury (its "full faith and credit," to use the official term), which promised to pay under any circumstances. These notes were used to build schools, bridges, and public hospitals. They could not be diverted for sports stadiums; voters and therefore legislators wouldn't stand for that. So the new governor needed a financing mechanism of some sort. Schaefer knew all about mechanisms. He and Benton had invented an entire parallel government made up of banking, real estate, and income tax—using mechanisms in Baltimore. But legislators were wary of that approach, and Schaefer knew it. So he, Rifkin, and the others tried a few of the usual ideas. A further tax on spirits was crushed immediately by the liquor lobby; a proposed increase in the beer tax met the same fate. "Next," someone told Rifkin, "you'll try to tax vegetables."

They knew they could get part of the way to the $280 million they needed by asking the city to put up a few dollars. Stadium revenues would provide money, but they couldn't close the gap. They were left with a $17 million window to close and almost no time to close it. Iannucci, Rifkin, Belgrad, and Mickey Steinberg, the lieutenant governor, met William S. Ratchford II, the legislature's financial adviser, a man whose acumen made him a worthy opponent of Schaefer and Benton. Ratchford, who never would have failed to see the difficulties in Schaefer's financing schemes or hesitated to reveal them, suggested another approach: What about a new sports lottery with proceeds dedicated to the stadiums? This, he asserted, would be found money, money provided by the fans themselves. No money would have to be taken from schools, roads, or economic development, they could claim. The lottery agency cranked out some numbers to show the likely take.

Schaefer loved the lottery approach because he loved lotteries and because no new tax dollars would be needed. City legislators often argued that the lottery was a tax on those who were least able to pay it. But in this case, the argument was not pressed forcefully. With the decision made, the team went to Bob Douglass, Schaefer's press secretary, to schedule a press conference. They wanted a poster at the back of the room for reporters to see as they walked in. It was to say: "Two new stadiums, for Maryland, No New Taxes."

Some had assumed that a scheming, calculating Schaefer and his geniuses had worked out everything long in advance and had done all their casting about as a dodge, an orchestrated prelude to the lottery. In fact, Iannucci and Rifkin had been wandering in the wilderness, absolutely without a clue about where to get the money. Meanwhile, the stadium bill was moving through the assembly with something like the same expectation: that Schaefer and Benton would provide.

A public hearing was scheduled in the joint legislative hearing room. Witnesses included Johnny Unitas, the Colts marching band, members of the Colt Corral booster club, and assorted economic development gurus who were prepared to talk about how much money would fly into the pockets of Marylanders if only they had twin first-class stadiums. Numerous studies suggested that the economic impact of stadiums was negligible. The ultimate question remained: Should the state be enriching the feckless barbarians of big-time sports? It *was* enriching them, of course, so the political challenge was to pass the bill over these very legitimate objections. Perhaps only a governor who had swept into town with an 82% electoral mandate could have hoped to succeed. Others criticized the projects as flimflam through and through. There was no such thing as found money, they said. If the state had a fund-raising capability of this sort, the proceeds could be used to build day care centers or to provide books for city classrooms that had none. If the money were used to build stadiums, it would be unavailable for other uses, by definition. Schaefer had heard that sort of opposition before, of course, from opponents of the *Pride,* aquarium, the Convention Center, and a hundred other big projects. But he believed that he was building or restoring spirit and standing and enhancing quality of life.

Windfall

Schaefer was the political leader as illusionist, faced with deciding something and doing it without benefit of polls—and not caring much about them—so confident was he of his instincts. And, of course, he had this $15 billion business called the state of Maryland to run. Before he could concentrate fully on stadiums, he had to answer another critical money question. In truth it was a political question, one in which many of the other questions were wrapped. What would Maryland do with a $450 million "windfall" resulting from the federal tax reform bill of 1986? Changes in the law that year gave states like Maryland, whose income tax is coupled to the federal levy, huge rebates of money the state's taxpayers had already paid to Washington. It was not exactly found money or even a windfall, though some in government saw visions of new public works projects. But shouldn't Maryland pass these savings back to the taxpayers? No, said Schaefer. The taxpayers know, he said, that no individual would get more than a few bucks. But government could have an impact with the aggregated cash, and people would want good programs improved or expanded. Here was Schaefer enunciating the covenant that was so welcomed in Baltimore. But Miller and Mitchell followed a fundamentally different imperative: Marylanders did not automatically endorse the spending programs that a poor city so clearly needed. Whatever the amount due the taxpayer, government should return it.

Contrary to the image accorded to such political bodies, particularly those dominated by Democrats, Maryland's assembly has been a conservative one, setting annual spending affordability caps on operating costs as well as construction. Senators and delegates of both parties agree that preservation of the state's AAA bond rating is an inviolable rule. AAA is the highest available credit rating granted by the big New York rating houses, reflecting prudent and skilled management of funds, and the higher the rating, the lower the interest or borrowing costs. With a perspective born of imminent disaster, Schaefer hated this confining restriction.

He was walking into another political trap. Wasn't his determination to spend the $450 million more arrogance and insensitivity from the new governor? Schaefer spent with more vigor than a drunken sailor, Speaker Mitchell said, recycling a tired line that gained new life and many repetitions over the next eight years. "If this money issue doesn't get resolved," Miller declared after weeks of back and forth, "we don't do stadium.

282 / WILLIAM DONALD SCHAEFER

We're not even going to discuss it." So they agreed, finally, to keep one third of the windfall and return two thirds. The likelihood that the stadiums would make their way onto the agenda increased.

But then, just as quickly, the old Schaefer with his old loyalties rose up almost by reflex as the former mayor of Baltimore, the man who always demanded more and usually got more, found himself for the first time at the other end of the highway, in Annapolis looking back at his city. His old friend Delegate Paul Weisengoff, long-time head of Baltimore's delegation at the general assembly and a master of the inside play, was in Schaefer's office asking for Baltimore's customary extra portion, the little bit more that the city's power, if not its needs, demanded. In this case, he wanted a piece of the $450 million. All he had to do was ask, he thought, and sure enough, Schaefer told his old friend, Why not? Go for it. A by-your-leave from the governor was a powerful lever, and Weisengoff was not shy about letting people know he had it. Out of Schaefer's office he came with a big smile on his face. Word of his coup ricocheted around the capitol building: Baltimore was at it again. Schaefer was emptying the state's pockets for his city. So he would be "governor of Baltimore" after all, Miller and Mitchell howled in unison. Rifkin, walking to a hearing, saw one of Miller's aides coming quickly toward him. The aide handed him a handwritten note: "Come to my office." He walked on past the door to the senate chamber and turned right, down the adjacent hallway toward the president's office.

"Stadium is off. Forget it. We settle something and this guy starts making side deals," Miller said. He assumed that Rifkin knew all about the Weisengoff arrangement. He didn't.

Rifkin ran back upstairs. Schaefer confessed and nodded a bit ruefully when Rifkin said that Miller felt betrayed. Other senators who are committed to the stadium construction project will bolt, too, if they think Baltimore is getting more special treatment, Rifkin said. Isn't $280-million worth of new stadium construction enough?

Once again, Schaefer was forced to admit a mistake, not his favorite thing. He had acted for Baltimore without thinking it through. The very political presiding officers would not accept that explanation, believing it to be a willful, deliberate threat and challenge. Rifkin knew that he would not be able to sell any other explanation and wouldn't try.

"Ask them to come back up here," Schaefer told him.

Rifkin ran back down the stairs. Near the end of the day, the speaker and the president were ushered into the governor's office. Schaefer sat behind his desk. Miller and Mitchell sat side by side in front of him. Rifkin slumped onto a couch at the governor's right. Schaefer rose and walked around to the front of the desk, where he stood with his backside against the front edge of his desk and the presiding officers of the Maryland general assembly sitting inches away. Suddenly, the state's chief executive grabbed his crotch and said, "Okay, you've got me right here. Will you please let go?" Miller and Mitchell were speechless. These two were not boy scouts, but they wondered: Is this the way they do it in Baltimore?

"I think they sensed the importance of the moment to the governor," Rifkin said later.

Miller agreed to schedule a committee hearing on the stadium proposals.

Tango

But the senate president did even more for the projects his governor craved. At the Legislative Follies that year, with Schaefer and Hilda Mae in the front row, Miller offered the concluding "rebuttal," which was often a witty and engaging summing up of the skits performed earlier. But this time, Miller provided an astonishing string of ribald and offensive jokes straight out of the junior high school locker room. He suggested that Schaefer's problems in politics—and in life, for that matter—had to do with sex. He needed more of it, Miller said. The governor of Maryland and his lady friend sat frozen, imprisoned almost, as Miller dumped an ashcan of off-color references on the state's first couple. The audience giggled and squirmed as the onslaught went on and on and on. Miller seemed trapped in the monologue, unable to end it. In the days that followed, as the senate moved toward its climactic vote on the two stadiums bill, Miller's performance seemed almost a boon to the chief executive, as some senators seemed to be thinking of voting for the bill as an apology for their leader's behavior.

Sympathy alone would not have been enough, and Schaefer knew he had to have the presence and the persuasiveness of Edward Bennett Williams. But the Orioles owner didn't want to look as though he was holding the state treasury hostage by threatening to leave Baltimore. Williams didn't want to testify and seem like a ruffian of sport, different from Irsay only by degree. He was also battling liver cancer.

Schaefer knew as much about posturing, playacting, and manipulating public sentiment as Williams, and he knew that his ally/adversary was right to avoid, as much as possible, the appearance of a power play in which Baltimore's team was used for leverage. Schaefer also knew that he needed Williams to make his case in person—but he refused to invite him. "The only way he will come is if you call him personally and ask him to come," Rifkin said.

Having dealt with Irsay and Williams and before them Jerry Hoffberger, the beer baron who had owned the Orioles until 1979, Schaefer was an experienced coddler. He had cooed over Irsay and rationalized him to reporters for years, calling him a friend and deferring to him in the most obsequious ways, only to see the infamous green and yellow Mayflower vans pull up to the Colts training facility at Owings Mills and leave with everything, down to the shoulder pads. Now he had to have Williams as a ratification of his authority, restoring of the city's dignity and his own effectiveness. If a man of Williams's eminence would willingly argue his case, Schaefer would be returned to the level of respect occupied by Vernon Eney, Bill Marbury, and the other men William Donald Schaefer so revered. Williams's qualms notwithstanding, Schaefer needed him to appear. When he was asked at a March 1987 press conference whether Williams would testify at the stadium bill hearing, Schaefer said, "Yes. He'll be here."

As the reporters rushed out, Rifkin and Iannucci thanked the governor for making the dreaded call.

"I haven't made it," Schaefer said. "You'd better get him."

Rifkin was stunned but not stunned, all at the same time. Schaefer regularly announced things that no one else knew anything about and would sometimes use his state of the state address as the occasion. Reporters and legislators would be asking questions of dumbfounded bureaucrats and aides who had no idea what the governor had in mind. He had a habit of naming people to do big jobs and doing it in public without informing them in advance, without giving them a chance to say yes or no and thereby exerting immense pressure on them. "A brain cell fired," Douglass would say when his boss announced something that no one expected. It seemed like government by impulse, by unexamined thought—though it was far more calculated. Episodic and emotional, the offhand dramatic announcement or declaration was emblematic of a man who had little regard for any government process, who wanted immediate action. It was government by Schaefer. But he was taking a very big chance this time.

Rifkin and Iannucci sprinted for the phone. They feared that a *Sun* sportswriter at spring training in Florida with the Orioles, where Williams was then, would be deputized by a statehouse reporter to get a comment from the unknowing owner. Iannucci called. Williams was not there. Iannucci left a message. After 5:00 P.M., the phone rang in his office.

"What the hell is going on up there?" Williams demanded, biting off the words. "I couldn't be there next week if I wanted to be, which I don't. I'll be in Boston for treatment."

Rifkin, who had answered the call, apologized and tried to move toward an explanation of how late it had become in the legislative day, how much was riding on Williams's appearance before this joint legislative committee, how much the governor regretted the imposition. Certainly they were not asking him to skip his treatment, but if there was any way. . . . He almost gasped when Williams asked, "What would they ask me if I did come?" Iannucci tried to answer, but Williams got off the phone. Later Lucchino called: Who would be at the hearing? What would they ask? Where would the hearing be held? Send us a list of questions they might ask.

Iannucci prepared a list of about eighteen inquiries, including: Why should the state of Maryland build you a stadium? Why haven't you come to testify on this issue before? What is your commitment to the city? How much will *you* be spending on the team's facilities? And what happens if you die?

Legislators repeatedly asked Schaefer's legislative team the final question. It was part of the stadium opponents' strategy to raise it ominously. It was also part of Rifkin's strategy to present it as a reason for getting the matter settled for fifteen years, the length of a lease that would be written if the stadium were built. Williams saw the dramatic leverage and looked for a way to use it himself. Several days after Lucchino's call, he said that he would show up at the governor's mansion by noon on the day of the hearing—if he could. They should look for him. But he made no promise. He had to be in Boston that morning.

The March hearing was scheduled for 1:00 P.M. At 11:30, Williams was not in sight. At 11:45, that was still no sign of him. Rifkin and Iannucci headed out of the statehouse, and Mickey Steinberg asked where they were going.

"We're going to brief Williams."

Steinberg laughed. "You two guys are going to brief Edward Bennett Williams?"

At about noon, a limousine parked on the circular drive around the statehouse and opposite the governor's mansion. Williams headed for the mansion's front door, helped by Lucchino and his driver, Leroy Washington.

Rifkin asked whether he wanted lunch.

"No."

"Would you like to rest?"

"No."

The four of them sat around an elegant maple table in the smaller of the mansion's two dining rooms: two 30-something no-names, Larry Lucchino, and Williams, one of the most storied lawyers of the generation, a man who entertained Supreme Court justices in his owner's box at RFK Stadium in Washington or at Memorial Stadium in Baltimore. He also appeared to be one of the sickest.

"Before we get started," he said, "I want to know who drafted this list and who put this question on it." Iannucci said that he had done both.

Williams nodded. "What does the bill say?" he demanded.

Iannucci answered.

They went over the questions quickly and then headed across the mall to the legislature's joint hearing room with its green stained glass skylight, Williams limping. This is our last shot, Rifkin figured, but Annapolis loves a show, whether it was pythons carried by zoo officials looking for millions in funds for renovations or new exhibits; rock star Frank Zappa, in town to testify against restrictions on free speech in song lyrics; or Ed Williams, the Clarence Darrow of his day.

Two of the senators began by telling Williams how honored they were that he was there. One had been a student in a class Williams taught at Georgetown University Law School. Williams grinned and said something about the joy of putting one's professor on the spot. Senator Larry Levitan, a Montgomery County legislator and chairman of the committee on budget and taxation, aimed his own videocamera at the great man.

Williams began by apologizing. He said he would have been more prepared, but he hadn't known until a day or so earlier that he was expected. Indeed. He dealt with the most emotional and inflammatory question—the question of his death—by saying that of course he would agree to a long-term lease that could not be broken even if he died before it expired. He mentioned that provision as if it were a mere legal necessity. And he had props. On their way to Annapolis from Washington that morning, Williams had ordered his driver to stop at a newsstand to buy that week's *Sports Illustrated*. At the right moment during the hearing, Williams reached into his briefcase to show the senators how important their deliberations really were. Baseball's most famous family, the Ripkens—shortstop Cal, second baseman Billy, and Cal, Sr., then the team's manager—were on the cover in uniform in Baltimore.

"This," said Williams, "is why the stadium is important to Maryland. It isn't the immediate dollars. All across this country, this city and this state stand tall with publicity they couldn't buy. It may not look economically to be a big thing to have a football team . . . but the visibility is so much more dramatic than the economic impact that it's indescribable." Here, the owner-lawyer made two contradictory points, both of which served him superbly. He said that he was shocked to learn that "the team's revenues were not equivalent to those of a large department store. "Yet . . . these are high, high visibility factors in the United States. So we have an opportunity . . . to have one of the most exciting attractions for a state in all America. We have a magnificent harbor complex, and I think the addition of a sport complex will be the equivalent of anything in the nation." Schaefer would have said something similar, and he would have added in some forums that Baltimore could not afford to lose its only remaining major league sports franchise. The stadium deal was critical, a must-win thing for the city and the state. Economists were thoroughly debunking the notion that sports franchises did much for the economy, so both men were talking up the public relations dividends.

The day belonged to Williams, but it was Schaefer's day as well. This was vindication for him because Edward Bennett Williams was *his* lawyer, in effect, his lobbyist, making his case before the jury of Maryland legislators. If Irsay had humiliated him and despoiled his city, Williams would wipe those memories away. The dying man appealed for a little vision among decision makers. "I like to think bigger than I am," he said. "I hope the state will think bigger and bigger, the legislature will think bigger, and that we'll have in this one little area a revolution so we can return to where we rightly belong. . . . When the stadium opens and later at the All-Star game, all of Maryland will be proud of what you are doing."

Legislative committees in both houses almost immediately approved the $280 million spending authorization, and the bill headed for final passage. An amendment was needed, usually not a good thing, since amendments can provide opportunity for opposition. But this one change probably saved the project from death at the hands of the voters. Opponents wanted supporters on record as having required the state to actually appropriate construction money—so they would have to bear the political fault. Instead, that explicit provision guaranteed that the voters would have no chance to block it: Under Maryland's constitution, an appropriation cannot be taken to referendum, lest every spending decision made by the legislature be subject to paralyzing delay, a possibility that would surely make governing impossible, or so the state's founders had believed. Therefore, when opponents tried to get the stadiums on the November ballot, Schaefer appealed, arguing that an appropriation was beyond the voters' reach. The state's highest and most political court, the Court of Appeals, ruled on September 7, 1987, that the constitution made the issue an easy one for them. The stadiums were a done deal. Schaefer hated process, but occasionally, even inadvertently, it saved him.

He had prevailed by manipulating one of the great manipulators of all time. He and Williams never spoke about Schaefer's brazen leveraging—perhaps because Williams had known that he would have to do what Schaefer wanted. He'd been Williams's prisoner at those dinner meetings at the Tremont Hotel, but in this case, Schaefer had the power. As in 1976, when he and Mandel managed a convention center and a subway system for Baltimore in the same year, in 1987 Schaefer gave Maryland two sports stadiums, as if Baltimore had to have two big public works projects every decade or so.

Ground couldn't be broken for the new park—nor could bank financing be arranged—until a lease was completed between the state and the team. Formal talks had to wait for the Court of Appeals to rule. The state and the Orioles had been talking informally since October 1987, but as usual, the talks went slowly. Finally, in late March 1988, with matters at what Schaefer always thought of as the Tremont stage, in honor of his dinner meetings with Williams, a bargaining session was held in the offices of Williams and Connolly in Washington, D.C. Williams sat at the head of the table. When everyone else had arrived, he asked, "Where are we apart?" As he leaned forward, his suit jacket, several sizes too big by then, slipped off his cancer-shrunken shoulders. The negotiators tried not to notice. The talks ended without agreement, and another session was scheduled for Sunday at a motel on Route 95 between Baltimore and Washington. Still no agreement was reached. Another meeting was set for Monday and another for Tuesday morning with everyone committed to making a deal in time to announce Tuesday afternoon at Memorial Stadium, when the Orioles were opening their home season. At noon on Tuesday, Belgrad suggested that they try to finish on the train to Baltimore. If they didn't leave, they would miss the drama they all wanted to create. The Baltimore group left their cars in Washington and went to Union Station, but they had no tickets for the train to Baltimore. Even Orioles brass had to have tickets. Eugene Feinblatt, then serving as the stadium authority's lawyer, approached the tracks and stood with one foot on the platform and one in the train car, refusing to move. "We had to have a place to sit in the club car," Belgrad said, "so we could work out the last of the details." Belgrad says that they put the last parts of the agreement on a napkin and finished it by the time they got to Memorial Stadium. Williams wanted the deal announced that night, but Schaefer said no. He wanted it typed, formalized, and signed first because Williams might then say, "No, that's not what we agreed to" and leverage more for himself.

"We've got a deal," Williams said. "How about a handshake?"

Schaefer said okay.

He and Belgrad and Lucchino went out on the field, Schaefer in an O's jacket to show what a fan he was, and they officiated at the announcement. Williams, too sick to join them, stayed in his box. The next day, when the agreement was committed to paper, the owner raised numerous questions, challenging the state's version of the lease, just as Schaefer had predicted. Another week of negotiating was needed to get a document both sides could accept.

Before Williams died, a mock-up of the first stadium proposal was brought around for him to look at. A cookie-cutter product, he said, nothing outstanding, not what we want. He ordered a whole new look, suggesting that the designers might try to make the new park fit with the city surroundings. Perhaps such an objective had never been more perfectly achieved. The stadium opened in 1992 to raves that have not subsided.

After Williams's death in August 1988, the Orioles were sold to Eli Jacobs, another extraordinary personality to be enshrined in the pantheon of big money owners. Virtually reclusive, Jacobs met dignitaries—former governor Harry Hughes, for example—without ever speaking a single word to them.

"Tomato"

In those early days of his tenure as governor, Schaefer wished to add staff to the executive department and imagined that he could do this on his own. But, no, he needed legislative approval, and each time he did something—added five or six people here, a few more over there—the assembly slapped him into submission or tried to. In the toils of budget deliberations one evening in his first year, Schaefer heard from his spies that a house of delegates subcommittee was cutting the salaries for the new positions. The committee on prisons, transportation, and the courts had control of these budget line items and was working late into the night at the Lowe house office building, no more than a city block from the statehouse, where Schaefer himself had stayed at his desk. Hearing of the cuts, the chief executive of Maryland churned down the stairs, past portraiture and statuary, down the outside steps, and into the chill evening air. He trudged across Lawyers Mall, a splendid preserve of crabapple trees and carefully placed park benches where a casual visitor might sit on warmer days to contemplate the wonder of democracy. Schaefer flew through the swinging door of the Lowe building, shot up the three flights of stairs to the committee room, and slammed into a seat in the back of the room, his entrance noticed by all. He fixed the Stare on Delegate Timothy F. Maloney, one of the assembly's most astute young members, who represented Prince George's County, a suburb of Washington. Known to reporters as "Tomato" because of his round red cheeks, Maloney had become a master of the budget, not to mention the assembly's own political dynamic. Close to some of the state's highest-ranking judges and an intimate of Speaker Mitchell, Maloney presided over an immensely important domain of spending, a position from which he built courthouses, ruled for or against judges' pay raises, and, in this case, several executive salaries. He called a recess when Schaefer arrived.

"Anything I can do for you governor?" he asked.

Schaefer could hardly speak, so Maloney suggested that they retire to a nearby office.

"Do you want me to kiss your ass?" asked the governor of Maryland.

"No," said Maloney.

"Okay, then," said Schaefer, "you can kiss my ass."

Maloney says that Schaefer began dropping the gubernatorial trousers. At about that moment, Mitchell and Miller rushed into the room, having been alerted by other committee members.

"This guy is cutting my budget," Schaefer shouted. "Tell him to stop cutting my budget." He then left the room and went back to his office.

The struggle over authority and prerogative in the governmental process continued so Schaefer's budget *was* cut, lest he think that he could overwhelm the process by fuming and disrobing. For two or three years of his first term, Schaefer literally prayed for the end of the legislature's annual ninety-day session.

As for Maloney, Schaefer went through a process familiar to the governor's friends: A rocky start would often evolve into a close partnership and warm regard. As an influential member of the appropriations committee, Maloney found himself going to Schaefer with ideas that the governor usually endorsed and promoted. The University of Maryland's performing arts center was one of these. Maloney's legislative district in Prince George's County included the university, and he wanted to see it achieve the distinction of flagship in the state's university system. Schaefer and Mickey Steinberg spent at least a year recalibrating aid formulas to pump more money into the school. And Schaefer eagerly endorsed Maloney's suggestion that three small public works projects planned for the campus could be aggregated more meaningfully into a single, $100-million project. The young legislator became a regular at the Governor's Mansion, where he struck up a friendship with Hilda Mae Snoops and began to win Schaefer's confidence. Near the end of Schaefer's second term, he, Maloney, and university officials stood on the wooded site where the arts center was to be constructed. The governor was noncommittal and full of questions that went on and on.

"We are going to do this, aren't we, governor?" Maloney asked finally.

"Yes, yes, of course, we're going to do it," Schaefer said, "but we're going to do it right." He went on to make a few design suggestions, which were reflected in the final plans.

12

Homeless

For the first months of his first term, Schaefer gave a fair approximation of being homeless. He refused to move into the governor's mansion, though that act had always symbolized a governor's investiture. In fact, Maryland's constitution requires the governor to live in the official state residence. Symbolically, this cements the relationship between governor and governed. Practically, it makes sense to have the state's chief executive live in the capital near the lawmakers and their assembly. Schaefer had various reasons for flouting tradition. For one, he hoped, as always, to avoid the airs associated with holders of high public office. To that end, he would remain a resident of Edgewood Street, West Baltimore. But this was at least partly camouflage. He also knew that Hilda Mae Snoops intended to live in the official residence, as remarkable as that notion was, considering that she was not the First Lady and never would be.

Politically and personally, Schaefer wanted to avoid the appearance of living with a woman to whom he was not married. When governor of Nebraska, Bob Kerrey, had lived for a time with the actress Debra Winger, it had been a somewhat risky though romantic adventure politically. The Vietnam war hero Kerrey more than survived, moving on to the U.S. Senate. Moreover, Schaefer and Snoops were sufficiently advanced in age that many Marylanders would have had no problem with their living arrangements. Some might have applauded. But Schaefer's reasons went further. He was unwilling to surrender his bachelor status or to subject himself to the demands of a woman who was ready to assert her dominion over him as no one else had done, with the possible exception of his mother. He might have been unwilling to share with her even the reflected glory of his eminence as governor, the title First Lady of Maryland, or any of the distinctions that would fall to her should she become Mrs. Schaefer. He might have seen her as a threat to his public image and his image of himself as a man who had made it to the top virtually by himself, his way, without help from any "woman behind the man." He was married to Baltimore, to his work, and to the vision he had of himself as an achiever. If he married Mrs. Snoops, the folklore would have been lost; the image so carefully crafted would have been shattered. Some saw an extension of the only child syndrome here. Others thought that he might have promised his mother never to marry Hilda Mae. A more likely analysis was that Schaefer had decided years earlier that he would not marry and had become irrevocably committed to his decision. He was, as his driver Chuck Fawley put it, a visitor, not a stayer.

By many accounts, the relationship between the governor of Maryland and his First Friend (no one knew what to call her) was not always a happy one. Angry with him for his refusal to marry and jealous of almost everyone around him, Mrs. Snoops administered large doses of reality when she thought he needed them. If a woman paid any attention to him, he told a reporter, Hilda Mae would observe, "She wouldn't even look at you if you weren't governor."

In Baltimore, she had thought that Schaefer never gave her the recognition she deserved; now she seemed determined to grab it for herself. If he would not marry her, the wags said, she would at least have the mansion. Eventually, Schaefer and Hilda Mae bought adjoining condominiums in Anne Arundel County, a decision that may have reflected a desire to reduce scrutiny of her status at the mansion as well as his growing unhappiness with Baltimore under his successor, Kurt Schmoke. Though Schaefer kept the old house on Edgewood Street, he was pointedly moving out of the city he'd been married to. But Hilda Mae's determination to be a house sitter without portfolio seemed undiminished. She evicted Schaefer's long-time hostess and arts maven, Jody Albright. She dictated which of his staff members could visit the mansion and how they should enter. One day, after Walter Sondheim met with Schaefer in his office before a reception in the mansion, the two men walked over to the party, ducking in the back door. When Hilda Mae spotted Sondheim, she stopped him. "How'd you get in here, Walter?" she demanded.

"Oh, hi, Hilda Mae," he said, "I came over with the governor. We came in the back door."

"Walter," said Maryland's official hostess, "when you come back, come in the front door."

If anyone was to feel welcome in the governor's house, they would feel that way on Snoops's terms. David Iannucci was invited into the kitchen one morning by the state police drivers to wait for the governor. The troopers had seen him standing by the fence in the cold and rain, and Snoops saw him too. She called down to the kitchen.

"Who've you got down there?" she asked the trooper.

"David Iannucci," the trooper said. "He's waiting for the governor, and it's raining."

Iannucci was to leave and wait outside and should not be invited in again, Mrs. Snoops instructed. She did not like Iannucci's beard.

She made other callers line up outside the front door until she was perfectly ready to receive them. The whole social thing annoyed her, since it highlighted her odd status. She hated getting invitations that said, "Governor William Donald Schaefer and guest." Those who wished to keep her favor began to include her by name. She was not above ordering state police troopers to do gardening and household maintenance chores. It was said that she even demanded that they be reassigned to different parts of the state, far removed from their families, if they fell into disfavor with her. If she was in Baltimore overnight, she would order dinner prepared in the mansion to be delivered by a trooper as if he were a pizza delivery man. Schaefer's staff, Lainy LeBow in particular, was outraged. "Here's a man ," LeBow said, "who never took a pencil from the state house unless he paid for it. And then this woman, I could never figure it. You know what he did, he buried his head in the sand and just hoped it wasn't true."

Guilt and Rubber Duckies

Just before Schaefer's famous swim in the Baltimore Aquarium's seal pool, while they were in Chicago for a promotional reception aboard the *Pride of Baltimore*, Hilda Mae gave him a inflatable toy duck. The pilots blew it up and put it on his seat. Schaefer was so nervous in airplanes and so apprehensive about the next day's events that he damaged the gift.

"He clutched that thing all the way back. He held it so hard on the plane he put a hole in it," said Chris Hartman, then his press secretary. "That's how I always knew if it was the real rubber duck or someone else's rubber duck."

In Baltimore, Hilda Mae had been virtually invisible, though anyone who knew the mayor in those days knew of her. Fifth Ward operative and city worker Dick Rudolph used to double-date with Schaefer and Hilda Mae. Herman Katkow, Schaefer's small business director, knew her too and thought Schaefer might marry her one day. "I tell you he had a roving eye, always noticed the pretty women. But he was true blue to Hilda Mae. While his mother was alive, I could understand why he didn't marry her. Total devotion there. But when she died, and rumors began about running for governor, I thought the time had come." Katkow had an idea. "'Why don't you have a press conference with Hilda Mae at your side and introduce her as the future First Lady of Maryland?' I thought it would be a nice way to announce that he was running. You know, a little bit of humor in it. He almost fell off his chair."

A Tough Cookie

When they met as adults in 1959, Hilda Mae Snoops was a handsome woman, a mother of three, and about to be divorced. Schaefer's question was more than a conversation starter. "Haven't we met?" he asked. They had indeed. His grandparents and Hilda Mae's were friends. Schaefer and Hilda Mae began dating. But Tululu remained the official woman in his life, and he kept them apart. His mother held the Bible when he was sworn into office, and at public ceremonial events it was Tululu, not Hilda Mae, who accompanied him. On Christmas Day, he spent time with his mother first, then visited Hilda Mae. They did not celebrate together.

City hall staff members began to realize that Friday nights were for Hilda Mae, and so did her neighborhoods on Lindsay Street, where, eventually, the mayor's chauffeur and sometimes the mayor would come to fetch her. But he kept her largely out of sight—not a happy situation for her but one that did not change.

He seemed to some to be perpetually on the brink of breaking up with her. LeBow remembered the prologue to a trip Schaefer and Sondheim were making to England or Germany in the early 1980s. "As it got closer and closer, he was like a lunatic, and the day before he was leaving, he said 'I'm canceling.' I said you'd be very foolish to cancel. You're not going with another woman. You deserve to have fun. I used to have to make him understand that he deserved to be happy. But the way he would deal with being happy was to be very miserable and then be happy so then he wouldn't feel guilty. I understood it. He and Hilda Mae played into each other. He felt guilty going without her, but he wouldn't want to go *with* her."

The two vacationed in Ocean City over the years and traveled abroad occasionally but took care to book separate, nonadjoining rooms. "There is no scandal about Mrs. Snoops and me," Schaefer said more than once.

Schaefer, LeBow said, made his own decisions about marriage just as he had made his own decisions about everything.

His mother would have hated anybody for taking Donny away, but you know it's one of those things where I think she always wanted him to marry, but it was very nice if he didn't. She thought that the governor's mother prevented him from marrying her. But I think the governor used his mother as an excuse. I think he just felt he was not going to be able to share his life with a family. He kind of knew that, and I think he was right. He made that decision and I think that's a decision he's regretted. He didn't regret it while it was going on. But I think he's regretted it since. You know, he used to tell me when he was mayor he never thought about family obligations. And he would say to his people, "We'll meet on Christmas Day." And then he realized he couldn't do that with people who had lives and families. And then as he got older, he would push everyone to spend time with their families. . . . I think he would have been a very tough father. He expected so much. The way he did with us. Never enough. You know, he would have been a tough cookie. But you know you have children and in the end they come back to you even if you don't get along with them.

So, he knew the price he was paying.

Circumstances

But Schaefer had almost married once. The lady's name was Irene Vincent. They met at a dinner party in 1955. She had been invited by her friend and supervisor at the phone company, the future Kay Waltjen, who would marry his law partner, Norman. Donald and Irene took an immediate interest in each other, and Schaefer asked whether he could drive her home. They got in his little gray Dodge, and on the way, he asked whether she would like to stop for a drink. They went to the Carousel on North Avenue, had a few drinks, and talked. He asked how old she was and was mightily taken aback when she said she was a few days shy of twenty-one—underage for drinking purposes. She guessed that he was about thirty-three. Those demographic details out of the way, he asked her to go with him to a bar association dance, and she did.

They began to date, and saw each other for three and a half years. They spent a fair amount of time with Schaefer's cousins Jeri and Anita in a house the sisters were renting in Mount Vernon just across the square from the Stafford Hotel. Vincent remembers how attractive Don seemed to other young women. "They always wanted to comb his hair. He'd say, 'Sure, for 25 cents.'"

Vincent recalls the postwar years as a time of self-absorption when the veterans were trying to adjust and others pondered a still unsettled world. She had been born in Czechoslovakia, and she watched with horror when Russia invaded Hungary in 1956. When a benefit was held at the Peabody Institute, she urged Schaefer to go with her. He was not particularly interested but finally said yes. When the time came to pay for the $20 tickets, he turned to her. "'It's your cause,' he said. 'You wanted to go.' I almost croaked."

She got over it, though, and the two continued to see each other until 1957, when, she said later, "We severed relationships." In the early 1960s, though, the relationship resumed. Then came a fateful accident, mundane and poignant. Irene traveled to Czechoslovakia to visit her family. While she was there, Schaefer wrote her a long, bulky letter, but by the time it arrived, she was on her way back to the United States. Her cousins wrote to ask what they should do with it. Not wishing to have them pay the postage back to the United States on such a large package and knowing she would see Donald in person, she said, "Just throw it away." Her relatives were poor after the war, and she did not wish to impose on them for such an expense. She told Schaefer what she had done, thinking nothing of it, assuming that he would understand. "He got his feelings hurt and didn't call me. Then I got my feelings hurt. That's the way the cookie crumbled." Before that, she said, they had talked of marriage. "Very definitely we talked about it." But a missed connection, a misunderstanding, hurt feelings, and perhaps other things got in the way. This time there was no reconciliation.

Irene remained close to Tululu Schaefer, though, speaking with her and visiting her periodically. When Irene married and had children, Mrs. Schaefer sent them birthday cards with dollar bills tucked inside. As the years went by, they talked about many things, including Hilda Mae.

"She wanted Donald to marry," Vincent said later. "She wanted grand-children and all of that. Once she told me, 'I know Hilda Mae thinks I'm the cause, but honest to God I'm not.' His mother always thought her son and Snoops would eventually marry." Vincent did not. "I knew he would not marry her. I could not see him doing that. He would not like to be giving his all to three children that were not his." His reluctance, she suggested, was partly financial, as it had been when she herself might have become Mrs. Schaefer. In those days, she observed, a man did not marry until he could provide for a wife and family. Schaefer had discussed this very issue with his lawyer pal, Milton Wisniewski, when they were careering around at the HiHo and in Ocean City. In the end, an accumulation of circumstances kept him single. Did he feel that he was too old for Vincent? Was he reluctant to spend his money on the bigger-ticket items of family? Had his other life taken over, marrying him to his work? All of these considerations figured into his decision, along with the mere passage of time. "People say he's gay," Vincent said. "I'm sure he's not." His cousins Jeri and Anita offered the same conclusion: "He was the least gay person I ever knew," Jeri said. Schaefer, who knew of the speculation about his sex life, said he was not gay.

He retained an affectionate memory of Vincent. They had been "mighty close," he said. "Irene was a very fine young lady. She wanted to get married. But she wasn't the only one." Vincent, Hilda Mae, and others were more than available, but the discussions seem to have been one-sided. People blamed his mother, but she seems to have been as close to Irene Vincent as her son, staying in touch over the years. If Tululu had offered a tacit endorsement in this case, it did not influence her son. "I guess I've never been the marrying kind," he said. "I don't know why." In terms of loyalty over time, Hilda Mae was his best girl, the woman he stayed with, the one he was loyal to for forty-five years through times that must have been at least as challenging as marriage.

Blue, Bland, and Boring

In March 1988, the governor of Maryland issued an executive order making March 30 Hilda Mae Snoops Day, calling her "a beacon of inspiration to all who are interested in nurturing and promoting a positive image for the mansion." He had made her an honest woman, sort of, by conferring a title: official state hostess. She had a calling card prepared with a picture of the mansion and her name engraved across the top. What might have been a sensational story in most states was a muted one in Maryland, owing largely to Schaefer's overwhelming popularity and to the fact that he was a character to begin with, a politician protected by his image. He was too cranky and too busy to be engaging in hanky-panky. Mrs. Snoops might have had one final hope: that a press-generated furor would be resolved at the altar. Furor there was, but it had more to do with the house than it did with the first couple and their relationship.

From the outside, it looked as though Schaefer and Hilda Mae were determined to trash their predecessors. Harry Hughes and his wife Pat had redone the mansion's first-floor rooms in styles that were intended to reflect periods in Maryland's history. Mrs. Hughes had engaged the services of noted architects and experts on the periods she wished to see represented. Stiles Tuttle Colwill, a noted collector and the chief curator at the Maryland Historical Society, had worked with her for many months to redo the six so-called public rooms. They recreated a Victorian parlor, "seductively," by one account. They also produced an elegant French reception room, an Empire parlor with chrome yellow walls, an eighteenth century neoclassical drawing room, a colonial revival dining room, and a contemporary conservatory done in the style of Baltimore-born designer Billy Baldwin. Baldwin's inclusion was curious to some and attributable to his designation as "dean of designers"; he certainly was not a period to be commemorated. Overall, though, the critics loved what Mrs. Hughes and the preservationists had done, and *Architectural Digest,* a bible of interior taste, gave it a rave review. The work had cost $1.5 million, all raised from private givers.

Colwill did what he could to save what he had accomplished over eight years with Mrs. Hughes. But, he recalled later, nothing in the new administration was shared with the old. Hilda Mae hated the Baldwin room especially. The Hughes family had used it for their portrait, but Mrs. Snoops despised the chocolate-brown lacquered wood and everything else about it. When Colwill and Mrs. Snoops met, one writer observed, the clashing of styles was jarring: his London tailoring, her housewifely pantsuit; his Greenspring Valley pedigree, her West Baltimore roots. "It got acidic very quickly," Colwill recalled later. Soon after the confrontation between Snoops and Colwill, the consultants used by Colwill, Brunshwig and Fils were sacked, and their New York City competitor, Scalamandre, was summoned. The Government House Trust was disbanded, and the Governor's Mansion Trust was formed to replace it. Mrs. Snoops's makeover of Colwill's eight-year effort was completed in three months. On

September 28, 1988, she conducted a tour of her new house for reporters, including some art critics who were decidedly sympathetic to Colwill. "The panache was gone and the rooms ran together in a sea of beige," wrote one of those who looked it over. John Dorsey of the Baltimore *Sun* called it "blue, bland and boring." Schaefer gamely defended Hilda Mae's work even as he felt that she was out of control.

At the same time, of course, he was still trying to acquire a new NFL franchise, build a light rail system, find ways to protect tidal wetlands without choking off development, and make Maryland more business friendly. He demanded the rail lines in spite of the unpromising revenue projections in a society devoted to its automobiles. He would push the project through the assembly, only to face suggestions later that he had deliberately lowballed the costs. Former governor Hughes, himself a former transportation secretary, thought that Schaefer's spending was a threat to the transportation fund if not to the state's own treasury. Schaefer and the assembly also reduced unemployment taxes and repealed onerous regulatory constraints, hoping to produce a record of accommodation that would attract new businesses, but none of these efforts improved the business climate. In part because his sense of public relations would never allow him to admit that the climate was poor to begin with, he could not develop a systematic campaign to make his state more business friendly.

Every Night Specials

In addition, Schaefer had the presidential election of 1988 to worry about, featuring the unpromising candidacy of Massachusetts governor Michael S. Dukakis, and a referendum on handgun control in Maryland. Given a choice in that year, Schaefer might well have gone with Republican Vice President George Bush, a man with whom he had become friendly. Dukakis's style was the polar opposite of Schaefer's. Restrained to the point of arrogance and clueless about making himself seem more human, Dukakis ran his campaign with a determination to control everything from Boston, including the distribution of bumper stickers. His very able Maryland campaign manager, June Streckfuss, despaired of ever having the tools to promote him. Voters in Montgomery County, always hungry to read about the candidates, had no campaign literature. There were no lapel stickers, no buttons, none of the palpable proof that an election was at hand.

Schaefer stepped in but not forcefully. Never anxious to endorse any candidate at any level, fearing that he would be hurt personally, he never-theless joined in a series of "zip trips" with state comptroller Louis L. Goldstein and Senator Sarbanes, who had been Dukakis's roommate at Harvard. After a swing through Prince George's County, during which Schaefer barely mentioned the name of the man he was supporting, the campaign day ended at the county office building in Upper Marlboro. Du-kakis's difficulties were much on the minds of other Democrats. "We didn't want to peak too early. I think we accomplished that," said Joel Rozner, chief of staff to the county executive, Parris N. Glendening.

Dukakis labored under an array of self-inflicted disadvantages going beyond the logistical delays in campaign paraphernalia. Early in the cam-paign he had allowed himself to be photographed in a tank commander's cap. Schaefer had worn such a hat years before at the Aberdeen Weapons Proving Ground and managed to look like a warrior. Dukakis looked like Alfred E. Newman, the *Mad* magazine character with the addlepated grin and the slogan "What me worry?"

Schaefer might have been criticized for doing less than his share for his party's candidate, but he had an immense personal stake in the 1988 cam-paign. At the urging of Attorney General J. Joseph Curran and members of the old Harborplace referendum team, including Rick Berndt, Schae-fer backed an effort to control the sale of the type of handguns known as Saturday Night Specials in Maryland. In that decision, he would be op-posing one of the most effective special interests in national politics: the gun lobby. Curran's father had been one of the victims of the 1977 Balti-more city hall shooting, so Schaefer, who had essentially ducked the issue before, began to think about going with Curran and Berndt. He tended to listen to Curran, a credit to the attorney general's calming and friendly demeanor on everything. The attorney general recalled the volatile and occasionally profane Schaefer stopping during one of their conversations to ask with sincere wonder, "How can you be so nice all day long?"

Schaefer might have been thinking that something less nice would be needed to defeat the National Rifle Association, which was certain to march into Maryland in force if the state seemed likely to deal it a signif-icant setback. Maryland had been an important battleground for the NRA in the past, the place where it had become the most feared lobby in U.S. politics by unseating Senator Joe Tydings in 1968. But Schaefer was im-pressed by the passion of his old friends and by the growing support he saw from law enforcement officials who wanted to get guns off the street. With an estimate of 1,040,000 legal and registered handguns in the state—

302 / WILLIAM DONALD SCHAEFER

and a similar number of illegal and unregistered weapons—every other Marylander might have had one. They were called Saturday Night Specials, but the state's police chief, Elmer H. Tippett, said they should be thought of as "Every-Night-of-the Week Specials." They would not succeed without a fight, however, and one that would be wounding to Schaefer politically. The NRA's "Stop the Gun Ban" bumper stickers showed up next to anti-Dukakis messages on the back of many a pickup truck. Analysts figured that President George Bush and the anti–gun control forces would be natural allies, since many of the GOP candidate's conservative supporters would oppose government intervention in gun control matters, among others.

The NRA was represented in Maryland by Fred Griisser, a thirty-four-year-old real estate salesman from Glen Burnie, who became chairman of the Committee Against The Gun Ban—a title that Schaefer and those on the other side said was misleading from the very start. The state law passed in 1988 did not ban guns, but it did require that guns would have to meet certain standards to get on a roster of permitted weapons. Griisser and his allies said that the law was merely a precursor to more complete prohibitions, a tack that had been taken with sublime success in almost every campaign the NRA had ever undertaken. As long as it is not an appropriations measure, a law passed by the Maryland General Assembly can be put on the ballot, so Griisser led a public effort to put the law to public referendum. "I don't believe the people of Maryland want to give up their right to choose anything—whether it's the right to have pepperoni on their pizza or whatever it is," Griisser said. He got his signatures, and the race was on.

At the start, the national NRA had wanted to avoid a fight in Maryland, having concluded that Schaefer's popularity and a high degree of antipathy toward guns would make a struggle difficult to win. When Griisser persisted, though, the organization decided that it had no choice but to support him. On Labor Day weekend, the NRA hit its stride, buying some $400,000 worth of TV advertising, a signal that it planned to wage the most intense battle it could. Vinnie DeMarco, formerly of the state attorney general's office, appealed to the Schaefer campaign—Berndt in particular—to raise money for a counterattack. DeMarco feared that moderate Marylanders would be persuaded to support the gun lobby if they believed that all handguns were to be banned, as the NRA claimed.

LeBow and Berndt went to work, and Schaefer became the TV star of advertisements that defied the NRA and sought to educate voters on just what the new law would do. In the Harborplace referendum the mayor and James Rouse had had to be moved offstage to avoid seeming to be a powerful two-man bullying crew. In this case, Schaefer could be David opposing the big outsider, and he had the popularity to pull it off.

His involvement meant money to put his voice on television. Every day or so near the end of the campaign, LeBow would call DeMarco. "Go over to so-and-so and pick up a check for $30,000," she would instruct, and Vinnie would comply. Schaefer's money people were instructed to contribute with as much energy as they would have if Schaefer himself were running. In a sense, of course, he was. If the NRA won, the loss would have been absorbed by Schaefer, its most prominent champion. From his point of view, it was a referendum on him. In all, DeMarco raised about $700,000, enough to do the job but only a fraction of what the NRA spent, a figure that was estimated to be as high as $7 million. Ironically, DeMarco thought, many of those who voted against the NRA did so because they believed that the law would, in fact, do what the NRA claimed: ban all handguns. When the battle was over and reformers realized that the ban was not a complete one, many were disappointed, to say the least.

DeMarco represented one further irony. In 1986, he had been a Sachs campaign worker, and after Schaefer had won, the new governor had sent a message to the attorney general's office, where Vinnie worked in the consumer affairs division. "Get rid of Vinnie DeMarchetti," the message said. But there was no such person, and the governor's office was so informed. Curran would not have fired DeMarco any more than Marion Pines would dismiss Paul Schurick—and Schaefer would be equally glad in the long run. Still, DeMarco was obliged to work out of public view. Even when the Saturday Night Special bill was pending in the assembly, DeMarco could not be in Annapolis for fear that someone in the administration would spot him. But without his tireless advocacy, Schaefer might not have had a bill to defend. It was DeMarco who quietly recruited a critical witness: Sarah Brady, the wife of the former presidential press secretary who was wounded grievously in an assassination attempt on President Reagan. Mrs. Brady's charm and her passion for workable gun control laws convinced the Maryland General Assembly eventually and helped to cement support from Schaefer. Once the campaign to defeat the NRA began, though, DeMarco moved out of the shadows.

Schaefer gravely doubted the political wisdom of allowing the voter to decide difficult issues by referendum. He had been worried about the Harborplace vote and, horrified to think what voters might do with the stadium bills, he made discreet inquiries about the disposition of judges who were asked to rule on whether that measure could be taken to referendum. No political scientist, he believed that the representative form of government wisely put difficult issues in the hands of a few men and women who had the time to fully understand them and let the voters speak on election day. With handguns, he set aside his concerns and put a huge portion of his political capital at risk. He knew the meaning of guns in the hands of criminals and madmen, of course, in the most personal way: his own near-death experience and the loss of his colleagues Leone and Curran.

Schaefer's campaign to defeat the NRA succeeded. Had there been no Bush-Dukakis race, Schaefer, Berndt, and DeMarco might have done better than the 58 to 42 margin that resoundingly defeated the NRA's campaign.

Sarah Brady frequently cited Schaefer's courage and leadership in Maryland as an essential first step toward passage of a nationwide gun control measure, which became known as the Brady Law. Even with Schaefer's decisive victory in Maryland, it would be eight more years before the Bradys, DeMarco, and others persuaded the U.S. Congress to require a seven-day waiting period before a gun could be purchased to permit background checks of the buyer. That law has been credited with keeping guns out of the hands of criminals and the mentally incompetent. Schaefer had been far ahead of the country, spending political capital—risking his own standing with some voters—to address a problem he might have ignored.

Dukakis lost to Bush in Maryland by 49 percent to 51 percent, a huge upset for any Democrat in a state that almost always goes Democratic in presidential elections. In 1976, when Schaefer was just moving into his second term as mayor, he had stayed out of a party primary in which Kovens and Mandel took on and defeated Jimmy Carter almost to prove that they could. They were in charge of presidential dummies and geniuses, too, and in that year, they had picked California's eccentric Jerry Brown—in part because Mandel and Carter had clashed in the National Governor's Association. There was irony in this for Schaefer because Carter had one of the last articulated national urban policies, and his assistant secretary of housing and urban development, Bob Embry, had given Schaefer and Baltimore a king's ransom of federal help.

Bush won in 1988 also because of low turnout in Baltimore that shocked the Democrats. The campaign had gotten ugly near the end as Bush's forces distributed sensational flyers reporting that the liberal Dukakis had furloughed murderers, one of whom had subsequently held a Maryland couple hostage and raped the woman. Dukakis was also charged in that campaign with opposing the Pledge of Allegiance and with having the dirtiest water in the nation, a finding heralded by Bush, who took a tour of the Boston Harbor to make that point. Bush's forces gave Americans hard images upon which to build animosity, if not doubt, about the man from Massachusetts.

The Fountain

The Hilda Mae saga simmered on as a curious sideshow to everything else. Schaefer's pain built but never reached the eclipsing, public quality of Marvin Mandel's. Mandel had divorced his wife Barbara, known as Bootsie, to marry Jeanne Dorsey, a blonde socialite from Southern Maryland. If Dorsey was a femme fatale, Hilda Mae might have been merely fatal—politically. Schaefer absorbed or deflected much of the damage but sometimes seemed as if he were dealing with an unhappy wife who seemed determined to let the neighbors know just how miserable she was. Schaefer was not married, but he could not or would not divorce. LeBow thought that Schaefer was on the verge of ending his relationship with Snoops several times. His sense of loyalty—and perhaps guilt for not being willing to marry—would not allow him to make the break.

Hilda Mae plunged on toward the mansion grounds, completely relandscaping the lawns, planning a Victorian fountain to be installed at the southeast corner, and having stately old cedars cut down to make room. Dutiful groundskeepers insisted that the trees were dead or dying, a contention that was refuted strenuously by state Senator Charles Smelser of Frederick County, who said he heard them moaning as the chainsaws ripped into their trunks. At about the same time, Snoops installed a bit of Baltimore folk art—a painted screen—on one of the mansion's rear doors. On Baltimore's east side, local craftsmen painted landscapes on common window and door screens, and the practice drew considerable scholarship and admiration. Outside the city, though, some considered the whole thing the urban equivalent of the suburban pink flamingo. Schaefer found the touch quite pleasing.

Snoops had asked her friend Ed Papenfuse, the archivist and Maryland historian, whether a Victorian fountain would be appropriate. Certainly, he said, recalling a precedent: a Victorian fountain on the statehouse grounds at the turn of the century. Mrs. Snoops wanted the statue to be authentic and proper. "If a fountain was to be installed, it had to be truly Victorian, she said," Papenfuse recalled, "done with care and with class and with accuracy that would reflect all of Maryland. Her biggest problem with the fountain was that she didn't know how to sell her idea."

By then, given her track record inside the mansion, everything Hilda Mae tried was seen with suspicion, mistrust, and foreboding. There she goes again, people said. What right did she have to be ripping out trees and wallpaper? She was not the governor's wife and not a state official, executive orders notwithstanding. Reaction to her work in the mansion and on the mansion grounds represented a reversal of Schaefer's symbolic successes in Baltimore, where virtually everything—even when opposed in the beginning—affirmed his leadership and Baltimore's progress. The *Pride*, the Aquarium, the World Trade Center, Harborplace, the renovated city hall, controversial outdoor sculpture, and Camden Yards were projects that some opposed in the beginning and all embraced in time, allowing even more acclaim to their progenitor and politically courageous exponent, William Donald Schaefer.

Yet, Hilda Mae's contribution *was* admirable. Her cast-iron fountain, designed by Lyle Beddes, was sculpture, a pastiche of native grasses, birds, and fish, evoking Maryland in all its glory—an outdoor version, it almost seemed, of Pat Hughes's vision for the mansion's public rooms. The finished work was installed in the fall of 1990, on a somewhat cold and overcast day. Once again, it was not well received, largely because Mrs. Snoops had seemed secretive, peremptory, arrogant, and willful—far more so, it seemed, than any of the blue-blooded antiquarians who had helped with the Hughes effort. What she wanted in the newly landscaped grounds, as well as inside the building, was something Marylanders would feel comfortable about, as a reflection of who and what they were. "She wanted to bring elements of Maryland together in a place on the grounds that people could enjoy and appreciate" said Papenfuse. "And she became intrigued with the idea of bringing a fountain, a public fountain."

Papenfuse conducted a press briefing on the work, but the image of Hilda Mae as unelected arbiter of taste—a barbarian inside the gates— had become indelible. To make matters indescribably worse, a surveillance camera was installed in a birdhouse near the fountain to record the efforts of any really aggressive opponent. "It turned into a public relations night-mare that didn't need to be," Papenfuse said. "It was an extraordinary monument, which I predicted at the time, and it's proven to be the case, was really appropriate, beautifully done, and well done, and what a con-tribution. In time, people will believe it was always there. They're going to have to come onto the grounds to see the plaque to see that it was Hilda Mae's idea." The fountain was a momentary disaster but perhaps an en-during contribution.

Several weeks after the fountain was dedicated, Hilda Mae lashed out at her critics and threatened to dismantle all that she had done. At the very least, she and the governor decided, they would do no more refur-bishing—a good thing, in the minds of many.

Piece of Ground

One thing led to another. Someone learned that Robert Pascal, the for-mer Anne Arundel County executive, Schaefer pal, and Republican can-didate for governor in 1982, had given the governor a nice deal: a below market price on a piece of land on Tilghman Island. At no other time in his years as a public official had anyone suggested that Schaefer was guilty of self-dealing. In this case, though, a gift was given by a man with devel-opment interests that might have been assisted by the state's chief execu-tive. Any number of environmental regulations harried builders, so, it was thought, Pascal might enjoy a better relationship with Schaefer and his administration if their friendship extended to price cuts on property. The suggestion infuriated Schaefer, who spoke at length about it one day dur-ing a press conference.

"I look over to my right and see Harry Hughes and think how smart he was," he said, referring to Hughes's portrait in yellow shirt, striped tie, and blue blazer.

He bought a lot on Fenwick [Island] and got one story. I bought a lot on Tilghman and we had two editorials and nine stories. . . . One of the things I've tried to do in public life was try to deal hon-estly. I don't have very much, but I did have some integrity, and now the integrity and my honesty is challenged by the purchase of a lot on Tilghman Island. I don't think anyone doubts that I had a hand-shake agreement with Bob Pascal two or three years ago. A lot of people knew it at the time. It wasn't any big secret. I've been interested in the Eastern Shore. I've been going down there some thirty-some years, enjoyed it. Now let's look at what happened between Bob Pascal and I. Bob Pascal is my friend. We became friends when he was Anne Arundel county executive and I was mayor. I admired him and I respected him. I watched him do things for the elderly. In fact, there was a senior citizen's center that was opened in his name, and many of the things that he did in Anne Arundel County, I also tried to do in Baltimore City.

Pascal sold him the land, in other words, before its value shot up, so the price was the price; there was no break because he was governor. Nevertheless, he said, he was going to get Pascal to buy it back.

The *Sun's* reporter asked Schaefer then whether he felt bitter. He said, "I really don't mind telling you that my integrity over a lot like this would be impugned. And a major to-do over what I thought wasn't a big deal. I don't even know what I can do now. I can't do what anybody else does."

Here was the poor-me, you've-ruined-me approach that Joe Sterne, the editorial writer, had observed. Schaefer was making a martyr of himself and—worst of all, he said—giving in to "trial by newspaper." Even if innocent, Schaefer should have realized that he could not accept a favor worth thousands of dollars from anyone. He had been advised to sell his three hundred shares of gas and electric company stock and various other holdings. Why? he wondered. People should trust him after all these years. He said he would sell the utility stock, bit by bit to avoid a tax liability. He would sell back the land. But wasn't it ironic? "I go all over the world and I say 'Invest in Maryland. Buy stock in Maryland,' but I can't do that myself." He had forgotten the cautions he himself had requested when he was treasurer of Bishop Cummins Church. He'd wanted a bond on his performance, particularly since his predecessor had absconded with precious church funds. Surely, he ought to have understood the principle perfectly. No doubt he did and was merely deflecting criticism as he had done with his shadow hat and cape.

His knowledge of the ethics law had in fact been refreshed by one of his closest and most trusted aides, Daryl Plevy. He had given her responsibility for learning just what he could and couldn't do, particularly in the area of gifts. As governor, she told him, he had to disclose his financial holdings and declare virtually any gift he received. What was reportable and what was not? Plevy wondered. She read the law and found it somewhat difficult, if not frightening. One could easily make a mistake, fail to report something, and pay for it with an embarrassing headline. Every time Schaefer was given something, Plevy called John O'Donnell, the smiling, snowy-haired enforcer of this intricate law. Gifts poured in, of course, and each one seemed to demand a query to O'Donnell. Annoyed but compliant, Plevy offhandedly mentioned to Schaefer one day that she was going to ask O'Donnell about yet another gift—a rockfish. Schaefer had a better idea. Why not mail the fish to O'Donnell so that he could inspect it up close and personal? She did.

Unmet Needs

Schaefer was pursuing his growth control and environmental preservation program, called "2020" for short, an allusion to the hope that by that year, Maryland would be taking care of its bay and using its scarce resources in ways that made sense for humans as well as animals, fish, and trees. But the initiative of the year—as far-reaching as "2020," as daring as gun control—was the tax study commission, which became known in Annapolis as "Linowes," after its chairman, R. Robert Linowes, a Bethesda and Washington, D.C., zoning lawyer. Linowes was an active Democratic fund raiser, helping D.C. Mayor Marion Barry and many others, including Bill Clinton in the 1990s. Linowes had attempted to vet both men before writing them checks. He met with Barry one day to say that further reports of drug use and womanizing would end their relationship. Barry swore that he was clean and committed to staying that way. On his way home from the office that evening, Linowes heard that Barry had been arrested for possession of crack cocaine in a Washington hotel in the company of a woman who was not his wife. Clinton, too, had sworn that rumors of his multiple affairs were no more than that—rumor. Gennifer Flowers, Paula Corbin Jones, and Monica Lewinsky would call that vow into question.

Linowes felt no need to conduct a similar interview with William Donald Schaefer, but the governor of Maryland was asking him to commit a year or two to a revolutionary study of Maryland's tax structure. Schaefer's intent was to modernize a thoroughly outdated system, to make it sensitive to the varying costs of providing public services, and to adjust state aid correspondingly. He wanted a more progressive system, one that helped poor individuals and poor jurisdictions. If a state government was to be an instrument for redistributing income, the mechanism should be as fair and current as possible. So Schaefer undertook a chore that legislators had been running away from for decades. Ben Cardin had promised himself to do that work, and Cardin was an expert in state finance and tax laws. But the time was never right to Cardin's political mind, and when he decided to run for governor, he would not have approached tax reform under any circumstances. Schaefer, who was always looking for more money to spend, did.

He appointed a range of Maryland citizens, including several legislators, to serve with Linowes. An unrepentant and even militant liberal, Linowes was perfect for the task. He came from Montgomery County, the state's wealthiest jurisdiction and the one that, by definition, would be asked to give most in any redistribution formula. Linowes knew that he would be accused of something approaching communism as he went about his task. Even the idea of redistribution was being challenged in those days by Maryland's newly muscular Republican Party. Hoping to generate controversy, the Maryland State Chamber of Commerce convened a discussion under the heading, "Redistributing the Wealth." That is our responsibility, thought Linowes. Ridiculous, thought Delegate John Morgan, a young legislator from Howard County, a rocket scientist employed by the Johns Hopkins University Applied Physics Laboratory. "It struck me as absurd," he told the *Sun*. "I thought we had abandoned all of that. Welfare isn't working. People don't think redistributing the wealth is a good idea."

Schaefer and Linowes thought government had an obligation to deal with casualties of the marketplace and history. If the poor were not taken care of, if the disabled child of an aging middle-income parent were not taken care of, if someone did not have compassion for the victim of a catastrophic illness, if people did not recognize interdependence, society was doomed. The haves would be forced to the burning barricades by *les misérables*. Beyond that, Maryland's system of taxation was antiquated, unfair, wasteful, and unlikely to produce the sort of smoothly efficient government that taxpayers were demanding.

The Linowes Commission's experts spent two years studying such arcane matters as tax effort—the amounts collected county by county even in those where the taxable property did not yield sufficient revenue for government to operate. The greater the effort, the more legitimate the appeal for help. Linowes wanted to know what $1 worth of public money bought in Montgomery County, where the cost of living was higher, and in Somerset County, a poorer Eastern Shore jurisdiction. He fed all of the data into computers in search of a new structure that would be fair to individuals, fair to counties, and likely to produce the additional revenue Schaefer wanted to address "unmet needs."

Irv

The tax reform effort was truly revolutionary, as monumental a task as Schaefer or any governor had undertaken in a generation. To craft a majority of lawmakers to vote for such a makeover would test every bit of strength and wisdom available to him. And he would have to do it without the Big Chief. Irv Kovens died on October 31, 1989. He'd had little if any role in anything Schaefer had done for many years, which was all to the good, many thought. Kovens had wanted Schaefer to make Edgar Silver his patronage chief in Annapolis, but Schaefer had demurred and dissimulated, putting Kovens off as he had sometimes done at city hall. Kovens was furious; Schaefer was fretful but unwilling to accommodate his friend and political godfather. The reformers still shuddered to think about the bad press that would come to them if they gave Kovens anything. When Schaefer was first elected governor, Bob Sweeney, chief judge of the state's vast district court system, thought Kovens would be his new boss, forcing him to put a robe on every hack lawyer in the state. Sweeney says he never heard from Kovens or from any Kovens messenger. "You had as much to do with Schaefer's judicial appointments as Kovens did," Sweeney told a reporter. Silver says that he couldn't get Schaefer to "make" an obvious insider. Sweeney said that Schaefer agonized over the choices he had to make, informing the chief judge that the men and women they appointed would be serving long after they were dead—and think of the responsibility of that! Occasionally, Schaefer would send Sweeney the names of all the finalists chosen by judicial nominating panels and ask Sweeney to pick. This was a far cry from the days of Pollack, George Hocker, and Tawes, when a governor's continuing campaign fund needed a $5,000 infusion.

Schaefer was one of Kovens's eulogists at Har Sinai Temple on Park Heights Avenue in Baltimore. He sat on the stage with the casket in front of him. He told the audience that he had not finished his grieving and that he would always remember Mr. Kovens, who, he reminded people, had always called him Shaky. There was a bit of laughter. Kovens had been the key to virtually every one of his election victories, Schaefer said. Someone had instructed him of a new reality: With Irv gone, the man had said, "You're not going to be president." There was more chuckling. Schaefer said he had lost his second father, a man who made the big and little problems go away, leaving him free to push the big projects. The political columnist Frank DeFilippo, who had been Mandel's press secretary and therefore knew all the players, asserted that Kovens, the scalawag so reviled by Rouse, was more responsible in the real world than Rouse for the development of renaissance Baltimore. Without Kovens's Fifth District clubhouse, DeFilippo said, Maryland might not have had Marvin Mandel or Schaefer—a mixed legacy, some would observe. Surely, though, Kovens had been part of the marvelous chemistry that included Rouse and Bereska; Clarence Mitchell and Emma Bright; the German General and Goldilocks; Lainy LeBow and Barbara Mikulski; thinkers like Charlie Duff; activists such as Lucille Gorman; and stalwarts Mimi, Du, Sol, Harry, Peck, Buddy, and Benton—all of whom were part of the soul of Baltimore. In coming years, people would see Schaefer working himself into one crisis or another and declare that he had absolutely no idea what to do or how to operate without Kovens to advise and soothe him. Schaefer would never disagree, though, of course, he did know what to do and had many people to help him when he asked.

Pronouncements were made before and after the service and in the newspapers that Maryland would never see the likes of Irv again. This was true in part because no one had inherited Kovens's fabled list of businessman check writers whose money had underwritten campaigns for a generation. Kovens had kept the phone numbers of the wealthy beholden—along with notes on the favors he had done for them—on a Rolodex, making it all available to Bereska, Hillman, or DiPietro. Some said that the magic data was really a well-annotated notebook. DeFilippo said it was a cigar box which Kovens took with him wherever he went, even to the hospital so he could work the phones from his bed. Schaefer's men had their own list by then—on computer disk. What they didn't have was Kovens's menacing scowl, his "Guys and Dolls" gangster voice, and his energy.

Schaefer would go over it all in his mind as he drove out to Finksburg around Christmas every year to visit Kovens's grave. He liked to take a holiday wreath, and he didn't care when LeBow shrieked at the thought of Christian symbols in a Jewish cemetery. She imagined caretakers lurking respectfully until the governor of Maryland left and then rushing in to dispose of the foreign object. Schaefer's real mission was to have his annual conversation, speaking aloud to stone and sod, bringing Kovens up to date on various things and waiting for word from the man who had made him councilman, mayor, and governor.

13

Tailspin

ADJUTANT: "We've got the weather report for tomorrow. We may have
to pull up and wait."
GENERAL PATTON: "Brave men are dying up there. We're not going to
wait. Not an hour. Not a minute. We're going to keep moving. Is that
clear? We're going to attack all night. We're going to attack tomorrow
morning. If we're not victorious, let no one come back alive."
ADJUTANT: "You know something general. Sometimes the men can't tell
when you're acting and when you're serious."
PATTON: "It's not important for them to know. It's only important for
me to know."   *Patton,* the movie

William Donald Schaefer knew when he was serious and when he was acting, when he was bluffing, and when he was frightening someone and why.
An important element of leadership for him was dancing along the line
between control and chaos, between predictability and uncertainty. He
seemed to prefer control in the end, no matter how much screaming he
might do. He never seemed to lose his place for long—until approximately
midnight on November 2, 1990, his sixty-ninth birthday. He was standing for election an eleventh time, and almost 40 percent of Maryland's
voters chose the Republican team of Bill and Lois Shepard, a husband-
and-wife ticket that was famous until then for nothing beyond the un-
orthodoxy of their political partnership. Even in the era of feminism, husband and wife did not run for office together. It was considered tacky and
transparent, an obvious case of having no choice—no other Maryland
Republican was willing to spend a summer in a hopeless cause. Never-

theless, William Donald Schaefer, who had secured a record 82 percent plurality in 1986, who had saved a hopeless American city, who had built stadiums and roads and railway lines, saw this unlikely pair of challengers reduce his winning margin of four years earlier by a full 22 percentage points. Though he imagined that his record was without parallel in Maryland history, many voters turned to Shepard, a recently retired foreign service officer who had lived away from Maryland for most of the preceding twenty-five years, the years when Schaefer was at his peak. Had Shepard found a more orthodox running mate, he might have done even better. He had no money and no real feel for the political game. Amiable and smart, he was nevertheless a bit lost. Though hardly known outside Montgomery County, the Republican standard-bearer campaigned one day at the Great Frederick County Fair without a nametag, explaining the omission in terms of home economics: A stick-on name tag would do a horrible number on a suede jacket, he said. But his amateurish moves were recommendations at a time in American politics when incumbents were, by definition, the problem. Voters were gleefully repudiating lifetimes of public service as mere careerism. The usual records of accomplishment—public works large and small, a smoothly operating and proactive system addressing unmet needs—had become proof of unworthiness in the mind of the voter circa 1990. Once the darling of voters, Schaefer was now a target.

Largely unaware of this dynamic, Schaefer and his team had begun that year campaigning as if he could resume his office by simply filing for reelection. He felt that he should not have to make his case, since the case was so obvious, and he frankly conceded as much to *Sun* reporters and editors. His record had earned him a free ride, he thought, particularly given the competition. Election by acclamation was his due. The Schaefer team had set up a series of celebratory events around the state, minimizing the act of actually asking for votes while inviting people to come and endorse his ascension to a second term. In Baltimore, his fund-raising parties had always been cast as "Reflections"—a stocktaking, a kind of subliminal or at least indirect calling upon citizens to recognize how blessed they had been to have Schaefer and his accomplishments. In 1990, the insiders were so confident of this approach that they made no effort to conceal it. The plaudits would roll in for this consummate man of the people, and he would be prepared to do even more for them. Schaefer was awaiting completion of the Linowes Commission's tax study, which, he seemed certain, would show Maryland that it could afford to spend even more money on government services. He anticipated another smashing mandate. His assessment of the climate was uncharacteristically optimistic, a complete reversal of form for the man known to intimates as Shaky. Grateful elected officials, having received a multitude of state grants for local projects, assured Schaefer and his agents that their people's votes were his already. His team had no current assessment of the electorate's mood—a mood most foul, as it turned out.

Reality Check

Schaefer had been challenged in the primary by Fred Griisser, the 1988 NRA standard-bearer from Glen Burnie, just north of Annapolis, and when Griisser piled up a substantial number of votes, Schaefer finally sensed the trouble. He fired the celebrationists, replacing them with a smaller group of more level-headed insiders: Wasserman, LeBow, and Gary Thorpe, a utilities expert and university professor who had been working for Schaefer as head of a small cities program and who might well have been Schaefer's chief collector of political chits. These three recruited the quietly astute press secretary Marvin Bond and his boss, Louis Goldstein, Maryland's irrepressible comptroller of the treasury, who was more politically folksy than Hyman Pressman or Schaefer himself, a man whose career in politics spanned the years of Roosevelt, the Kennedys, and every other Democratic winner since 1940.

"What we consciously tried to do was tie the comptroller's campaign to the governor," said Thorpe. "We knew the comptroller was popular."

So there Schaefer was, the colossus of Maryland politics, whose approval ratings had been "godlike" for years, grabbing onto Goldstein's coattails, looking for help from a down-ticket running mate whom Schaefer regarded as somewhat goofy, difficult, and racially insensitive—to put the best face on it. But they were running hard together now as both had always done, taking nothing for granted.

Still, "We had all this snappy campaign stuff," Thorpe recalled. "People came out with bands. They were happy to see us. We looked at a bridge on a business block and said 'We're gong to fix this for you.' These mayors were so damn appreciative, sincerely appreciative, and you could see it. They loved the guy. So he was feeling pretty good about the second half. He expected to get 90 percent, and it was reasonable. But we were still completely wrongheaded. We were talking to the wrong people—mayors, councilmen, business guys. We weren't talking to citizens. *They* were sitting home grumbling about the son of a bitch who was spending all their tax money."

Yet, looking back on it, the animosity did come out amid the walking and talking of the campaign. In the burgeoning bedroom community of Belair, northeast of Baltimore, Schaefer got into a bit of an argument with a seventy-five-year-old voter about taxes and "that damned stadium and that damned cesspool, Baltimore." Thorpe tried to show the man what he was getting for the $500 he paid in state and local taxes every year: 911 emergency call service, trash pickup, state police, the public schools. This elderly man, completely unconvinced, sneered at his governor. In the old crabbing community of Crisfield on the Eastern Shore, "an insurance guy, very influential, lobbied like hell for money to renovate their decrepit theater. It was water damaged, snake infested. It was hopeless. But he wanted to get it renovated and saved. He wanted $145,000 in state money to stabilize it. And while he was talking he started trashing the stadium in Baltimore. Totally irrational," Thorpe thought. His own project, in other words, was a worthy one, but the Baltimore work was obviously corrupt and wasteful.

The Schaefer team scheduled a stop at a huge convention of junk collectors at Martin's West, the political catering hall on Baltimore's west side. Senator Mikulski, who usually went along on such outings, dropped out in a rage at whoever it was that had scheduled such a stop. Everyone would be drunk and abusive, she thought. But 2,000 people were on hand at Martin's, where one of the officers of the organization took Schaefer, a bit nervous about the lion's den of scavengers he was about to face, and led him through the hall. There, finally, was the adoration he had been expecting. "These people went crazy. They took pictures of him. They loved him," Thorpe recalled.

Like Schaefer, himself, everything about his 1990 campaign was ad hoc, random, and episodic. Nothing the campaign stuff did was guided by polling. "When celebration is the theme," Thorpe said later, "you don't imagine you need to take the temperature. I never saw a poll number. We focused on officials and business guys, who kept assuring us that these communities would be with him—but it was a year when the folks weren't with the pols. We didn't see what was happening."

On the Eastern Shore and in western Maryland, Schaefer's standing was taking a hit for a number of reasons: Hilda Mae, Hilda Mae in the mansion, state spending in the mansion, the 1988 handgun referendum, and the nationwide anti-incumbency fever. "When Shepard is elected," said a Western Maryland Republican Party official, family values will return to the Maryland State House." In this sense, the two-Shepard ticket was genius, playing as it did off the "scandal" of Hilda Mae Snoops and William Donald Schaefer living in sin.

As the campaign closed, Thorpe and Wasserman were betting on the final winning percentage: not the 90 percent Schaefer imagined, but 65 percent (Wasserman's prediction) or even as low as 62 percent (Thorpe's). Both were above the mark, and neither was confiding in their boss how much they imagined he had slipped. When they saw him on the stage for the victory celebration that night, they could see the gathering emotional storm. "He was most upset by his numbers on the Shore. He'd been out there. He'd spent time there. He was sincerely interested in the problems he saw, and he'd worked on solving them. We spent hundreds of thousands of dollars, and most of those counties went against him."

Landslide

When the votes had been tallied and reported, Press Secretary Douglass and others urged Schaefer to understand that his 60 to 40 victory was a landslide. "Cuomo and Bradley almost lost," Douglass told him. "You've won by a huge margin compared to all of them." For a moment, Schaefer bought it. He mouthed the spin even as his psychological pout was tightening the pit of his stomach, pulling his face into a tight frown, and piling up a huge reservoir of boiling hurt and invective. After the election, he put maps of the offending counties on the walls of his office and pointed to them when anyone visited him. He ordered an end to certain projects in offending areas. He cut them off, all over the state.

"The son of a bitches. Let them do it themselves," he told Thorpe. "They didn't do it for me."

"I'd say, 'Governor, you did carry Crisfield.' He'd shout, 'God damn it, I didn't!' He'd tick off the numbers again and go on for four or five minutes."

There was plenty of precedent for this monumental pique, of course. When Schaefer beat Steve Sachs, he railed against those such as Herbie Belgrad who had not been with him, as if their individual defections were more important than his smashing victory. When he ran against Russell in 1971, he didn't carry his own precinct, though he had done far better there than many had predicted. A few days after that election, the mayor-elect had gone door to door, asking, "Aren't I a good neighbor? Why don't you like me?" He saw the returns of 1990 in precisely the same way. He had been in the houses of people in these Eastern Shore communities, and they had voted for Shepard.

"He took it as a personal rejection," said Thorpe. "It wasn't a happy time." It would get worse.

Privy Governor

Schaefer's habit of gathering motivation from a day's events allowed him often to make his public speaking personal and immediate even when it was difficult for outsiders to see the points of reference. After the 1990 election, though, the whole state would get a glimpse of what LeBow and the others saw.

On January 20, Schaefer walked down the white marble steps from his second-floor offices to perform an unavoidable duty: his fifth state of the state address to members of the Maryland General Assembly. He had been at a meeting that morning with poverty warriors in Baltimore, and one of them had whined a bit about some things she thought the governor and the state of Maryland should be doing for them. Even before he had heard the pitch, Schaefer had asked one of his aides to close the door. In private, he had lashed out at the ungrateful wretches arrayed in front of him. He was doing everything he could, and no one, not one single soul, gave him an ounce of credit. The entire Eastern Shore had gone against him in the election after everything he'd done there, and so on. Later, on the way to Annapolis, he had read a newspaper story in which Hilda Mae's activities were once again being criticized. This time, she had . . . it hardly mattered. On this day, he had perhaps too much stimulation, particularly since he was still feeling the pain of the election results. He fumed all the way down the grand statehouse staircase, passing the 1859 painting of General George Washington, a halo of righteous light around the patriarch's head as he resigned his commission as commander-in-chief of the recently victorious Continental Army. General Washington had delivered his statement to the Continental Congress in Maryland's Old Senate Chamber only a few feet away. Thomas Jefferson and James Madison had been members of that body then. "The great events on which my resignation depended, having at length taken place," Washington had said, "I retire from the great theater of action; and bidding an affectionate farewell to this August body under whose orders I have so long acted, I here offer my commission and take my leave of all the employments of public life." He would accept other public jobs, of course, but for the moment, Washington was headed into retirement.

Schaefer felt none of Washington's affection for the assembly he was about to address. He was inclined to offer a leave-taking of his own, but he continued down the steps, saw the great doors swing open, and heard a state police officer announce his arrival. He shambled into the room, glancing left and right, scowling all the way as if nothing he saw pleased him a bit. Hands reached out to Maryland's governor as he moved slowly down the center aisle. But he was feeding on anger and sending it back into the landscape of unsuspecting faces that turned to greet him. As rambling and chatty as Washington was crisp and efficient, Schaefer's speeches almost always offered as much information about the state of Schaefer as they did about the state he governed. He got to his oratorical point even before he reached the rostrum, delivering one of the most enduring lines of his career well before he reached the speaker's podium. He spotted newly elected Delegate Bennett Bozman, a friend and supporter from a district near Ocean City, now transformed in Schaefer's mind into another disloyal face in the crowd.

"How's that shithouse of an Eastern Shore?" asked the governor of Maryland.

Legislators who heard and who knew him did not pause. Bozman smiled and then, having expected a more pleasant greeting, frowned. The governor had probably been rehearsing his rude question or one like it for weeks, knowing that some deserving target would appear. Bozman's Somerset County, along with Cecil, Caroline, Worcester, and Talbot Counties, had gone to the Republican candidate. Someone had to pay for that, and it was Bozman. When Schaefer was mayor, he banished those who displeased him to a sort of purgatory, where offenders were required to find some way of restoring themselves in his eyes. In city hall, this was known as "going to Siberia." Those who saw how peremptorily he acted predicted that he would soon disenfranchise whole counties when he became governor.

Bozman and others near him in the house chamber told reporters, who dutifully told their editors what the governor of Maryland had come up with. The punchy little bit of text was printed with comments from anyone who wanted to comment. He was the governor, after all. Bozman, by contrast, was a pharmacist, a member of the Veterans of Foreign Wars, and a volunteer fireman in Berlin, the small town outside Ocean City where he lived. Maryland prided itself on sustaining its citizen legislature, one that limited its deliberations to three months a year, balanced its budget, and overcame spending phobias to put more money into public education. Bozman and his colleagues, most of them having the same broad spectrum of community affiliations, spoke with wonder about their colleague's encounter. A day or two later, after the story was widely read, Eastern Shore men and women drove over the Bay Bridge to Annapolis with outhouses on their pickups and trailers, handing out bags of manure, and marching around the brick-paved street encircling the State House, acting offended.

Schaefer had always said what was on his mind. But he had always been on top, and the degree of approbation that greeted most of his public acts provided an ambient, unconscious forgiveness if he crossed the line. No one reported to the media the pungent letters they had received from the exalted mayor of Baltimore. City businessmen said nothing when he ordered them to do what he wanted on pain of some unspoken municipal retribution. His own aides never complained about the tongue lashings they received. On the contrary, they told stories of how he had badgered them into glorious exertions for the greater good. He was insulated from criticism by his good works, by his good humor and optimism, by the manic energy that seemed to send up a protective force field, by his very eccentricity. Until the shot he took at the Shore's ingrates via Bozman, Schaefer had contained the worst of the hurt and anger he harbored from the election. To be sure, people had puzzled over his tantrums. They wondered whether he was out of control. This uncertainty had always been what he wanted. He was the man holding the nuclear bomb of disapproval, retribution, and intimidation. Intimates worked hard to please him, not wishing to disappoint him and not wanting him to upbraid them. He seldom did, but people always thought he might. One of his opponents observed that something like an autistic child syndrome had risen to protect him. People gave him what he wanted so that he wouldn't hurt himself, or them, by an errant swipe of the hand. These outbursts weren't his fault, they said. And look at all the good he does.

He had been given to reflexive, creative swearing and to novel formulations of profanity that could raise the eyebrows of the worldly. The one he tried on Bozman was right out of that imaginative lexicon. The difference, of course, was that until then, he had kept it all in house. The things he said were often not appropriate for family newspapers, but when the papers did use some of his rhetoric, he prospered even more famously. What reporters and editors thought was unseemly and undignified made him seem more human. People began to take for granted that their mayor, later their governor, was a bit off. It was a fact of their lives, like crabs and marble steps and the Orioles. Suddenly, though, people began to wonder whether his idiosyncrasies would begin to overwhelm the rest of his life, a fog of vituperation creeping in to obscure and sully his accomplishments.

This time, some wondered whether his mood was not, finally, a signal that professional help was needed. His perfectionism, his unwillingness to set priorities, and his demand for service to the people now congealed at the core of his being. He could not escape the feelings of rejection and could not accept the "spin" of his own managers. Spin was for the reporters and for the citizens, of course, but if the man himself wasn't buying it what could you do? What was happening was a rapidly accumulating crisis of principle, of life habit, and of borderline imbalance: Nothing was ever good enough, allow no priorities, use the outrageous, exaggerate offenses into the dimension of holy war, confront your tormentors (Romney, Orlinsky, Hughes, Pomerleau, even Kovens) and reporters, and never relent. Now this attitude had become so extreme that it was sounding alarm bells throughout the executive offices of the statehouse.

Schaefer had fallen into a major-league funk, LeBow and Thorpe agreed—or perhaps worse. "There were days," she said, "when I went home and cried. I didn't think I could go back the next day. I was listening to him. And listening and listening. He needed somebody, and I knew I was the one. But I didn't know if I could keep doing it. He was really very miserable. And it was so sad."

Wasserman told a reporter he hoped it would not be long before the governor came "back to balance." Thorpe found him profoundly and unalterably "unhappy." Outside the governor's office, few had any idea of the worry that gripped Schaefer's friends and associates. His lifetime of nutty performances, towering rages, and fights with the world at large insulated him in an odd way. He's crazy? No kidding. Off the deep end? Really?

Psychiatrists were consulted informally. "I called several people. He knew it, but he wouldn't have seen anyone. We talked about [treatment] and he said 'I'm not going to do it.' I talked to several people about it. . . . Politically, I understood he couldn't do anything. And I talked to a lot of people about things I should say to him, without telling them what was going on, looking for ways to deal with it. . . . It was so hard and trying to keep him afloat. He did all kinds of dumb stupid things. You were afraid to let him out of your sight, you didn't know what the hell he was going to do. . . . He was so depressed."

There was no refuge for Schaefer in religion. He had been active, if not devout, when he was a parishioner of Bishop Cummins Church, but he had transferred to Old St. Paul's on Charles Street. At the urging of Bill Marbury, the eminent Baltimore lawyer who had represented Alger Hiss, the suspected Soviet spy, Schaefer was elevated to deacon at St. Paul's.

Schaefer had wanted to be governor at one point in his career because, by a quirk of Maryland law the governor was also head of the Episcopal Church. When Mandel become governor, though, that law was changed, apparently because Mandel was Jewish.

As mayor, Schaefer was fascinated for a time with Bob Harrington, a preacher from New Orleans who had decided to "save" Blaze Starr, the famous stripper whose act Schaefer had admired when he was younger. Harrington's speaking style and dramatic approach to the gospel appealed to something in the renaissance mayor, who attended a few prayer meetings conducted by Harrington.

"He knew his audience," Bailey Fine said, "forty- or fifty-year-olds, heart attacks waiting to happen. We'd just finished our eggs and sausage — this was before people knew that eggs and sausage could kill you. And the whole time Harrington's talking, he's snapping his fingers, and then suddenly the light drops and he says, 'Like that! Your heart stops and there's no future.' Schaefer was jumping up and shouting 'I believe!' I almost dove under the table. I didn't know if we should quit or sign on. And then it just kind of went away."

"He captivated me," Schaefer said. "Maybe it was a time in my life when I needed saving." He needed saving in general, he said, not from anything in particular. Schaefer and the preacher read scripture to each other over the telephone after Harrington returned to New Orleans, and the mayor visited Harrington. Schaefer says that he began to wonder what Harrington's attraction to Starr really was, and then he wondered why he himself had been so taken with what he realized was a bit of a con. Schaefer left the gospel train one day when he watched Harrington shrug off the request of a poor supplicant who wanted the minister to visit his modest church — it was too modest, apparently. Schaefer says he had a similar falling-out with Old St. Paul's Church.

"They had a homeless man, and they were willing to get rid of the guy as a nuisance," Schaefer said. Always ready to help panhandlers and the homeless, Schaefer watched them materialize on city streets and then decline step by step. He tended to identify with them and urged others to realize that they could be in the same boat. Many of these people, he thought, were refugees from the state's mental institutions, exiled to the streets during the process called deinstitutionalization, in which the hospitals were closed and patients were sent back to the "least restrictive environment"—a huge policy mistake, Schaefer thought. Some of these refugees did not wish to be helped, he knew, but he tried anyway. "I'd give them a little money. People would say 'You're encouraging them. You give them money and they stay.' But there are two sides to that. Maybe it's God in disguise."

"Notting Brain"

Then one day the funk lifted. "He just sort of came out of it," LeBow said. "We had been trying to get him excited about what was going on, about being governor again. Which he did. He came back." He had adjusted more successfully (though sometimes stormily) to problems in his public life—Romney, Hughes, the Reagan years—but when his own accomplishments, his own sacrifices, and his own devotion to the public good were questioned, it threw him. Sure, editorial writers and reporters would carp at him. He called them "Hit Men." He could manage them. He could frighten them out of the way and neutralize if not stop them. But now the tirades were almost self-directed. He could not put an entire state into Siberia, so finally he sent himself there.

After the 1990 election, people saw how vulnerable he was. Some began to take liberties with his dignity. Republicans sold T-shirts with a cartoon likeness of him, the results of the election, and a legend next to the anti-Schaefer total that read: "I know where you live." All of this was pretty tame stuff, the kind of hectoring that goes with the job. But Schaefer hated it more than most, and in fact he did know where his tormentors lived.

He began to write letters, giving back as good as he was getting. He didn't much want to, but one morning a few days after the 1990 election, he dutifully positioned himself next to a commuter highway outside Annapolis holding a placard that said, "Thank You." A woman flashed him a sign in return. The finger, the governor said. A thumb, said the woman. The governor of Maryland had her automobile license number traced through Motor Vehicle Administration license and registration records. Then he wrote her a note.

"Your action only exceeds the ugliness of your face," wrote the state's chief executive. The papers wrote about that, of course. (Among members of Bill Clinton's campaign staff in Maryland, it became an inside joke to stop anyone who disagreed with you even slightly by saying, "Your action is exceeded only by the ugliness of your face.") They were laughing at him now. He had always avoided that. It seemed to make him crazier. He would have the state police drive him to the houses of his tormenters, and he would march into their kitchens. A farmer from Kent Island, Dan Shortall, made some disparaging remarks about the governor one night at a banquet. Later, as Shortall and his wife were getting into bed, a helicopter flew over. "Better get your clothes on," his wife said, "the governor's coming." It was just a joke, of course, but the whole state was beginning to expect a gubernatorial visit.

A man named Nottingham from Frederick wrote to complain about taxes. Schaefer replied by return mail, "Dear Notting Brain. Your letter sounds like a frustrated little boy. How old are you? I pay taxes on real estate, federal and state! Most likely more than you." A complaint about the governor's "tax and spend" proclivities merited this response: "You are everything that speaks of stupidity." And he wrote to Annett Lavell of Stevensville on the Eastern Shore, a thirty-four-year-old school bus driver who had come to Annapolis to demonstrate after his outhouse eruption. As she demonstrated against the governor in front of the statehouse, Ms. Lavell had been photographed by someone—the state police? Schaefer himself? He loved to take pictures. It had been "eerie," she said, to open a letter from the governor and find the pictures, as if some Mafia godfather or Iron Curtain secret police chief had sent them along for her to think about. What she thought the governor seemed to be saying was this: "'I know who you are and I can find you if you cause trouble.' I don't know if that was the message he wanted to send, but that was the message I got."

Shades of George Orwell and 1984, several years late, a *Sun* columnist said. A newspaper editor in Chestertown was reminded of Shakespeare's Julius Caesar: "Upon what meat doth this our Caesar feed that he is grown so great?" When the uproar ensued, Schaefer put on his best look of innocent surprise. "They were nice pictures," he said. "Nice, clear pictures." He was not nearly that obtuse. He understood exactly what he was doing. He had used intimidation throughout his career. It had been one of his bedrock methods, something he used with tight focus on individuals he thought could take the heat. The hell of it was, his friends said, Schaefer really did care about people. On a grand scale, he wanted to make their lives better and very frequently did. He had over the years occasionally let fly a bit of epistolary bile and then allowed one of his staff members— even arranged for one of his staff members—to save him. He would ask someone to preview something he had written. "Better hang on to that one?" he would ask rhetorically with a smile of recognition. "I think so, boss," would come the immediate reply. And he would set the work aside, his anger slaked. Later, though, his team was populated by people who were too much in the thrall of his anger and quirkiness, who bought a little too deeply into his idiosyncrasies. He also became more determined himself. One day he called LeBow. "You're not going to be happy with me," he said. "I mailed it."

"You mailed what?" she asked.

He had mailed one of his diatribes, and he had done it on his own, outside the command and control of those who were still able to say no to him, including LeBow.

He had always had his cadre of loyalists, men and women who appeared willing to follow him anywhere, validate his intemperate remarks, and even encourage them. Occasionally, during the dark days immediately after the 1990 election, a constituent letter would land on his desk with a note suggesting that it cried out for his special touch, as if they thought he ought to be lashing out at these ignorant critics.

With Bozman that day in the State House, the damaging remark flew out beyond the reach of a smart and loyal censor. Even then, he probably thought he would be protected, that the offended and outraged legislator would not wish to think his governor had been so intemperate or to punish him for it if he had. The protecting syndrome had been internalized even by Schaefer. His guard was down, defiantly. He had feelings, after all, and now that there probably were no more elections in his future, he was going to let people know they were hurting him. Sad to say, he was hurting himself.

Looking back, historian and Schaefer friend Ed Papenfuse thought that some semblance of meltdown was inevitable for public figures in the modern American democracy, and not just those of Schaefer's personality. The demands of leadership created a volatile psychic brew that was certain to produce an explosion or implosion. "For him to be able to lead, he had to have that sort of quirky personality—jumping into the pond with the rubber ducky synthesized it. The whole idea of promotion, boosterism. That is the essence of what America is. I mean if you really get down to what America is, America is boosterism and how effectively you push ideas. He was extraordinary at that, the most American of mayors and political leaders. At the same time he wasn't taken as seriously as he would have liked to have been taken as a statesman." The paradox was this: To lead, you sometimes had to be a bit daffy, but at the end of the day, your daffiness competed with your aspirations to leadership. Schaefer's individual version of this was tempered, Papenfuse thought, with a rootedness and sense of community. "He saw the picture whole, its pragmatic truth, an understanding that friends who were developers and businessmen would benefit from the boosterism, but his real love and his real concern was with his neighbors on his home street. He realized in the end that what really counts is that a guy like him coming from humble beginnings and origins, can progress through this world and do well, and serve other people, and he always thought, 'I owe it back to them to serve them so that it does help them within the context of their community.' He didn't always agree with the community leaders. He had his drawbacks like any human being would have. Too volatile a temper, which got in his way sometimes and his ability to sort of reflect. So he spoke too quickly, too impulsively, and rejected those who were trying to help him not make that mistake, lose control, and retreat."

The demands of leadership and Schaefer's own personality evolved and became even more combustible. Papenfuse thought that he suffered a degree of madness, controlled for the most part but subject to the occasional full-blown manifestation—not always, like Patton, under control, apparently.

Bunky and Buzzy

Imploding emotionally or not, Schaefer had the completed Linowes Commission tax overhaul to consider. Fairness unfortunately meant higher taxes overall. If no county was to be damaged, then current levels of taxation and state aid had to be maintained. The cost would be $900 million in new service industry taxes to be imposed in the area where the modern marketplace produced taxable economic activity—where the money was, in other words. The commission said that the new levies would be used to begin equalizing distribution—a re-redistribution of the wealth, in other words. As that direction became clear, state legislators began leaping off the boat, resigning from the commission lest they be caught endorsing anything that increased taxes for whatever purpose. Linowes said good riddance, in effect.

The report was completed two years after Linowes was appointed and presented just before the 1990 election—for politicians, one of the most unsettling of the twentieth century. Government was falling into deepest disrepute. When the 1991 general assembly convened, Schaefer may have been in a deep spiritual trough, but he was determined to push for passage of a bill based on his report despite the anti-incumbency that had almost sunk Mario Cuomo and Bill Bradley. His chief legislative manager, Lieutenant Governor Mickey Steinberg, urged him not to push it, to wait. But Schaefer was determined.

Linowes was prowling the halls, cigars tucked in the breast pockets of his pinstriped suits, an impish smile on his face. He believed in the product his team had produced at a cost of $500,000, and he wanted to see it pass. He found the legislative landscape a bit comic and made his way from office to office with an occasional quip about the wheelers and dealers he was meeting. Among them were Charles "Buzzy" Ryan of Prince George's County, chairman of the Appropriations Committee, and Tyras "Bunk" Athey of Anne Arundel County, chairman of the Ways and Means Committee, in which the tax laws were rewritten or repealed. At one point, Linowes pretended to be a bit confused: "I have been to see Buzzy—or Bunky—whichever the case may be, and I have given them my best shot." He knew perfectly well who he was speaking with, of course, but it hardly mattered. The price tag on his proposal was $900 million, and the general assembly of Maryland saw it as politically fatal.

As the chief legislative pulse monitor, Steinberg so informed Schaefer who should have required no such tutoring. However, Schaefer was as determined as Linowes. He wanted Steinberg to be his point man, but Steinberg demurred. He would not squander his credibility with legislative leaders who had already made plain their fear and opposition. Steinberg intended to run for governor, and he hardly wanted to run on a tax increase platform. In a meeting with Linowes, Schaefer extracted a promise that Steinberg would at least refrain from criticizing the proposal. That promise lasted one day, Schaefer thought, after he saw a headline in the *Washington Post* quoting Steinberg's reservations. Schaefer never forgave Steinberg. The lieutenant governor became a minister without portfolio, free to stop and make jokes with reporters—and nothing else.

Schaefer became his own lobbyist on this issue, appearing before committees to make his pitch. The bill was referred for "summer study," a painless death in most cases. With the Linowes bill—as it was called by the end—bits and pieces of the proposal were written into law over the remainder of Schaefer's tenure. With a little more luck, perhaps, he would have passed his bill, however tweaked and amended it might have been by Buzzy and Bunky, leaving Maryland a model tax code that was fairer and better for the citizens. But the times were inauspicious. The 2020 environmental protection plan, authored by former Congressman Michael D. Barnes, died as well.

Assemblies are slow learners. At least one legislative session and sometimes many are needed before major initiatives are sufficiently understood to gain approval. As glacial as the pace might seem, it can help to guarantee that lawmakers actually do understand what they are doing before they do it. Buzzy and Bunky, Ben and Mickey were canny and principled, but the assembly runs on its own clock, encumbered as it is by thousands of bills and hundreds of individual agendas each year. An overhaul of environmental regulations or of the tax code almost always needs the step-by-step approach Schaefer was forced to follow in the area of redevelopment, bringing voters along slowly and carefully with constant efforts at public education. He could do it personally in Baltimore, giving a sense of the big picture even as he built the projects one by one. Annapolis presented him with more abstract chores and a tougher sell by far, since, increasingly, Marylanders saw that Schaefer could build only if they gave him more of their money.

With both Linowes and 2020, though, he initiated the biggest of big picture discussions, requiring him to spend even more of his political capital. He failed. But he grasped the importance and went for the big win—and not the sort of campaign one might have expected an essentially establishment pol to undertake. In this case, the residue was a positive one, not the negative momentum he feared failure would create. In 1997, Schaefer's successor, Parris Glendening, found a way to convince the assembly that his smart growth proposal was a necessary thing. It might not have always been a comforting thought for him, but Schaefer would realize later that, even if he could not always complete the buildings, he had laid the foundations.

Hitting Bottom

When recession struck in 1991, Schaefer said that he had given fair warning. He'd said the tax structure, as analyzed by Linowes, should be over-
hauled. It hadn't been and now the price had to be paid. He hadn't been
prescient, of course; he hadn't foretold the unraveling of good times and
the tax revenue shortages. Nor had anyone else, including the canny Louis
Goldstein. Schaefer's support for Linowes had been based on his desire to
spend more, to do more. He had wanted a fairer, more rational, and more
effective system as well, setting himself a goal that no other governor or
legislator had been willing to pursue, as it was considered too politically
difficult and dangerous. Some jurisdiction or interest group would be too
deeply wounded, and another would be seen as the major beneficiary. Had
he been successful in passing the Linowes plan intact, it would have been
a further demonstration of political power and acumen, of leadership and
courage. Then it was seen as another Schaefer excess, another political
miscalculation—easy meat for the Annapolis insiders who were always
ready to pounce on and discredit something that does not work in the
assembly's sometimes foreshortened sense of priorities. Now, in referring
to the Linowes idea as a cushion for recession, he was rewriting history.
He had not asked the commission to create a bigger rainy day fund. But
it was pouring now, so the big spender suddenly had to cut: reduce services already provided, eliminate jobs, slice into the slim paychecks of state
workers, order unpaid furloughs, and start down the long road of re-
trenchment. This was not what he was wired for and not why he had
always wanted to be in charge. Suddenly, he was running another founder-

ing governmental entity, a state that had been transformed fiscally into something like a city.

The recession of 1991 would thoroughly debunk the myth that Maryland was, thanks to the proximity of Washington, immune to unemployment and bankruptcy. The recession came down on a relatively rich Maryland (always fourth or fifth in per capita income) with as much ferocity as it did any state. Almost monthly for eighteen solid months, Goldstein checked in with another set of discouraging revenue receipts, figures that showed Maryland had budgeted more than it would collect. Goldstein's instincts had occasionally been superb, moving him in 1987 to withdraw Maryland's pension fund from the stock market just before it crashed in October of that year. But that seat-of-the-pants acumen was insufficient to help Schaefer through the downturn of 1991. The governor's advisers were furious with Goldstein, who they thought was transparently eager to separate himself politically from the bad news he was delivering on tax collections, failing to measure the depth of the economic decline and then overstating signs of recovery.

Should Schaefer be cutting or standing pat? How much pain had to be inflicted? "The governor lost all confidence in his numbers," said Paul Schurick, then a senior adviser to Schaefer. These weeks were embarrassing as well as trying. Schaefer was meeting constantly to find and cut "fat" he had sworn wasn't there. More than ever before, he needed ideas. One of the most lucrative came to him from Capitol Hill via Nelson Sabatini, his veteran health secretary, who had come to the state from the Social Security Administration, a man who had navigated governmental white water for years. From Schaefer's representatives on Capitol Hill, Sabatini heard about something called a provider tax that could be imposed on doctors in a way that allowed states to pretend they had doubled the cost of physician services, simultaneously doubling the amount of money they received from Washington for the then-mushrooming health care insurance program for the poor called Medicaid. Congress had been ordering states to expand coverage under this program, mandating services without providing money to cover the costs. They were proving a point that Marvin Mandel had made when Medicaid was first introduced in 1969. Mandel refused to have the program in Maryland. He already had a small medical assistance system and would not be lured into a larger one by the promise of federal help. He said, "'If you really hate a guy,' my father told me, 'give him a baby elephant as a birthday present. Eventually it will get so goddamned big it will eat you out of house and home and there'll be shit all over the place.'" Mandel had been unable to withstand the pressure ultimately, but his view had been an astute one. Twenty years later, medicaid costs were out of control, forcing Maryland to carry over a $120 million deficit in one year, contrary to the state constitution's demand for a balanced budget every year.

Sympathetic to the plight of the states, California congressman Henry Waxman, a Democrat, came up with a proposal under which states could get what they needed after all. Democrat Waxman wanted to undermine Republican budget cutters, who, he thought, were deliberately sabotaging worthy programs that he had worked hard to create. It worked like this: Physicians would pretend to charge twice as much for the services they provided. Higher costs meant higher reimbursements. But the additional payments from Washington would be captured by the states before they could be returned to the doctors. Doctors would have to be willing participants—and were given no choice in the matter. Some of them were outraged, worrying that their reputation for overcharging would be etched more deeply into the public consciousness. To make this flimflam work, the state legislature would have to pass a law permitting it. At Schaefer's urging, Maryland went ahead with the so-called enabling act, even as the newspapers referred to the plan as "fool the feds" or the "Sabatini scam."

Schaefer loved the sheer outrageousness of it. It served them right over there in Washington, he thought. He loved it even more when the health care financing bureaucrats howled. He had just come back from a trip to Russia, where he had suggested a Maryland health care partnership with European countries. With no authority to do so, he offered the help of Maryland-based institutions, including the National Institutes of Health in Bethesda. He could be of assistance to these newly free nations. He had talked to President Bush and others in the Bush administration, and they sent him to see Lawrence Eagleburger, then an assistant secretary of state. Eagleburger was direct with the governor of Maryland: Why don't you do something you know something about? Why don't you try cleaning up the Chesapeake Bay?

So, already unhappy that the federal Health Care Financing Administration was refusing to move its offices into downtown Baltimore, where its many employees could boost the city's economy, and as angry as all governors were about unfunded federal mandates, Schaefer told Sabatini to go ahead with his scam. Schaefer had asked Attorney General Curran whether the thing was legal, and Curran said it was but also, Curran thought, preposterous and offensive. "I'm a citizen of the United States, so why am I ripping myself off?" he asked the governor, whereupon Schaefer's enthusiasm grew. If the lawyers didn't like it, it couldn't be all bad. Steering gleefully around what Sabatini called the "righteous bull-shit" of Curran and others, Schaefer and his troops took on officials in the Health Care Financing Administration, which was attempting to block Waxman and the states that adopted his plan. The agency tried to force Maryland to accept half of what it claimed, simultaneously imposing onerous requirements for collecting the bogus tax: The state would have to collect it from the doctors. Sabatini's plan simply grabbed the money on its way to the doctors, who were, of course, shrieking about how bad the plan made them look.

Benton, who had joined Schaefer as budget secretary, wanted to take the half-loaf and run, fearing that even less might be available when the federal government came to its senses. His Medicaid books were unconstitutionally in the red. Sabatini thought that Schaefer should decide and arranged to call on the governor with Benton at his side. Sabatini later said, "We went in there, and the boss was not in one of his best moods. I laid it out for him. And that vein in his forehead started to throb. Charlie immediately bailed: 'I never did think it was a good idea,' he said." The budget secretary could read Schaefer's moods as well as anyone.

Schaefer exploded: "God DAMMIT. GAAAH-dammit. I knew I shouldn't have let you do this. I thought you were in it for the long haul."

Once begun, Schaefer knew, the scam had to be rammed through to conclusion; otherwise, you looked like a fool and a scoundrel for nothing. You would be conceding what the critics said, and you'd have far less money or no money at all. So they hung in, and finally, since it was an election year, candidate Bush interviewed, and Maryland got the full $75 million. The effect on Schaefer's budget was double that figure: Had Sabatini been forced to cut Medicaid spending, he would have lost a federal dollar for every state dollar saved. But the stakes were even higher: The essence of the Medicaid program was at risk, as government downsizers knew full well. But Bush needed help if he was to be reelected. Several other states, including the first presidential primary state of New Hampshire, were getting similar breaks, so Maryland's version of the scam (one of the more modest such enterprises) was allowed to stand.

Less spectacularly, Sabatini said, Schaefer worked his way through the downturn with several other budget cuts that would not have been possible in a strong economy. Some $18 million that was budgeted annually for so-called non-emergency transportation—cab fare to get welfare recipients to doctors' offices and hospitals—was lopped off with pleasure. This was all state money, with no federal participation, so the savings did not have a downside. Recessions were painful, but they allowed sensible cuts that were not possible in good times when the affected group could rally legislative support to protect them.

Schaefer also cut the $7 million state-only kidney program, knowing that it was unnecessary. Everyone called it "the dialysis program," and it did provide that service to a very few people with very expensive needs that Medicaid did not already cover. But the program that was being eliminated served primarily the families of foreign diplomats who were not eligible for Medicaid. Its main uses and expense came from transplants, an extremely expensive offering that, at that moment, the state could not afford to continue. It might not have wanted to provide the coverage even in the best of times. Now, like the cab fare allowances, it could be dropped. During public hearings on the proposal, witnesses told state lawmakers that they would die if the program was cut, and Sabatini couldn't contradict them because federal laws requiring confidentiality prohibited a state official from saying anything about a "case"—here, a witness claiming to be in mortal danger as a result of a state government action. "We just sat there and got beat up," Sabatini recalled. But the program was dropped.

Don Donaldo

Schaefer turned with ferocity then to the public relations side of budget cutting. He ordered economies in the ranks of the Maryland State Police, ordering them, along with other state employees, to take a three-day, unpaid furlough. From outside the bunker of state government, that action looked perversely calculated. Washington journalist Charlie Peters called it the "firemen first" approach to budget cutting, a ploy focusing cuts on something the public needs and would be willing to save through new taxes or some other way of dealing with revenue shortages. This time, though, the tactic very nearly backfired. Delegations of demonstrating troopers in uniform arrived at the statehouse to protest. A few of their wives showed up to lobby with babes in arms. The police themselves, burly, frowning men with sidearms, skulked about the capitol grounds. "They were really an intimidating group of guys. They were not particularly friendly. They were hostile," Sabatini remembered. A briefing was convened in a nearby state office building, and Schaefer announced the furloughs to a packed hall, including several rows of unhappy tan-jacketed cops, wedged into their seats shoulder to shoulder.

Schaefer was coping, but his standing with Marylanders fell with each state police pay protest, each cab fare complainant, and each patient who had allegedly been unhooked from a dialysis machine. Already in tatters after his vituperative letters and unannounced visits, his approval rating began to plummet. What he needed was a bailout, so he turned again to gambling.

The state's lottery was already the fourth largest producer of income for government in Maryland, funneling hundreds of millions of dollars into the state treasury.

He had begun a separate sports lottery to pay for the baseball and football stadiums, but perhaps the well was not dry. Over dinner one night in the mansion, Benton suggested that Keno might offer a way out. A fast-paced game with the poorest of odds for players, it could be put into operation by Schaefer alone because it had been anticipated in the state's controversial contract with GTECH, a Rhode Island–based computer company specializing in lottery terminals. Schaefer was receptive, since his money needs were urgent and keno could be installed quickly in restaurants and bars. In practice, these establishments became downscale mini-casinos in which the players could place repeated bets while having a smoke and a beer.

Schaefer and his lottery agency had taken care to ensure that Maryland's new lottery computers could handle the addition of Keno, and GTECH was happy for the opportunity that now presented itself. Some observers thought that GTECH had won the lottery contract by offering to supply new computers and marketing of the lottery for a remarkably low price in anticipation of Keno's arrival. But that point came later, in 1990, when Schaefer announced that he was instituting the Keno game and instructing GTECH to proceed with it as specified in the contract. In 1989, Schaefer had appointed a commission to examine bids for the lottery computers, taking that process outside normal channels because so many of his friends were lobbying for the business. GTECH had hired Bruce Bereano, by then the leading lobbyist in Annapolis, and Bereano had hired former governor Mandel. Both had longstanding relationships with Benton, whose staff did the special commission's detail work in reviewing the contract bids. As always, Bereano had worked every angle he could think of, using leverage afforded by other clients. For example, he sent Hilda Mae Snoops free cigarettes supplied by him or by his tobacco clients. The idiosyncratic Benton coveted a complete set of the miniature flags and miniature license plates GTECH handled as marketing tools, each symbolizing a state where the company had won the lottery computer business. Bereano got Benton his flags and plates.

The lobbying war was intense. Schaefer's former legislative aide Alan Rifkin, the man who had helped to steer the stadium bill to passage, had represented Control Data Corporation, one of GTECH's rivals. Rifkin had Schaefer's friend Edgar Silver, by then retired from the circuit court, on his lobbying team. Several other skilled lobbyists had represented other bidders, and all of them had applied pressure on the assembly as well as on the governor's office. A bit cornered—he could have appeared to be making an ally or a friend rich no matter who won the contract—Schaefer had decided to appoint a commission, which had decided in due time that GTECH was the best vendor. It certainly was the low bidder—breathtakingly low, in fact; GTECH's bid was $20 million under the next lower offer. Now, though, it looked as if GTECH was recovering from an intentionally low initial price that had been based on the likelihood that Keno would be added later. The contract specifications, in fact, required that the new vendor be Keno-ready.

Schaefer had been accused of dancing around conflicts of interest by knowing when to leave the room—a term of political art meaning that one sensed when something questionable might be in the works and not wanting to even know about it. One always needed insulation from one's political friends, though, and blue-ribbon commissions were a favorite device. Nevertheless, the newspapers had a field day. Schaefer was depicted in editorial cartoons by Kevin Kallaugher of the Baltimore *Sun* as Kaptain Keno, a lumpy figure in superhero's tights and cape with a large "K" on his chest. U.S. Attorney Richard D. Bennett would later investigate the Keno contract and find nothing illegal. Bereano, though, was indicted after the GTECH probe on mail fraud charges stemming from the government's belief that he had used expense money from his lobbying clients to hide campaign contributions.

The recession and his unrestrained public antics were eroding Schaefer's once-lofty approval rating. Cartoonists and writers began to have even more fun with him. Dan Rodricks, a *Sun* columnist, began to write a series of mock operas called the Don Donaldo Ring Cycle (with apologies to Richard Wagner), based loosely on the life and times of the Lord

High Governor of Maryland. The first of these chronicled Schaefer's rise to power and was called "Don Donaldo." It was followed by "The Merchant of Menace," which featured "Don Donaldo's Operatic Grail," and "Rigmarole on the high C's." Then came "Il Padrone Irato," chronicling his travails with the general assembly, his tantrums, and the efforts of his legendary companion, Brunhilde Mae, to redecorate the mansion. This was followed by "L'Infuriato," outlining the "demoniacal rage" that proceeded from the 1990 election and his proposal to annex the District of Columbia (an unpopular idea Schaefer had floated earlier). "Don Donaldo: On The Edge" told of an encounter with the devil, who promised a way out of the budget wilderness. Finally came "Il Disperato" ("the Desperate One").

Featured players in "Il Disperato" were Padre Michino (Lieutenant Governor Steinberg); Paolino (Fish Powell, the mayor of Ocean City); and Guiseppe Currano (Attorney General Curran). To the theme song of *Beauty and the Beast,* these three sang to the Don:

PAOLINO: No one whines like the Don.
CURRANO: No one snipes like the Don.
MICHINO: No one gripes like the Don.
DONALD: Yes, I'm especially good at bel-ly-aching.
But he unexpectedly brightens, and a chorus dances into the room, singing.
PEASANT: He sometimes is angry and mean-o.
PAOLINO: He wants you to gamble on ken-o.
PEASANT: It's cheaper than flying to Ren-o.
MICHINO: Next time why not vote for Michin-o.
CHORUS: He's a Keno head . . . He's the Don!

Schaefer hated the Kaptain Keno cartoons, but he loved the "operas."

The Grand Stroke

The hell of the recession was clear to all. It wasn't just the budget cutting that tormented Schaefer, though he tried to make people understand the real pain of cutting back. The anguish for him was the loss of projects, being unable to show Marylanders how great they could be. "He couldn't make the grand stroke," said Bruce Poole, a legislator from western Maryland who had seen the Schaefer style in many incarnations over the previous eight years. Poole had been the house majority leader at the age of thirty-five. Young and ambitious, he'd been elected on a wave of outrage directed at another Washington County lawmaker, Paul Muldowney, who in 1984 courageously (with a bit of macho flair thrown in) led the assembly's effort to reform the state's excessively generous pension system. The teachers' union's determination to defeat Muldowney swept Poole into office in 1986, and the young newcomer moved rapidly up in the political structure. He was a lawyer, a quick study, and one of the assembly's best quotemen: he could explain the most complicated bill or legislative maneuver in a tight, colorful sentence. Reporters sought him out. His name was in the paper. He moved up quickly. But then he moved a half-step over the line of legislative protocol, offending some of his superiors in the Democratic Party. He looked like a threat, like a pretender to someone else's throne. So he lost his majority leader post in a coup. Schaefer called him in.

"I know you're upset," Schaefer said, "but don't hit back."

"Governor," Poole said, "I've watched you over the years. I've admired you. And I just know that if you were in my position, you would not be silent. I'm mad as hell and I'm not going to bottle it up."

Schaefer listened, said nothing for a minute, and then made another effort. "Can't you learn something from me?" he asked. "Can't you see how you might make matters worse? I've done exactly what you say all my life. I've never let anything go by. It's one of the things I might do differently if I had another chance."

Poole knew that Schaefer was attempting to help his friend Casper Taylor, the new house speaker—and the man who had disciplined Poole. But the young legislator thought Schaefer might have been admitting to a bit of rare self-criticism, insight, and stocktaking. The moment was a brief one, not because more incendiary activities were on the way but because the two men had work to do.

Poole and Schaefer's transportation secretary, Jim Lighthizer, had discovered another way to make the federal government solve a big Maryland problem: a program designed to preserve historically important lands. The lawmaker and the bureaucrat hit upon an idea one afternoon in a duck blind, where they sat waiting to shoot Canada geese. Poole talked about the encroachment of developers on South Mountain, the approach to sacred battlefields outside Antietam, site of the bloodiest Civil War engagement. These developments, bringing crowds, traffic, and the need for schools, threatened the way of life in that part of the state. There was a program called ISTEA (for Intermodal Surface Transportation Efficiency

Act), Poole learned from Lighthizer, through which federal money could be used to buy the rights to historic lands. Schaefer loved it. In the next few months, they applied for and received $15 million that was used to preserve hundreds of acres. Maybe the grand stroke could still be made. Maryland used ISTEA more aggressively and successfully than any state in the nation, prompting historic preservation organizations to move their headquarters to the area near the battlefield—just the sort of small, discreet and non-service-using business Poole and his constituents hoped would move into their mountains.

Opening Day

Schaefer did feel reflected glory from his long years of toiling in defense of Baltimore's role in professional sports. But the struggle to assert the city's prerogatives continued. The Orioles' new owner, Eli Jacobs, insisted on naming the stadium that Maryland was building for him. Jacobs wanted it to be called Orioles Park. But Schaefer wanted Camden Yards in celebration of a Schaefer priority: city neighborhoods. Others say that the governor's choice included the name Schaefer, but the owner was the owner—Schaefer was only the governor. They settled on Orioles Park at Camden Yards, a long handle that was quickly shortened informally to Camden Yards, as Schaefer had hoped.

The ballpark opened on April 6, 1992, to raves from the sportswriting and architectural communities. In photographs that day, Schaefer appeared unusually pensive. He always felt a bit let down when a big project was completed—anxious that others would not decide that total victory had been won—but on this day, he seemed almost to wonder for a moment whether the struggle had been worth it. Any doubt was erased a year later when the old-style park he and Williams wanted proved to the be real star of the celebrity-studded All-Star Game and All-Star week in Baltimore. Willard Scott, in town with the CBS *Morning Show*, did the weather from the infield. NBC's *Today* was broadcasting from the Yards, too. Michael Jordan came for the celebrity homer-hitting contest with actor Tom Selleck, comedians Bill Murray and Jim Belushi, and track star Florence Griffith Joyner. Tourists posed for pictures under the spot where Seattle's Ken Griffey, Jr., became the first player to hit a ball to the B&O Warehouse wall beyond the right field fence. A U.S. Postal Service van came by to stamp out special Orioles Park at Camden Yards postmarks. The Reverend Jesse L. Jackson came to town to use the park and the game as foils for his cause. "We are marching for jobs. The All-Star game is for the economic development of others," he said.

Over the course of the six-day, mid-July festival, visitors spent $30 million in Baltimore's hotels, at Harborplace, at the National Aquarium, at the Maryland Science Center, at a memorabilia extravaganza called Fan-Fest, in Little Italy, Haussner's Restaurant in East Baltimore, maybe even at the Sip 'N Bite, a rowhouse restaurant in Canton.

Taken by camera beyond the bald pate of weatherman Scott, television viewers from Miami to Spokane saw a ballpark that was as homey and comfortable as the bar in *Cheers*. They saw the green dome of Johns Hopkins Hospital, the Babe Ruth Museum and Birthplace, the Walters Art Gallery, and the Baltimore Museum of Art with its priceless Cone Collection. Baltimore had hosted the big game in 1958, when Schaefer was president of the city council, and attractions had been meager: Fort McHenry and the Block were about it. Visitors had hopped on trains and went to Washington. Baltimoreans had understood if no one wanted to see the sights in their city. What sights? they would have asked.

Now there were plenty of sights, and the centerpiece was Orioles Park at Camden Yards. "This stadium is the future of baseball," said Pittsburgh centerfielder Andy Van Slyke. "A stadium like this is an amazing example of what can happen when a city does something right." Ed Williams had died almost four years earlier, but the park had come along as splendidly as he and his partner, Schaefer, might ever have imagined.

Bill and Don

With his popularity plummeting, Schaefer was a bit toxic when the 1992 presidential primary season opened. Campaign organizers for Arkansas Governor Bill Clinton studiously avoided him. Schaefer fumed. He knew Clinton from Governors' Association meetings and did not like him, regarding him as an out-of-control womanizer. Schaefer had his own thoughts about the presidency as well, and getting wind of them cartoonist Kallaugher put Schaefer on Mount Rushmore with Teddy Roosevelt and Abe Lincoln.

In the end in Maryland, the 1992 presidential primary game came down to endorsements, and since the Clinton team had openly rejected him, Schaefer turned to Paul Tsongas, the former U.S. senator from Massachusetts whose thoughts about government and the economy were giving Clinton and the other Democrats a real run for their money. Looking as though he had never heard of or met the candidate before that moment, Schaefer stood with Tsongas on a small stage at the Hilton Hotel as the Massachusetts senator took questions.

Bill Clinton's Maryland managers made sure people on the Eastern Shore knew that Schaefer was for Tsongas, putting the news on the radio and hoping the governor's endorsement would backfire in the part of the state Schaefer had so offended. Tsongas won the Maryland primary, but his campaign fizzled quickly as the primary moved into Clinton-friendly, Massachusetts-wary southern states. Schaefer, meanwhile, continued to rebuff the overtures of Clinton's people. When the candidate was in Washington or moving through Maryland, he frequently tried to get Schaefer on the phone, but the governor of Maryland refused to take his calls. Secretaries and state troopers, who occasionally answered the phones, were instructed to tell the Arkansas governor that Maryland's chief executive was preparing his budget or otherwise unavailable. When Hillary Clinton campaigned in Maryland—on the statehouse steps one day—Schaefer refused to greet her.

But when the national nominating convention opened in New York, Schaefer wanted to announce how Maryland's Democrats would vote. For months, he and the state party chairman, Nathan Landow of Bethesda, had been struggling over control of the party. A potent fund raiser and deal maker, Landow had tried to put himself at the center of several presidential campaigns, particularly Albert Gore's. Landow's position as chairman was a joy to some Maryland Democrats because they thought he would try to give the party financial and organizational strength. No one had paid much attention to party building since Marvin Mandel had been governor. Landow and Schaefer were immediately at odds, with the party chairman attempting to supplant the governor whenever he might. Landow had been a supporter of Steve Sachs until Schaefer announced, and then he immediately shifted to the Schaefer team.

The two men had come into real conflict in 1991, when Maryland, like every other state, had to redraw its legislative district lines to match the 1990 census results. Landow and Schaefer clashed on a number of issues, particularly the lines to be drawn for the center-state district that was then represented by Tom McMillen, the former University of Maryland basketball star. Here again he clashed with Senate President Miller. "I wanted to send Democrats to Congress" said Miller. "He wanted to help Helen Delich Bentley, a Republican. Period. I didn't mind—but not at the expense of Democrats." Miller wanted the new districts to attain the needed balance of about 500,000 voters each by poaching on Bentley's district, which was centered in Baltimore County. Instead, the cutting and balancing focused on Anne Arundel County and McMillen. (The redistricting commission also had to create another African American district that year, putting even more pressure on the congressional map makers.) McMillen, who had the second misfortune of not being a favorite of his Maryland colleagues in Congress, was the odd man out, landing in a district much less favorable to a Democrat than the one he had been representing. He lost eventually in the 1992 general election to Republican Wayne Gilchrest. This moment of Republican favoring by the Democrat Schaefer turned out to be a precursor to an even more dramatic endorsement of the GOP by Maryland's governor.

Schaefer remained at odds with Landow as the party delegation headed off to New York, ready to shift votes from Tsongas to the obvious winner, Clinton. On the night when governors, favorite sons, or other luminaries stood to be on television for thirty seconds, announcing in silly boosterish language who the state's delegates had voted for, Schaefer arrived. As the governor, he would certainly have that honor if he wanted it. But when the moment approached, Landow began elbowing his way toward the microphone. Schaefer did not shrink from the confrontation, and when the two men appeared to be headed for physical contact, Senator Sarbanes stepped between them and said, "For God's sake, Nate, he's the governor. What're you doing?" Others joined the usually unflappable senator to hold Landow at bay. With the national TV cameras focused on him for a brief moment, Schaefer announced that Maryland was casting all its votes for Bill Clinton. He personally remained a Clinton critic.

Indeed, some Marylanders wondered whether Schaefer might not endorse George Bush in the general election. Schaefer and Bush had become friendly, meeting in various parts of western Maryland when the president flew in to Camp David and playing golf in Carroll County just north and west of Baltimore. Schaefer even bought a pair of shoes like the president's. Despite his determination to represent Maryland in Madison Square Garden, Schaefer was not a Democratic partisan. He was a member of the Schaefer party, a man made by Kovens, and his loyalties were a bit transferable. Still, the governor's chief political adviser, Pam Kelly, said that there was no way he would publicly endorse Bush. He was a Democrat, wasn't he? Hadn't he been elected for thirty-five years under the Democratic banner? He was. He had been. But this was the United States of America. And this was William Donald Schaefer.

Edgar Strikes Again

In late October 1992, with Clinton moving ahead of Bush in enough states to make his election seem certain, Schaefer and Edgar Silver sat in the upstairs dining room at Harry Browne's, a comfortable Annapolis restaurant just across State Circle from the statehouse. Schaefer was going after Clinton. He considered the Democratic nominee virtually a turncoat. Not only had Clinton never served in the military, he had demonstrated in Russia against the war in Vietnam. How could such a person be allowed to take the presidency from Schaefer's friend George Bush? From their table, Schaefer and Silver could almost see the steps where Hillary Clinton had campaigned for her husband without so much as a perfunctory handshake or greeting from Maryland's governor. Now, a week before the election, Schaefer and the retired judge—a somewhat mischievous practitioner of the political arts—talked about what was left of the race. They knew that Bush was in trouble.

"They'd love to have you endorse him, you know," the judge said.

"Could you arrange that?" Schaefer asked, knowing the answer. Arranging things was Edgar's forte. They called him "the judge," but it should have been "the arranger." In the morning, in the criminal court, he slammed jail cell doors. In the afternoon, his docket clear, he opened doors, working his contacts, talking to his friends for his friends. He was so active in this enterprise that after a while, the supervising judges grew restive: Wasn't Edgar too political? Silver observed wryly later that the chief judges were not so concerned when he was lobbing for their pay and pension issues before the general assembly. The questions eventually grew annoying, though, and nearing retirement, Silver turned to full-time arranging. As a result of a deal he was working for an airline company, he knew a former cabinet member who knew Jim Baker, manager of Bush's campaign.

By midafternoon, after Edgar's call, Baker called the governor of Maryland. "The president would love to have you come along on *Air Force One* to St. Louis. We understand you're thinking you might endorse us," said Mr. Baker.

"Sure, sure," said Schaefer in his perfunctory way, imparting, perhaps, a tone of hesitancy, as if he needed a more authoritative invitation.

"Would you like to speak with the president?" Baker asked.

"No, no," Schaefer said, "I'll take your word for it."

It was left to their various staffs to coordinate flight times and the like. Thus did William Donald Schaefer make one of his last great political plays. It was not widely applauded. When the word went out, the wrath of every Democrat in the state came down on his head, as he knew it would—wanted it to. He wanted to spite the people who, he thought, had aided and abetted his fall from grace. His approval ratings were now in the teens and dropping.

Senators Barbara Mikulski and Paul Sarbanes, usually tolerant of the governor's quirky behavior, nailed him rhetorically in the local press. The Clinton campaign in Maryland had worried this would happen. They had worked all summer to make him happy, deferring to him when they could, asking his permission to do various things. They were not worried about Maryland voters, but they thought the defection of a Democratic governor might hurt elsewhere, where William Donald Schaefer's good works were better known than his temper. In Baltimore, Clinton workers picketed the house on Edgewood Street with signs that said, "Who Asked You?"

Schaefer's airplane ride temporarily cost him at least one longtime friend: chief fund raiser Bob Hillman, a Baltimore lawyer who had been his labor commissioner in Baltimore. Hillman, who had been with him from the beginning, angrily took every bit of Schaefer memorabilia off his office walls.

"Edgar, you caused all this trouble," LeBow moaned.

"It's not me. He wants it," the judge said, and she knew it was true.

It's a free country, Schaefer said over and over when people asked him why he was running out on the party that had supported him in thirty-five years of public office seeking—as if freedom were the issue. He'd always been good at shifting the ground. People tried to explain it for him. He was Bush's friend—an interesting suggestion, since few who knew him thought he had any close friends, let alone such exalted ones. President Bush had invited Schaefer to Camp David, had come to Maryland to announce a major, campaign-year infusion of funds for Head Start, and had taken the governor along in his limo on a campaign swing to the Johns Hopkins Hospital. Schaefer had loved being included. But he was also quick to say that he thought Bush was out of touch, not appreciative of the anguish recession had visited upon the city's streets. As they rode through poor city neighborhoods during the campaign, Schaefer pointed it out to him, asking the president to see the pain in the faces of people who waited on the sidewalks to wave. "It's not getting better," Schaefer said to this president, who had seemed to believe advisers who thought the recession was ending.

The real bond between these dissimilar men was World War II: Clinton had avoided service in Vietnam, perhaps even organized demonstrations against the war when he was a Rhodes Scholar in England, and Schaefer thought him repugnant for many reasons. Beyond that, what grand political stroke was left to this wounded and virtually shunned governor? Where else was he going to go in the presidential election of 1992? Hadn't Irv always been flexible, finding a place to hang his political hat if the Democratic candidates did not please him? Hadn't Irv helped McKeldin, of all people? Clinton had given Schaefer an opportunity to do what he would have done anyway, partisan considerations aside.

For several hours after the White House called, Schaefer and his closest aides calculated the pluses and minuses. Unaccountably, they saw mostly pluses. Their lobbyist in Washington said that there was little likelihood, based on the polling, that Bush could win. Bush's own political electoral vote counters said that the president's count was "soft." But Schaefer's aides were euphoric, for the most part, at the opportunity that Baker was offering. If Bush won, Schaefer was sure to get a payoff. He could be made an ambassador. Think of all the great jobs they themselves might get. Schaefer was warned that the press and party reaction would almost certainly be punishing and unremitting. His political adviser Pam Kelly was not invited to this skull session—and almost quit the next day. Bush and his party opposed everything William Donald Schaefer had worked for in government, but Schaefer was not completely concerned with the interests of government here. He was concerned with the bitterness and hurt of William Donald Schaefer. He had taken private shots at Clinton, but now he had a chance to fire one publicly. And the dividend could be phenomenal. Suppose the wild card Ross Perot hurt Clinton and Bush actually snuck through at the end. Wouldn't Schaefer have made a strong friend for Maryland? For himself? In the meantime, Edgar Silver said, Schaefer got a great airplane flight. He actually hated to fly and had bought himself a bus for getting around Maryland. Now, though, he would be flying in *Air Force One*. "He told everybody how grand it was, two galleys and places to sleep. It really impressed him," Edgar said.

At Lunch with Bill

Clinton won, of course. His victory margin in Maryland, where he took more than 50 percent of the vote, was second only to the 54 percent he got in Arkansas—yet another repudiation of Schaefer. During inauguration week, the president threw a luncheon in the Great Hall of the Library of Congress for his former colleagues, the nation's governors, including Schaefer. Maryland's governor arrived early and began making his way around the fabulous room searching for a card with his name on it, as if the Clinton team might have seated him in the hallway, since he was the only Democrat who had defected to Bush.

"Surprised to see you here," said a reporter who saw him hovering near his table.

"He's the president now," Schaefer said. "I support him 100 percent. We're in America. We can do what we want." He then defended the man he had opposed in the election: "The press is starting to tear him apart before he goes in." Schaefer had written the president a letter, promising to help in any way he could.

The New York Times anticipated the Clinton-Schaefer meeting in its Sunday magazine the day before. Hillary Clinton, in particular, had Schaefer on her enemies list, according to the article, remembering, no doubt, how she had been treated in Annapolis.

When the president-elect arrived, he was applauded by his colleagues—governors and former governors, including former Maryland governor Hughes. Mr. Clinton moved slowly around the room, circling counterclockwise toward Schaefer. "He's the bald guy in the corner," a reporter whispered to a cameraman. The man from Arkansas had been indulging in his penchant for hugging. He embraced almost everyone in the room, Republican and Democratic governors alike and an assortment of television stars—the actor Hal Holbrook, his wife, Dixie Lee Carter, and others were on hand to provide entertainment and moral support. When Clinton and Schaefer came face to face, there was a momentary silence and even a gasp from the reporters. It was a moment of humiliation for a man who had wondered whether he, and not a guy named Bill from Arkansas, might actually have been on the threshold of the Oval Office. Hadn't cartoonists at the Baltimore Sun rendered his face with its long, ruler-straight nose on Mount Rushmore? He had served in the military, and he had rebuilt a great American city. George Will had compared him to Fiorello La

Guardia, Richard Daley, and even Franklin Delano Roosevelt. But he had endorsed the loser.

When the president-elect got to the governor of Maryland, he seemed to pull back a bit, to stand a bit taller, more stiffly. There were no hugs at this stop. He put out his hand. "Glad you came," Clinton said. Schaefer thanked him and smiled, seeming to peer into his eyes. "You'll find that I will be one of your most loyal backers," Schaefer said. By then, loyalty and William Donald Schaefer might not have been synonymous for the Democratic president-elect. Schaefer ate seafood salad and chicken Devonshire while Governor Ann Richards of Texas introduced president-elect Clinton.

"He's been in your shoes," she said, "and he knows just where they pinch. He knows how hard it is to move forward when someone puts an eighty-pound weight in each heel." Clinton reminisced a bit. He said he knew his colleagues were as stunned as he that one of them had become the nominee. He pointedly singled out Harry Hughes as someone with whom he had discussed the frustrations of being governor. When Clinton finished speaking, Schaefer disappeared instantly. He had known that reporters were leaning over the marble banisters to see him in his elegant pit of embarrassment. He had even thought about staying in Annapolis, but finally, he sighed and muttered something about making his bed and lying in it.

When he got back to the statehouse, he gave his account of what happened: "He humiliated me. Showed me up in front of all those people." Then he smiled ruefully. "I'd have done the same thing to him if he did what I did. If I gave a lunch like that, I would've parked him in a different building."

Later that week, on Inauguration Day, the governors assembled for breakfast at a Capitol Hill restaurant called La Colline. Schaefer was even more mortified to be along for this part of the ceremony, having been so publicly identified as an enemy at the Library of Congress. He sat by himself. Staff members who usually found a place off to the side at such official functions joined him.

While Schaefer worked on his eggs, Bob Casey, the governor of Pennsylvania, stopped by for a moment. Casey had been scheduled to speak at the Democratic National Convention the previous summer in New York but had then been disinvited. Clinton favored abortion rights. Casey was an outspoken opponent. Schaefer was not consoled. "Great," he said, when Casey was gone. "Another outcast."

The Street Guys versus the Moguls

Schaefer enjoyed life more when he was dealing with his home boys, Hank Butta and others, and he desperately needed them in his quest for the holy grail of a new NFL franchise. Baltimoreans, and perhaps even Schaefer, thought that the NFL owners would be moved to do the right thing—to redress the grievances felt by one of their storied founding cities. Butta realized almost immediately that he was dealing in a singular realm with men who saw the world in terms that were unimaginable beyond its well-protected gates.

Butta's confident, friendly bearing earned him the occasional hearing from the owners, and one day he found himself in a conversation with Lamar Hunt, owner of the Kansas City Chiefs. A bit awestruck to be sitting with these men he'd read about for years, Butta nevertheless asked Hunt a fairly direct and personal question. In preparation for his mission, he'd been studying the profit and loss statements of the league's teams, he said, and he was surprised to find that several of them had racked up $4 million or more in losses the previous year. Since he knew that Hunt, his brother Nelson "Bunker," and father, H. L., were the shrewdest of businessmen, he said, "Does it bother you to be involved in an enterprise that loses that much money?"

"No," said Hunt.

"As a guy who fires his broker if he loses $10,000 in a year, I don't understand that."

"Well, Hank, let me put it to you this way. When I walk into Chiefs' Stadium every Sunday, everyone turns around to look at me."

"You could get them to do that by streaking across the 50-yard line," Butta said.

Hunt said he could also go into the Chiefs' locker room. Then he stopped teasing. He and Bunker had cornered the silver market, "but what in this world can I own that only twenty-seven other guys in the world can own?"

Butta later saw an interview with H. L. Hunt, who was asked the same question: What do you think of your son's losing $4 million on a football team. "Lamar did that? Well. He's only got 125 years to go before he runs out."

However, not every owner had the same resources. Butta and Schaefer had to hope that some of them were as hungry and faithless as Irsay.

Schaefer's twenty-year struggle was a reflection of its warring participants. The Boys of Baltimore—Peter Angelos, a street kid with a fortune built by attacking big steel; Herb Belgrad, the technocratic Baltimore lawyer; Hank Butta, a former telephone lineman; and Schaefer himself were arrayed against the Long Knife Knaves of the NFL, guys who bragged about owning something no one else, however rich, could hope to own. From the NFL's viewpoint, Baltimore was a joke, an unwitting and unwilling stalking horse kept in motion by clever operatives to set a standard for the cities that the league did want.

The NFL had staged a magnificent charade designed to boost the value of its properties by convincing politicians that people would support huge public outlays to keep their teams. When the Maryland General Assembly acted in 1987 under the direction of Schaefer and Ed Williams to authorize two stadiums, it set the standard for all other teamless big cities. Schaefer's deal made it impossible for the league to ignore Baltimore, but not in the way Schaefer had hoped, thought Jon Morgan, a Baltimore *Sun* writer who has studied the finances of major league sports. "The league saw it could drive up the bidding in other cities. It worked like magic for them." Maryland was a hapless player that was never in the running. Morgan believed that the state and Schaefer could have done little to change the early outcome. Before Charlotte and Jacksonville got new teams, Baltimore was the only city offering a new stadium. Therefore, when NFL representatives talked with other contending cities, Maryland's offer started the bidding—a pledge of $200 million that, as everyone predicted, rose and rose, reaching $500 million by 1998. Every supplicant city would be required to match or exceed Baltimore's offer, yet Baltimore was itself never really competitive. Baltimoreans watching Schaefer in his pursuit of redemption might have assumed that the city could rely on a degree of sympathy from men whose partner, Irsay, had treated it so shabbily. This generous, rather naive outlook was shared to some extent by Schaefer himself. To a remarkable extent for a man of politics, Schaefer expected people to do the right thing because it *was* the right thing. He would sometimes invite legislators to his office for a discussion of important legislation and never ask directly for a vote, expecting the bill's merits to prevail. He was not above pressuring people who resisted him, but he could go a remarkable distance professing and believing in the honorable way. This approach perhaps stemmed from a luxury afforded early in his poitical life by Kovens, who had done the tough talking for him.

In this case, the governor of Maryland thought he was being blocked by Jack Kent Cooke, the diminutive and cocky owner of the Washington Redskins. Yet many in the league were as alienated by Cooke as Schaefer had been. They obliged Cooke, but only in service to their own needs. Morgan concluded that Baltimore's problem was nothing more or less than geography and market, which were beyond Schaefer's power to alter. "You can't expand into an area you're already serving," Morgan said, referring to the Redskins in this case. It was not primarily Cooke the owners were protecting, but their league's desire to grow in unserved areas. Ironically, Schaefer's men were helping the league and Baltimore's competitor cities by setting the financial terms. Baltimore's offer drove up the bidding.

At the same time, Schaefer might not have been completely candid in his public determination to avoid stealing a team. "I think he was willing to do it," Morgan said. "He kept saying he wouldn't, but they talked to the Cardinals and the Patriots until the league told them not to. If Modell had said back then 'I'm yours,' they would have found a way to justify it. Schaefer said he felt comfortable talking with teams that seemed to be marketing themselves, but that could have been said about any city at any time."

For twelve years, then, Schaefer struggled against forces that were as immutable as outmigration to the suburbs—almost. By engineering passage of the stadium construction legislation and by dangling a delicious lease, he had prepared the ground for Baltimore's only real hope: that circumstances would some day make the Maryland offer too rich to ignore. Then Schaefer would get his team. The beginnings of that process could be traced, according to Morgan, to 1985 when Schaefer and Art Modell, then owner of the Cleveland Browns, met secretly at Martin State Airport. Among the scenarios they discussed was one that would have brought the Browns to Baltimore then, replacing them in Cleveland with a team owned by Alfred Lerner, a banker who had done business in Baltimore for several years. Virtually all of that plan came to pass, though it took fourteen years. In the meantime, Schaefer was spared a decision that would have been difficult even if these men had been able to make Baltimore whole without harming Cleveland. He was left to hope that Modell would be his ally in league councils. Before one of the votes, the infinitely pragmatic governor of Maryland subjected himself to Irsay's humiliation one more time, appealing for a vote in favor of Baltimore's bid to be an expansion city. Irsay said no. As for the league's obligation to Baltimore, NFL Commissioner Paul Tagliabue removed any lingering doubt by saying that the city never had any right to think it would get a team. Maybe, he said, it should think about building a museum.

Savile Row Meets Off-the-Rack

Schaefer had dealt with the titans of sport in the way that some people tried to deal with him—as if their power obliged him to indulge their eccentricities, and of course it did. He had given his obeisance to all of them, and they had acted often without regard to his needs, all but extorting public money by the millions under threat of midnight abandonment. It was a nightmare in which the hero is forced to humble himself repeatedly. "It was like going to one used car dealer after another," he said later. He was batting .500, actually, having lost the Colts and won the Orioles. Now he would try to find what the sports writers called redemption—a comeback from the humiliation of defeat at the hands of Bob Irsay and Jack Kent Cooke. As a member in good standing of the NFL ownership council, Cooke had, Schaefer was certain, blocked the governor of Maryland cleanly out of the Baltimore-Washington sports marketplace. He wanted no competition. But Cooke also wanted a new stadium, and he had his eye on property in Maryland. To get it, he would need various land use concessions, so a meeting was arranged in the governor's mansion on a Saturday morning.

"My dear man," Cooke began, "I want you to know you have my utmost respect. I know there is speculation that I blocked your expansion plan, but I want you to know I had nothing to do with it." Neither statement was true. Cooke regarded Schaefer as a rube, and he certainly had done everything he could to keep football from returning to Baltimore. Cooke's denial killed the talks, if they weren't doomed already. Schaefer would have preferred a frank admission: Yes, I blocked you. I didn't want a team in Baltimore. Where do we go from here? Instead, Cooke laid on charm like an encyclopedia salesman, hoping to remove some hostility from the atmosphere. He failed. Schaefer rehearsed in detail how the league, driven by Cooke, had been abusing Baltimore for almost a decade. "My good man, that's not how it happened," Cooke would say. It did too, Schaefer would respond, and so on.

The two titans began yelling at each other. Schaefer instructed his emissaries to do the same, somewhat naively. But he had no illusions about

Cooke, who seemed anxious to assert his superiority intellectually and financially as a means of intimidating his host. Schaefer suggested that everyone could be happy if Cooke simply brought the Redskins to Baltimore. After all, the state was prepared to assist with construction of the new stadium. Cooke said that wouldn't do. His team was the *Washington* Redskins.

A good face was presented to reporters after the meeting, but it had been characterized largely by bouts of shouting between the two principal negotiators. Maryland House Speaker Taylor, Senate President Miller, and others had been in the room, but their roles had been minor. Cooke had promised to build a training facility at Frostburg State College in Taylor's legislative district, and since he already had the allegiance of Miller, whose constituents included many Redskins fans, he felt that he had a winning hand. But Schaefer, who controlled the money and the environmental permit process, was the key, and he would never accept anything short of a new team for his home city. "When we parted," Schaefer understated later, "we were not friends."

Cooke kept pushing, inviting the governor of Maryland to his estate in Northern Virginia. Schaefer refused. With Cooke, he thought, accepting an invitation instantly made you weaker. Miller had allowed himself to be overcome by Cooke and his wealth, Schaefer thought, so he said no. But he did send an emissary, Peter Angelos, the former city councilman and union lawyer. Angelos was himself a prospective NFL owner, having made a fortune representing workers suffering from asbestosis. He was already principal owner of the Baltimore Orioles and a man who would not hesitate to confront the NFL crowd. Schaefer, as governor, had been able to help Angelos buy the Orioles in 1993 by appealing to New York bankers who had liens on the team in connection with money owed them by Eli Jacobs, who had bought the team after Williams's death. The subsequent auction kept the team out of the hands of an Ohio buyer backed by Baltimore banker Furlong Baldwin.

With former congresswoman Bentley running interference, Angelos went to see Cooke at Cooke's house. Bentley took along a lunch of Maryland crabcakes from Haussner's, wine, and plastic cups. Angelos quickly decided that nothing good could come of the session and began to antagonize "the Squire," as some had started calling Cooke quite derisively. Cooke responded in kind. "Who is your tailor?" he asked the pugnacious and short-tempered Angelos.

"My tailor? I don't have a tailor. I'm just a poor boy from the other side of the tracks. I buy my clothes off the rack."

Cooke held out the lapels of his jacket and said, "Savile Row. Of London. You ought to try it sometime." Then he said, "Why are you asking me to bring my football team to Maryland?"

Angelos wasn't asking but turned the matter around, suggesting that Cooke should be so lucky as to have his team in the Free State. "I don't know what gives you the right to come to Maryland," he said.

Cooke began to squeeze his plastic cup, and a bit of wine spilled in his lap.

Angelos leaned forward with a napkin and a consolation. "Oh, Mr. Cooke," he said, "this is so sad. You've got wine all over your Savile Row pants."

Angelos says that Cooke began to shout for Bentley: "Helen! Helen! Get this cur away from me!"— or words to that effect. Angelos and Bentley left.

By then, Schaefer may have been depending on the actuarial tables to remove his rival from the scene. Cooke seemed determined to live exuberantly into his eighties or nineties. If he did not, perhaps Maryland would have a better shot at getting a team. Conversely, the owner knew that Schaefer was not governor for life. Cooke thought that he could roll over Schaefer's successor.

Schaefer finished his final term without a team. He had vowed to have one in place by then, but the moment was not yet right. The deal he put on the table would ultimately regain the franchise, with a few adjustments in the owner's favor. All of this energy and money had been expended for an amenity, something to enhance the quality of life and restore Baltimore's status as a big-league city. Few were willing to do as Bob Lanier, the mayor of Houston, had done: bid farewell and good riddance to its Oilers. A big-league city, said Lanier, was one that worked hard on its schools, enforced its housing codes, and tried to promote industrial growth. When he was mayor of Baltimore, Schaefer had done everything Lanier recommended. But Schaefer could not bring himself to believe that the city would be better off without professional football. It was too much a part of the city's self-image, and even if people did not hold him responsible for the team's loss, there was a residue of that setback in his own consciousness. His can-do psychology would not permit him to think otherwise, and he had hoped he might do with the team owners what he had done with A. N. Pritzker and the city fathers of Baltimore. He found instead that Mr. Irsay and Mr. Cooke were worlds removed from Mr. Eney and Mr. Marbury, the lawyers and civic leaders Schaefer so revered. Irsay and Cooke were probably more like Mr. Kovens, happy to deal with politicians when that seemed a route to success and willing to discard them otherwise.

CHAPTER 15

The Return of the Native

The pursuit of NFL football continued until the end of Schaefer's eight years in Annapolis. He set a deadline for the league, had it endorsed by the assembly, promised to stick with it—and then, when the league didn't fall for his maneuver, persuaded Angelos to convince legislators that they should extend things once again, leaving the offer on the table. He labored on many other fronts at the same time, of course. He never liked being governor, so his efforts in that job seemed even more remarkable. He did well despite his unhappiness, though he seldom missed an opportunity to vent. Mayor was the best job, he said. He'd never wavered from that view. Years earlier, Chris Hartman, one of his city press secretaries, wondered amid all the speculation about a Schaefer gubernatorial candidacy whether Schaefer had any interest in being governor.

"No, no, no, I don't ever want to be governor," Schaefer had said, "except they do have that nice fireplace in the governor's office." Near the end of his eight-year lease on that particular amenity, Schaefer told a reporter that he'd first noticed the fireplace while he and Mandel were cooking up deals for the city. "Marvin would sit with his feet in the drawer smoking his pipe, and the fire would be blazing, and we all just had a good feeling," Schaefer said.

He had fewer of those feelings later when it was his office, but there were some—when the stadiums bill passed and the oversized football and baseball were tossed about, when he tried to give Delegate Bruce Poole advice about moderating anger, and when he sat with Anne Arundel County Senator Gerald Winegrad, an uncompromising environmentalist. Schaefer's concerns about water and wildlife always seemed a bit foreshortened by his concern for business development, yet his stewardship of nature got high marks from the Chesapeake Bay Foundation, Maryland's best-known citizens environmental group.

"You haven't always agreed with me," Schaefer told Winegrad, "but I can say this about you: Unlike some of those people down there in the assembly who don't do anything or believe anything, you're a zealot."

Winegrad was perfectly happy to think of himself as a zealot, but was this a compliment?

Schaefer smiled. "I'm a zealot, too," he said.

Zealotry was always easier and more effective in Baltimore. Yet he had immediate impact in Annapolis, more than he thought. While he was settling in, someone heard that the new governor did not like to see anything on the top shelf of bookcases. He wanted that one surface uncluttered. Suddenly, a survey of state agencies would have detected this odd bit of top shelf uniformity. Within months, moreover, according to Ed Papenfuse, the archivist, Schaefer had achieved an atmosphere of accountability enforced by the view that he might drop in unannounced—via helicopter, striding across the statehouse grounds to confront a committee chairman, or lying in wait for some hapless functionary preparing to explain a contract to the board of public works.

As episodic and tantrum-oriented as he seemed, Schaefer knew that he needed a system. In a sense, he was a system. He locked the doors at 8:00 A.M. when he convened cabinet meetings, leaving cabinet secretaries and even the lieutenant governor waiting in the hallway if they were even a minute late. In his first mayoral campaign document, "Where I Stand," Schaefer had written, "To strengthen and tighten the management of city government, we must seek a way of institutionalizing executive authority and accountability. City government is a big business with an annual budget of over 900 million dollars, nearly 40,000 employees and hundreds of operating departments and programs." If this formulation was at all abstract, Schaefer gave it concrete form. "I used to call people just to ride their ass a little," he said later. "I did it because the bureaucracy will go as slowly as you allow it to go."

Sally Michel, the Baltimore activist who had "won" Schaefer for lunch in 1971 and who put together seventy-five or so dinner forums at his request, remembered the softer side of his encyclopedic approach to getting things done. Her daughters had a bake sale one day on a street corner near their house, and Schaefer made a point of stopping by to see how it was going. The Michel girls gave the mayor the proceeds—a bag full of nickels—for some cause or other, and each one of them got a thank you note.

"He was always happier as mayor," Michel said, "because he could be closer to people."

As the end approached, Schaefer's Annapolis minions began tabulating and plotting the accomplishments of his eight years. Year by year, in a dozen categories, they logged hundreds of high spots, including 10,600 memos commanding someone to fix something. His own assessment was a mixed one, as always. He agreed with Marion Pines, who worried that Schaefer's footprint—her own as well—would not be as deep as she had hoped. City neighborhoods—from Charles Village, where the houses were being repainted in multihued Victorian styles, to Otterbein and Canton, where young people were buying houses and taking over—thrived the way Schaefer knew they could. An effort was being made to create a real downtown neighborhood, linking the Inner Harbor hotel planned by Peter Angelos to the bristling hive of life at the University of Maryland Hospital. The old Hippodrome Theater was to be restored along with a wide swath of buildings in need of rejuvenation. As always, shopkeepers were being asked to recognize the greater good and get out. But the idea seemed to have momentum reaching back to the Shadow Government's investment in conversion of the old textile plants into offices and loft apartments. Streets around these buildings, rescued by Schaefer's trustees, looked as promising as any downtown street anywhere. The footprint seemed likely to grow with the help of strong institutions like the hospital, the salutary presence of Angelos, the reawakening of various charitable foundations, and money from the State of Maryland.

Pines' thoughts about Schaefer's lasting impact went to the area of social services. Schaefer knew what she was talking about and sympathized with her anguished reflections. He wished in the end that he done more with Baltimore's schools. Education was a nettle he had feared to touch, and he had realized that he could do more with redevelopment downtown. As governor, he saw the price of his decision: He had to cope with the appalling costs of prison construction and then of incarcerating more than 20,000 offenders, many of them young black men. A better school system, he thought, might have kept this number down. His support for Nancy Grasmick, his state superintendent of schools, deepened as he watched her cope with—and threaten to take control of—Baltimore schools. With Delegate Howard A. "Pete" Rawlings of Baltimore, chairman of the House Appropriations Committee, Schaefer had attempted to set up a voucher program that would allow parents to shop around for the best school, hoping to introduce competition into a stagnant system. He continued to push for special math and science instruction and insisted that Maryland high schoolers participate in some community service as a requirement for graduation.

As governor, he had more control over higher education, and with Mickey Steinberg, his lieutenant governor, he accomplished a thorough-going reform of the state's thirteen-campus university system. He wanted to focus unprecedented financial resources on the University of Maryland at College Park, hoping that it might achieve higher national ranking. The recession of the early 1990s made College Park a victim, though, and it would be almost a decade before his successor could recommit state government to the goal that Schaefer had set in 1988.

The two stadiums and the light rail system were completed before the downturn, and despite continuing criticism of priorities, the state seemed to agree, finally, that his view was the correct one. The state's drivers might be years in accepting the wisdom of mass transit, but the beginnings of a smart transportation system—light rail—would be in place if they did. He had completed his "Reach the Beach" project along Route 50 to Ocean City, and even that effort had been accepted finally by the Eastern Shore residents who were so inconvenienced by the work when it was under way. He had tackled tax reform, the NRA, and an effort to protect the environment, particularly the endangered Chesapeake Bay.

Schaefer had taken many of his Baltimore "children" with him to Annapolis, but inevitably, they began to leave. Bob Douglass, the reporter and press secretary, joined Bill Marbury's law firm, Piper and Marbury. Daryl Plevy went to work for Senator Mikulski. And on May 30, 1993, Lainy LeBow married Leonard Sachs, a Baltimore developer. Schaefer's major domo, his woman for all seasons, continued at his side as Lainy LeBow-Sachs. She was just as devoted to the governor of Maryland as ever, but her marriage reminded him of his decision to remain single— and might have made him wonder, if only for a moment, how he would cope when his successor was sworn in.

History

In the week before Schaefer left office, a state trooper ran into the executive offices looking for LeBow-Sachs. It was eight full years into Schaefer's Annapolis tenure, and the governor of Maryland's chief aide was about to get her first tour of the mansion. She had been in the building only twice and never upstairs. The governor and his friend had laughed about her alien status, about the tyrannical Hilda Mae. It was one of their private jokes. "Hurry," the trooper said. Mrs. Snoops was out for a doctor's appointment, so Lainy would get her tour, something Schaefer could not manage with the official hostess on the premises. They hit all the rooms: his, Hilda Mae's, the bathrooms, the kitchen, the closets. Their giddy whirl veiled the difficult time just ahead of them. A week later, Lainy was in Schaefer's office, sobbing. The Schaefer years were ending. "What's the matter?" he asked, as if he really didn't know.

He was at peace on that final day, or so it seemed. Against all odds, he seemed to have achieved some perspective, to be capable finally of handling an emotional moment, in this case his transition to private citizen. His friends had feared that he would fall into yet another slough of despondency and emptiness. For the moment, these concerns seemed unwarranted. He floated above the end-point ceremonies, the final questions thrown by reporters, the attendant foreboding.

On the final day, in the throng just below the famous Washington painting and on the edge of the black and white marble floor of the statehouse's main lobby, *Sun* reporter Sandy Banisky remarked on Schaefer's tranquility. What accounted for that, she wondered. "I realized I'd had my time," he said. Minutes later, right after Parris Glendening was sworn in as governor, Schaefer and Hilda Mae drove away, not bothering to stay for the speeches. Perhaps this was just as well, since former governor Hughes said he hoped Schaefer's departure would permit a return to normalcy. (Attorney General Curran had said during a period of conflict with Schaefer that he yearned for the arrival of 1994: "Then we can call it the Free State again," he said.)

Weeks before the final day, LeBow-Sachs had gone to Glendening to plead for a state police driver to remain with the ex-governor for a few weeks. "You'll remember this conversation," she told him. "The way it usually works is at 12:01 P.M., like, 'Get in your own car, honey, and drop dead.' It is a really pathetic thing. The man didn't even know there was a world out there." Fortunately, Glendening said yes. Weeks before, she and Schurick had taken Schaefer to a big parking lot—the kids with their dad, but in a reversal of the usual order—to give him some driving instruction. He couldn't or wouldn't concentrate. Now Schaefer was history, a man without a title unless it began with "former" or "ex." It was over.

LeBow-Sachs couldn't go with Schaefer that day, but they talked on the telephone "about 18 times," she said. Some of the gang met for breakfast the next morning at the Center Club in Baltimore, the Charles Center–era businessman's club on the USF&G Building's fifteenth floor. Wasserman, Schurick, Sabatini, LeBow-Sachs, and the former governor sat and said little. Tired, dazed, and melancholy, they scanned the Inner Harbor they had helped to build, unconsoled by its sweep and bustle.

For the first time in his adult life, Schaefer had nothing pressing to do. LeBow-Sachs had provided for various elder statesman–style activities, including a joint lectureship underwritten by his business friends: the William Donald Schaefer Chair in Public Policy to be situated jointly at the Johns Hopkins University Homewood campus in Baltimore and the University of Maryland at College Park. He had an offer to provide commentary on a local television station. Later, he joined Eugene Feinblatt's law firm on Redwood Street, where he was given a fine office with a splendid harbor view. As always, friends were picking him up, hand-carrying him into retirement.

Schaefer had made virtually no personal preparations for that move, no psychic adjustments and no practical plan, either because he could not face that chore or because he knew by then that others would try to do it for him. He got lost driving his car, found himself unable even to get former associates on the telephone, was rebuffed in his effort to sell an idea about senior citizen employment to McDonald's. "You or I," thought Sondheim, "would have considered the possibility of being depressed, unhappy, lost. He never thought about it for a moment." The steep emotional decline so feared by LeBow-Sachs and others began almost immediately. "He just didn't even know what to do with himself" she said. "And then I went away. My husband had arranged for us to go away for two weeks. Which was really hard for me to do—you know, leave him. But then on the other side of the coin, it was hard for me to balance everything out. And then I came back, and we saw each other every single day."

Depressed as he was, he was not beyond responding to the mischievous instincts that often arose in him. His friend Ed Hale, the banker, businessman, and professional sports team owner, wanted to take Schaefer and Lainy to lunch. They decided on Victor's Café, a new place then on the east side of the Baltimore Harbor that was usually empty on a Tuesday. But when she and Schaefer entered, LeBow-Sachs noticed a group of "wheelchair people," and started over to see who they were. Something made her stand back as the former governor walked ahead. "I'm waiting and waiting and something told me not to go. You know I usually go over, and he always likes to introduce me. Something said to me don't go over there. I'm waiting, waiting, and I'm looking, and one woman looks familiar."

Schaefer came back. "You aren't going to believe this."

"Is that Hilda Mae?"

"Yes," he said and began to hustle LeBow-Sachs up the steps, getting her out of Hilda Mae's line of sight—just as in the old days.

"I forgot she was going to be here," Schaefer said.

"You forgot? You set this up!" said LeBow-Sachs.

It pleased Schaefer to know that he had created this sort of collision, she thought. Marion Pines thought that it was part of his nature to demand reaffirmation of love twenty-four hours a day—and to do everything he could to make it more difficult for people to show how they felt about him. This time, perhaps, the conflict was a way to get back to the center of things.

These vaguely desperate efforts to stay connected with his former life were unnecessary because Schaefer's friends stayed in close touch with him. Hale had taken him to lunch. Sabatini and his wife would have Schaefer and Raynor to dinner. Mandel, Bereano, and the former state police chief, Larry Tolliver, met with him regularly at the Double T Diner in Catonsville. Raynor and Dr. Jay Platt had breakfast with him several times a week at Jimmy's in Fells Point. And every day, LeBow-Sachs called him at least once, the first time from her car after her early morning jog with Mark Wasserman.

"Hello? Superman here," he would say, picking up the phone.

"Wonder Woman here," she would reply. They might chat about his schedule for that day: Some group would be having him for lunch, conferring yet another official tribute for his years of public service. And she would help him with one chore or another—sale of the Edgewood Street house, for example. She had urged him to make that break finally, arguing that the house was an unnecessary financial burden. He hung on, though, as if 620 Edgewood were the only official address he would ever have. He remained a bit rootless. He had not moved out of the condo in Anne Arundel County, but he bought a place in Baltimore on Lancaster Street, around the corner from Jimmy's, but he stayed there only occasionally.

On the Shelf

What Schaefer really wanted was to get back into the political game—immediately. He wanted to run for mayor as McKeldin had done successfully in 1963 after two terms as governor. He was furious with Kurt Schmoke and certain that Schmoke's 1995 opponent, Council President Mary Pat Clarke, could not win, though he supported her. Schmoke and Larry Gibson pretended to want Schaefer in the race, hoping to humiliate him. They had called his work as mayor "cosmetic," virtually turning their back on the state's—and Schaefer's—$100 million Convention Center expansion, taking some pains to disrespect it as another project of the downtown white business establishment, which they had to oppose lest they seem less attentive to their base constituency. The renaissance mayor might have run for mayor again, seeking a fifth term, but he feared that he could not win and knew that Gibson would love to drive him into the political earth like a tent peg. Schaefer went to see the mayor and his political man at one point, offering to do just about any job they could think of for him, only to have them say no, unequivocally. Who, they must have wondered, would want as independent a man as William Donald Schaefer loose in city government? His dalliance with running again hurt him in his retirement plans: WJZ said that he would have to give up his television commentaries if he was preparing to run for mayor. And Glendening, hoping to solidify the support of the Gibson-Schmoke team, withdrew his appointment of Schaefer to the St. Mary's College Board of trustees.

Schaefer had been of great help to this small liberal arts school in southern Maryland when he was governor, granting it extraordinary budget status outside the channels through which the system's other twelve institutions of higher education had to swim. If Schaefer was running for mayor, said Glendening, he shouldn't be on the board. Glendening was going out of his way to discipline his predecessor and help his ally, Schmoke. Indirectly, however, the governor was taking on several of his Democratic brethren, including Congressmen Ben Cardin and Fifth District Congressman Steny Hoyer, who were on the St. Mary's board and were eager for Schaefer to join them. In time, Glendening relented, and the former governor took his seat with some of the most prestigious men and women on any college board in the nation. Former *Washington Post* editor Ben Bradlee served, along with former NATO commander Andrew

Goodpaster and Paul Warnke, the John F. Kennedy intimate and famous nuclear disarmament negotiator.

Life was actually less dramatic most of the time. Schaefer often had dinner alone at the house in Anne Arundel County—or almost alone. "My dog Willie comes and sits beside me. I have my TV dinner and my bottle of nonalcoholic beer. I'm getting to be an expert on TV dinners. Have to turn 'em, stir some of the vegetables. I'm learning which ones to buy, such as Healthy Choice. I look to see what they look like. Last night I had salisbury steak. Fettucini. Stuff like that."

Snubbed

Glendening's unkindest cut came after the new governor had taken Schaefer's deal, made it sweeter, and convinced Cleveland Browns owner Art Modell that Baltimore could be his salvation. Using the lease outline drawn by Belgrad and the other Schaefer soldiers, Glendening and his stadium authority chairman, John Moag, were in place at the right moment. Schaefer had spent a dozen years in pursuit of an NFL team. Now, with the Browns in serious financial difficulty and no prospect of a new stadium, what Schaefer had prostrated himself to make possible was happening, though not in the way he had hoped. Modell agreed to abandon Cleveland, a city that was no less a part of NFL history than Green Bay—or Baltimore. He agreed secretly to move the Browns to Baltimore as if the team could make such a trip and still be the Browns. Indeed, the team would be renamed the Ravens. Glendening's deal went far beyond the one he inherited from Schaefer, which was already the best untaken offer in NFL franchise history. Chief among the new blandishments were personal seat licenses—authority to charge season ticket holders thousands of dollars simply for the right to purchase their seats. Schaefer was critical of the deal's generosity and lamented the impact on Cleveland fans, but his criticisms were muted. And now his successor would treat him the way the NFL owners had treated him.

On November 6, 1995, Glendening stood on a dais at Camden Yards, prepared to bask in the glow of the victor who had come home with a team after so many years. Schaefer was not invited, and the legislature's two presiding officers were asked to attend only at the last moment. Both declined. Schaefer stood in the audience that day. Had he accorded Schaefer credit for a decade of humiliating, groveling efforts to win over one of the owners, Glendening would have insulated himself a bit from the storm of criticism that was about to break over his unsuspecting head. Columnists showered the governor of Maryland with the type of invective that was usually reserved for for spoiled super stars. Glendening had allowed himself to become the political version of Irsay. Glendening responded to the critics by reminding them that franchises were not delivered by the Easter Bunny. He had chosen to play NFL tennis without the net of moral rectitude demanded by Schaefer—naively, some had said. Glendening's snub actually helped Schaefer, bringing him renewed credit for the years he had fought to win back a team. Still, he was faced with conflicting emotions: He wanted to be pleased that the struggle was at an end and Baltimore had an NFL team once more, but he sympathized with the mayor of Cleveland and the Browns' fans.

First Citizen

Although Schaefer's transition to private life was not a smooth or happy one, some moments of recognition for his life in public service occurred without the urging or intervention of the ex-governor's team. Senate President Miller made him Maryland's "First Citizen" in 1995, an award that Schaefer's old nemesis created to honor former colleagues and others. As part of that moment, the honoree offered some thoughts on the occasion of George Washington's birthday. The ceremony was held in the Old Senate Chamber, where Washington had resigned his commission as general in charge of the just victorious Continental Army. Schaefer began by observing that Miller actually looked a little like Washington. The resemblance, if any, was slight, but Miller sat on a raised dais and was positioned between Schaefer and another portrait of the first president that hung on the chamber's east wall.

"This is the first time I've been back since I was removed," Schaefer said, as if he had been the victim of a coup. By then, after almost forty years in public office, he had begun to appreciate the privileges he had taken for granted. "Your importance is made known to me," he said. "People depend on you. Give thought to what you are doing." What had Washington been thinking on that day 218 years earlier on the occasion of his departure from the Continental Army? Surely, Schaefer said, the great general had wondered "how he would tolerate the peace of retirement." Schaefer was certain "his hand trembled as mine would have" when he signed the official document in that flowing, somewhat enigmatic script. Washington had realized within the weeks after he left Annapolis that he had more power than he realized. Some had wanted Washington for king, and he had said no. Yet the new country was treading into the realm of the unknown, and the general must surely have reflected upon his continuing responsibilities. "I've done my duty. Let others carry on," he might have said. But that was a vain delusion, and soon Washington realized the truth: He could not retire. For duty's sake alone, with no thought of aggrandizement, he would be the nation's preeminent First Citizen.

Then Schaefer confided something: He felt he had a psychic line to the nation's father, a line that had opened to him when, as governor, he walked down the marble steps to sit in this chamber. "I really did come into this room," he said. "Sometimes with the lights on. Sometimes with the lights off." As some other householder might sit alone on a sunporch or in a library or family room, Schaefer could have and did repair to one of the republic's most hallowed places, as momentous as it was modest in size and furnishings. Washington must have wondered, the former governor went on, what posture to take when he relinquished command. "He never spoke out," Schaefer said, adding a question for his audience: "I wonder if that was the right course? I wonder if he would have done that again if given another chance?" Schaefer seemed both frustrated and comfortable with the decision he had made for himself. He felt that he should, in all conscience, comment on things that troubled him. But how could he? "You never really know what's going on," he said. "You're out of it."

Honor Roll

A former governor is never out of it for long, of course, even one who endures a bit of payback for his own personal mistreatment of others over the years. Politics has a way of rescuing people as irrationally as they are punished. One day, LeBow-Sachs got a call from Glendening's aide, Eleanor Carey.

"You know Parris would like to hang the governor's portrait," Carey said.

"You mean it's not hung?" LeBow-Sachs said, as if the matter was of so little consequence that she hadn't kept up with it. "I said, 'Ellie, Look, let's not fool each other, it's a great idea for Parris. He should be doing this. He made such a fool of himself with Schaefer. Whether Schaefer hates him or not, Parris'll come out looking good.'" Glendening then asked whether Schaefer would accept appointment to a commission on the millennium, an honorary position that someone like Schaefer might actually turn into a useful enterprise. LeBow-Sachs reported Glendening's desires, and Schaefer began to shout about "that son of a bitch." But he said he would accept, and Glendening put LeBow-Sachs on the commission as well. Schaefer also agreed to advise the governor on various things, including how to deal with the business community, and the two began meeting over lunch. The portrait-hanging ceremony was scheduled.

Wearing a black tie festooned with lime green, orange, and yellow Christmas tree ornaments, Schaefer sat to the right of a smiling Glendening as various speakers told of Schaefer's contributions to the state of Maryland and to the ideal of public service. Peter O'Malley, who had been chairman of the University of Maryland Board of Regents during Schaefer's first term, presided. He reminded Schaefer of their standing joke about the former governor's constant unhappiness—and about a recent phone call. Schaefer had called when O'Malley was out and left a message on the answering machine. "I had to call and tell you how happy I am," Schaefer said. "I'm standing here with a $25,000 check for community health programs. I met this guy at a party and told him what I was doing, how I was raising money for one of the centers, and the next thing I know there's this check." O'Malley, once the boss of Prince George's Democrats, was nearly in tears as he recounted the story.

Then came an eloquent speech by Louis Goldstein, the comptroller. Glendening spoke next. He had asked his staff to find the famous elegy to heroes written by Teddy Roosevelt: "The credit belongs to the man who is actually in the arena; whose face is marred by dust and sweat and blood; who strives valiantly; who errs and comes short again and again, . . . who knows the great enthusiasms, the great devotions; who spends himself in a worthy cause; who, at the best, knows in the end the triumph of high achievement; and who, at the worst, if he fails, at least fails while daring greatly, so that his place shall never be with those cold and timid souls who know neither victory nor defeat."

Glendening was the supporting player here; Schaefer, the has-been governor, once again dominated this grand room where he had growled, huffed and puffed, and once pointed an assault weapon at reporters. The guests of honor moved to their right to stand in front of the portrait, draped in black. A cord was pulled and pulled again, the drape catching a bit and the frame tilting before falling away. There was Schaefer-for-the-ages with Willie at his side. Everyone applauded. "Nice of the dog," someone said.

Schaefer gazed up at his likeness for the photographers. He posed with members of his cabinet and friends. Then he moved around the room, hugging and chatting with this somewhat small crowd. He signed copies of the official program, as did the white-bearded artist Joe Sheppard, smiling broadly from beneath his gold-colored beard and ponytail. The portrait of the fifty-ninth governor of Maryland took its place next to that of Schaefer's least-favorite Maryland politician, Harry Hughes. LeBow-Sachs pointed this out repeatedly, knowing just how to insert the needle. Schaefer curled his lip for just a moment. Spiro T. Agnew, Harry Nice, Albert Cabell Ritchie, and Ted McKeldin were all there on the wall, of course, joined now by a more contemplative likeness of Schaefer than the man of action Sheppard had painted when Schaefer was the mayor.

The ex-governor took another glance at his portrait as if to confirm for himself that, yes, he had been governor of Maryland—quite an accomplishment for someone who believed that he might well have been a street person. The distance between accomplishment and failure, he always thought, was shorter than most people realized. He always conducted himself as if a nudge of fate would park him in some shelter for the hungry and homeless.

He stopped with a reporter briefly to marvel at the course of his life. "Pretty amazing the way things turn out," he said. He turned again to the painting, knowing for once whose likeness it was—not Mencken's, not Uncle Willie's or Mr. Eney's, or any of the other role models, but his own. He had been the governor of Maryland for eight years, and now he had a moment to realize and accept that history as fact. He had done it again. He had made the honor roll.

Struggling

Still, he could not find his balance. The plaques and the portraits, the buildings named for him, the honorary degrees, and the adulation of people on the street did not fill the gap in his existence. He recalled his sojourns in Ocean City with Hilda Mae, sitting in their boat, catching the occasional flounder. "I didn't think I was having fun," he said, "but I was." She was too ill to join him now, and if he went alone, he said, he was lonely.

He spent a fair amount of time complaining publicly and privately about the Schmoke administration, sounding cranky and bitter or worse. He was certain Schmoke and Gibson wanted to make Baltimore an all-

black city. The old integrationist ideal was fading under Schmoke's housing and neighborhood revitalization policies, Schaefer thought, and he
resented it. He resented Schmoke personally because he thought his successor had not paid his dues and had not accorded Schaefer the honor of
recognizing that the job was a hard one, one that had to be learned.
Schmoke was, in a sense, an accident of history, a man whose résumé made
him the ideal bridge from Schaefer's era to a new one. Schmoke had enormous promise, education, and charm, but he was not in a job he seemed
particularly well suited for or one he might have chosen for himself on the
basis of his talents and interests. History had chosen him, and he did well
enough, keeping the city afloat with almost none of the federal help Schaefer had had. He would have benefited from Schaefer's tutelage, but it was
a sad fact that neither man was prepared for a close relationship. Schaefer was unwilling to share with someone he regarded as insufficiently
committed, and Schmoke seemed, at times, at risk of losing his base if he
seemed to rely on his establishment predecessor.

Schaefer once offered this appraisal of his mayoral successor:

> When I came in, there was a difference: The city had a leader, a
> cheerleader, maybe not too bright, as the Sunpaper said, but we had
> someone who was dedicated to making things better. I couldn't
> fail—because anything I did had to go up. Schmoke is driving the
> city down, but yet the city is poised to move up. . . . With Schmoke,
> when he came in, everyone wanted him to be the greatest thing since
> applesauce. First of all [the *Sun*] wanted to promote a black man.
> That was the vogue and it's still the vogue, make a black man the
> greatest thing in the world, and the Sunpapers tried. No matter
> what he did, he was right. Joe Sterne told me that. We're never going
> to criticize him. We're never going to be the catalyst that starts a
> race riot. He told me that. He told a business group that. So first
> four years, honeymoon, honeymoon, honeymoon, great man. Oh,
> a little mistake, we'll slap him on the wrist. . . . The business com-
> munity kept alibing him. He'll learn now, they said. He wasn't com-
> petent to learn. However, the city itself is a great city. It knew glory
> days. There are still remembrances of the glory days. There it is out
> this office window. The Inner Harbor is symbolic. The Orioles are
> symbolic. All the things that happened never happened during the
> reign of Schmoke. He's made no major improvements in the city. He
> didn't do the Convention Center. I did it. I gave him the money,

forced him to take it. He didn't do the Science Center. He didn't do the Aquarium. He didn't do the Columbus Center. Camden Yards. I did it. His glory [neighborhood] is Sandtown-Winchester. Take a ride and see the beauty of that place, and you'll see vacant land. You'll see some nice housing, but it's going to go to hell because there's no supporting structure.

Rouse had been Schmoke's partner in Sandtown-Winchester, an ambitious community reclamation effort northwest of downtown. Schaefer had urged Rouse to find another site, arguing that without some sustaining institutions—churches, solid families, businesses—the project would inevitably fail. Schmoke thought that criterion was a limiting one, since some inner-city neighborhoods were by definition without institutional strength. If you red-lined them, there would be no hope for the thousands who lived there. Schaefer said,

Rouse had a vision, and the vision was that Sandtown-Winchester would be a model for the United States. He couldn't see he was dragging all the money in there and ruining the rest of the area. He kicked the Koreans out and put in the blacks. All he could see was the vision. A vision, but he couldn't do it. He didn't have anybody like me to be quite frank who would help make it a success. There was a way to make it right. I wouldn't have made it that big. I would have staged it. I would have moved in with certain parts of it. I wouldn't have cleared out every thing without a plan. Housing inspectors, special police, code enforcement. I lost interest. I didn't want to fight him. I wanted a marriage between vision and practicality. When I looked at it, I said, 'What the hell are you doing?' A new market coming in, but it won't last. Didn't bother with the merchants on Pennsylvania Avenue. His theory was—I was hoping he was right—we'll make this great and it will radiate out. I don't think it can do that. Schmoke can't keep the area clean. That to me is an insult to the black community. That's saying you're willing to accept the trash, the needles, the people that don't work. I think that's a tragedy. I think that's the wrong thing to do to people. That's this idea of the black culture versus the white culture. What we tried to do was make it one culture. You don't need trash. You don't need rats. You don't have to have vandalism. And you don't have to accept them. . . . My theory was and will be that black people deserve to have a good clean community.

Rouse actually agreed with Schaefer on the need for strength to build on but acceded to Schmoke's wishes, knowing that he would have to accommodate the mayor who was then in office.

"This Man"

LeBow-Sachs turned away when Schaefer talked like this, plugging up her ears and looking around for some refuge against this politically incorrect venting. He felt that it was his obligation by then to say something about the mistakes he saw all around him, whether people accused him of jealousy, second-guessing, sour grapes, or whatever. He would not adopt George Washington's studied silence; he would speak out. But even that frustrated him because he was so dyspeptic and sometimes so personal that he got no serious hearing in the newspapers, before the Greater Baltimore Committee's board, or anywhere. It was not that people didn't agree with much of what he said. They were simply unwilling to take on the charges that would surely follow a full airing of his complaints. His troops—Wasserman, Sabatini, Hoffman, Plevy, and even Barbara Mikulski—were off on other occupations, necessarily, and were just as fearful as LeBow of the repercussions that would greet his views.

They contented themselves, as he did, with nostalgia for their one shining moment in Baltimore civic life, spectacular yet all too brief, when people could be pulled together for community projects of great significance. Even the cerebral Benton longed for days on the street. Benton remembered Schaefer ordering everyone to meet at a certain corner with green garbage bags. Benton snorted and brought a U-Haul truck. He recruited his handyman, Arthur McHugh, the dealmaker who carried a bowie knife on his belt. They both showed up for the Saturday command performance with sidearms. Benton loved direct action, the immediate sense of accomplishment, and the response of the people who met them with six-packs and grills already fired up to make lunch. That was what they all missed.

No one missed it more than Schaefer. Almost every day, some group somewhere in Maryland held a luncheon in his honor or gave him a plaque or a picture. He did some work with a dozen organizations, many of them very important but none of them imparting the sort of power lift he wanted. "I can't find anything I really like," he said. Yet he did. Each of these events was like a family reunion in the city he had once married. What he liked most were sessions in Baltimore neighborhoods, such as the nineteenth anniversary of the city's purchase of a Little League ball field in Hamilton. If the city would buy the property, Hamilton citizens had said, they would maintain it. When he got there, when he sat on a stone wall to watch a bit of the game, Schaefer surveyed the neatly trimmed fields, the kids playing with the parents, the young ballplayers.

"It looks great. Just like it did nineteen years ago," he said.

The award he'd gotten as a child—the one that so thrilled his father—was eclipsed by honorary degrees, portraits, memorial buildings, and even a church service at Old St. Paul's, which came close to a living funeral service with a succession of eulogists. It was not as if he had been in a drought of recognition. In 1984, he had received the Brandeis University distinguished Public Service medal, previously given to only three others: Eleanor Roosevelt, U.S. Supreme Court Chief Justice Earl Warren, and House Speaker Thomas P. "Tip" O'Neill. The William H. and Tululu I. Schaefer Scholarship was established at Brandeis in his parents' honor. A year after his last day in office, Trinity College in Connecticut awarded him an honorary doctorate of laws. The citation read, "Your imposing, eclectic legacy includes a cleaner Chesapeake Bay, higher performance standards for public schools, health and welfare reform, and Oriole Park at Camden Yards, arguably the best new baseball stadium in the world. . . . With a self-described style of governance that made everything an adventure, you revitalized the state bureaucracy with fresh ideas, hard work and a well-known flair for the dramatic. . . . For your lifetime of public service."

The credit for these awards and commemorations belongs to LeBow-Sachs, who labored feverishly on Schaefer's behalf and was giggled about by those who found the cult of personality a bit overwrought. She told *Baltimore* magazine once, in the flip way that her friends saw as vintage Lainy, that she "did Don for a living." She had been the proud leader of his Kool-aid drinkers, having had her picture taken taking the powder directly from its packet without benefit of mixing it with water. She seemed desperate to make sure Schaefer would not be forgotten, as if, without her exertions, he would vanish from public consciousness. But she saw the essential truth of his legacy as a political figure: A man reaching desperately for the mantle of self-fulfillment had been, at the same time, a model of the public man. He would leave an upscale waterside shopping center, two grand stadiums, a light rail system, and three-word manifesto: "Do it now."

"I never thought Donald was a brilliant man, but he had the instinct to know when to act," said the Reverend Marion Bascom, a civil rights leader who had battled Schaefer over promotion of blacks in city government. "He had just the right amount of bull and mule—and tenderness—to make him successful. He had the honesty and willingness to change, and he loved the city. Without the city, we are all doomed. The city is the crucible, the source of everything good man has done for his society."

LeBow saw Schaefer as a singular man striving restlessly to reach something just over the horizon, something better, something that would last— but knowing that such a quest would never end, accepting that reality. He was a gift to the state and to the city as preposterous as that suggestion had been when made after he was first elected governor, and he was a gift that the city and state hardly deserved. There was no way to find a suitably tangible, big or important, thing to name in his honor. He was what he was, a public man determined to make the honor roll. "It took me a while to figure that out. It wasn't that he was 'the governor,'" she said. "It was that, of course, that was always mixed into it, but what you really dealt with was this man."

Comeback

It was not unusual for one-time public figures to have difficulty in private life. Jimmy Carter adopted the "think globally, act locally" approach, devoting himself to building houses with others in the program called Habitat for Humanity. George Bush threw himself out of an airplane with a parachute. Jerry Ford played in celebrity golf tournaments. Schaefer fretted and kvetched about the small world left to him when he was "removed" from office in 1994. Only death, it seemed, could rescue him— and it did, but not in the way most would have imagined. On July 3, 1998, Schaefer's colleague on the board of public works, Louis L. Goldstein, the eighty-four-year-old state comptroller, died after a swim at his Calvert County home. The man Marylanders called Louie had suffered a fatal heart attack. Goldstein had been Maryland's tax collector since 1958 and president of the state senate before that—over a half-century of public service. It was difficult to imagine anyone but Goldstein in the job, but in the midst of the mourning and eulogizing, his colleagues had to select a successor. The pressure was particularly great in this case because Goldstein had died three days before the official filing deadline for the 1998 election.

Schaefer called his new best friend Glendening to say he was interested in the job. It must have been like getting a call from the movie monster Freddie Krueger, cooing, "I'm back!" The governor said he was thinking of naming Montgomery County Executive Douglas M. Duncan to the post, hoping that might help him carry the state's most populous county and one where Glendening had various problems. A Duncan admirer, whose style had been likened to his own, the former governor said he would not run if Duncan did. But if Duncan said no, "get back to me," Schaefer said. Glendening said okay.

Duncan did decline, but the promised call from Glendening never came. The weekend stretched on with plenty of speculation about who might be interested, and by Monday, Glendening had contacted a handful of other potential candidates. Schaefer went into what Schurick called "nuclear meltdown."

Not famous for keeping his word in such matters, Glendening was stiffing his predecessor yet again. After declining to invite Schaefer to the ceremonial return of NFL football, denying him a seat on the St. Mary's College board, and refusing for two years to hang his portrait—putting the image of a disgraced Spiro Agnew on the hallowed wall first—Glendening now picked Mike Barnes, the former congressman from Montgomery County, to fill Goldstein's office immediately and to run for comptroller on Glendening's ticket in the fall. The governor had hoped Barnes could help him in Montgomery precincts, where the state's financial aid for stadium construction had been damaging to Glendening.

Taking Barnes meant ignoring Schaefer, whom Glendening had spent the better part of a year courting to offset the offense he had given over the NFL's return and the rest. With the help of LeBow-Sachs, Glendening had gotten Schaefer's endorsement for reelection—given finally over the objections of other Schaefer loyalists. The former governor began taking Glendening around the state, introducing him to people and counseling him on how to win the support of those who tended to see the incumbent Democrat as purely political in everything he did. Because Kovens insulated him at first and because, over time, he had developed his own armor against such pressures, Schaefer had avoided a similar reputation. Unlikely as it seemed for a career politician, Schaefer often declined to do the things that some thought were reflexive political behavior: David Iannucci, who had worked for Glendening and Schaefer as a legislative aide, said that Schaefer would sometimes talk to legislators about a bill but fail to ask them directly for a vote, much less promise a bridge, a judgeship, or a community center.

LeBow-Sachs had been the intermediary between Schaefer and Glendening forces, but now, with her old boss on the brink of disrupting Glendening's plan, she was on a safari in Africa, unavailable to talk him out of such an adventure. In her stead, Douglass and Raynor were urging Schaefer back into the game and trying to convince Glendening that having Schaefer on the ticket would help him to defeat Ellen R. Sauerbrey, the Republican candidate for governor. When LeBow-Sachs returned to find that the world had changed, she declared herself as energized as the rest of the Schaefer team.

Though Glendening handled the matter badly, there was some sympathy for him in the political community. What governor would want his predecessor horning in on matters of public policy? Schaefer wouldn't have wanted it, and Glendening didn't either. Some predicted that Maryland would have two governors, since Schaefer had never been a power-sharing, go-along kind of player.

As angry as he was, Schaefer told his friend and law partner, Zelig Robinson, that he probably would not run. What did he know about being comptroller?

Robinson laid into him. "You have to do it," he said. "You must." He worked Schaefer over in every way: the guilt trip, the challenge, and the praise. Schaefer had done the same thing any time he had to keep talented people who wanted to move on. You owe it to the city, Schaefer would say. You owe it to me. We'll do exciting work. Who else would give you such responsibility? Your judgment is important to me. When some people left him anyway, he virtually disowned them, banning the use of their names in his presence.

Schaefer said it would cost him $290 to file as a candidate. Robinson slapped a $20 bill on the desk and said, "There's your first contribution."

Schaefer was elated by the number of calls he got making the same vehement appeal. His judgment, his integrity, and his independence were needed. *He* was needed. "I felt alive again," he told a reporter.

Glendening was whipsawed by events and by his own misjudgment. His staff had assured him and Barnes that Schaefer would not run. It would be, if not a cakewalk, at least a winnable race for a man such as Barnes, who had been highly respected in his day and still was in Montgomery County, which he had represented in Congress and where he still lived. But he had been out of politics for twelve years. Some Democrats in the Maryland General Assembly did not even know who he was.

Schaefer was in the race, but before he decided finally, he gave Hilda

Mae an opportunity to talk him out of it. Perhaps she knew he would have done it either way, or maybe she thought he was looking for a way out—in which case she was denying him an escape route. "Sounds like a good idea. Do what you want," she said.

With two hours remaining before the 9:00 P.M. filing deadline on September 9, with the governor's men trying to get Schaefer on the phone, Gene Raynor and Dr. Jay Platt, a member of Schaefer's breakfast klatch at Jimmy's Restaurant, hauled their friend out of his office, down to Platt's creamy white Cadillac, and then to Annapolis. He could file, he agreed. He could do that much. He could preserve his options.

"And then," Raynor said later, "he said the dumbest thing a politician's ever said. He tells a TV guy, 'I've got ten days to change my mind.'" A ten-day cooling off period is provided by state law, to allow a candidate to withdraw. Schaefer also told the TV guy that he wanted to come back so he could work on economic development, not exactly the province of the comptroller. Glendening's crowd tried frantically to get him out, driving Schaefer farther in with every move they made. Schaefer's men told Glendening's men they should be grateful for the former governor's help in the Baltimore area. The colorful old warhorse would bring out Democrats on election day, and his presence might help the incumbent governor seem more human and put some excitement into a Democratic Party and a political climate that had been demoralized by Bill Clinton, special prosecutor Kenneth W. Starr, and the U.S. Congress.

Acting comptroller for less than a week, Barnes withdrew from the race, officially in the name of party unity but surely because he knew that he could not beat Schaefer, whose name recognition was a light-year ahead of his. Glendening told reporters he hadn't realized how eager Schaefer was to run—and, of course, what a wonderful thing it was! A glow of redemption settled around the soon-to-be seventy-seven-year-old candidate, lifting him grandly from the depths into which he had sunk in his retirement. Nowhere was it written that a public man, especially a man as quirky and defiant as Schaefer, should have another chance, an invitation to become, as it were, a monument to himself. The *Washington Post* ran file pictures of him in his googly-eye, spring-loaded glasses and in his Shadow cape and hat and declared him just what the political system needed. News photographers captured Glendening and Schaefer wearing the same silly headgear and Schaefer looking at his successor as if to say, "Not everyone can pull this off, you know."

As governor, Schaefer had pushed hard and angrily against Goldstein and others whose conservative approach to taking on debt had curtailed his gubernatorial ambitions, holding back his propensities to expand and grow. Goldstein had been the chief caretaker of Maryland's Triple A bond rating, a measure of creditworthiness conferred by Wall Street on governments that demonstrated fiscal prudence and restraint. Now Schaefer declared himself a born-again Triple A kind of guy. He was quick to say that he was not Louie, though, and presented himself as one who knew the ins and outs of state government generally, not in the specialized way Goldstein had known finance. Elected officials across the state were enthusiastic. "He locks," said state senator Tommy Bromwell of Baltimore County. (A "lock" was a certain winner.)

At a fund-raiser for Mary Dulany James, daughter of the state's former treasurer, the late William D. "Billy" James, Schaefer ambled down the fifteenth floor Center Club hallway to attend the party, wincing a bit on his bad knees and showing that he would not be the dogged campaigner Louie had been, but his blue eyes were dancing. So were the hearts of those who wanted Schaefer back in Annapolis. Three days later, his lieutenants, bankrollers, loyalists, and many of those who he had beaten at the polls over the years rallied at the East Baltimore truck stop conference center owned by John Paterakis, founder of H&S Bakery and a developer with an interest in getting casino gambling allowed at the Inner Harbor. Glendening's 1998 reelection platform included implacable resistance to new gambling of any kind, so Paterakis and others saw the former governor's candidacy as an opportunity to be heard in the state's highest councils once again. Moreover, Paterakis was an old Schaefer loyalist, a man who had always played the political game along with the bakery business and who might have taken his company out of the city in the 1980s but for Schaefer's pleading.

When the rally began, Nancy Grasmick called Schaefer a tonic to government and to political leaders because they knew he had the courage and the heart to give Maryland the leadership it needs. George Russell, who had railed against electing dummies in service to the divine right of bosses, came to speak glowingly of Schaefer, as did Billy Murphy, whom Schaefer had beaten in the 1983 race for mayor.

Steve Sachs, who had been trounced by Schaefer in the gubernatorial primary of 1986, called organizers of the rally repeatedly to ask whether he could speak. He told the crowd that Schaefer would be the perfect replacement for Goldstein and a perfect partner for the next governor, whoever he or she might be in 1998—pointedly referring to Glendening's primary opponent, Eileen Rehrmann. As Sachs's accolades flowed, Schaefer sat nearly stunned. "Oh, my," he said. "Oh, my." Former House of Delegates member Tim Maloney of Prince George's County observed that, since Schaefer had filed for comptroller, the stock market had gone up eighty points, the Orioles had won four straight games, and Maryland would have a new-old leader who was far more interested in raising test scores than in raising campaign funds. Said Schaefer, "There'll only be one governor. But I'll still be me. I know I had trouble with Louie when he wanted to limit how much money we spent. But I'll have a different job now."

The initial forecasts indicated that, in fact, he would have that job. All he and his team had to do was explain to Marylanders why they should take back as a rookie comptroller a man who was independent, sure, but a big spender, and a man whose mental health had seemed precarious and who seemed to have too little regard for checks on the power of individuals. Still, writers observed that Schaefer had a huge advantage over the remaining competitors, Baltimore's neophyte comptroller Joan Pratt and the GOP's range of hopefuls. Schaefer could raise plenty of money, and he had almost 100 percent name recognition. He would almost certainly be returned to public life even more vigorously and enthusiastically in the general election by Democrats *and* Republicans. Hadn't he endorsed Bush?

A poll that was taken immediately after Schaefer's declaration of candidacy in July 1998 suggested that Marylanders remembered him with a fondness that forgave, even understood, what had prompted the nasty letters, the photographs, and the snits. Only 3 percent of the 1,200-person sample polled by the *Sun* did not recognize his name. Some 64 percent remembered him with approval, a standing that came close to the exalted figures of his prime and were far ahead of those of Glendening and the Republican candidate for governor, Ellen Sauerbrey, both of whom were having trouble staying above 40 percent. A full 43 percent of the sample said that they would "definitely" support Schaefer. In March 1993, his approval rating had been no more than 16 percent by one survey, with a full 83 percent of Marylanders saying that they didn't much care for his governing. But voters are fickle creatures. By the time of his reentry effort, only 16 percent said that they would definitely be against him.

A few commentators, including Montgomery County's Blair Lee, wondered how the electorate could be so amnesic. "Once we sober up, we'll see that Don Schaefer is not Louie Goldstein," he said. Schaefer's opponents began immediately to suggest that the electorate was under no obligation to relieve its elder statesman of his retirement blues or to lift him up somehow to the grandeur he felt of old. And he certainly knew that. But the bandwagon was rolling, and he was waving to the crowd.

Glendening, who had refused to share the credit with Schaefer for Baltimore's NFL team, was getting all the blame for public spending to build a new stadium, and his approval rating stood far below Schaefer's. If there was perversity in the public's attitude, someone else was suffering it this time. Schaefer had resumed his position as the people's favorite. His support was strong statewide. In the city, 66 percent were in favor of his return. In Baltimore County, the figure was 56 percent; and in Howard, 48 percent. His support was slightly higher among African Americans than among whites, a finding that seemed to augur well for both the primary and the general election. He fared well among those whose personal finances were up or down. He was equally well regarded by liberals, independents, and conservatives. Schaefer's team felt validated once again in their belief that their leader had given them, their city, and the state a uniquely committed and honest leadership. The people had, more or less, caught up with the truth about Schaefer, they thought.

On August 25, Paterakis and Ed Hale, the banker, organized a fundraiser for Schaefer at Martin's West. LeBow-Sachs decorated the hall. She hung the red and white "Schaefer For Comptroller" banners, set out the bumper strips, and checked the guest list for the $1,000-a-head reception, at which more than two hundred people were expected. Now and then, as immersed as she was in the work she knew so well, she asked herself, "Am I really doing this?"

One of the many influential men who saw the inevitability of Schaefer's return was Furlong Baldwin, the Mercantile Bank man who had battled with him over so many issues when Schaefer was governor. One of Baldwin's friends, Louise Hayman, said that there was no mystery in Baldwin's presence: "He's a member of the pragmatist party, you know," she said.

Patriarch

A week after the campaign began, Schaefer threw his annual birthday dinner for Hilda Mae at D'Alesio's Restaurant in Little Italy. He presided as head of household, greeting guests, introducing them or reintroducing them or announcing them to his stricken friend, slumped in her wheelchair but looking, even in her debilitated state, as if she could and would like to have everyone for lunch. Schaefer called her Hilda Mae or Old Girl. She was, as usual, up for the program, ready to be there for the event, but looking a bit wary. She was frail and weak, her limbs narrowed to bone. Her guests wondered whether she was aware of anything going on around her. Dr. Platt, who sat with Raynor, said that her problems were largely circulatory. She was a smoker still, and her heart and lungs could not function efficiently. Her nurse, Zina Scheyer, occasionally hoisted her back into a sitting position. Zina had been a godsend, acting almost as a daughter to Hilda Mae. She was strong and willing to take her patient's periodic tongue lashings. "Hilda Mae fires her about twice a day, and Zina just laughs," Schaefer said.

These were Hilda Mae's friends, for the most part, though they were Schaefer's friends first. Nancy Grasmick had come with her husband Lou. Raynor was there. The late R Adam Cowley's wife Roberta, as Bobby, attended because Cowley, founder of Maryland's Shock Trauma Center at the University of Maryland Hospital, had been a close friend of both Schaefer and Hilda Mae. Roberta was a bit shell-shocked by the high circle her late husband had brought her to, but she was a genuine character like Raynor, Platt, Lou Grasmick, and all the rest of these intimates. Cowley had died seven years earlier, but when he was alive, he had loved Hilda Mae. Bobby reminded her, "My husband said if Schaefer hadn't met you before he did, he'd have been after you." Hilda Mae gave a big smile, a sign of life in the Old Girl.

Everyone else slid into Schaefer's seat for a moment to visit with the guest of honor, who was holding court even in decline. Brice Phillips, owner of the Phillips seafood houses, who had traveled to Baltimore in his Cadillac limousine, showed her a snapshot of himself with her in Moscow, a McDonald's in the background. They had been on a trip with Schaefer when he was governor. In the photo, Hilda Mae was smiling, radiant, more like the lovely young woman Schaefer had met on the Hill thirty years earlier. Marty Resnick, owner of the fund-raising venue known as Martin's West and caterer to Maryland politicians for forty years, arrived with his wife. Bruce Bereano came in with a huge white flowering chrysanthemum in a pasteboard box. Schaefer's former state police driver and bodyguard, Jim Spicer, and Larry Tolliver, the former superintendent of state police, and his wife Sheila, by then an Anne Arundel County councilwoman, arrived—Larry in shorts, Sheila in a business suit.

The candidate for comptroller, meanwhile, moved around the room taking pictures of the guests with his little flash camera and then sat with Lou Grasmick. Honey blond and wary-eyed, Grasmick was talking about the power of magnets to cure various ankle and knee ailments, a remedy that he recommended to the gimpy Schaefer, who couldn't figure out how to wear them and didn't try.

Grasmick really wanted to talk about how Nancy shouldn't be working so hard, how he would like her to retire. Once, at lunch with Schaefer and Raynor, Lou had pulled an hourglass out of his pocket to count the minutes he was away from his beloved. "Get that thing off the table," Schaefer had ordered. On this night, the former governor said that it would be a mistake for Grasmick to push his wife into retirement. "She will wilt like a rose," he said. Schaefer knew the hammer blows of inactivity, of power loss, of having nothing momentous to do. Once you have been a public servant, he said, once you have known the power and the prestige and the thrill of decision-making, you could not get it out of your system.

Not every recollection was shared with Hilda Mae. Out of her earshot, Raynor told a group of a breakfast meeting at the governor's mansion one morning with members of this very same special birthday crowd: Grasmick, Phillips and his wife, and Elmer Horsey, once the mayor of Chestertown and one of the keepers of a Schaefer slush fund, which had been used for mansion expenses. On the day recalled by Raynor, Hilda Mae had had history in mind, legacy. She wanted to raise money for a portrait.

"The state will pay for the governor's portrait," the assembled bankrollers told her somewhat wearily.

"I mean *my* portrait," she said.

They sat in silence.

"Don't you think the people of Maryland would like to see a portrait of the woman who made all these changes in the mansion?" she asked.

"No," said Raynor.

But the money was raised, and the Snoops portrait was done.

At the end of the evening, Schaefer and Zina put Hilda Mae in her car. He stood with the door open, making sure her seat belt was in place and her head was cushioned against the reclining seat. He kissed her good night and closed the door while Zina wrestled the wheelchair into the back seat. As Zina drove Hilda Mae away, he fretted angrily about her condition, a real damper on a big day. This was typical of Schaefer. He had been in the spotlight all day long, just as he had been when Harborplace had opened, when A. N. Pritzker had come to town for the Hyatt opening, at the seal pool, and on the first opening day at Orioles Park at Camden Yards. On that day, he had stood in front of 70,000 football fans at Raven's Stadium with no sense of crowning accomplishment, though his work had resulted in a $200 million stadium, the second of his career. He had labored for more than a decade to guarantee major league football for his city, and here it was. But if anything, he was a bit deflated. "It was done," he said, restating his well-tended suspicion of celebratory moments. What many people didn't understand was this: He was not ever building buildings. He was building momentum, progress, confidence—a feeling that could be sustained only by more building and even more good feeling. Therefore, *his* project would never be finished. "Everything we did, soon as it was over, you looked for the next thing to do. It was nice, though, today. Everybody walked by, [at the stadium], waving. You know, it makes you feel good. It was good."

The Covenant Restored

In the race for comptroller, candidate Schaefer hardly campaigned. His old team—Wasserman, LeBow, Douglas, Raynor, Sabatini, and assorted others—rallied around to run things. One of them told him sternly at the beginning of the fall that he was as good as elected if he could refrain from saying anything outrageous. No more outhouse remarks, nasty letters, or offensive hand signals, they said—as if they still didn't really know him, as if they had not tuned in on him much since the last days in Annapolis. Those who had spent time with him thought he had become a mellower man, a citizen finally who saw what a privileged life William Donald Schaefer had led.

"I still write letters in my head," he said. "When the *Evening Sun* died, I wanted to write the publisher and say, 'Why not make a clean sweep of it [and close the morning paper as well]?'"

But the letter writing had been forgiven and his earlier image as a selfless public servant came back into focus. Suddenly, he had the extraordinary status he had wanted in 1990 when he made his second run for governor. Now, finally, he could declare his intentions and be elected without a campaign. This was a good thing for him because, when he walked now, he looked as if his feet or his knees were anchored in broken glass. His side-to-side rocking gait looked excruciating, so the less it had to be seen, the better. This was not a problem. He appeared a few times with Glendening, coaching the governor and issuing report cards on his successor's performance. His team congratulated itself on fooling the known world by making their candidate seem so very energetic, so omnipresent, so youthful. Where would he have been without them?

With or without them, he would have been elected comptroller. It was a year when the people of Minnesota threw over Skip Humphrey, son of former vice president Hubert H. Humphrey, to elect a former professional wrestler. Skip had just won for the state a $4 billion settlement from the tobacco industry, a wonderful achievement, yet Minnesota chose Jesse "The Body" Ventura. Who could be shocked, then, if Marylanders picked a man to be comptroller who had virtually no qualifications for that particular job? So maybe the Shore was an outhouse after all. To give the voters credit, the cranky and independent Schaefer was being elected not so much to the post of comptroller as to the board of public works, a job for which he was probably more qualified than anyone else in Maryland, having served on that board for eight years when he was governor.

During the campaign, the *Sun* ran a feature page series of reminders for Marylanders who had not been on hand for the high jinks of Schaefer's heyday. One of its reporters did a story about the former governor's return to the Eastern Shore—for the inauguration of a new public restroom, of course. Every other newspaper also did a feature on the return of William Donald. A *Washington Times* reporter had breakfast with Schaefer at Jimmy's in Fells Point, his favorite retirement haunt, and then followed him on one of his campaign jaunts. Head in hand, leaning forward and looking tired, he told the reporter that he'd had no second thoughts. It wasn't true, of course. "If Lainy hadn't been walking around in elephant doodoo," he had said to his team, "I wouldn't be doing this." Even if she hadn't been in Africa, she couldn't have kept him out, she thought. "Glendening tried to push him out and then it became a challenge, and everyone got all excited," she said.

He wanted to be back, but he knew the price he would pay, the hard work and anguish he was in for. He knew the right public lines of course: "I can do this," he told the *Washington Times* reporter. "There isn't a learning process for me. I've been mayor. I've been governor. Louie's got a great office there. People know they'll get an honest shake. . . . You don't have to be an accountant. You have to be an administrator. I've been an administrator." But what if he lost? He said he could handle that. This was easy for him to say, since there was no way he could lose—almost as if the Big Chief Kovens were directing things once again. The money guys ponied up for Reflections '98, laying a cool half-million into his campaign account virtually overnight. Schaefer's Republican opponent, Larry Epstein, had won his party's primary by about a dozen votes, so Schaefer led a chorus of worried Democrats urging Marylanders to turn out. It could come down to a handful of votes again, he told the world.

On election day, Schaefer was the first to vote at Lemko House, a community center and elderly housing project he and Wasserman had nursed into being on South Ann Street when he was mayor. Then he headed, as he had for twenty-five years on election day, to Iggy's, a breakfast and sandwich joint in Little Italy. Schaefer and the gang had started eating there when one of its number had been shocked to learn he could not get ham and eggs at a kosher deli. On this day, Schaefer was joined by Lieutenant Governor Kathleen Kennedy Townsend, her daughter Maeve, her sister Rory Kennedy, and the usual election day crowd. That night, the gang gathered at the Harborview Hotel to watch the returns on television and to wait for Raynor's educated guesses about the outcome. On the basis of a few selected precincts, the former Baltimore elections chief could predict outcomes race by race. He sat in a room away from the rest of the crowd, away from Schaefer, and waited for his still-loyal poll-watchers to call.

Schaefer fretted. "Gene's not coming out," he said. "Why doesn't he come out? It's trouble."

LeBow-Sachs went into the room. "Give him some numbers, Gene," she said. "Make 'em up."

Raynor came out minutes later without trying too hard to build Schaefer's confidence. "Well, these numbers aren't great, but they're early and you're fine. Better than fine."

Schaefer, shaky as ever, made what was supposed to be a victory speech. He made it conditionally, as if he could still lose, thanking everyone he could think of, beginning with his mother and father, Mr. Kovens, Lainy, Zelig Robinson, and other members of his law firm. He was usually not nervous on election night, he said, as if it were a laugh line for the faithful. This time, he seemed to be saying, he really could have lost.

He won big, of course, though not as big as he had hoped. He took 63 percent of the vote to 37 percent for Epstein, a huge triumph for someone whose popularity had been in the teens when he left office four years earlier. His 26-percentage-point margin was wider than his 20-point victory margin over the Shepards in 1990. No other public official—not Mandel, not Goldstein, not any of the men whose portraits hung in the statehouse—could match his record.

The baker and businessman Paterakis ribbed him gently. "Do you really have to go to work with this job?" he asked. Was it possible that Boss Kovens's man had achieved the ultimate patronage deal: a no-show job? Paterakis knew, of course, that showing up was everything for Schaefer. He would show up before he had to. A week after the election, the comptroller-elect dropped in unannounced on the comptroller's Glen Burnie office to quiz a few of its staff, to see whether they were on the ball, serving the public and to begin finding out what exactly a comptroller's staff did. He demanded transition meetings with Louie's team in Annapolis. He noticed peeling paint on the flagpoles outside the treasury building's main entrance and ordered them refinished. Inside, he found a scrawny, lightless Christmas tree and asked why it was so meager. No lights were allowed under the regulations, he was told. A day later, though, there were lights. It wasn't the Washington Monument again, but it was bright and colorful.

His friends, egged on by Mandel, began taking bets on how long it would be before Schaefer and Glendening went to war on the board of public works. People had been saying for weeks that Maryland was about to become the only state in the union with two governors. Schaefer always deflected that talk, somewhat mischievously sometimes. "There's only going to be one governor," he'd say and then raise his hand as if the one he had in mind was William Donald Schaefer.

LeBow-Sachs planned a gala swearing-in party, inviting several hundred people to sit in the House of Delegates chamber as Schaefer returned to public life. Marvin Mandel and his wife Jeanne, who was in a wheelchair, robbed of her voice and virtually paralyzed by Lou Gehrig's disease, sat up front. Charlie Benton, Bob Douglass, Sally Michel, and many other members of the Schaefer crowd came to see the reascension of their old boss. During the ceremony, Hilda Mae was on the speaker's dais with him. Schaefer helped her to stand for the Pledge of Allegiance. He thanked the Goldstein family, sons and daughters of Louis, asking them to stand, and he thanked Jeanne Mandel for coming. He knew that she heard him because her right hand moved slightly in recognition. She had been with him in that very chamber's balcony twenty-three years earlier when his convention center bill, backed and pushed by Mandel as governor, passed on the last night of the 1976 assembly session.

In his speech, Schaefer said he had run into someone that morning who asked him if he was happy. "I'm never happy," he said. His friends laughed. Here was the old Schaefer. In a sense, he said, he felt as if he'd never left. He was picking up where he had left off four years earlier. He made pointed criticisms of Glendening and Schmoke, suggesting that he would have an agenda as comptroller that could make him a rival of both, ready to move into their business if they weren't adequately sensitive to his concerns.

A few weeks before—as if directed by the fates to tantalize Schaefer—Schmoke had announced that he would not run again for mayor of Baltimore. Schaefer immediately persuaded a few of his friends that he might try for a fifth term in the only job he'd ever really loved. He was half-serious. He rode through the city as he had always done but with more focus: "I wanted to see if there were any blocks I could save if I did go back to city hall," he said. The Schmoke administration was bulldozing bombed-out rowhouse blocks with no apparent plan for dealing with the pockmarked cityscapes. Schaefer spoke publicly about running, but mostly he was playing the old pol, stirring the pot—hoping by making himself available to coax Mfume into the contest. What he wanted for Baltimore, he said, was what he had always wanted—"somebody good." But Mfume walked away from a draft movement orchestrated in part by Schaefer.

Speculation flared again that Schaefer would run now. But he quickly said no. Some of Schaefer's backers wanted him to stay in the comptroller's post and on the Board of Public Works. And Lainy said he absolutely would not endure another campaign. She promised to clear her schedule of safaris and anything else that might take her away. His friends thought his capacity to campaign, even to govern, was undermined by his wobbly legs and by a decline, at age seventy-seven, in his legendary energy. He might not have another hurrah to give. Still, the option would be open until July 6, 1999, the filing deadline.

In a sense, there was, finally, nothing to run for. He had gotten into the comptroller's race because he wanted to serve—and to win one last measure of proof that he was wanted. Even he had no doubt of that respect now. He worried that pretending to be a candidate for mayor would call into question his promise to be a splendid comptroller. He was as ready as he could be for that challenge. For his seventy-seventh birthday, coming on the eve of his comeback election, he'd gotten a slate gray Brooks Brothers derby hat from Raynor. And his press secretary, Mike Golden, had given him a copy of *Accounting for Dummies*.

The reader will see that remembered dialogue has been used liberally, with the sources quoted by name in the text. These passages reflect the views of the speaker, and, to the extent possible, more than one participant in various conversations verified the discussions, action, and import of scenes and conversations.

Over more than twenty years of covering William Donald Schaefer for the *Baltimore Sun,* I interviewed him, his aides, his friends, and his associates often. For this book, I spoke with him at length on at least twenty occasions between 1994 and 1998, when it appeared to him and others that his public career had ended.

It is possible that some of those I interviewed would not have been as open and frank had they known that he would return to public office. If so, added candor should be to the advantage of history yet of little likely embarrassment either to the speaker or to Schaefer.

Chapter 1: "Dummy"

3   "You can't send a dummy . . ." *Baltimore Sun,* August 24, 1971.

7   "b'hoys." Variation on "boys," as in members of a political clubhouse, clan, group, or team; used derisively by editorial writers, pridefully by the b'hoys.

4   "Nothing more than a title search lawyer . . ." Author's interview with James Rouse.

7   "He's got to win this damn thing . . ." Author's interview with Ted Venetoulis.

10   "The house had a precise . . ." Author's interview with John Steadman.

14   "The 5a Class Presents . . ." Schaefer Collection, Maryland State Archives.

19   The story of Schaefer's mother turning down his covers is from the author's conversation with Leon Sachs.

22   The letter from Betty Wise Lonergan is in a Schaefer family album, Maryland State Archives.

25   ". . . slightly off my nut." More than thirty annotated or captioned photos of Lolita B. Cook ("Cookie") are in Schaefer's albums, Maryland State Archives.

28   "Pass the salt . . ." Schaefer was mortified at the recollection of his dinner

table expletive, but he told the story to a few friends, one of whom repeated it to the author.

Chapter 2: Apprenticeship

35 "An average life . . ." Accounts of Schaefer's life around Court Square after World War II are drawn from interviews with him and with one of his law partners, Judge Mary Arabian; their friend Milton Wisniewski; and others.

37 "You ought to take a look . . ." Former House of Delegates member and former circuit court judge Edgar P. Silver and Schaefer supplied accounts of their discussions with Irv Kovens about running for city council and for governor.

39 "Big John." *Baltimore Sun*, March 15, 1977.

39 "Strained mash." *Baltimore Sun*, January 16, 1923.

44 "Up-up." Remy Marks was a political type named not in Baltimore, but in Democratic Providence, Rhode Island, by the keen political observer Paul Goulding, an aide to former U.S. Senator Claiborne Pell. Such personages are also known as coat holders, retainers, body slaves, and gofers.

44 "Talent pool." A boss could elect a hack, to be sure, but Kovens and Pollack often felt a responsibility to run good candidates, men they could be proud of. "He knew I would never embarrass him," Schaefer said.

45 "Mr. Schaefer surely deserves re-election . . ." *Baltimore Sun*, April 1959.

47 Roosters and chickens, even goats, are often housed with high-strung race horses for company and to approximate barnyard life, providing a calming presence.

48 "Dad's down." According to the death certificate, Uncle Willie had been treated for heart problems for six years before his death.

48 "A bit of a nerd." Until then, no one had thought being a council member was a full-time job, but Saturdays and Sundays found Schaefer in his office. He accepted any assignment; at the same time, he was thought of as "disputatious," always ready for a fight.

51 "I think the citizens of this city . . ." *Baltimore Sun*, March 2, 1962.

54 "It seemed that this highway . . ." *The Baltimore Book: New Views of Local History*, ed. Elizabeth Fee, Linda Shopes, and Linda Zeidman (Philadelphia: Temple University Press, 1991), p. 147.

57 "I don't drink . . ." Author's interview with former mayor Thomas J. D'Alesandro III. Schaefer's announcement was more evidence of discipline, which was underappreciated by many in Baltimore, perhaps because his sometimes hilarious public relations escapades made him seem unrestrained.

Chapter 3: Schaefer's Turn

63 "He'd stand by . . ." Mildred Momberger, Maryland Historical Society's Oral History Project on the Baltimore civil rights years dominated by Theodore McKeldin and the African American leader Lillie Mae Jackson.

71 The "continuing campaign fund" tale is from an interview with Edgar Silver.

73 "The real possibilities." From Schaefer's basic campaign document, "Where I Stand," 1971.

75 "What conflict of interest?" Staszak's line was uttered in the presence of *Baltimore Sun* columnist Barry Rascovar, then a State House reporter.

78 The story of Venetoulis's meeting with Schaefer in Little Italy is from an interview with Venetoulis.

88 "I can't get 50 together." Author's interview with Elmer "Peck" Jones, chief clerk of the Baltimore city council.

90 "I never thought George should run . . ." William L. "Little Willie" Adams, Maryland Historical Society oral history project.

92 "Transparent honesty, appetite for municipal housekeeping . . ." *Evening Sun*, September 3, 1971.

Chapter 4: Charm City

95 The description of the parades is from Bert Smith, *Greetings from Baltimore* (Baltimore: Johns Hopkins University Press, 1996), p. 26.

98 "When you live in Baltimore . . ." William Gildea, *When the Colts Belonged to Baltimore: A Father and a Son, a Team and a Time* (1994; rpt. ed., Baltimore: Johns Hopkins University Press, 1996), p. 169.

98 "You're dead and rotten . . ." Francis B. Beirne, *The Amiable Baltimoreans* (Baltimore: Johns Hopkins University Press, 1984), p. 154.

98 "Unutterably charming . . ." Fred Hobson, *Mencken: A Life* (1994; rpt. ed., Baltimore: Johns Hopkins University Press, 1995), p. 76.

99 "Mile after mile . . ." Hobson, *Mencken*, p. 208.

101 "All too often . . ." Jo Ann E. Argersinger, *Toward a New Deal in Baltimore* (Chapel Hill: University of North Carolina Press, 1988), p. 57.

101 "Summoned by church bells . . ." Samuel G. Freedman, *The Inheritance* (New York: Simon & Schuster, 1996), p. 89.

103 "Wow, Mr. President . . ." Thomas J. Alesandro, Jr., "The Tommy Tapes," *Baltimore Evening Sun*, 1976.

104 "Loud and cantankerous . . ." Kweisi Mfume with Ron Stodghill, *No Free Ride: From the Mean Streets to Mainstream* (New York: Ballantine Books, 1996), p. 56.

105 "The armpit of the east . . ." *The Baltimore Book* (New Brunswick, N.J.: Temple University Press, 1995), p. 236.

105 "Three times before World War I . . ." *The Baltimore Book*, p. 235.

106 "Back from the war . . ." *The Baltimore Book,* p. 222.

106 "The rate of decay . . ." Clarence W. Miles with Jacques Kelly, *Eight Busy Decades: The Life & Times of Clarence W. Miles* (Queenstown, Md.: White Banks Press, 1986), p. 58.

107 "Unless radical action is taken . . ." Report of the Commission on Civic Arts, *Baltimore Sun,* November 1952.

111 Images of Bill "Sweetie Pie" Adelson are from Gene Raynor, Baltimore and Maryland elections administrator; Peter Marudas, an aide to Baltimore mayors and U.S. senators; and Marvin Mandel, the former governor.

113 The chronology of construction projects is from Barbara Bonnell's invaluable chronology of the city's urban renewal history, project by project, beginning with the report on declining tax revenue in 1952.

Chapter 5: Caretaker

116 "Never cross me . . ." This warning and other aspects of Schaefer's takeover as mayor are from the author's interviews with Schaefer, Joan Bereska, and others.

117 Dome anecdote is from G. Jefferson Price, foreign editor and former city hall reporter for the *Sun.*

123 "Actual or customary . . ." Author's interview with Charles L. Benton, finance director for Schaefer as mayor and later state budget secretary when Schaefer was governor.

128 Palughi's unorthodox greetings were reported by Bereska and Schaefer.

132 "Thanks . . ." The memo is from Bereska's files.

133 Bereska's friend Jim Beek, who worked in city hall for a time, had this observation about Schaefer's staff: "It was a little like the *Star Trek* crew: Everybody was brilliant and everybody was a little bit crazy."

132 Various memos are from Daryl Plevy.

136 The reported tacit agreement by which, politically, the schools would become the patronage territory of African Americans is lore reported by Superintendent Nancy Grasmick and in *Time,* October 27, 1998.

140 "But I wanted to be." Author's interview with Scott Livingston.

Chapter 6: The Cheerleader Cometh

143 Some of the steps taken as Schaefer imposed hope on a demoralized city came from Bailey Fine, his aide and former head of the Baltimore school board.

143 "Maybe we can survive . . ." Author's interview with Mark L. Joseph, president of Yellow Cab in Baltimore (not to be confused with the developer Mark K. Joseph, his cousin).

145 "Schaefer Begins Second Term," *Baltimore Sun,* December 3, 1975.

155 "What in the hell are you people . . ." Nicholas Lemann, *The Promised Land: The Great Black Migration and How it Changed America* (New York: Alfred A. Knopf: 1991), p. 167.

155 "Bent stick of a man . . ." Michael Olesker, *Baltimore Sun,* April 15, 1976.

155 Joan McQuade, Joe Coale, Bereska, and others gave accounts of the city hall shooting.

160 Elements of the new design are taken from Baltimore Department of Planning Outline of City Hall Renovations, p. 7. This work was supervised by Joanne McQuade, whose meticulous checking detected one door among several hundred in the building that opened in, not out as required by the fire code. McQuade saved Schaefer's political life in many ways and perhaps saved his physical life on the day of Charles Hopkins's rampage.

161 "I'd like you to be the HUD Secretary . . ." Author's interview with Bob Embry.

162 The city needed a luxury hotel, Schaefer and his advisors thought, but for a time they couldn't get much interest from hotel operators of any rank.

166 Stories of how hotel magnates and financiers were persuaded to take a chance on Baltimore came from M. Jay Brodie, Schaefer's development chief, and Schaefer's aide, Joan Bereska.

Chapter 7: Wild Man

170 HUD Secretary Romney's visit to Baltimore and Schaefer's visit to Romney's office were described by Jay Brodie, Baltimore's housing chief, and the developer Mark K. Joseph, then an aide to Schaefer.

171 Lucille Gorham's comment is from *The Baltimore Book,* p. 149.

172 "He cannot bring himself to do that . . ." Author's interview with Schaefer's friend Walter Sondheim.

173 "He knew better than to thank us . . ." Author's interview with the *Sun's* long-time editorial chief, Joseph R. L. Sterne.

176 Harborplace as the city's front porch was a formulation of Jay Brodie.

177 Rich Berndt, lawyer, political strategist, and Baltimore city father, kept detailed notes on his Harborplace campaign.

177 Furlong Baldwin's observation on the Harborplace referendum is from Berndt.

178 "Political center of gravity . . ." Laslo V. Boyd, "Political Power in a Referendum, Baltimore's Harborplace as a Case Study," University of Baltimore, 1985.

183 Trueschler concluded, in the end, that Schaefer was the most important Maryland politician of the half-century.

193 Interview with Evans by *Sun* reporter Sandy Banisky, fall 1994.

Chapter 8: Reinventing Main Street

194 "Cannons boomed . . ." *Baltimore Sun,* July 1, 1980.

199 "They were trying to get more money . . ." Author's interview with Willard Hackerman, the construction magnate and philanthropist, who almost never talked to reporters but agreed to offer accounts of his efforts on behalf of Schaefer at the Pyrolysis Plant, Hackerman House, and the Pulaski Highway Incinerator rescue effort.

199 The Shadow Government series was written by the author, then a city hall reporter for the *Sun.*

199 "He thinks he knows what's best for us . . ." The CPHA's Frances Froelicher's comments appeared in a *Sun* article.

200 "You just can't win . . ." *Baltimore Sun,* April 20, 1980.

215 "Blankie." Plevy and LeBow-Sachs rose in the Schaefer firmament as Bereska fell. Schaefer says that he never lost faith in Bereska's ability, but she began to slip as the undisputed leader of what Richard Ben Cramer called "the all girl gestapo."

Chapter 9: "The Best Damned City"

221 "I have never seen the equal of Schaefer." *Baltimore Evening Sun,* September 12, 1983.

226 "I saw a side of him . . ." Mfume and Stodghill, *No Free Ride,* p. 250.

233 Baltimore's public golf courses, like the voting machines and the water-metering system, were rescued with the help of Baltimore Gas & Electric. A BGE man named Henry Miller put the golf courses under sound management control, and they began to make a profit even with very low greens fees.

235 "I was trying to bear the image of the corpse . . ." Gildea, *When the Colts Belonged to Baltimore,* p. 2.

Chapter 10: Moving On

244 "Modell and Schaefer met secretly . . ." Jon Morgan, *Glory for Sale* (Baltimore: Bancroft Press, 1998), p. 4.

251 "I have to get to court . . ." This exchange was reported by Edgar Silver.

254 "I was so pleased . . ." Author's interview with Steve Sachs.

255 "Look me in the eye . . . I have it on tape." Doug Birch, *Baltimore Evening Sun,* July 17, 1986.

258 "It was not aimed at Schaefer . . ." Author's interview with Blair Lee.

260 "Hatfields and McCoys . . ." This scene is from an interview with Robert DiPietro.

262 "Rot beneath the glitter . . ." From "Baltimore 2000," an assessment of the city's prospects sponsored by the Goldseker Foundation, 1987.

Chapter 11: A Gift

271 "Farewell you pompous clown." *Baltimore Sun,* January 21, 1987.

272 "Why does he think . . ." David Iannucci's observations are from an interview with the author, March 1993.

273 "Please take me back . . ." Author's interview with Linda Rossi.

274 "The whole import . . ." Author's interview with Dr. Ed Papenfuse, July 1997.

274 Mark K. Joseph's comments are from an interview with the author, July 1998.

277 "You're not married . . ." Author's interview with Herb Belgrad.

283 "Okay, you've got me . . ." From a variety of sources.

286 "Would you like to rest . . ." Author's interview with Rifkin.

290 "Would you like me to kiss . . ." Author's interview with Timothy Maloney.

Chapter 12: Homeless

293 Comments by David Iannucci and Walter Sondheim are from interviews with the author.

293 "She wouldn't look at you . . ." "It's Not Easy to Be Hilda Mae," *Baltimore* magazine, May 1991, p. 50.

293 Schaefer confided wearily and understatedly to a *Sun* reporter that Mrs. Snoops could be a bit headstrong.

298 "A beacon of inspiration . . ." Official declaration of the state, 1988.

299 "It got acidic . . ." *Baltimore* magazine, May 1991, p. 50.

300 "Blue, bland and boring . . ." *Baltimore Sun,* December 30, 1990.

303 "Go over to so and so . . ." Author's interview with Vincent DeMarco.

306 "Done with care . . ." Observations by Dr. Papenfuse are from an interview with the author.

Chapter 13: Tailspin

316 "What we consciously . . ." Schaefer's 1990 reelection strategy, its abrupt revisions, and its subsequent execution were recounted by Schaefer aide Gary Thorpe, an all-purpose adviser and later member of the Maryland Public Service Commission; Marvin Bond of the comptroller's office; and others.

317 Washington's Farewell Address, December 23, 1783.

322 "There were days . . ." Author's interview with Lainy LeBow-Sachs.

323 "I believe!" Author's interview with Bailey Fine, one of Schaefer's aides. Schaefer acknowledged a strong attachment to Bob Harrington, an evangelist and friend of Blaze Starr.

326 "This is the essence . . ." Papenfuse.

Chapter 14: Hitting Bottom

338 "I'm mad as hell . . ." Author's interview with Bruce Poole, March 1998.

346 "He's the President . . ." Reported to the author by Tim Phelps, former *Sun* reporter and now foreign editor of *Newsday,* who spoke with Schaefer before the Clinton lunch.

347 "He humiliated me . . ." Author's conversation with Page Boinest, a Schaefer press secretary.

351 "My good man . . ." Author's interview with Paul Schurick.

352 Accounts of Schaefer's continuing efforts to land a professional football team are drawn from interviews with the *Sun*'s Jon Morgan, former Baltimore County Executive and Schaefer friend Ted Venetoulis, Orioles principal owner Peter Angelos, former C&P Telephone's Hank Butta, and others.

353 "I'm just a poor boy . . ." Author's interview with Peter Angelos.

Chapter 15: The Return of the Native

364 "His hands trembled as mine would have . . ." From Schaefer's First Citizen Award remarks, President's Day, 1996.

366 "The hero" quote is from Theodore Roosevelt.

375 "He could file . . ." Had Schaefer arrived a few minutes earlier, he would have seen a cortege of official vehicles bearing Goldstein's body back to southern Maryland for his funeral. Worried already about appearing to capitalize on Goldstein's death, he might not have filed at all.

376 "He locks . . ." Senator Bromwell's observation was made to the author at the fund raiser for Mary Dulany-James, April 1998.

377 "Once we sober up . . ." Blair Lee's observation is from his newspaper column in the *Montgomery Journal,* July 15, 1998.

380 "The State will pay . . ." Comments from Mrs. Snoops's birthday party were made to the author, who was present at the party.

1. *Do* sweat the small stuff: "I knew the bridge would be built. I didn't know if the trees would be trimmed," he said.

2. "Do it now": Start. Also, beware of planners.

3. Do not set priorities: Everything is critical and essential. Identify your strengths and consolidate them. Define your problems and go after all of them with everything you have. "Time is not on our side," he said.

4. Follow up: You're dealing with human beings, no matter how talented. Put one of your best people in charge of following up—someone whose sole responsibility is to check up on progress—to see, for example, whether the work has started.

5. Build strength/build *on* strength: Never simply give in to demands. Ever. Get something in return because you must have the investment of people. If there's nothing to build on, you will fail—and waste money.

6. Demand ideas/use ideas: Leadership is finding talented people and proving to them that ideas will be tried. That recognition will put a further dimension of responsibility in play: He's going to do this, so it better be good or we'll all be embarrassed.

7. Stand by your women: Instinctively, he believed that women were better team players, more loyal, less ego-driven. After she was challenged by state government unions, Schaefer's director of juvenile services Linda Rossi had to keep him from firing unhappy union members. "Governor," she said, "we still have to run this place."

8. Practice pragmatism, especially when it hurts: Defeated by neighborhood groups in his effort to build a better highway to and from Baltimore, he met with his tormentors and proclaimed himself a member of their team. Though he endorsed George Bush for President in 1992, he went to a gala luncheon thrown by President-elect Bill Clinton at the Library of Congress.

9. Avoid what he called the "residue" of failure. Act quickly when possible, but wait for the right moment. The failure of good ideas for whatever reason leaves a new level of opposition beyond the mere merits.

10. Act out: Most people will back down in the face of outrageous behavior. Don't worry when they accuse you of throwing tantrums. When you're right, you're right. And you're always right.

Abortion rights, 347
Abramson, Leon, 37, 46, 50
Ackerman, Charles, 162–63, 165
Acting mayor, Schaefer as, 61
Ad Council, 217
Adams, William L. (Little Willie), 3, 5, 42, 73, 74, 90
Adelson, Bill (Sweetie, Sweetie Pie, Sweets), 70, 111–12
Afro-American (Baltimore), 180, 221
Agnew, Spiro T., 58–60, 73, 86–87, 112, 367, 373
Albright, Jody, 168, 293
Alder, Louise (Goldilocks), 178, 180–81, 312
All-Star game at Orioles Park (1993), 339–40
Ameche, Alan, 235, 241
American Legion, 29
Americans for Democratic Action, 108
Amey, Edgar, 13
Amiable Baltimoreans, The, 98
Angelos, Peter, 44, 49, 349, 352–54, 357
Applefeld, Floraine, 224–25
Aquarium, 65, 151, 177, 202, 204–10, 294, 340
Arabian, Mary, 29–30, 32–34, 36, 135, 143, 213, 214
Argersinger, Jo Ann E., 101
Army service, 14, 22–28, 127
Arts: in Baltimore, 101, 167–68, 202; Baltimore High School for the Arts, 168; Baltimore Museum of Art, 167, 340; Baltimore Symphony Orchestra, 19, 183, 189, 203; Morris Mechanic Theater, 110, 113, 134; Municipal Art Society, 107; University of Mary-

land performing arts center, 291; Walters Art Gallery, 202, 340
Association of Commerce, 188
Athey, Tyras (Bunk), 328–29
Awards after retirement from public office, 370–71

Babe Ruth Museum and Birthplace, 340
Babusci, Frankie, 260
Baker, Jim, 343
Baker, Will, 22
Baldwin, Billy, 299
Baldwin, H. Furlong, 177, 187, 232, 233, 266, 352, 378
Ballot tailoring, 42
Baltimore & Ohio Railroad, 100
"Baltimore 2000" report, 262–65
Baltimore Beltway construction, 54
Baltimore Board of Elections, 79
Baltimore Book, The, 105–6
Baltimore Boys Choir, 145
Baltimore City: the Block in, 30, 32, 96, 128–30, 340; Board of Estimates of, 119, 130–31, 204; bosses of, 3–6, 39–40, 83; budget issues in, 119, 120, 126, 131; Fifth councilmanic district of, 35–37, 41, 46, 49, 52, 312; First councilmanic district of, 52; Fourth councilmanic district of, 40, 41, 45; parking in, 247–48; population of, 262–64; pothole repair in, 245–47; poverty in, 53, 84, 101, 113, 160, 169–70, 220, 263, 265, 319, 344–45
Baltimore City, opinions of, 94–100, 103–5; derogatory, 82, 96–98, 103–5; Mencken's, 98–100; Schaefer's, 94–96, 113–14, 143–45, 166, 264–65

Baltimore City business district, 94–96,
181; Charles Center, 108–9, 121,
165, 181, 187, 194, 195; deterioration of, 107–8; Harborplace, 97,
147, 175–181, 194–195, 221. *See
also* Baltimore City preservation and
renewal
Baltimore City Council, 3, 6; election in
1959, 45–46; in 1950s, 6, 44; "reorganizations" of, 71; Schaefer's first
term on, 43–45; Schaefer's presidency
of, 56–57, 61, 66, 72, 115; Schaefer's
second term on, 48–51
Baltimore City Hall, 115, 155; Ceremonial
Room of, 159, 183; renovation of,
153–54, 158–59; shootings in (1976),
153–58
Baltimore City neighborhoods, 104–5, 116,
145–50; Embry's work with, 161–62;
Mayor's stations in, 224; partnerships
with, 155; preservation and renewal
of, 104–5, 145–50, 170–71; Schaefer's commitment to, 145–50, 187,
357
Baltimore City preservation and renewal,
32, 69, 72, 79–80, 104, 143; Baltimore City Hall, 153–54, 158–59; Baltimore neighborhoods, 104–5, 145–
50, 170–71, 357; the Block, 128;
Camden Yards sports stadiums, 178,
202, 258, 276–89, 339–40; Charles
Center, 108–9, 121, 165, 181, 187,
194, 195, 265; convention center,
150–53, 202; creating partnerships
for, 154; creating public approval for,
149–50; Department of Housing and
Community Development, 121;
Embry's contributions to, 44, 121,
161–62, 165, 170; financing of, 148,
153–54, 160–61, 164–66, 169–74,
181–83, 196–202; Greater Baltimore
Committee, 107–10, 113, 175, 180,
181, 186, 200; hotel construction,
162–66, 219, 228–30; Inner Harbor
area, 162–66, 174–81, 194; Lexington Market, 127; National Aquarium, 65, 151, 177, 202, 204–9; in
1960s, 112–13; in 1980s, 228–29;
"Outer City Conservation Program,"
79–80; plethora of projects for, 197;

project-by-project approach to, 148–
50, 182; public opinion and fear of
Baltimore in 1971, 82; Rouse's contributions to, 4–5, 107–8, 148–49, 175–
79; Schaefer taking credit for, 368–
69; Schaefer's "edifice complex,"
113–14, 210; Schaefer's holding
actions during, 193; Stirling Street
Renewal Area, 138–40; subway sys-
tem, 151–53, 228; "urban pioneers,"
139
Baltimore Colts, 109, 235–44, 351
Baltimore Development Corporation, 121,
161
Baltimore Emergency Relief Commission,
101
Baltimore Gas & Electric Company (BGE),
188–89
Baltimore High School for the Arts, 168
Baltimore magazine, 371
Baltimore Museum of Art, 167, 340
Baltimore Orioles, 10, 44, 69, 107, 189–
91, 217, 235, 244, 265, 352
Baltimore Ravens, 363
Baltimore School Board, 51
Baltimore Symphony Orchestra, 19, 183,
189, 203
Baltimore Urban Renewal and Housing
Agency, 69
"Baltimore's Best/Baltimore Is Best," 218,
225
"Baltimore's Gift to the State," 271
Banisky, Sandy, 359
Bank holidays, 102
Barnes, Michael D., 329, 373–75
Barry, Marion, 309
Bascom, Marion, 60, 62, 371–72
Baseball stadium, 149, 151, 190–92, 202,
258; Memorial Stadium, 151, 190,
192, 235, 239, 251, 258, 288–89;
naming of Camden Yards stadium,
339; passage of bill for Camden Yards
stadium, 276–89
Baseball team, 10, 44, 69, 107, 189–91,
217, 235, 265
Beirne, Francis B., 98
Belgrad, Herbert J., 277–79, 288–89, 318,
349, 363
Belushi, Jim, 339
Bennett, Richard D., 336

Bentley, Helen Delich, 341–42, 352–53
Benton, Charles, 122–29, 150, 152, 159, 184–86, 196–98, 203–5, 229, 259, 272, 276, 280, 312, 333, 335–36, 370, 384
Bereano, Bruce, 335–36, 361, 379
Bereska, Joan Burrier (Dragon Lady), 18, 47–48, 50, 56–57, 67–68, 74, 77, 116–19, 122–24, 128–33, 159, 173, 177, 206, 207, 214–16, 245–47, 312
Berman, Edgar, 67
Berndt, Rick (German general), 154, 177–81, 185, 224, 253, 255, 260, 261, 301, 302, 304, 312
Berry, Raymond, 235, 241
Bertorelli, Joe, 117
Beuchelt, Walter Eric, 116–19, 123, 124, 146, 214
Bible reading, 10, 12, 323
Biddison, Tom, 229–30
Birch, Doug, 255
Bishop Cummins Memorial Reformed Episcopal Church, 12, 33, 35, 308, 323
Black Panther Party, 82
Blatop, Bill, 82
Blockbusting, 106
Blue Chip-In, 233
Bohemian Pleasure Clubs, 88
Bomb shelters, 275
Bond, Marvin, 316
Bond issues, 197
Bond rating of state, 281, 376
Bonvegna, Joe, 158
Boosterism, 208–9, 326–27
Booth, John Wilkes, 144
Bopps family, 13
Borders, William, 145
Bosses of Baltimore, 3–6, 39–40, 83
Boucher, William, III, 64, 66–67, 72, 74, 108, 180
Bozman, Bennett, 320–21, 326
Bradlee, Ben, 362
Bradley, Bill, 328
Brady, Sarah, 303–4
Brady Bill, 304
Brandeis University, 371
Brantly Baptist Church, 7, 12
"Breakfast with the Experts," 83
Brewster, Danny, 32

Bright, Emma Gaskins, 53, 60, 312
Briscoe, John Hanson, 152, 153
Brodie, Jay, 163–65, 170–71, 220
Broening, William F., 116
Bromwell, Tommy, 376
Brown, Benjamin L., 120
Brown, Jerry, 304
Budget issues: during 1991 recession, 330–37; in Baltimore, 119, 120, 126, 131; unpaid furloughs for state employees, 334–35
Bumbry, Al, 217
Bush, George, 300, 302, 304–5, 332, 333, 372; Schaefer's 1992 endorsement of, 342–45, 377
Business connections of Mayor Schaefer, 66–67, 74, 181–87, 232–33, 257, 265
Butler, Thomas B., 108
Butta, Hank, 183, 232–34, 240, 348–49
Byrd, Harry C. H. (Curley), 125

Cade, Jack, 160
Calvert Cliffs nuclear plant, 188
Camden Yards sports stadiums, 178, 202, 258, 276–89, 358; All-Star game at Orioles Park (1993), 339–40; consideration of dual-purpose stadium, 278; financing of, 279–83, 287–89, 335; naming of baseball stadium, 339; purchase of land for, 278; value in search for new NFL team, 349; Williams' support for, 284–89, 339, 340
Camp David, 342, 344
Campaign fund raising, 66–67, 72; Reflections, 85, 315, 383; in Schaefer-Russell race, 74, 77, 85
Capital Center, 278
Caplan, Harry, 88
Caplan, Reuben, 40–41
Cardin, Benjamin L., 150, 152, 160, 251–53, 259, 310, 362
Carey, Eleanor, 365
Carrick, Julian (Fats), 87–88
Carroll, John S., 211
Carter, Dixie Lee, 346
Carter, Jimmy, 44, 162, 230, 277, 304, 372
Casey, Bob, 347
Casino gambling, 376
Center Club, 67

Charles Center, 108–9, 121, 165, 181, 187, 194, 195, 265
Charles Center-Inner Harbor Management Office, 121
Charm City, 94–101, 246
Chauffeurs, 129–30
Chernoff, Michael, 239, 241–42
Chesapeake Bay, 21–22, 44, 279, 332, 358
Chesapeake Bay Bridge, 111
Chesapeake Bay Foundation, 356
Christmas, city celebration of, 122–23, 133, 384
Citizens' advisory committees, 199–200
Citizens Planning and Housing Association (CPHA), 5, 29, 47, 72, 73, 199–200
City College, 16–17, 135
City Fair, 218
Civic pride, 144–45, 266
Civil defense plan, 275
Civil rights, 44, 49–53, 58–59, 65, 80, 105–6, 155. See also Racial issues
Civiletti, Benjamin R., 277, 278
Clark, Jim, 160
Clarke, Mary Pat, 147, 155, 177, 362
Cleveland Browns, 350, 363–64
Clinton, Bill, 5, 309, 325, 340–47, 375
Clinton, Hillary, 341, 343, 346
Coale, Joe, 155
Cold Spring, 198, 200
"Colossus of state politics," 251
Columbia, Maryland, 149, 175
Colwill, Stiles Tuttle, 299–300
Commission on Government Efficiency and Economy, 107
Committee Against The Gun Ban, 302
Committee for Downtown, 107
Community Action Agency, 169
Community development, 7, 45
Community health programs, 366
Commuter trains, 252
Comprehensive Employment and Training Act (CETA), 119, 230–31
Comptroller of the Treasury, Schaefer's campaign for, 372–85
Cone, Claribel, 101, 167
Cone, Etta, 101, 167
Constitution (Atlanta), 84
Convention Bureau Advisory Committee, 220
Convention center, 150–53, 202, 362

Cook, Lolita B. (Cookie), 25–28
Cooke, Jack Kent, 350–54
Coolahan, John (Lion of Halethorpe), 160
Cornish, Monroe, 145, 259
Cosell, Howard, 251
Cowley, R Adam, 379
Cowley, Roberta, 379
Crane, Charles P. (Skipper), 108, 188
Criticism of Schaefer, 201, 221; by D'Alesandro, 61–64, 124; Don Donaldo Ring Cycle, 336–37; for purchase of Tilghman Island property, 307–8; by Rouse, 4–7; self-criticism, 338
Crooks, Robert, 210
Culotta, Samuel, 68, 180
Cuomo, Mario, 328
Curkey, James Michael, 120
Curley, Michael J., 102
Curran, Joe, 156–158, 160, 301, 304
Curran, Joe, Jr., 158, 160, 301, 303, 332–33, 337, 359
Curran, Willie, 40, 69

D'Alesandro, Thomas J., III (Young Tommy), 5, 20, 34–35, 39, 41, 56–58, 60–64, 71, 82, 83, 89, 117, 124, 135, 146, 154, 182, 250; burnout and retirement of, 63–64, 73; criticism of Schaefer by, 61–62, 124; stand on racial issues, 62–64
D'Alesandro, Thomas J., Jr. (Old Tommy), 5, 20, 34–35, 39, 45, 60, 102–3, 168, 187, 210–11
Daley, Larry, 197–98, 259
Daley, Richard, 64–65, 154, 347
Darden, Alonzo, 24
Davis, Eddie, 22
De Francis, Joe, 239, 240
DeFilippo, Frank, 151, 312
Deinstitutionalization of mental patients, 324
Della, George W., 176–177
DeMarco, Vinnie, 302–4
Democratic Club, 37
Dialysis program, 334
DiPietro, Bobby Jo, 252–53, 260–61, 312
Disharoon, Leslie, 233
"Do it now" approach, 215, 371
Dobson, Rev. Vernon S., 180
Docter, Charles A., 152

Don Donaldo Ring Cycle, 336–37
Donovan, Artie, 235
Dorf, Paul, 45–46, 249
Dorsey, John, 300
Douglas, Robert C., 280, 284, 318, 358, 374, 381, 384
Douglass, Robert, 139
Drug abuse in Baltimore, 82, 169
Duff, Charles B., Jr., 149, 150, 187–88, 312
Dukakis, Michael, 205, 300–302, 304–5
Dulles, Allen, 144
Dump sites, 184–86, 198–99
Duncan, Douglas M., 373
Dundalk Marine Terminal, 96

Eagleburger, Lawrence, 332
Eastern Shore of Maryland: pfiesteria outbreak on, 382; "Reach the Beach" project on, 358; voting in 1990 election, 318–21
Eckman, Charlie, 16
Edelman, Leon, 37, 44, 50
"Edifice complex," 113–14, 210
Education issues, 51, 69–70, 82, 135–38, 168, 258, 263–64, 357–58
Eisenhower, Dwight David, 68, 261
Elkins, Wilson H., 125
Elkridge Club, 107
Embry, Robert C., Jr., 4, 44, 61, 66, 72, 74–75, 83–84, 121, 143, 161–62, 165, 170–72, 183, 220, 224, 229, 304
Eminent Domain Bill, 239, 242
Employment issues, 100–101
Eney, H. Vernon, 20, 181, 192, 224, 238, 284, 354
Entitlement programs, 170
Environmental issues, 255, 257, 279, 300, 355–56; "2020" program, 309, 329
Erickson, Milton, 33
Ethnic festivals, 225–26
Evans, Randy, 193, 212

Family Assistance Plan, 170
FanFest (1993), 340
Fawley, Chuck, 130, 193
Federal Hill area of Baltimore, 140
Federal Housing Act of 1959, 110, 140
Federalism, 121, 196
Feinblatt, Eugene, 163, 289, 360

Finan, Thomas B., 86
Financing for Baltimore projects, 148, 153–54, 160–61, 164–66, 169–74, 181–83; Benton's role, 203–5; by businesses, 232–33; "creative," 196–202; in 1970s, 230–31; in 1980s, 231–33
Financing for state projects: Camden Yards stadiums, 279–83, 287–89; health care, 331–33; University of Maryland, 291; "windfall" from federal tax reform bill of 1986, 281–82
Fine, Bailey, 134, 143, 168, 181, 213, 217–18, 323
Finney, George, 76
Finney, Jervis S., 76
Finney, Redmond C. S., 76–77
"First Citizen," 364
Fitzgerald, Carroll, 156, 158
Flannery, Tom, 258
Flowers, Gennifer, 309
Football stadium, 237–41; Cooke's desire for new football stadium in Maryland, 351–52; passage of bill for Camden Yards stadium, 276–89
Football team: Baltimore Colts, 109, 235–45, 351; Baltimore Ravens, 363; pursuit of new NFL team, 348–55, 363–64, 381
Ford, Gerald R., Jr., 372
Fort McHenry, 340
Fowler, Jeri, 23, 28, 227, 271, 297, 298
Frederick, George R., 158
Freeman, Lawrence, 259
Froelicher, Frances M., 199–200
Furloughs for state employees, 334–45

Gaigler, Anna Mae, 227
Gaither, Thomas, 156
Gallagher, Francis X., 73
Gambling, 335–37, 376
Garrett, John Work, 100
Generosity, 10
"Genius mayor," 251
Gephardt, George, 189
Gibson, Larry, 62, 90, 136, 224, 254, 362, 367
Gifts given to Schaefer, 308–9
Gilchrest, Wayne, 342
Gilman School, 76, 140, 178
Glauber, Bill, 238

Glendening, Parris N., 301, 329, 359, 362–66, 372–78, 382, 385
Golden, Mike, 385
Goldseker Foundation report, 262–65
Goldstein, Louis L., 301, 316, 330–31, 366, 372, 375–76, 384
Golf courses, 233
Goodman, Phillip H., 37, 46, 52, 56, 60, 71
Goodpaster, Andrew J., 362–63
Gore, Albert, 341
Gorham, Lucille, 170–71, 173, 195, 312
Government House Trust, 299
Government Services Agency, 110
Governor's mansion in Annapolis: fountain on grounds of, 305–7; Hughes' decorating of, 299; relandscaping of grounds of, 305; Snoops living in, 292–94; Snoops' redecorating of, 299–300
Governor's Mansion Trust, 299
Grady, J. Harold, 41, 56, 83, 146
Grantley Improvement Association, 5, 29
Grasmick, Lou, 73, 379, 380
Grasmick, Nancy, 135, 137–38, 357, 376, 379, 380
Great Depression, 10, 20, 35, 55, 60, 69, 101, 253
Greater Baltimore Committee (GBC), 64, 107–10, 113, 175, 179–81, 186, 200, 370
Green, Abraham, 12
"Green bag" appointments, 88
Greenmount (Green Mount) Cemetery, 144
Griffey, Ken, Jr., 339
Griisser, Fred, 302, 316
GTECH lottery contract, 335–36
Gun control legislation, 158, 300–304

Habitat for Humanity, 372
Hackerman, Willard, 186, 199, 202–3, 266, 278
Hague, Frank, 120
Haldeman, Bob, 229–30
Hale, Ed, 360, 361, 378
Haller, Keith, 251
Harbor Court Hotel, 230
Harbor tunnel, 97
Harborplace, 97, 147, 175–81, 202, 340; approval of, 181; campaign for, 179–81; criticisms of, 221; new jobs related to, 220; opening of, 194–95; opposition to, 176–81
Harrar, Haywood, 263
Harrington, Bob, 323
Harris, Pat, 162
Hartman, Chris, 206, 208–10, 294, 355
Harvey, F. Barton, III, 189
Hatch Act, 77
Hayman, Louise, 378
Head Start program, 344
Health care financing, 331–34
Hicks, Louise Day, 64
Hillman, Bob, 84, 178, 224, 344
Hillman, Sandy, 84, 216, 224, 259
Historic Preservation Commission, 73
"Hit Men," 324
Hocker, George, 70–71, 111, 311
Hoffberger, Jerry, 108, 189, 284
Hoffman, Janet, 150–52, 160–61, 183, 227, 370
Holbrook, Hal, 346
Hopkins, Charles A., 155–58
Hopkins, Johns, 96, 101
Horsey, Elmer, 380
Hotel construction in Baltimore, 162–66, 219, 228–30, 357
Houck, Jim, 256
Household income, 263, 331
Housing issues in Baltimore, 7, 44, 79, 106, 107, 110, 121, 161–62, 169, 193; Department of Housing and Urban Development and, 169–72; federally subsidized housing, 161; Stirling Street homesteaders, 138–40
Houston Oilers, 353
Hoyer, Steny H., 160, 362
Hubble, John D., 145
Hudnut, William, 243
Hughes, Harry, 28, 153, 211, 227, 234–36, 239, 240, 252, 257, 277, 278, 289, 299, 300, 307, 346, 347, 359, 367
Hughes, Pat, 299, 306
Humphrey, Hubert H., 67, 382
Humphrey, Skip, 382
Hunt, H. L., 348
Hunt, Lamar, 348
Hunt, Nelson (Bunker), 348
Hurricane Agnes, 128
Husted, Stephen C., 108

Hutchins, Diane, 90
Hyatt Regency Hotel, 163–66, 219, 220, 229

Iannucci, David, 272, 273, 276, 278–80, 284–86, 294, 373
Incinerator, 186, 199
Inner Harbor area of Baltimore, 32, 109, 110, 113, 121, 143, 162–66; hotel construction in, 162–66; Rouse's proposal for development of, 97, 147, 174–81. *See also* Baltimore City preservation and renewal; Harborplace
Intergovernmental relations, 65, 120–22
Intermodal Surface Transportation Efficiency Act, 338–39
Inventory tax, 210–11
Irsay, Robert, 236–44, 278, 283, 284, 348–51, 354, 364

Jackson, Howard, 35, 101, 102
Jackson, Jesse L., 90, 222, 339
Jacobs, Eli, 289, 339, 352
James, Mary Dulany, 376
James, William D., 376
Jefferson, Thomas, 319
Job appointments, 88, 117–18
Jobs and joblessness in Baltimore, 101, 169, 220, 263; Public Service Employment (PSE) program, 231–32
Johns Hopkins Hospital, The, 97, 203, 340, 344
Johns Hopkins University, The, 360
Johnson, Lyndon B., 53, 58, 60, 76, 104, 154, 169
Jones, Paula Corbin, 309
Jones, Peck, 87–89, 223, 312
Jordan, Michael, 339
Joseph, Mark K., 7, 55, 83, 86, 109, 138, 171, 172, 174, 178, 212, 224, 263, 266, 267, 271, 274
Joseph, Mark L., 143, 219, 220, 224
Joyner, Florence Griffith, 339
Jubilee Baltimore, 149, 187
Junior Boy's Brigade, 12
Juvenile detention centers, 273

Kallaugher, Kevin, 336, 340
Kansas City Chiefs, 348

Katkow, Herman, 295
Keelty, James, 9
Keinzle, Anita, 227, 271, 297, 298
Kelly, Pam, 248, 342, 345
Kemp, Jack, 231
Kennedy, John F., 78, 100, 259
Kennedy, Robert F., 117
Kennedy, Rory, 383
Keno gambling, 335–37
Kerrey, Bob, 292
Kidney program, 334
King, Martin Luther, Jr., 51, 53, 57–58, 62, 228
"King of Concrete," 83
Knott, Henry J., 184–85, 192, 198–99, 203, 204, 230
Kopp, Nancy, 261
Kovens, Irvin (Big Chief; Furniture Man), 3–6, 37–39, 41–43, 45–47, 49, 56, 60, 66–69, 90, 111, 114, 120, 129, 162, 187, 227, 255, 345, 349, 354, 373, 383; death of, 311–13; gifts from, 68–69; grand jury indictment of, 151, 249–50; management of Schaefer's 1971 campaign, 66–68, 74–76, 86, 89, 92–93; Schaefer's loyalty to, 249, 255; support for Schaefer's building projects, 151–52; support for Schaefer's candidacy for governor, 249–51, 255, 260
Kuchta, Frank, 182, 183

La Guardia, Fiorello, 251, 346–47
Labor relations problems, 100–101
Lacy, Jim, 81
Lanahan, W. Wallace, 108, 189
Land preservation, historical, 338–39
Landfills, 184–86, 198–99
Landow, Nathan, 341–42
Lane, William Preston, 3, 40–41
Lanier, Bob, 353
Lapides, Julian L. (Jack), 139
Lavell, Annett, 325
LeBow, Lainy, 127, 195, 216, 248, 253, 255, 260, 294–96, 302–3, 305, 312, 316, 319, 322, 324, 326, 344, 358–61, 365–67, 370–74, 378, 381–85
Lee, Blair, III, 160, 254
Lee, Blair, IV, 254, 256–59, 262, 377
Legislative Follies, 283

Legislative redistricting in 1991, 341–42
Lehman, Arnold, 167
Leone, Dominic, 156–57, 304
Lerner, Alfred, 350
Levine, Hartge, 13, 48
Levine, Mark, 219–20
Levitan, Larry, 286
Levitan, Sar, 231
Lewinsky, Monica, 309
Lexington Market, 127, 228, 229
Lidinsky, Richard, 223
Light rail system, 300, 358
Lighthizer, James, 338–39
Lindley, Daniel, 108
Lindsay, John V., 65
Linowes, R. Robert, 309–11, 315, 327–30
Linthicum, Doris, 13
Liss, Sol, 37, 44, 45, 50, 51
Little Italy area of Baltimore, 35, 41, 45, 62, 78, 89, 102, 124, 180, 260, 340, 378
Loan and Guarantee Fund, 197
Loden, Dan, 217
Lonergan, Betty Wise, 22–23
Lonergan, Harry, Jr., 23
Lottery, 335; sports, 279–80, 335
Lucchino, Larry, 191, 285, 286, 289

Mach, Joe, 51
Madison, James, 319
Magna Carta, displayed in Maryland, 274
Mahoney, George P., 73–74, 86
Maloney, Timothy F. (Tomato), 290–91, 377
Mandel, Barbara, 305
Mandel, Jeanne Dorsey, 152, 153, 305, 384
Mandel, Marvin, 67, 86, 111, 112, 129, 131, 150, 162, 188, 254, 260, 305, 312, 335, 341, 355, 361, 384; grand jury indictment of, 151–53; objections to Medicaid, 331–32; support for Schaefer's building projects, 151–52
Marbury, William L., Jr., 20, 284, 323, 354, 358
Marks, Remy, 43, 47
Marudas, Peter, 63, 111, 112
Maryland Association of Counties, 209
Maryland Club, 81

Maryland Department of Housing and Community Development, 121
Maryland General Assembly, 35–37, 80, 102, 116; cutting of salaries for Schaefer's staff positions by, 289–90; filibustering against Baltimore convention center in, 152; fiscal conservatism of, 281; Legislative Follies of, 283; Schaefer's 1991 state of the state address to, 319–20; Schaefer's distrust of, 276
Maryland Historical Society, 299
Maryland National Guard, 58
Maryland Science Center, 145, 147, 340
Maryland Sports Authority, 277–78
Maryland State Boxing Commission, 40
Maryland State Parole Commission, 103
Maryland State Police, 334
Maryland Title Guaranty Company, 16, 20, 29, 31, 94
Mathias, Charles McC., Jr. (Mac), 171, 172
Maurer, Lucille, 274
Mayor's Advisory Committee on Equal Rights in Education, 200
McCormick, Charles P., 103, 108
McCormick Spice Company, 96–97, 229
McCoy, Dennis, 150
McGowan, George, 232
McGuirk, Harry J. (Soft Shoes), 75, 87, 89, 257
McHugh, Arthur, 370
McKeachie, William N., 226
McKeldin, Theodore Roosevelt (Ted), 5, 7, 35, 41, .62, 63, 68, 70, 74–75, 102, 110–13, 118, 120, 154, 168, 196, 250, 345, 362, 366
McMillen, Tom, 341–42
McQuade, Joanne, 155–58, 205
Medicaid, 331–34
Memorial Stadium, 151, 190, 192, 235, 239, 251, 258, 288–89
Mencken, H. L., 15, 18, 60, 98–100, 209
Mental institutions, 324
Merchants Club, 50–52
Metro Crime Stoppers, 220
Metro Democrats, 88
Meyerhoff, Joseph, 110, 266
Mfume, Kweisi, 44, 104, 228, 385
Michel, Sally, 7, 224, 356–57, 384

Mikulski, Barbara, 44, 54–55, 177, 187, 227, 312, 317, 344, 358, 370
Miles, Clarence W., 107, 108, 110–11, 224
Military service, 14, 22–28, 127
Miller, Thomas V., Jr. (Mike), 272–74, 282–83, 290, 341, 352, 364
Millspaugh, Martin L., 109
Mitchell, Clarence M., Jr., 59–60, 76, 81, 312
Mitchell, Clarence M., III, 76, 90–92
Mitchell, Juanita Jackson, 59
Mitchell, Parren J., 81, 180, 256
Mitchell, R. Clayton, 273–74, 281–83, 290, 352
Moag, John, 363
Model Cities program, 104, 169
Modell, Art, 244–45, 350, 363, 364
Momberger, Mildred, 63
Mondale, Walter C., 234, 258
Monsanto pyrolysis plant, 184–86
Mooney, Thomas J., 262
Morgan, John, 310
Morgan, Jon, 240, 349–50
Morlock, Laura, 231
Morris Mechanic Theater, 110, 113, 134
Moseley, Jack, 232–34
Mount Vernon Flower Mart, 205
Moyers, Bill, 154
Muldowney, Paul, 338
Municipal Art Society, 107
Murdoch, Robert, 229–30
Murphy, Arthur, 223
Murphy, Reg, 84
Murphy, William G., 221–24, 376; charge of "two Baltimores," 222–23, 226
Murray, Bill, 339

National Aquarium, 65, 151, 177, 202, 204–10, 294, 340
National Association for the Advancement of Colored People (NAACP), 44, 59, 104, 228
National Football League negotiations, 348–55, 363–64, 381
National Industrial Recovery Act, 101
National Institutes of Health, 332
National League of Cities, 202
National Rifle Association (NRA), 301–4, 316
National Welfare Rights Organization, 170

News American (Baltimore), 92, 129
Nice, Harry W., 367
Nixon, Richard M., 70, 169–70, 229
Nolan, Kathleen, 155–56
Non-emergency transportation budget, 334
Novak, Frank, 195

Ocean City, Maryland, 31–32, 296, 298, 337, 358, 367
O'Donnell, John, 309
Off Street Parking Commission, 121, 161
Old St. Paul's Episcopal Church, 221, 323, 371
O'Malley, Peter, 366
O'Neill, Thomas (Tip), 371
Only Child Law, 11, 24
Orioles baseball team, 10, 44, 69, 107, 189–91, 217, 235, 244, 265, 352
Orioles Park at Camden Yards, 339–40. See also Camden Yards sports stadiums
Orlinsky, Walter S., 62, 76, 78, 152, 156, 211, 231
Orphan's Court in Baltimore, 40
Orr, Marion, 136
"Outer City Conservation Program," 79

Palmer, Jim, 217
Palughi, Buddy, 127–29, 260, 275, 312
Panhandlers, 193, 323–24
Papenfuse, Edward C., 177, 274, 305–7, 326–27, 356
Parks, Henry G., 44, 49–51, 75, 110
Pascal, Robert, 185, 307–8
Paterakis, John, 376, 378, 384
Patronage, 3–6, 39–41, 69–70, 83; "green bag" appointments, 88
Patterson, Roland, 135–36, 224
Patton, George S., 24
Paul, Daniel, 203
Peabody, George, 96
Peabody Institute, 297
Peck, H. Stephenson, 232
Perot, Ross, 345
Peters, Charlie, 334
Peters, Tom, 216
Pfiesteria outbreak, 382
Philanthropy, 265
Phillips, Brice, 379, 380
Phillips, Wendell, 80
Pines, Marion, 182, 196, 202, 203, 211–

Pines, Marion (*cont.*)
13, 215–16, 231, 233, 234, 259, 303, 357, 361
Platt, Jay, 361, 375, 379
Plevy, Daryl, 132–33, 213–15, 231, 308–9, 358, 370
Poe, Edgar Allan, 205, 209
"Police aid," 160–61
Pollack, James H. (Jack, Yankel, Big John, J. P.), 4–6, 30, 35, 37–42, 45–46, 69, 73, 74, 223, 311
Pomerleau, Donald, 129–31
Poole, Bruce, 337–39, 355
Port of Baltimore, 96
Pothole repair in Baltimore, 245–47
Powell, Fish, 337
Pratt, Enoch, 96, 101
Pratt, Joan, 377
Preakness, 144
Pressman, Hyman (Rhymin' Hyman), 48, 74–76, 81, 234, 243, 250, 316
Pride of Baltimore clipper ship, 162, 167, 248, 294
Prisons, in Maryland, 357
Pritzker, A. N., 164–66, 192, 219, 220, 229, 354, 380
Prohibition, 39
Property taxes, 160, 169, 196–97, 220
Proven Democratic Organization, 88
Provider tax, 331–33 ·
Public relations: budget cutting and, 334; Schaefer's hi-jinks, 205–10, 217–18, 271
Public Service Employment (PSE) program, 231–32
Public works projects, 150–54, 230–31. *See also* Baltimore City preservation and renewal
Pyrolysis plant, 184–86

Quayle, Vinnie, 180

Racetracks, 151
Racial issues, 14, 44, 49–53, 57–60, 155; affirmative action and set-asides in government contracts, 155; Baltimore city school administration, 135–38; black candidates for mayor in 1971, 73–77, 83, 91–92; black migration into previously white areas of Balti-
more, 105–6; campaign for approval of Harborplace project, 180; D'Alesandro's responses to, 62–64; educational gap, 263–64; flourishing black businesses in West Baltimore, 104–5; riots in 1968, 58–60, 63.65, 71; "safe" men on, 75; Schaefer's belief that Schmoke wanted Baltimore to be an all-black city, 267–68; Schaefer's support by black voters, 80–81; "sleeping giant" of black political consciousness, 221; urban renewal and, 109–10; voting by blacks in 1971 election, 81, 89–90
Ramsey, Norman, 137
Ratchford, William S, II, 279
Ravens football team, 363
Rawlings, Howard (Pete), 221, 357
Raynor, Gene, 79, 89, 90, 92, 361, 374, 375, 379–81, 383, 385
"Reach the Beach" project, 358
Reagan, Ronald, 231–33, 303
Recession of 1991, 330–37, 344–45
Rehrmann, Eileen, 377
Republican Party, 4, 59, 314–15, 341–42; Schaefer's 1992 endorsement of Bush, 342–45, 377
Resnick, Marty, 379
Revenue sharing, 230–31
Richards, Ann, 347
Rifkin, Alan, 272, 276, 278–80, 282, 284–86, 336
Riots in 1968: Baltimore, 58–60, 63, 71; Chicago, 65
Ripken, Billy, 287
Ripken, Cal, Jr., 287
Ripken, Cal, Sr., 287
Ritchie, Albert C., 101, 367
Rizzo, Frank, 64
Road construction, 54–55, 83, 187, 358
Robinson, Zelig, 374, 383
Rodricks, Dan, 336
Romney, George, 169–74
Roosevelt, Eleanor, 371
Roosevelt, Franklin Delano, 35, 60, 102–3, 347
Roosevelt, Theodore, 366
Rosenbloom, Carroll, 236
Rosenberg, Henry, 233
Rossi, Linda, 273

Rotary Club, 145
Rouse, James, 4–7, 14, 45, 62, 83, 107, 108, 110, 114, 138, 148–49, 181, 187, 196, 224, 229, 246, 255, 312; commitment to urban renewal, 4–5, 107–8, 148–49; Gallery project of, 229; Harborplace project of, 175–81, 194, 303; opinion of Schaefer, 4–7, 221; planning of Columbia, Maryland, 149, 175; Sandtown-Winchester project of, 368–69; at Schaefer's swearing in as governor, 271
Rozner, Joel, 254, 301
Rudolph, Dick, 295
Rusk, David, 263
Russell, George, 3, 4, 66, 67, 119–20, 266, 376; in 1971 mayoral campaign, 72–74, 76, 79, 81–82, 89–92, 222, 249, 318
Russell, Richard, 84
Ryan, Charles (Buzzy), 328–29

Sabatini, Nelson, 331–35, 360, 361, 370, 381
Sachs, Jerry, 278
Sachs, Leon, 19
Sachs, Leonard, 358
Sachs, Stephen H., 19, 234–35, 249–59, 261–62, 275, 318, 341, 376–77
Safdie, Moshe, 198
Sales tax, 4, 40, 258
Sandtown-Winchester project, 368–69
Sarbanes, Paul S., 111, 177, 227, 277, 301, 342, 344
Saturday Night Specials, 301–3
Sauerbrey, Ellen, 374, 377
Schaefer, Emma, 8, 9
Schaefer, Louis, 8, 9, 11
Schaefer, Tululu Irene, 7–10, 15, 17–20, 22, 135, 226–28, 295–97
Schaefer, William Donald: birth and family of, 7–22; campaign for Comptroller of the Treasury, 372–85; homes of, 7, 9–15, 20–21, 80, 106, 159, 292–93, 361; law practice of, 29–36; schooling of, 11–12, 14, 16–17, 22, 135; service in World War II, 22–27; views on marriage, 126–27, 293, 295–98
—on Baltimore City Council: first term,

43–45; presidency, 56–57, 61, 66, 72, 115; second term, 48–51
—as mayor: advisory committees to, 199–200; approval ratings in 1985, 251; City Hall shootings (1976), 153–58; commitment to neighborhoods, 145–50, 187; communication abilities, 146; demand for respect and loyalty, 115–16; drivers for, 129–30; election in 1971, 66–68, 71, 73–93; election in 1975, 145–47; election in 1979, 181; election in 1983, 221–26; evaluation of, 266–67; first term of, 115–40; focus on big picture, 187–88; optimism about city, 143–45, 166; personal notes and attention from, 132–33; public works projects of, 150–54; pursuit of money for projects, 153–54, 160–61, 165, 170–74, 181–83, 196–202; qualifications of, 71, 83; state of city before and after, 219–20; support of arts by, 167–68; team of, 127–28
—as governor: assertions of authority, 272–73, 289–90, 356; as "Baltimore's Gift to the State," 271; election in 1986, 249–62, 315; election in 1990, 314–19; Hilda Mae Snoops and, 291–300; institution of snow emergency plan, 275; learning to share power in Annapolis, 273–74, 289–90; leaving office, 359–61; legislative agenda in 1987, 278–79; overview of accomplishments of, 357–58; portrait of, 365–67, 373; preparedness for job, 271–72; during presidential campaign of 1988, 300–305; during presidential campaign of 1992, 340–47; pursuit of new football team, 348–55, 381; during recession of 1991, 330–37, 344–45; support for Camden Yards sports stadiums, 276–89; support for handgun control legislation, 300–304; support for keno gambling, 335–37; support for Linowes Commission tax overhaul plan, 309–11, 315, 327–30; unexpected announcements of, 284
Schaefer, William Henry (Willie), 7–10, 15, 17–18, 22, 24–25, 48–49

Scheyer, Zina, 379, 380
Schlenger, Jacques, 197
Schloeder, Nick, 76, 178
Schmoke, Kurt L., 63, 90, 223–24, 250, 264, 293, 362, 367–70, 385
School issues, 51, 69–70, 82, 135–38, 168, 258, 263–64, 357–58
Schurick, Paul, 211–12, 232, 303, 331, 359, 360, 373
Schweinhaut, Margaret, 161
Scott, Willard, 339, 340
Seal pool swim, 205–10, 294
Segregation, 14, 44, 49–53, 57
"Self-Denial Day," 101
Selleck, Tom, 339
Set-asides in government contracts, 155. *See also* Racial issues
"Shadow Government," 199–202, 259, 272, 357
Shellhase, Otto, 50
Shepard, Bill and Lois, 314–15, 317–19
Sheppard, Joe, 367
Shortall, Dan, 325
Shula, Don, 235
Sickles, Carlton, 77–78, 86
Silver, Edgar, 36–38, 42, 68–71, 151, 249, 251–52, 311, 336, 343–45
Skipper, Anita, 8, 18, 19, 23, 28
Skipper, Clara, 8, 21–22
Skipper, Clarence, 8
Skipper, Fielding Copperton (Fred), 7–8, 21–22
Skipper, Harry, 21, 22
Smart growth proposal, 329
Smelser, Charles, 305
Smith, Bubba, 235
Snoops, Hilda Mae, 13, 130, 134–35, 206, 216, 227, 271, 283, 291–96, 336, 359, 361, 367; fountain for governor's mansion grounds ordered by, 305–7; impact on Schaefer's political career, 305, 317, 319; living in governor's mansion, 292–94; nature of Schaefer's relationship with, 294–98; as official state hostess, 298–99; portrait of, 380; redecorating of governor's mansion by, 299–300; relandscaping at governor's mansion by, 305; during Schaefer's election as comptroller, 374–75, 378–79, 384

Snow emergency plan, 275
Solid waste disposal, 184–86, 198–99
Sondheim, Walter, 51, 52, 69, 86, 166, 172, 173, 181, 187, 212, 229, 273–74, 278, 293–95, 360
Sorenson, Joanna, 226
Southeast Council Against the Road (SCAR), 54
Spicer, Jim, 379
Sports: All-Star baseball game in Baltimore (1993), 339–40; Baltimore Colts, 109, 235–44, 351; Baltimore Orioles, 10, 44, 69, 107, 189–91, 217, 235, 244, 265, 352; baseball stadium, 149, 151, 190–92, 202, 258, 339–40; Cooke's desire for new football stadium in Maryland, 351–52; economic impact of teams, 287; football stadium, 237–41; Maryland Sports Authority, 277; passage of bill for Camden Yards stadiums, 276–89; pursuit of new NFL team, 348–55, 363–64, 381; Schaefer's participation in, 16–17
Sports lottery, 279–80, 335
St. Claire, Rita, 159
St. Mary's College, 362, 373
Stadiums. *See* Baseball stadium; Football stadium
Starr, Blaze, 30–31, 323
Starr, Kenneth, 375
Staszak, Joe, 50–51, 75, 87
State employees, unpaid furloughs for, 334–45
Steadman, John, 10, 240
Steadman, William, 10
Steiff Silver Company, 146
Steinberg, Melvin A. (Mickey), 256, 261, 276, 279, 285, 291, 328–29, 337, 358
Steiner, Marc, 222
Sterne, Joseph R. L., 173–74, 308, 368
Stevenson, Adlai, 261
Stirling Street Renewal Area, 138–40
Stonewall Democratic Club, 75, 88–89, 176, 223
Streckfuss, June, 300
Suburban growth, 108, 109, 113, 194, 264
Subway system, 151–53, 228
Sun (Baltimore), 5–7, 15, 40, 45, 62, 82, 84, 92, 98, 103, 112, 144, 173–74, 194, 199–202, 205, 211, 221, 238,

255–58, 284, 300, 308, 315, 325, 336, 346, 349, 359, 368, 377, 381, 382
Swann, Ruth, 153
Sweeney, Bob, 311
Swisher, William L., 90, 223, 250

Tagliabue, Paul, 351
Tawes, J. Millard, 70–71, 111, 311
Tawney, Doug, 122
Tax savings, 197–98
Taxes: as 1990 campaign issue, 316–17; inventory, 210–11; Linowes Commission for overhaul of, 309–11, 315, 327–29; property, 160, 169, 196–97, 220; provider, 331–33; sales, 4, 40, 258; "windfall" from federal tax reform bill of 1986, 281–82
Taylor, Casper, 338, 352
Thomas, Evan, 191
Thomas, Henry, 13
Thomas, Sister Mary, 221
Thorpe, Gary, 316–18, 322
Tidal wetlands, 300
Tippett, Elmer H., 302
Tolliver, Larry, 361, 379
Tolliver, Sheila, 379
Tourism in Baltimore, 143, 162, 166, 175, 266; during baseball All-Star week (1993), 340
Townsend, Kathleen Kennedy, 383
Townsend, Maeve, 383
Trashball, 216–18
Trinity College, 371
Trueschler, Bernie, 159, 181–83, 189, 203, 210, 232, 233, 265
Tsongas, Paul, 340–42
"2020" program, 309, 329
"Two Baltimores," 222, 226
Two O'Clock Club, 30
Tydings, Joseph D., 301
Tydings, Millard E., 102

Unglesbee, Alvie, 36
Unitas, John, 235–36, 241, 280
United Christian Citizens' Organization, 17
United States Department of Housing and Urban Development (HUD), 44, 162, 165, 169–74, 196

Univerity of Maryland Hospital, 357, 379
University of Maryland at College Park, 125, 291, 358, 360, 366
University of Maryland Law School, 264
Urban deterioration, 107–8, 143–44, 169, 174, 195, 220, 262–63. See also Baltimore City preservation and renewal
Urban Development Action Grant (UDAG), 165, 197, 230
Urban Renewal Study Board, 107
USS Constellation, 176

Valentine, Jeff, 204
Van Slyke, Andy, 340
Venetoulis, Ted: role in Baltimore Colts negotiations, 241–42; as Schaefer's campaign manager, 6–7, 77–79, 82–87, 131
Ventura, Jesse, 382
Venture capitalist lenders, 5
Veterans of Foreign Wars, 29
Vincent, Irene, 17, 36, 48, 296–98
Violence, in Baltimore, 82; City Hall shootings in 1976, 153–58; gun control legislation, 158, 300–304; looting in 1978, 254; riots of 1968, 58–60, 63, 71
Volstead Act, 39
Volunteers for Schaefer, 224–25
Voting: in 1990 governor's election, 318–19; in 1971 mayoral election, 89–92; in 1975 mayoral election, 145; in 1979 mayoral election, 181; in 1983 mayoral election, 226; in 1988 presidential campaign, 304–5; in 1992 presidential election, 346; black turnout for, 81, 221; democratic road map ballots for, 88; Schaefer's independence in, 38–39; Schaefer's record of, 45
Voting Rights Act of 1964, 76

Walking-around money, 87, 260
Walters Art Gallery, 202, 340
Waltjen, Kay, 296
Waltjen, Norman, 29–31, 36, 296
War on Poverty, 53, 104, 169
Warnke, Paul, 363
Warren, Earl, 371
Washington, George, 319–20, 364–65

Washington, Leroy, 286

Washington Monument (Baltimore), 122–23, 133, 265, 384

Washington Post, 206, 256, 328, 362, 375

Washington Redskins, 350, 352

Washington Times, 382

Wasserman, Mark, 253, 255, 259, 260, 316, 318, 322, 360, 361, 370, 381, 383

Waters, John, 98; 101

Waxman, Henry, 332

Weaver, Earl, 217

Webster, Marvin (The Eraser), 217

Weisengoff, Paul, 282

Welch, Agnes, 88

Weldon family, 13

Wetlands, 300

Wharton, Henry M., 7

White, Kevin, 65, 204

Wiley, George, 170

Wilke, Anton, 51

Will, George, 251, 346

Williams, Edward Bennett, 189–92, 244, 283; support for Camden Yards stadiums, 284–89, 339, 340

Winegrad, Gerald, 355–56

Winger, Debra, 292

Wisniewski, Milton, 30–32, 99, 104, 298

Work ethic: in Baltimore, 100–101; of Schaefer, 62, 63, 71

World Trade Center, 167, 197, 207

World War II, 345; Baltimore during, 98; Schaefer' s service in, 22–27

Wyatt, Joseph, 88, 89

Yellow Cab Company, 144, 219

Young, Andrew, 223

Young Men's Bohemian Club, 51, 223

Zemansky, Stanley, 122–23

Library of Congress Cataloging-in-Publication Data

Smith, C. Fraser, 1938–
    William Donald Schaefer : a political biography / C. Fraser Smith.
        p.   cm.
    Includes bibliographical references and index.
        ISBN 0-8018-6252-3 (alk. paper)
        1. Schaefer, William Donald.   2. Governors—Maryland
    Biography.   3. Mayors—Maryland—Baltimore Biography.
    4. Maryland. Comptroller's Office Biography.   5. Maryland—
    Politics and government—1961–   I. Title.
    F186.35.S33S55   1999
    975.2'043'092—dc21
        [B]   99-21399
                                                                    CIP